# SPLENDOURS OF JAPAN

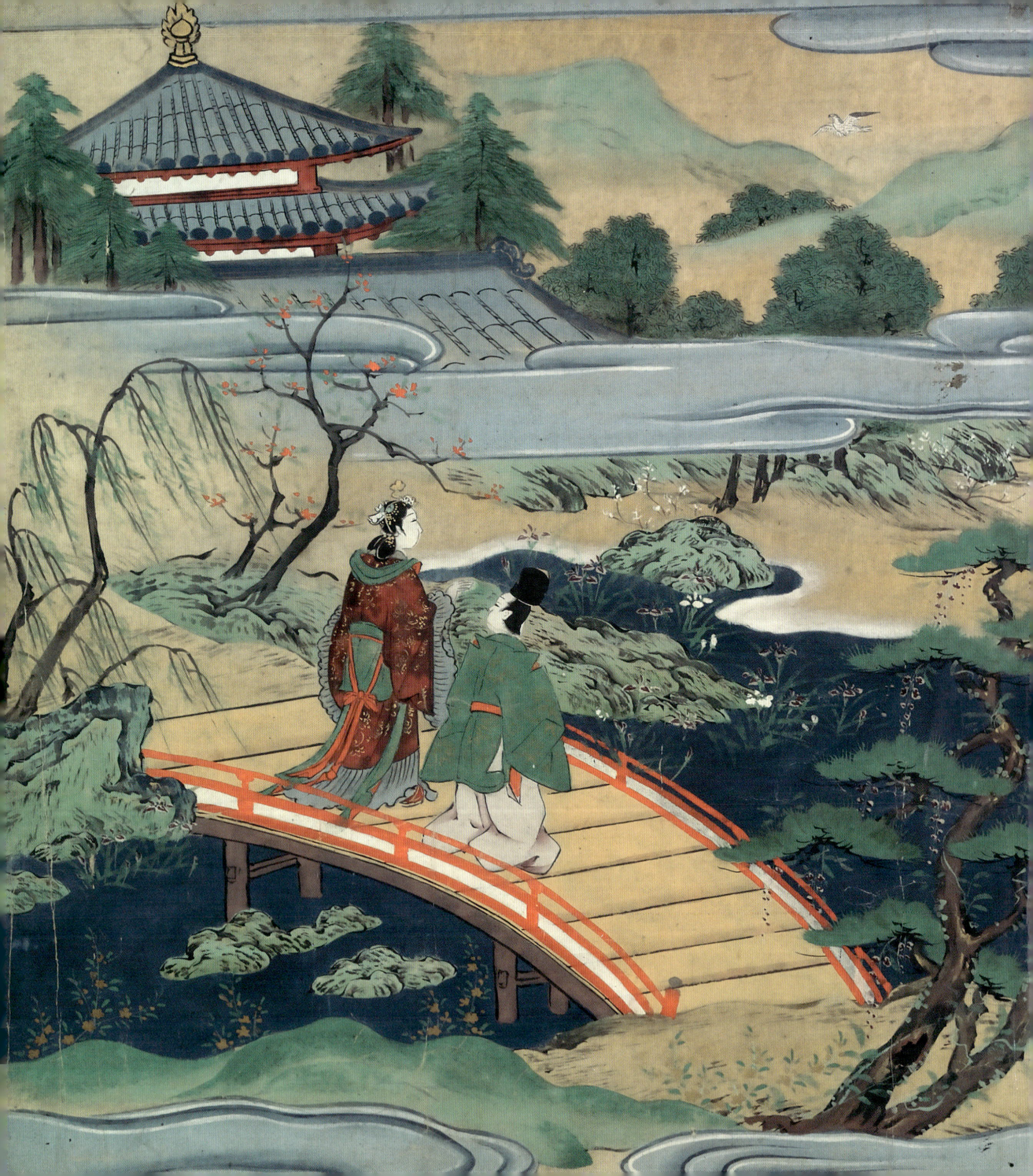

# SPLENDOURS OF JAPAN

## HIGHLIGHTS FROM THE BODLEIAN LIBRARY

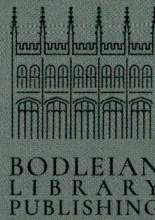

BODLEIAN
LIBRARY
PUBLISHING

# CONTENTS

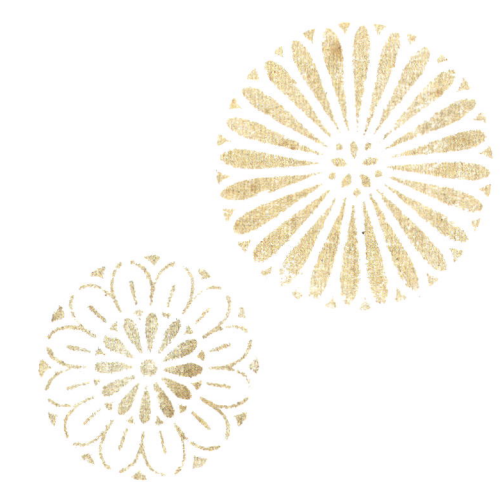

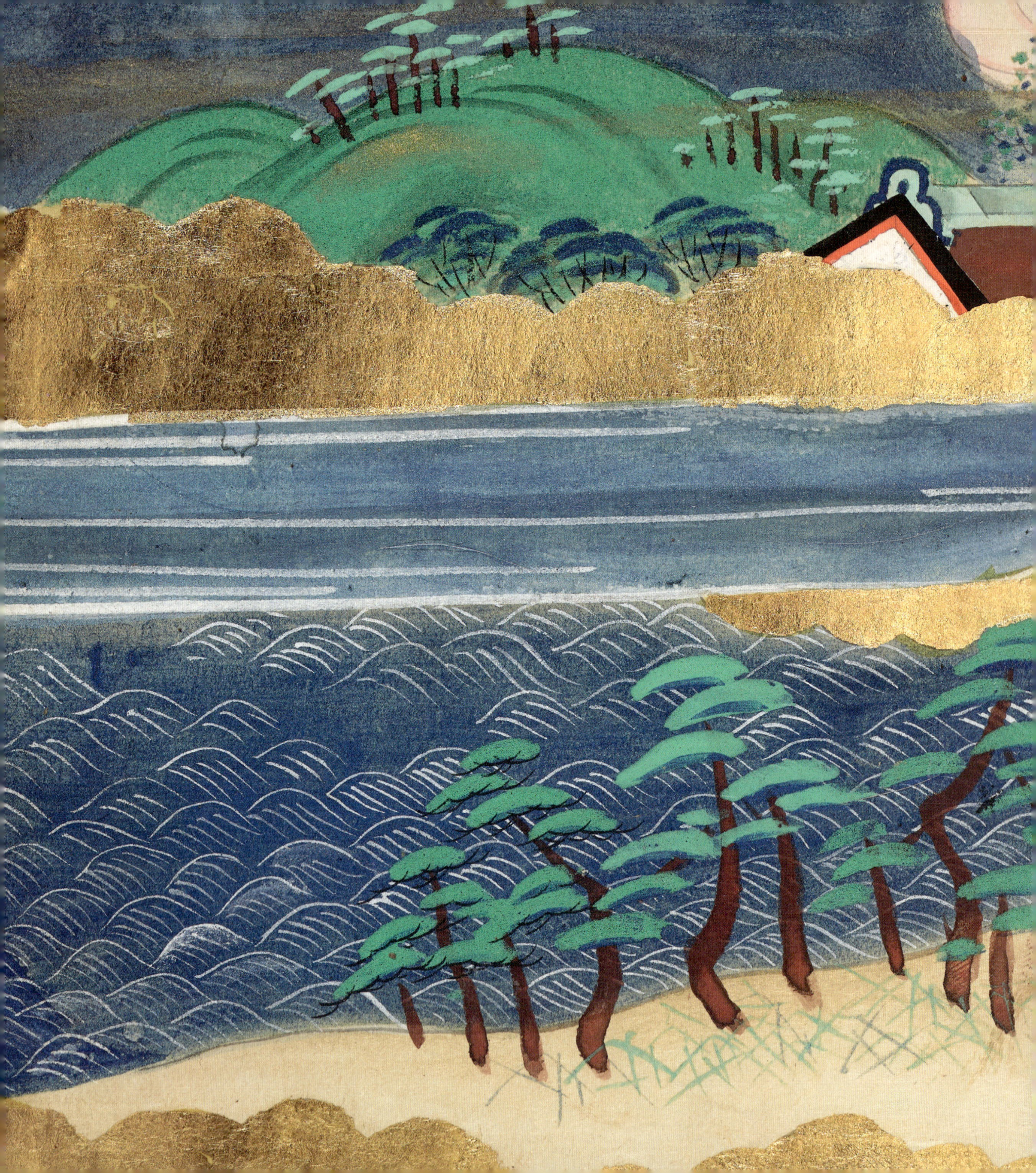

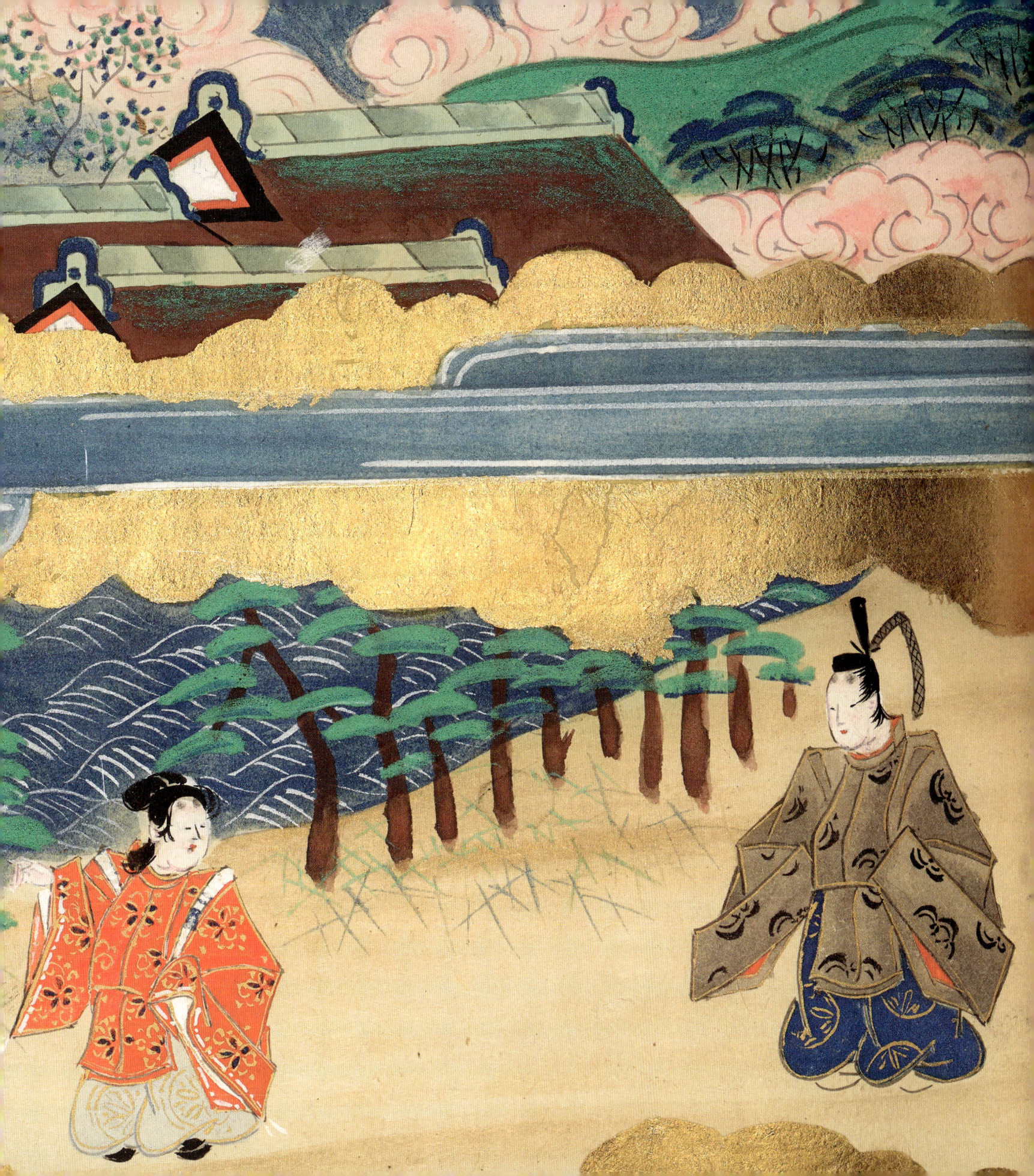

# FOREWORD

THE BODLEIAN LIBRARY houses one of the oldest institutional collections of Japanese rare books and manuscripts in Europe. As early as 1629 three Japanese books containing chanting texts of Noh plays arrived at the Library, and not long after a *Shuinjō* – a charter that marked the earliest trading agreement between England and Japan, dated 1613 – came into the collections. It is extraordinary that these items were carefully preserved and catalogued at a time when it was unlikely that anyone in Oxford could read Japanese – and indeed the significance of the charter was not fully understood until 1985. These important early acquisitions were joined by a stunning seventeenth-century painted handscroll of *The Legend of Urashima Tarō*, beautifully illustrated poetry anthologies and many other lavish manuscripts and narrative scrolls as the collection grew. At first the Library benefited largely from donations by merchants and travellers to Japan in the seventeenth and eighteenth centuries, before it developed a collecting policy and actively purchased Japanese manuscripts and important books.

As we approach the landmark of four hundred years of collecting Japanese books and manuscripts in the Library, it is fitting to celebrate the provenance of this magnificent collection with a volume of specially commissioned essays, featuring cross-disciplinary contributions from leading scholars on Japanese material culture and in the fields of Japanese literature, history and the arts. Each chapter examines a particular aspect of the collections: from the exquisite examples of handmade paper, inks and brushwork unique to Japanese culture, traditional narrative art and woodblock printing, to the sixteenth- and seventeenth-century publications of the Jesuit mission press.

I would like to express profound thanks first and foremost to Edward Kamens, Peter Kornicki, Melissa McCormick, Laura Moretti, Marinita Stiglitz and Katja Triplett, for their time and scholarly expertise in writing this book. Great thanks are also due to Gillian Evison, Anna Sharko, Mamtimyn Sunuodula, Mike Webb, and all the staff, past and present, in the Bodleian Japanese Library and in Special Collections, without whom

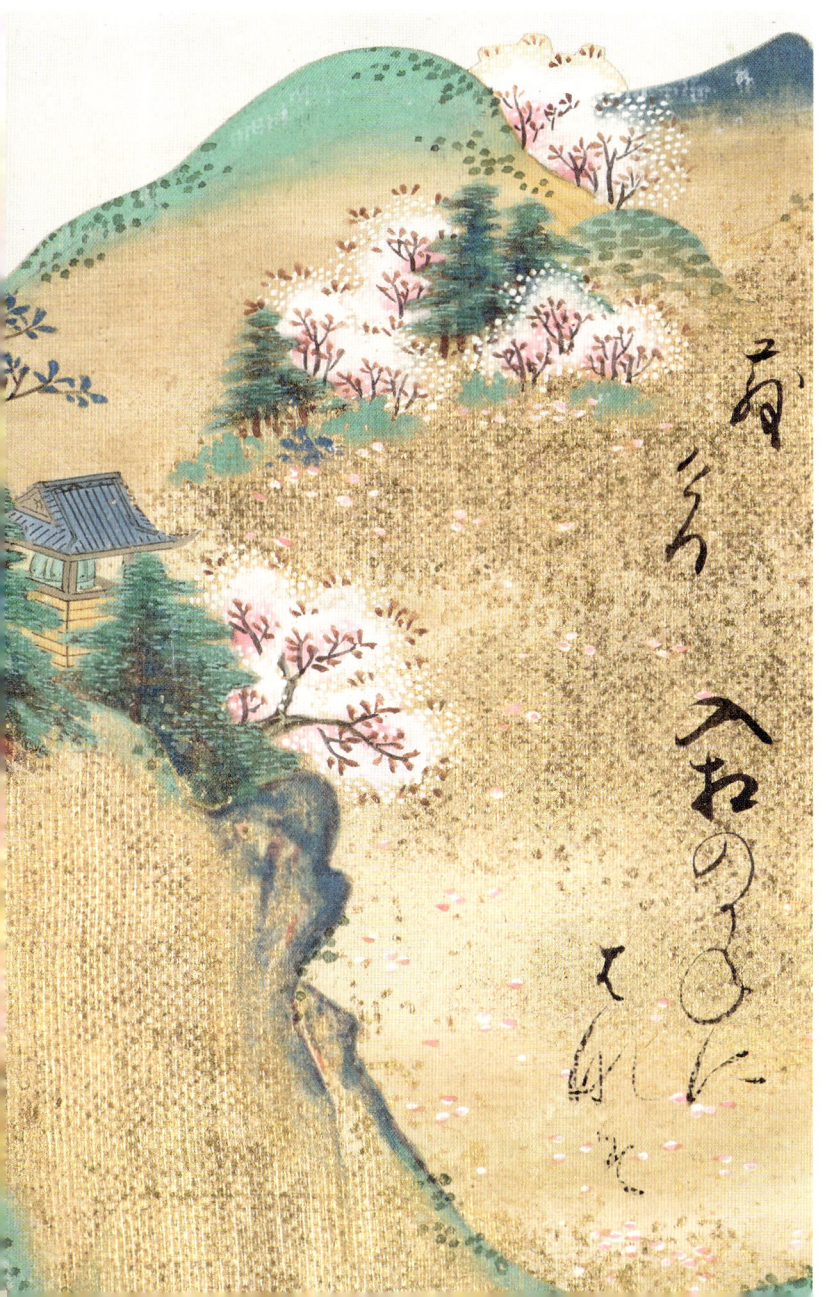

the production of this volume would not have been possible.

The study of Japan in Oxford continues to thrive, across the disciplines studied in the University. The Bodleian's Japanese collections continue to be built, four centuries on from those early acquisitions. They are today mostly modern printed and digital materials. Occasionally, new holdings of spectacular early materials come to join those that came before them, to enrich our holdings and to reaffirm our intellectual and cultural connections with Japan.

**RICHARD OVENDEN**

*Bodley's Librarian and the*
*Helen Hamlyn Director of University Libraries*

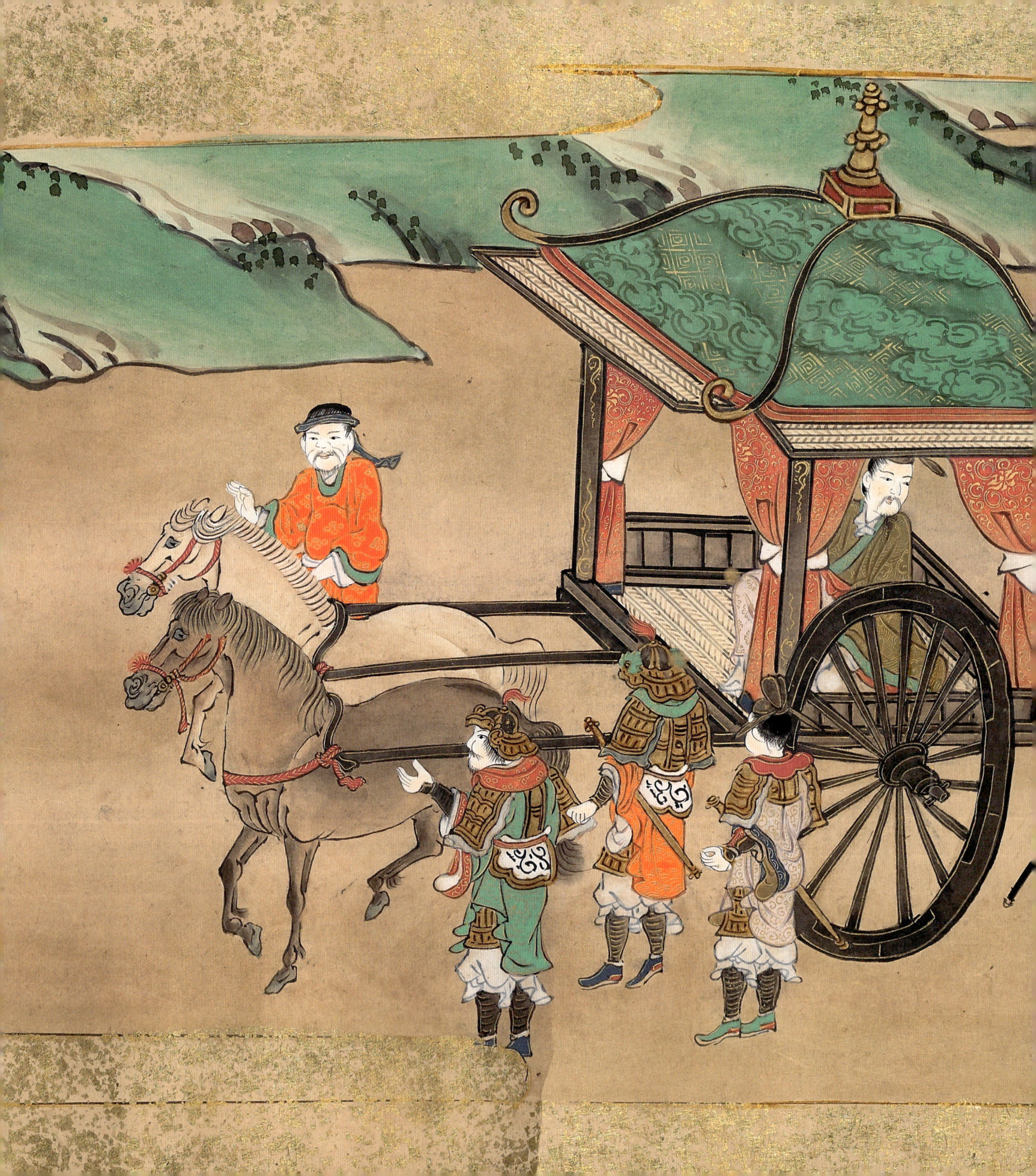

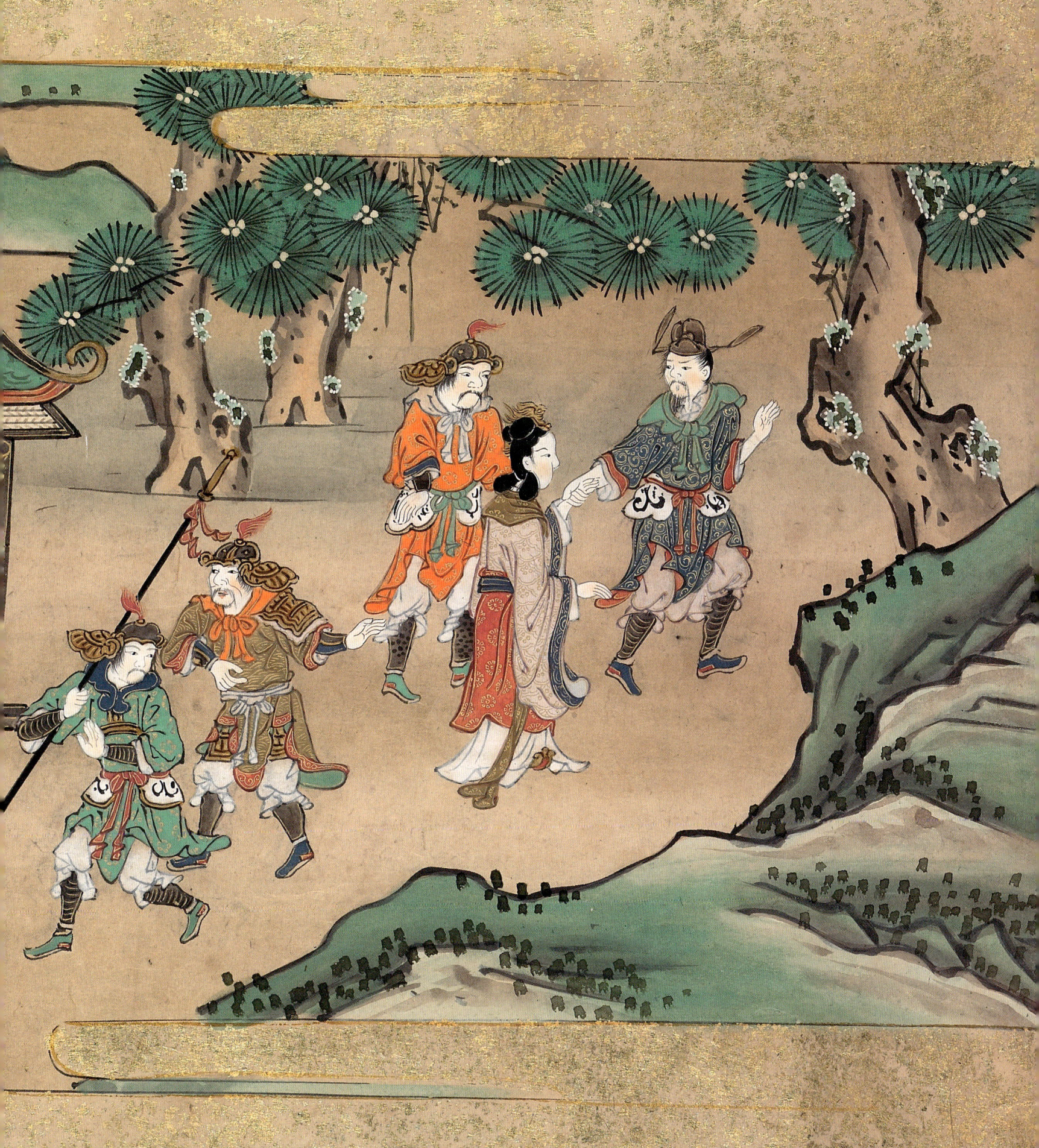

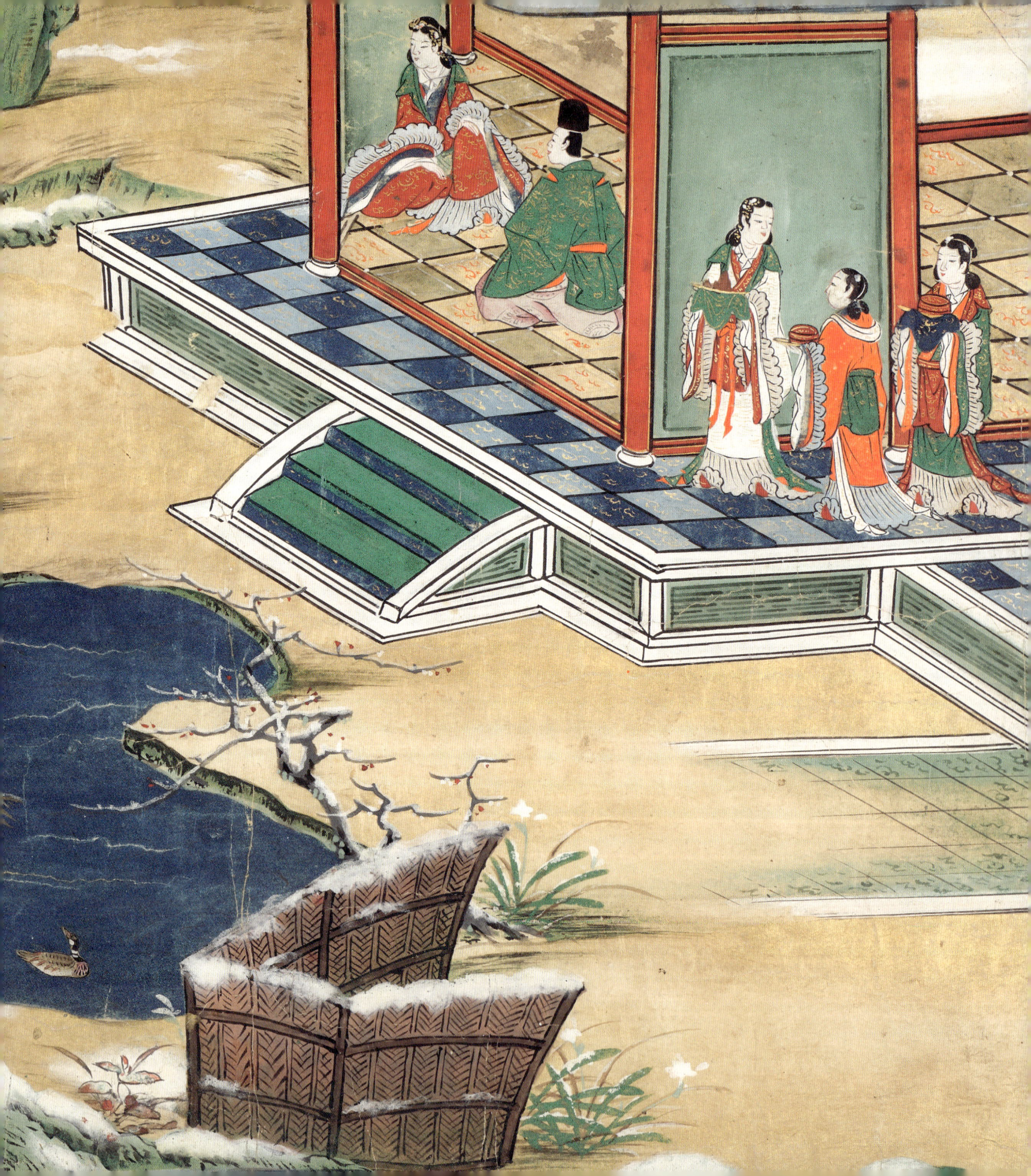

# History and provenance of the Bodleian Japanese collection

THE BODLEIAN houses one of the oldest institutional collections of Japanese rare books and manuscripts in Europe, with a rich and multifaceted history that spans almost four hundred years – it started in the early 1600s and continues uninterrupted to today. This introduction offers a glimpse into the provenance and history of the Japanese collection, showing how it has developed over time not only through a proactive acquisition policy, but also thanks to the generosity of donors and patrons who chose the Library to be the keeper of their legacies.[1]

The Japanese collection can claim to be almost as old as the Bodleian itself. Scholars and students in Oxford had access to knowledge about Japan at the very beginning of the seventeenth century. The first catalogue (1605) of books and manuscripts in the Bodleian listed a few publications on Japan under the section *Libri Artium*.[2] By the third quarter of the century more specialized books could be found on the library shelves. For instance, the 1674 *Catalogus Impressorum Librorum Bibliothecæ Bodlejanæ in Academia Oxoniensi* records various titles about Japan, and further groups of anonymous works on the same subject under the heading 'Japonia'. Among these, there are three important publications compiled by the Spanish missionary Diego Collado (d. 1641): *Ars Grammaticæ Iaponicæ Linguæ* (Rome, 1632); *Dictionarium siue Thesauri Linguæ Iaponicæ Compendium* (Rome, 1632); and most notably *Niffon no Cotōbani Yô Confesion* (Rome, 1632), an edition of the *Modus Confitendi* with a parallel Latin–Japanese translation (FIG. 1).[3] The size and scope of this section of the collection continued to grow over the centuries, as the Library accessioned numerous European books about Japanese history, customs and language. This eventually formed the basis for a remarkable research collection that vividly illustrated Europe's encounters with Japan from the sixteenth century to the nineteenth.

While European books about Japan were indeed valuable and treasured possessions, far rarer objects entered the Library collection in the seventeenth century. From its inception, the Bodleian housed books in various languages – for instance Arabic, Hebrew and Chinese. As the Library increased its holdings, the range of world languages

# Niffòn nò cotõba ni iô confefion vo mófu iõdai to màta confefor iòri gò xensá cu mefarùru tàme nò can iônàru giô giô nò còto dàngui xà no mònpa no Fr. Didaco Collado to iù xùcqe Roma ni voite còre vo xitáte mòno nàri 1632.

**P.** Itçu, ve litçũgòro confeffion vo mòxi àtta ca?

**R.** Sorégàxíga cotòxi Deus no vòn jifino vie iòri Chriſtian ní nàri maràxitẽ gozàru iùie, ni, mãda confefion vo mófaĩdẽ gozàru.

**R.** Vel, vàrégà xígò ròcu nẽn sàqi iòri Chriſtian de vòri àtta rẽdomo, go zõnji nõ gotòqu, padre sàma no von fiſsòcu ní iòtte, rèn rèn confefion vo mùxi ãgueô tote, chicàra no voiòbi faicàcu ità ità rẽdomo, tçùini fono chôbí ga gozaràíde, ìma màde confeffion vo mòxi ãgue maraxenàndẽ gozàru.

**R.** vel, vatacùxí ga jũ gonen màie võ mizzu vò sãzzucàri maràxitẽ gozarẽ domo, sòre và mùsàto fito nàmi ni tçucàtçutta tocòrõ dè; còno fõdo màde xpàn no von voxìie ni tçùite, imàda xìca xìca fũnbèt tòcuxìn to mófu còto va gozaràíde, Chriſtian no guiõ gui tatoiẽba, mainen, zzutçu xemète ichídò no confefion no coto, mata tòvo no go vòqite vo tamòtçu còto, nando ni càma vàíde, tãda vqi iò no nànde monài còto ni tã zzufa vàtte macàri itẽ gozàru. Sàri nagàra còno giũ go dàngui vo fucòxi vqe tamòtte càra, xingiũ ni Deus ni taĩ xite xinjĩn no cocòro vo mòiọ vòxi, tocàcu, dàí jinàru goxõ vo tafu càru t-me ni, mãzzu Chriſtian no còto vo ichi ichi gàttèn xi, mimòchi vo aratàme, còre ni nòmi xeɨ jei vo tçùcu faíde va, to, vomòi acàtta ní iòtte, sòre càrà funa vàchi Chriſtian no còto vo mìna naràí maràxitẽ màta confefion no càcũgò mo itàitẽ gozàru. Sàri nàgàrà sùie no confefion và sòionèn no màie de gozàtta.

**P.** Sàte mo sàte mo võqinaru Deus no von jifí cana! ma còto ni

ni

# MODVS CONFITENDI

## & examinandi pœnitentem Iaponensem formula suamet Lingua Iaponica.

### Auctore F. Didaco Collado Ord. Prædicatorum Româ a die 20. iunij ann. 1632.

*P. Quando fecisti confessionem Sacramentalem ?*

*R. Ego ex Dei misericordia hoc anno Christianus factus, nunquam confessionem Sacramentalem feci : vnde hæc, quam modo incipio, erit prima.*

*R. Vel: etiam si a quatuor, quinque, vel sex iam annis fuerim Christianus, quia tamen sicut uestra experitur paternitas, sacerdotes ob persecutionem sunt absconditi, etiam si sæpius ad confessionem faciendam, quoad potui, diligentiam adhibuerim, non potui tamen occasionem nancisci : vnde vsque modo nondum sum confessus.*

*R. Vel: etiam si à quindecim iam annis fuerim baptizatus ; quia tamen baptismum sine consideratione alios imitatus suscepi : circa Doctrinam Christianam vsque ad dies præteritos nondum conceptum formaueram, neque curabam de Christianorum exercitijs sicut, verbi gratia, de confessione annuali ; neque de decem legis Dei præceptorum obseruantia ; sed fui tantus occupatus & intentus rebus momentaneis, & huius sæculi vanitatibus. Sed cum diebus elapsis Dei sermones audissem, ita in cordis mei visceribus excitata est erga Deum animi deuotio ; quòd ex illo tunc decreuerim addiscere omnia & singula mysteria fidei Christianæ, ex quorum fide cum morum perfecta reformatione, & omni ex parte secundum, quod vires suppeterent virtutum exercitio, possem meam salutem æternam operari, vnde ex tunc omnia didici, & ad confessionem cæpi me etiam disponere. Sed a quatuor iam annis non sum confessus.*

*P. O bone Deus, quàm magna est misericordia eius! profecto non*

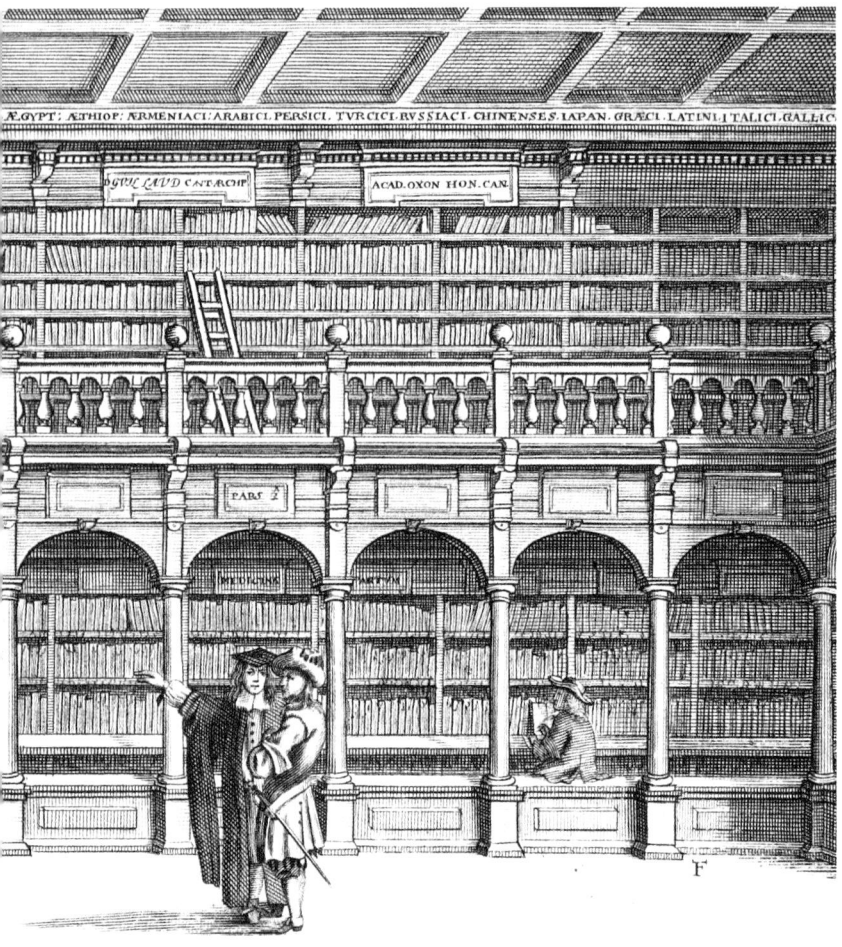

that were represented in the collection grew accordingly. This is evident from a plate in *Oxonia Illustrata* (1675) by David Loggan (1634–1692), which portrays the interior of the Old Library. Looking closely at the inscription at the top of the bookshelves in Selden End (the west-facing section of the library), one can see an extensive list of languages represented in the Bodleian's books at the time the plates were engraved. The inscription celebrates the rich and diverse global heritage of the Library collection, which counted books written in various Asian languages including Japanese (FIG. 2).

The first books produced in the archipelago to reach the Bodleian arrived in the third decade of the seventeenth century. These were three volumes comprising texts from Noh plays for chanting, which were entrusted to the Library in 1629 (see chapter 1). This exceptional gift shows the international reach that the Bodleian had from its early years. More significantly, it marks the very beginning of the exchanges between the University of Oxford and Japan, and it represents the inception of a relationship that has lasted for almost four hundred years.

In the decades following this initial donation, several gifts arrived at the Bodleian. Along with two printed almanacs, we have a record of Japanese objects entering the Library collection at this time. Jeremiah Carter, a merchant active in Asia, donated a Japanese fan in 1663, while Robert Ward, a surgeon from Northampton who had travelled to Asia in the second half of the century, gave a large gold coin in 1679.[4] By the 1680s, the Bodleian had also accessioned one of its greatest treasures: the *Shuinjō* (vermilion seal document).[5] This charter

1 PREVIOUS SPREAD  An opening spread (pp. 4–5) from *Niffon no Cotōbani Yô Confesion*, Rome, 1632. Ink on paper. This rare edition of the *Modus Confitendi* (*Manner of Confessing*) has parallel translations in Japanese (*left*) and Latin (*right*). The Japanese text is transliterated using the Roman alphabet. 4° B 48(8) Th.Seld.

2 The interior of Duke Humfrey's Library, where the earliest collection of Japanese books was housed. From David Loggan's *Oxonia Illustrata*, E Theatro Sheldoniano, Oxford, 1675, plate VII. Douce L. Subt. 27. The detail ABOVE shows the top of the bookshelves in Selden End, Duke Humfrey's Library. An inscription lists the languages or locations, including Japan, of manuscripts housed in the library in the seventeenth century.

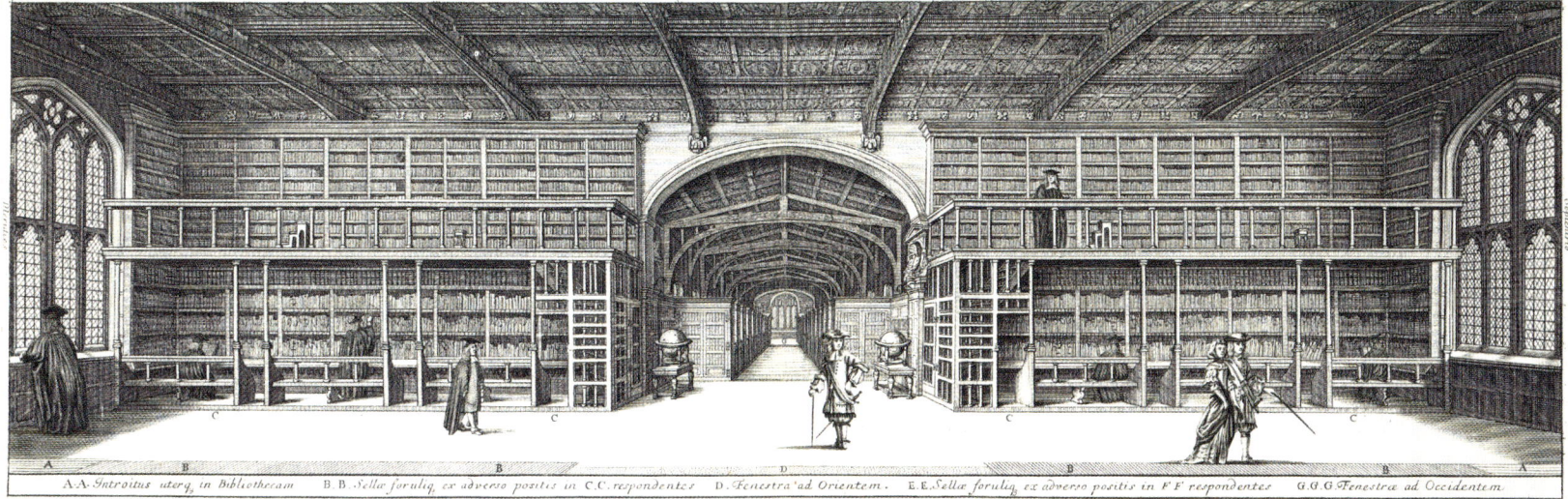

A.A. *Introitus uterq. in Bibliothecam.* B.B. *Sellæ foruliq. ex adverso positis in C.C. respondentes.* D. *Fenestra ad Orientem.* E.E. *Sellæ foruliq. ex adverso positis in F.F. respondentes.* G.G.G. *Fenestræ ad Occidentem.*

BIBLIOTHECÆ. BODLEIANÆ. OXONIÆ. *Prospectus interior ab Occidente.* THE *Inside of* y.ᵉ Public or BODLEIAN LIBRARY in OXFORD from y.ᵉ West

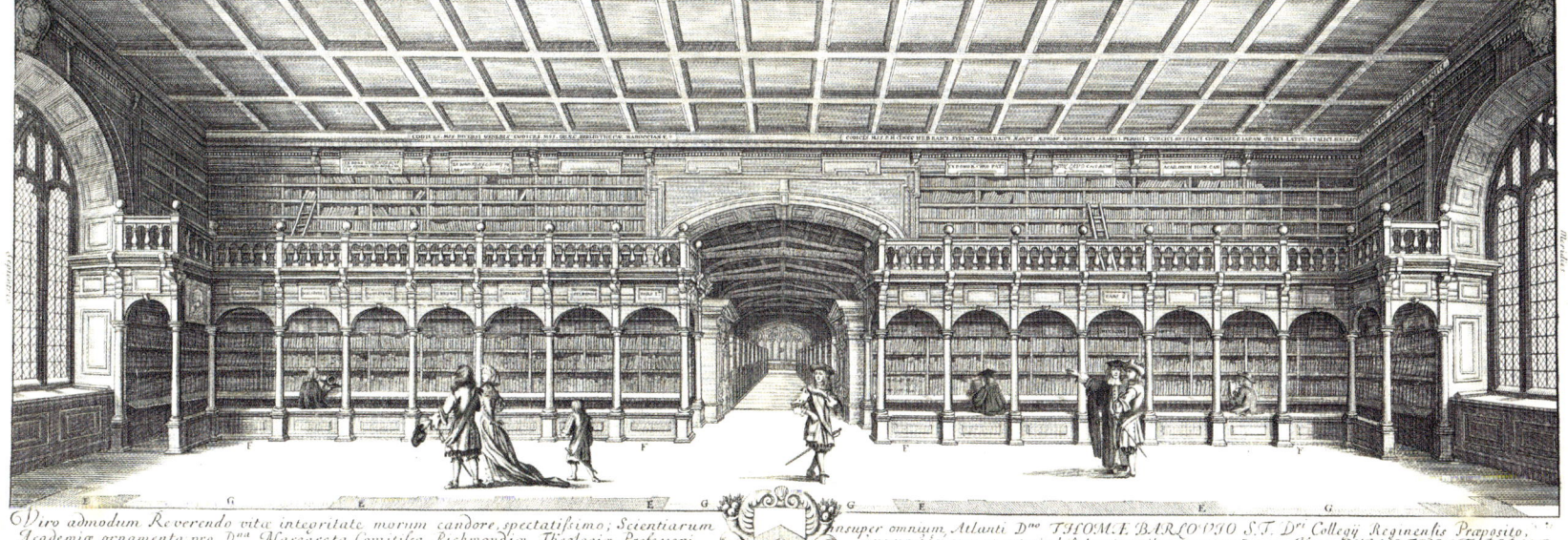

*Viro admodum Reverendo vitæ integritate morum candore spectatissimo, Scientiarum*     *Insuper omnium Atlanti D.ᵐᵒ THOMÆ BARLOVIO S.T. D.ʳⁱ Collegij Reginensis Præposito.*
*Academiæ ornamento, pro D.ⁿᵃ Margareta Comitissa Richmondiæ Theologiæ Professori*     *ΧΡΑΩΤΙΖΡΝΤΩ, et exteris hic hospitantibus semper Patrono Hunc BIBLIOTHECÆ BODLEI-*
*AN.Æ Typum, Cui (dum IPSE præfuit) AVCTARIVM SELDENI Pelion se Ossæ gigan-*     *teo nisu, sed felici conjecit, optimo jure, debitiq. observantiâ.     D.D.C.Q.   Dav. Loggan.*

*Dav. Loggan Delin. A.*     *Sculp. cum Privil. S.R.M.*

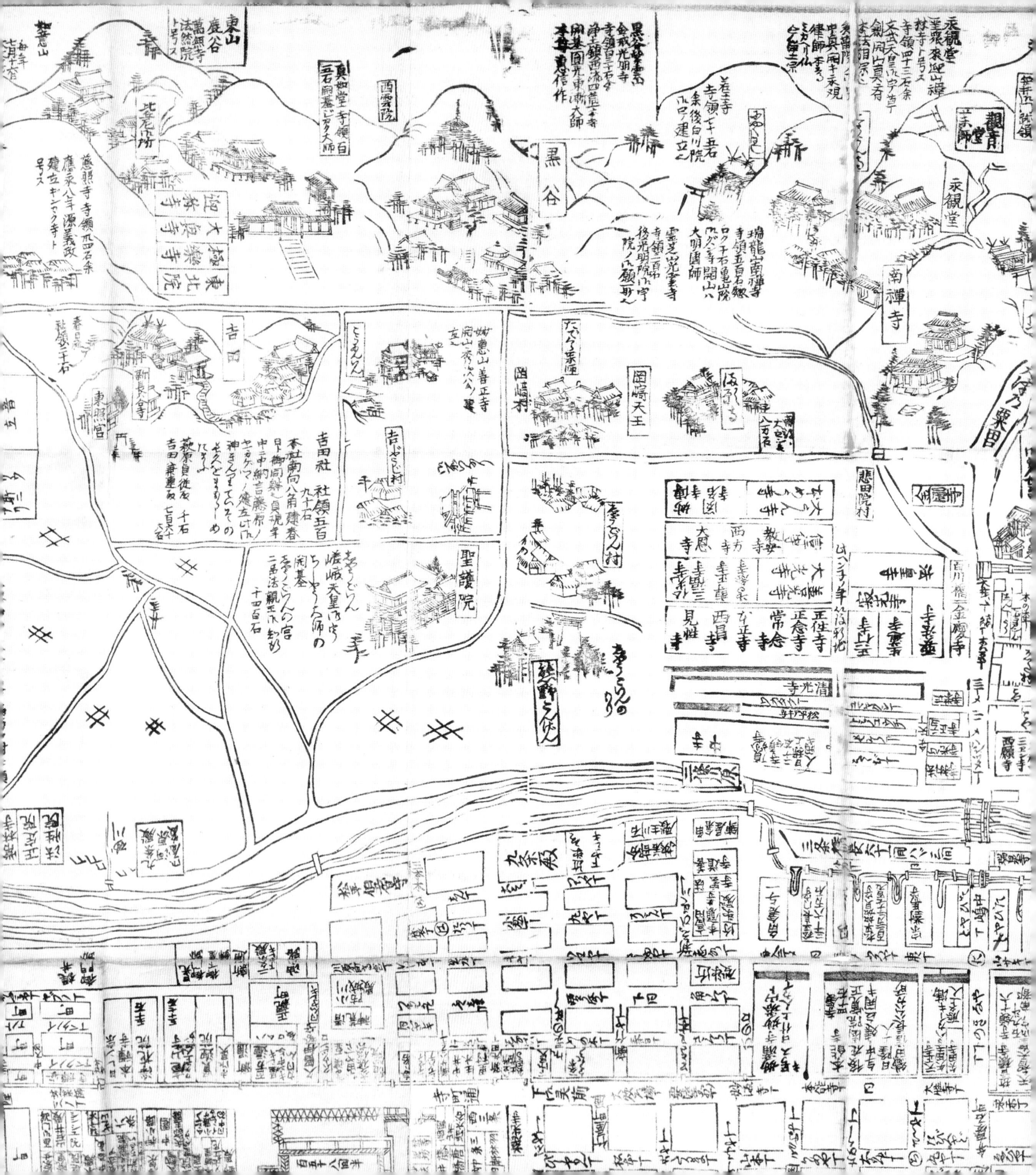

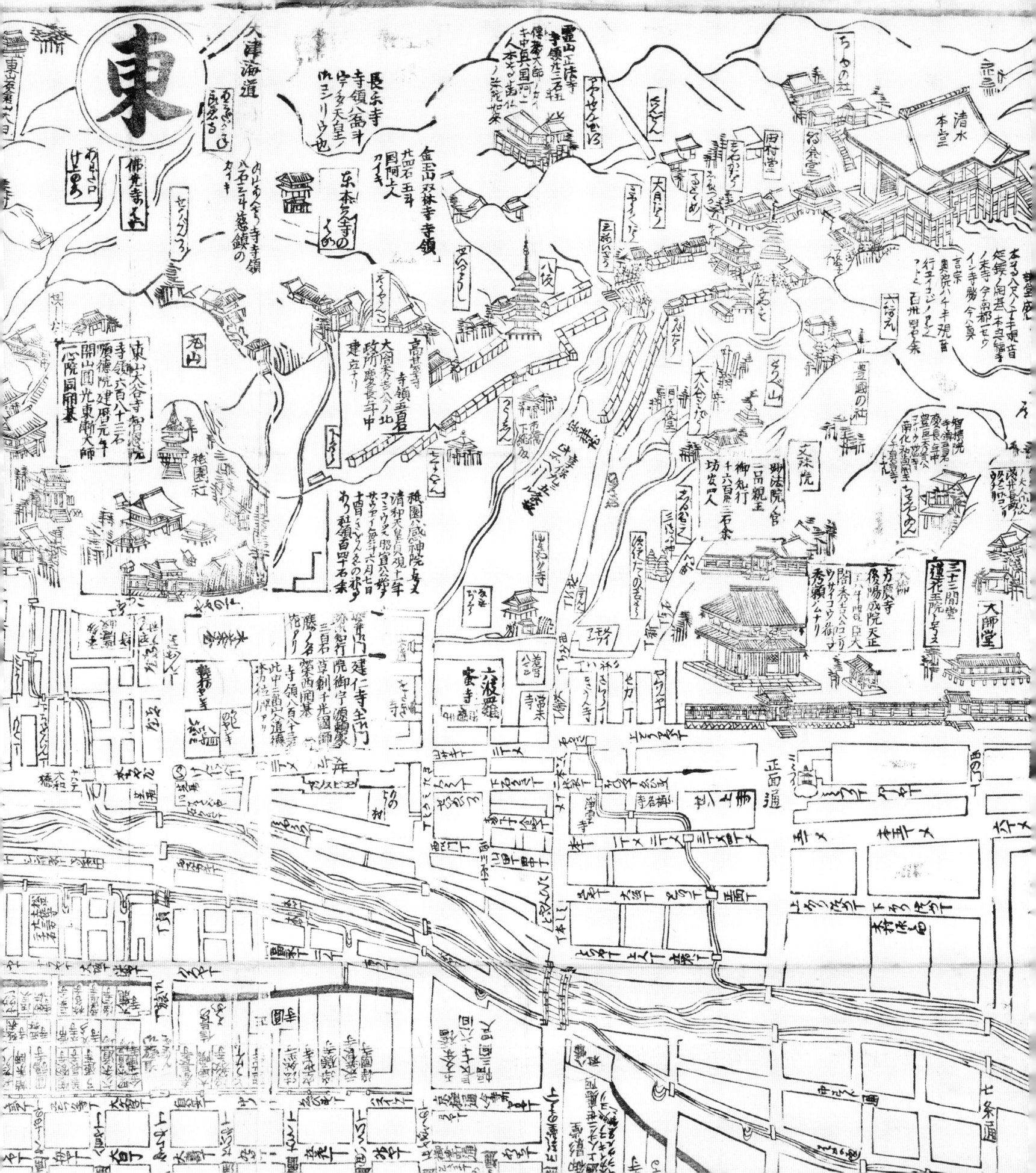

ratified England's trade privileges in Japan, and represents the oldest memorandum of understanding between the two countries.

Two further gifts of exceptional importance arrived at the Bodleian in the second half of the seventeenth century. The first came with the collection of John Selden (1584–1654) in 1659. This was *Sanctos no gosagueô no vchi nuqigaqi*, an anthology of the lives of Christian saints and martyrs. The second, a Japanese translation of Thomas à Kempis's *De Imitatione Christi*, was donated in 1695 by John Evans, chaplain for the East India Company who later became Bishop of Bangor and Meath. These two books represent a milestone in the history of printing in Japan, and testify to the prolific publishing activities of Christian missionaries stationed in Asia (see chapter 4).

Following this surprisingly high number of accessions of Japanese books, the exchanges between England and Japan were not so numerous in the eighteenth century. This is perhaps a long-term consequence of the closure of the Japanese borders to most foreign merchants in 1635, as well as the failure of the English East India Company in the archipelago. Nevertheless, a few sporadic donations arrived in those decades. In 1750 a large map of Kyoto was donated to the Bodleian by Frederick Pigou, a merchant who was possibly director of the East India Company (FIG. 3).

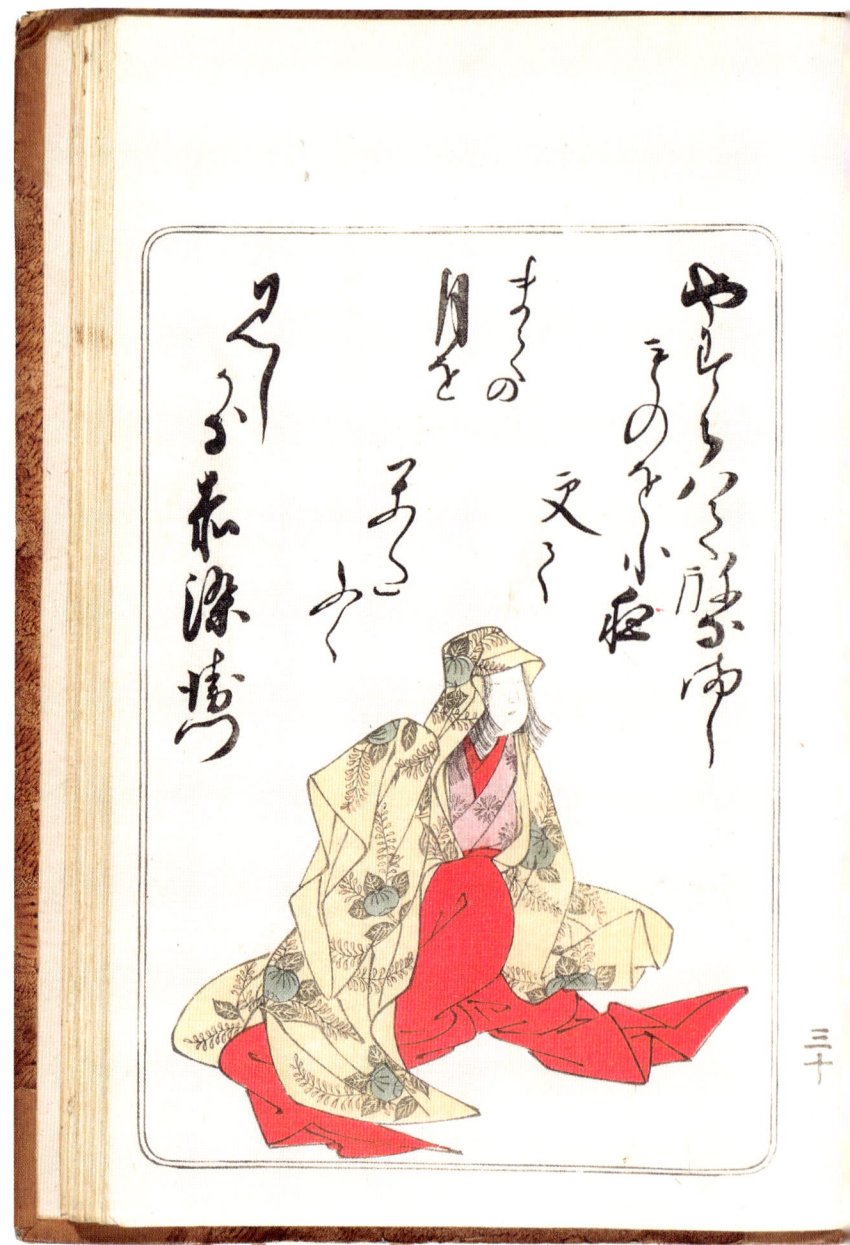

3 PREVIOUS SPREAD Map of Kyoto donated to the Bodleian by Frederick Pigou in 1750. *Shinsen zōho Kyō ōezu*, published in Kyoto possibly in the early eighteenth century. Nipponica 637.

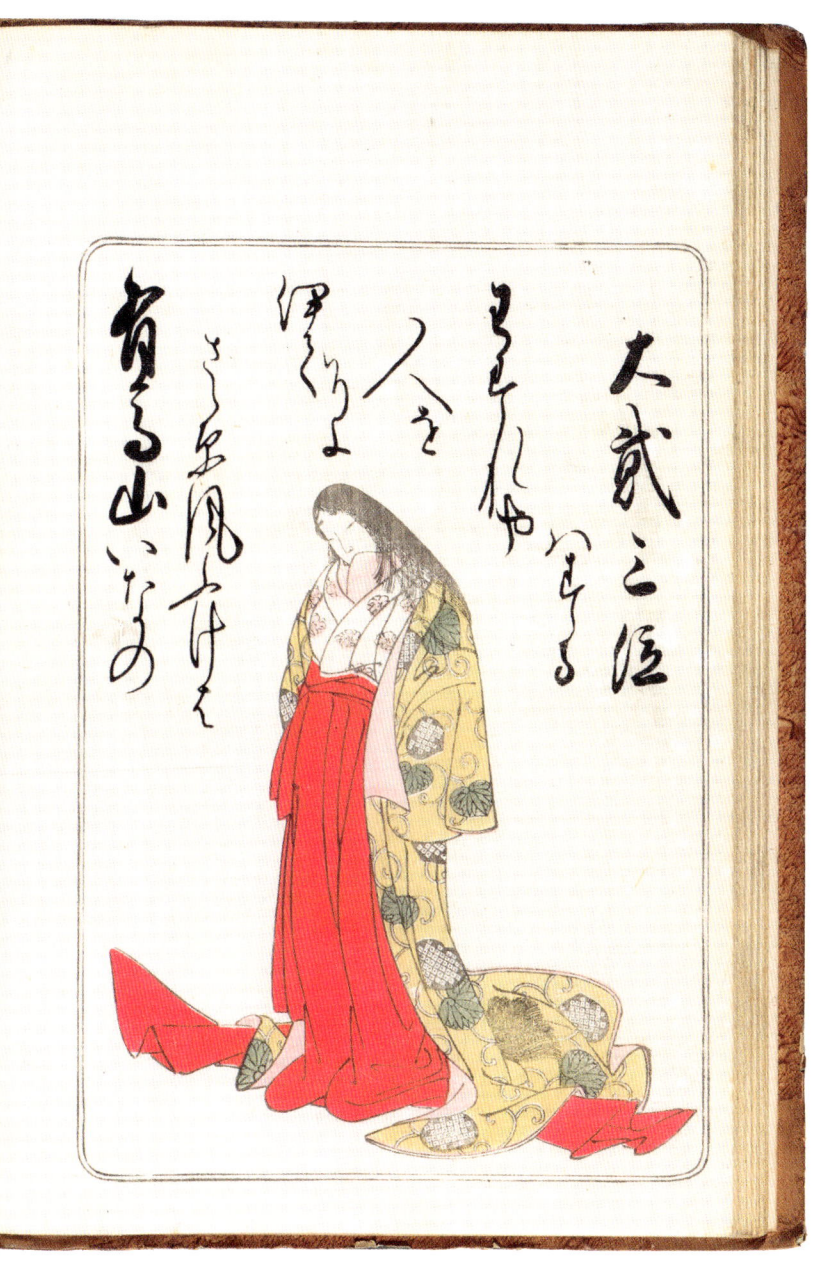

From the nineteenth century, Japanese books begin to arrive with renewed impetus, mostly via donations and subsequently thanks to the development of a more systematic acquisition policy. This included materials procured at auctions and specialized sales, as well as through formal exchanges with other institutions.

In the 1820s, the Bodleian acquired two important publications formerly owned by Louis-Mathieu Langlès (1763–1824), a renowned French orientalist and keeper of oriental manuscripts at the Bibliothèque Royale.[6] Langlès managed to amass a significant collection of rare editions and hard-to-come-by books, which were sold at auction on 24 March 1825.[7] Among these, purchased by the Bodleian, were two volumes published by the Jesuit mission press in the early seventeenth century: *Arte da lingoa de Iapam* (Arch. B d.14), a Japanese grammar in Portuguese published in 1604, and *Vocabulario de Iapon declarado primero en Portugues* (4° L 67 Jur). The latter, a Spanish translation of the first Japanese–Portuguese dictionary printed in Manila in 1630, seems to had been in the possession of Isaac Titsingh (1745–1812), who was intermittently head of the Dutch trading station in Japan during the late eighteenth century.

A small number of illustrated Japanese books arrived in 1834 with the bequest of Francis Douce (1757–1834), antiquary, bibliophile and former

4 A two-page spread (fols 29v–30r) of *Nishiki Hyakunin Isshu Azuma Ori*, 1775, published in Edo by Kariganeya Gisuke and illustrated by Katsukawa Shunshō (1726–1792). Ink and colour on paper. Douce Jap. d.1.

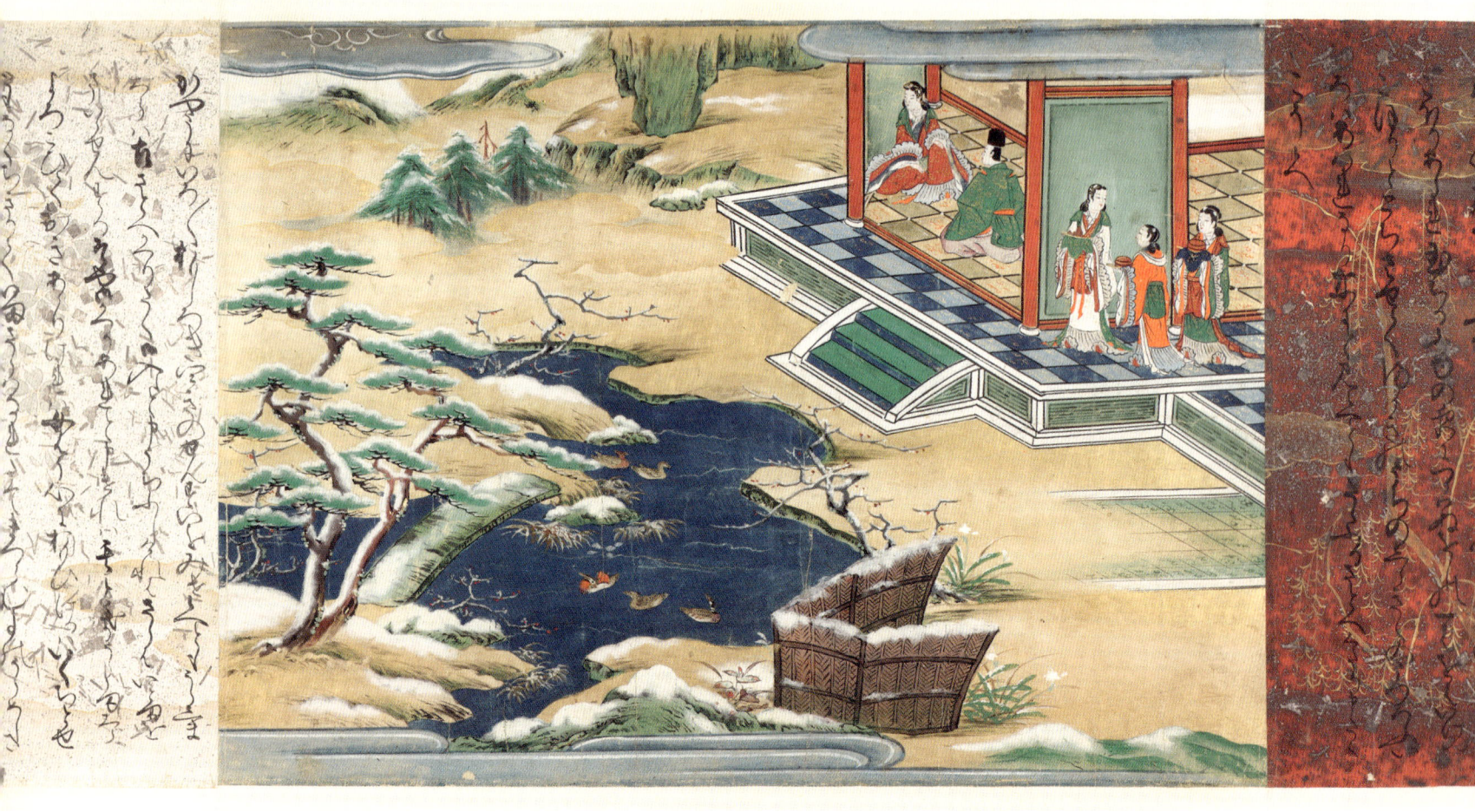

5 ABOVE & OPENING PAGES A section from a painted handscroll narrating the tale of Urashima, possibly seventeenth century, Japan. Ink, colour, gold pigment and cut gold leaf on paper. MS. Jap. c.4 (R).

Keeper of Manuscripts at the British Museum. Douce was not interested in Japan specifically, but had a general curiosity for the arts of Europe and Asia, as demonstrated by his extensive collection of illustrated books, which also encompassed fine examples of Chinese and Persian painted manuscripts. Among his collection of Japanese illustrated books there was an etiquette manual, a war tale and a poetry anthology (FIG. 4). Some of these books were formerly in the hands of Dr Johan Arnold Stützer (1763–1821), a Swedish naturalist and physician who was stationed in Japan between 1787 and 1788.[8] It is likely that Douce secured these publications at an auction in London in 1823, possibly with the aid of the bookseller Robert Triphook (1781–1868).[9]

Towards the end of the century, a few more Japanese books were gifted to the Bodleian by Mr. S. Amos and later by Friedrich Max Müller

(1823–1900), professor of Sanskrit philology and the religions of India at the University of Oxford. This was a small yet significant donation, which comprised Japanese editions of Chinese classics, legal texts and Buddhist literature, reflecting the growing interest in Oriental Studies as a research subject taught at the University. The Amos and Müller donations were catalogued and described together with the Japanese books formerly in the collection of Alexander Wylie (1815–1887), whose library was purchased by the Bodleian between 1881 and 1882.[10] This first printed catalogue of Japanese holdings in the Bodleian Library was compiled by Nanjō Bun'yū (1849–1927), a Japanese Buddhist priest who was at the time studying under Max Müller's guidance.[11]

Donations of manuscripts and printed books remained the primary means by which to grow the collection, but the Bodleian also began purchasing manuscripts written in Japanese around the turn of the century. According to an entry in the *Oxford University Gazette*, the first Japanese-language manuscript to be acquired by the Library was an anthology of poetry (MS. Jap. b.1) inscribed on gilded cards, which was purchased at auction for the sum of £4 8s in 1888 (see chapter 3). Other purchases followed in subsequent years: two Japanese manuscripts (MS. Jap. c.2 and MS. Jap. d.3) were purchased in 1896, two more – MS. Jap. c.4 (R) and MS. Jap. c.5 – were acquired in 1901 (FIG. 5), and three additional manuscripts were purchased in 1903, registered as MS. Jap. d.6, MS. Jap. d.7 (R) and MS. Jap. d.8 (R).[12]

The collection kept growing throughout the twentieth century, thanks to new acquisitions and donations. In 1908, distinguished British diplomat and scholar Sir Ernest Mason Satow (1843–1929) presented the Bodleian with a substantial collection of 328 volumes of Japanese Buddhist texts and commentaries. By this time the Bodleian had built up a sizable number of Japanese books, as suggested by the hiring of a 'special assistant' for the cataloguing of books in Japanese languages in the same year.[13]

Between the late nineteenth and early twentieth centuries, the collecting patterns begin to change. It is in this period that the collection grew to include lavishly illuminated manuscripts and handscrolls (see chapter 2), painted albums and polychrome prints – all objects which reflected a collecting informed by a new aesthetic sensibility fostered by the spread of Japonisme across Europe.

6 Postcard written by Paget Toynbee during his sojourn on Mount Kōya on 13 April 1887. Ink on paper. MS. Toynbee d.23, fol. 20r.

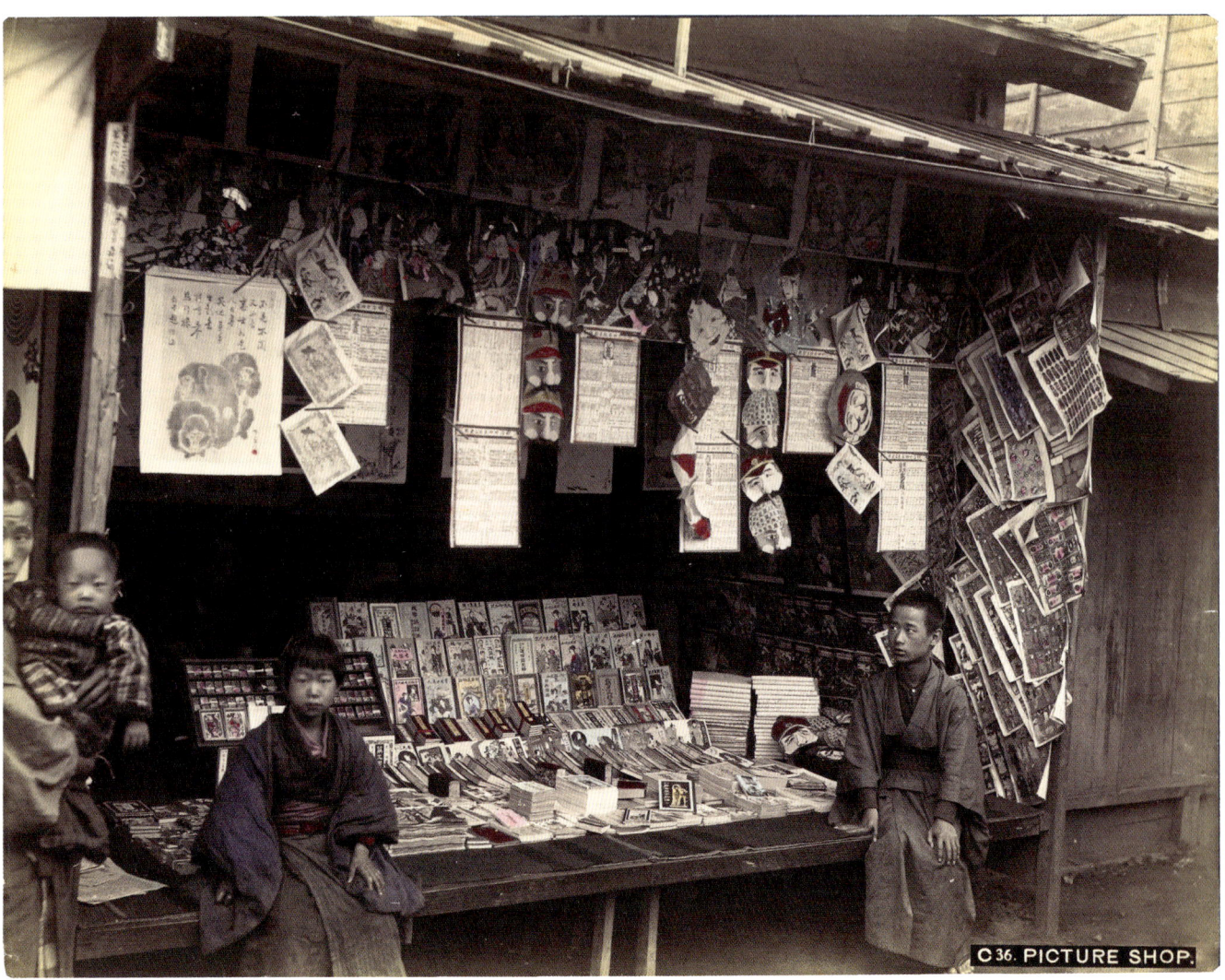

C 36. PICTURE SHOP.

7 A Japanese bookshop in the late nineteenth century. Possibly taken in Tokyo around 1890–91. Hand-coloured photographic print, unmounted. British Museum.

This shift is evident when we look at several gifts presented to the Bodleian by travellers, researchers and intellectuals who visited Japan at the turn of the century.

For instance, the preeminent Dante scholar Paget Jackson Toynbee (1855–1932), alumnus of Balliol College, made numerous donations of books and manuscripts to the Bodleian between 1912 and 1923.[14] Among the first donation of 1912, we count twelve manuscripts and approximately forty woodblock-printed books that he acquired while travelling through Japan in 1887. Toynbee was entranced by this journey. In a postcard (FIG. 6), written during his sojourn at Mount Kōya in Wakayama Prefecture, Toynbee writes: 'I am writing this in a Buddhist priest house at the top of a mountain ... Japan is a fine country and the people are delightful, most hospitable, kindly, and good humoured.'[15]

While for the most part Toynbee's donation comprised works relating to Dante and to Horace Walpole, his interest in Japanese printed books and illuminated manuscripts was conveyed in letters addressed to the then Bodley's Librarian Falconer Madan (1851–1935). In his correspondence, Toynbee recalls visiting local booksellers and confessed his personal preference for a long silk handscroll, now registered as MS Japan. c.7 (R), which was illustrated with attractive paintings of celebrated Japanese poets and inscribed with one of their most famous verses. In a letter dated 30 January 1913, Toynbee praised this painted scroll:

> I believe the most valuable thing of the whole lot is the simple roll of portraits of Japanese poets and poetesses – not only on account of the portraits, but also because it contains specimens of calligraphy ... Perhaps, someday, when a change of exhibits is made in the showcases, space might be found for the roll, with one or two of the figures shown. I used to have it so, unrolling different bits at intervals.[16]

Madan welcomed Toynbee's proposal and arranged for the handscroll to be displayed in the Library: 'I am glad to say that there will be ready, within a fortnight, a new case in the Picture Gallery in which I shall be exhibiting "Recent Acquisitions". In that I will put in a prominent place your Japanese roll, with all care that it be not injured by the light.'[17]

Only a few years after Toynbee's donation, another gift of illuminated manuscripts was presented to the Bodleian in 1914 by Annabel Nevill Gwyn Jeffreys (1855–1928), the widow of Henry Nottidge Moseley (1844–1891).[18] Moseley was an Oxford-educated British naturalist, who participated in various expeditions around the world and played a crucial role in securing the anthropological collection now housed at Oxford's Pitt Rivers Museum. He travelled on board HMS *Challenger*, a British vessel that reached Japan in 1875, where he remained from 11 April until 16 June. During this period Mosley purchased various picture books, which he described as 'full of interest'.[19] By the time Moseley visited the archipelago, Japan had developed a thriving publishing business (see chapter 6) and books had become a widely available commercial commodity (FIG. 7). In his *Notes by a Naturalist on the Challenger*, Moseley writes: 'In Osaka, I spent much of my time in the booksellers' quarter, where there is nearly a mile of continuous book-shops. I bought here a large collection of illustrated books.'[20] During this visit, Mosely likely acquired the printed books and manuscripts that were later presented as a gift to the Bodleian. The donation included an album (MS. Jap. d. 25) containing fine examples of poetry cards richly decorated with gold, painted with seasonal themes, and inscribed in a sophisticated calligraphic hand (see chapter 3). Furthermore, he presented the Library with twenty-one manuscript volumes (MS. Jap. d. 30-50), each furnished with indigo-dyed covers decorated with hand-painted floral motifs or landscapes, and further embellished with lavish doublures (the ornamental lining on the inside front and back covers of a book) made of patterned silver foil (see chapters 2 & 4).

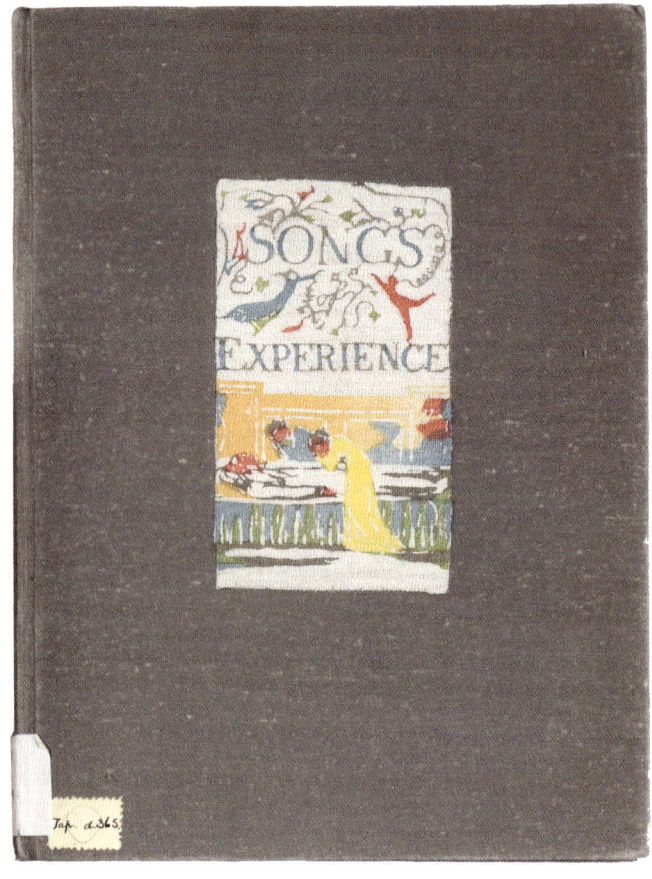

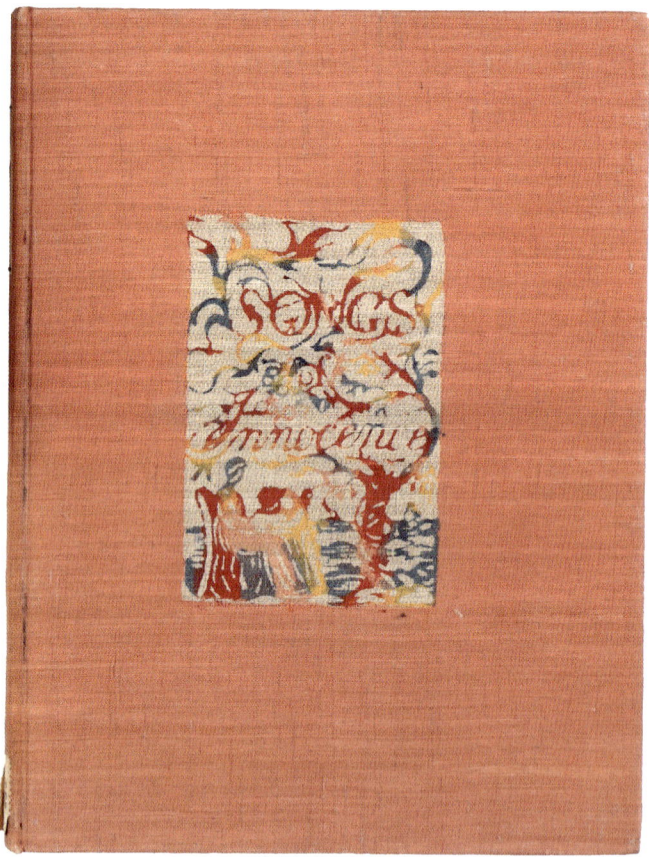

In the immediate post-Second World War period, the development of the collection was chiefly connected to the teaching of Japanese Studies as an academic subject at the University.[21] Consequently, in the following decades the Library substantially increased its holdings to support teaching and research. Books in Japanese or about Japanese Studies remained split across various branch libraries and affiliated centres until 1993, when the Bodleian Japanese Library opened its doors in the newly constructed Nissan Institute Building at 27 Winchester Road. Over time, the Japanese collections were centralized there, in response to the academic community's desire to rehouse all books and journals about Japan in one location. Although collection-building efforts were now focusing on supporting the broader academic community, sporadic donations of rare books and materials arrived throughout the twentieth century. For instance, in the 1950s a group of Japanese translations of William Blake (1757–1827) was presented to the Bodleian by surgeon and bibliophile Sir Geoffrey Keynes (1887–1982).[22] These limited editions are splendid examples of the artistic and aesthetic influence that the Japanese Folk Craft

8 Three fine press limited editions published in Japan during the interwar period. RIGHT *Wiruyamu Bureiku shoshi*, 1929, Guroria Sosaete, Tokyo – a bibliography of the works of William Blake (1757–1827) edited by Jugaku Bunshō (1900–1992). TOP LEFT *Muzen no uta*, 1933, Kyoto, Kōjitsuan Press (Blake's 1789 *Songs of Innocence*). BOTTOM LEFT *Mumyō no uta*, 1935, Kyoto, Kōjitsuan Press (Blake's 1794 *Songs of Experience*). These volumes were donated to the Bodleian Library by Sir Geoffrey Keynes in the early 1950s. [CF] JAB 14, [CF] JAB 15, [CF] JAB 19.

Movement had on books produced by small and private presses during the interwar period (FIG. 8).

In the twenty-first century, the Bodleian continues to expand its holdings about Japan, including pre-modern rare books and manuscripts as well as modern and contemporary works of art. The Library acquired its first Japanese artist's book in 2019, and a year later it received a donation of three prints by contemporary artist Yoshimura Yoshio (1950–2013).[23] A rare book of fiction for young adults (see chapter 6) was acquired in 2021 with the generous support of the Friends of the Nations' Libraries. In 2022 the Library was presented with various gifts, including an anthology of Japanese poetry by thirty-six female poets (FIG. 9), a printed album formerly in the collection of Edmond de Goncourt (1822–1896), who purchased it from the renowned Paris-based dealer Hayashi Tadamasa (1853–1906). Furthermore, in the same year, the Bodleian received the collection of early-modern Japanese printed books, manuscripts and ephemera donated by Professor Peter Kornicki.[24] This is arguably one of the largest collections of Japanese materials that has entered the Library since the time of Sir Ernest Satow. It comprises some remarkable items, including two specimens of early printed books (FIG.10): a volume dated 1278 (Kornicki 1)

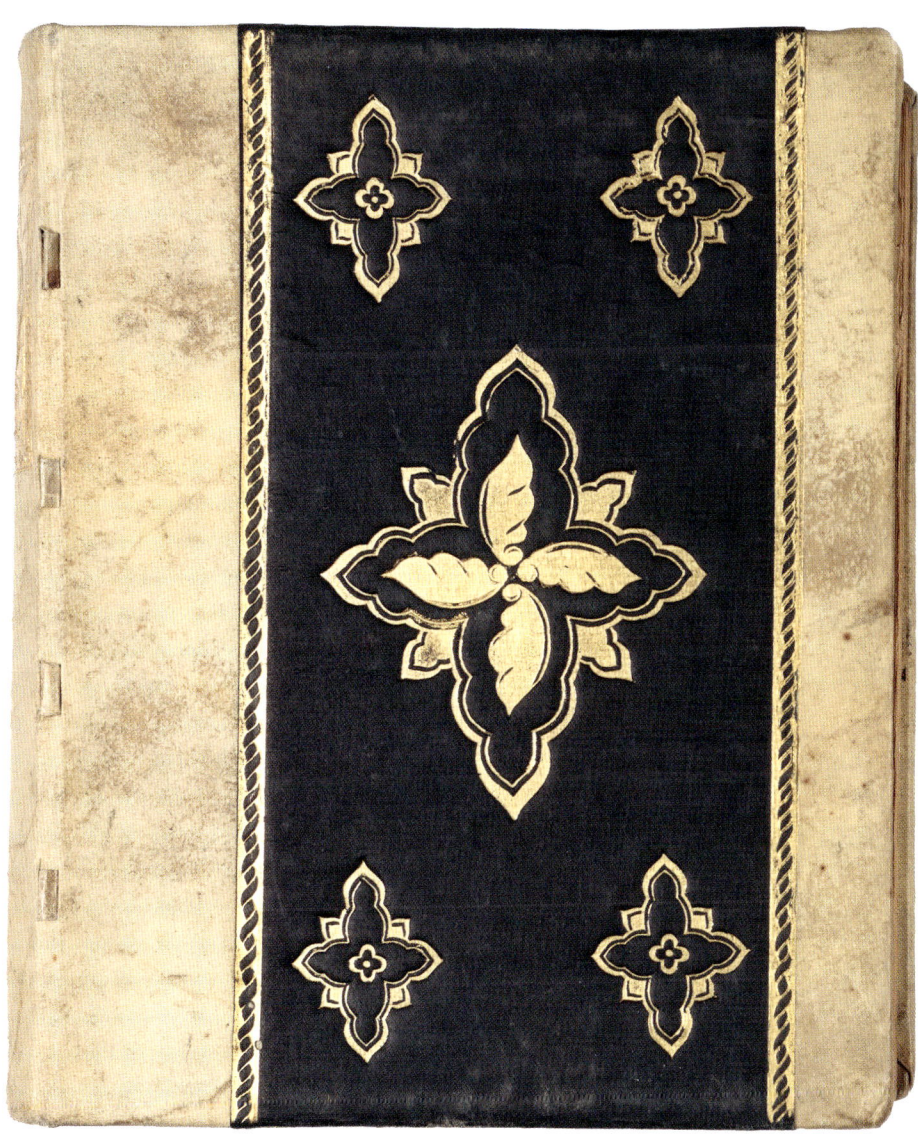

9 OVERLEAF  Woodblock-printed illustration by Katsushika Hokusai (1760–1849) from *Nyōbō Sanjūrokkasen*, 1801, published in Edo by Nishimuraya Yohachi, illustrated by Chōbunsai Eishi (1756–1829) and Katsushika Hokusai. Ink and colour on paper. Nipponica 1003.

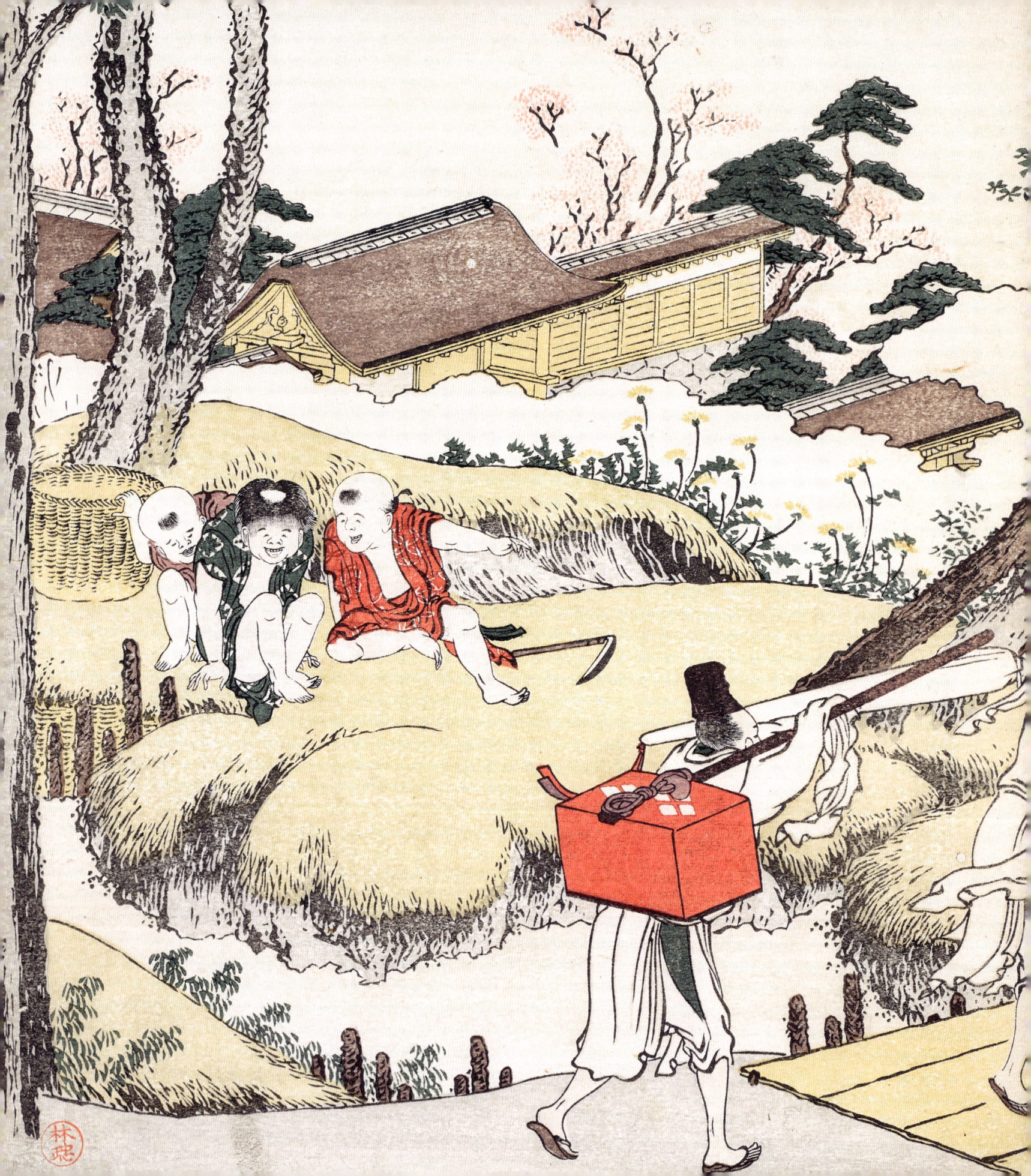

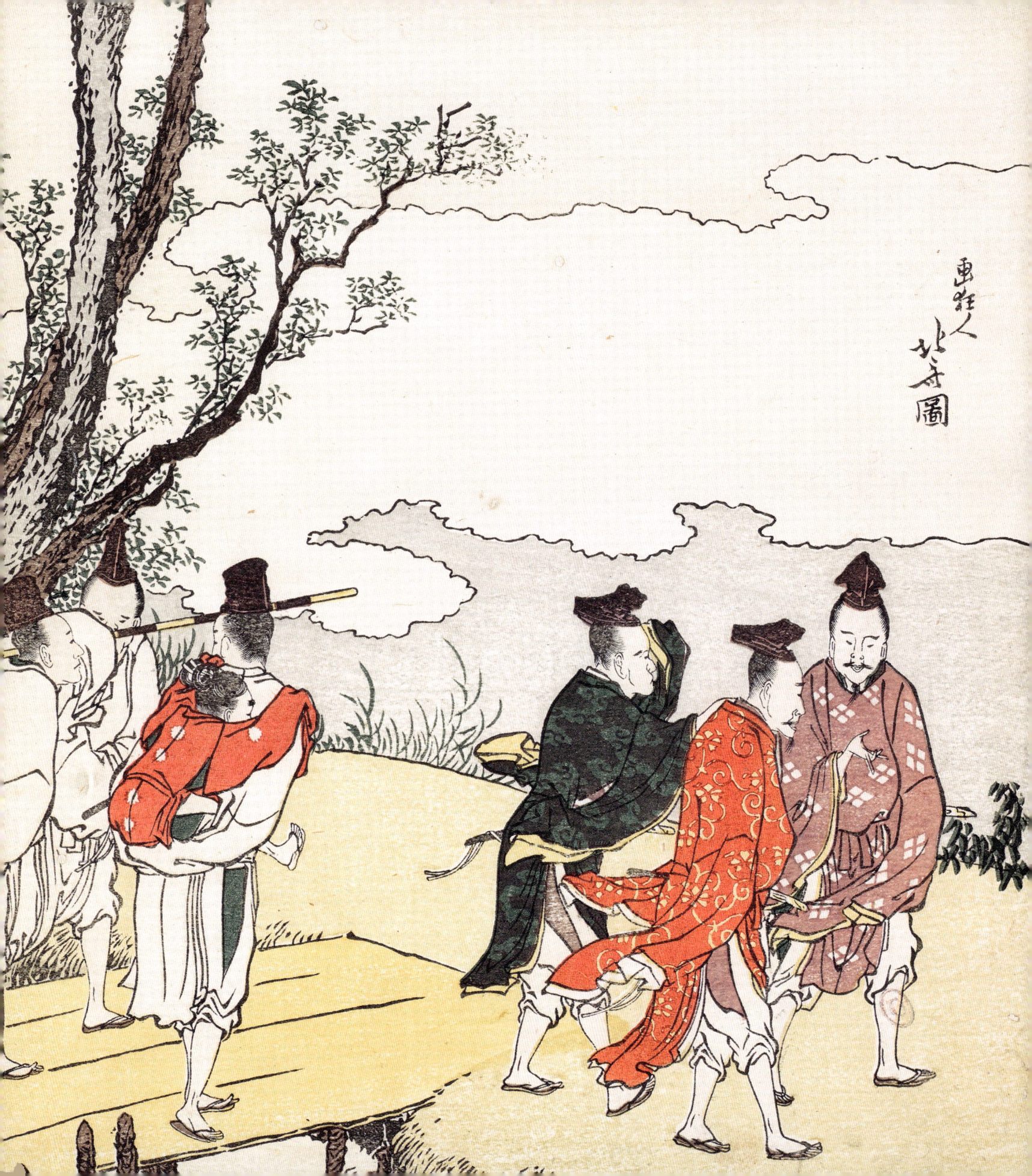

and a handscroll printed in the fourteenth century (Kornicki 2).

*Splendours of Japan* explores the Bodleian Japanese collection with six independent essays authored by leading scholars and experts in their respective field. Each chapter analysesa different theme by shedding new light on representative works in the collection. Peter Kornicki (chapter 1) investigates early encounters between England and Japan, explaining how Japanese books and manuscripts arrived in England from the archipelago in the seventeenth century and later entered the Bodleian Library. In chapter 2 Melissa McCormick examines a narrative handscroll from the Toynbee donation, and observes it along with other lavishly illuminated manuscripts, which were possibly created for nuptial libraries. In chapter 3, Edward Kamens offers new insights about the artistic and literary dimensions of two never-before-translated poetic anthologies which arrived at the Bodleian at the turn of the century. Marinita Stiglitz (chapter 4) delves into the study of the materiality of Japanese manuscripts and printed books in the Bodleian Japanese collection, focusing on the production and use of handmade paper, colour pigments and ink. In chapter 5, Katja Triplett discuss the production of printed publications by the Jesuit mission press by investigating some of the works formerly in the hands of John Selden, John Evans and Louis-Mathieu Langlès. Finally, Laura Moretti (chapter 6) offers an overview of the thriving publishing market in the early-modern and modern period by analysing works from the Douce gift along with some more recent acquisitions.

## A NOTE ON JAPANESE TRANSLITERATION

Romanization of Japanese words has been used throughout this book, following the modified Hepburn style in *Kenkyusha's New Japanese–English Dictionary*. The only exception to this is the occasional instance where citing the original Japanese characters is relevant to the narrative. Macrons are included, except where anglicized words have become an established part of the English language (for example, shogun). Place names follow the same principle (for example, Tokyo). For both singular and plural renditions of romanized words, the same form is used (for example, the third and seventh Tokugawa shogun).

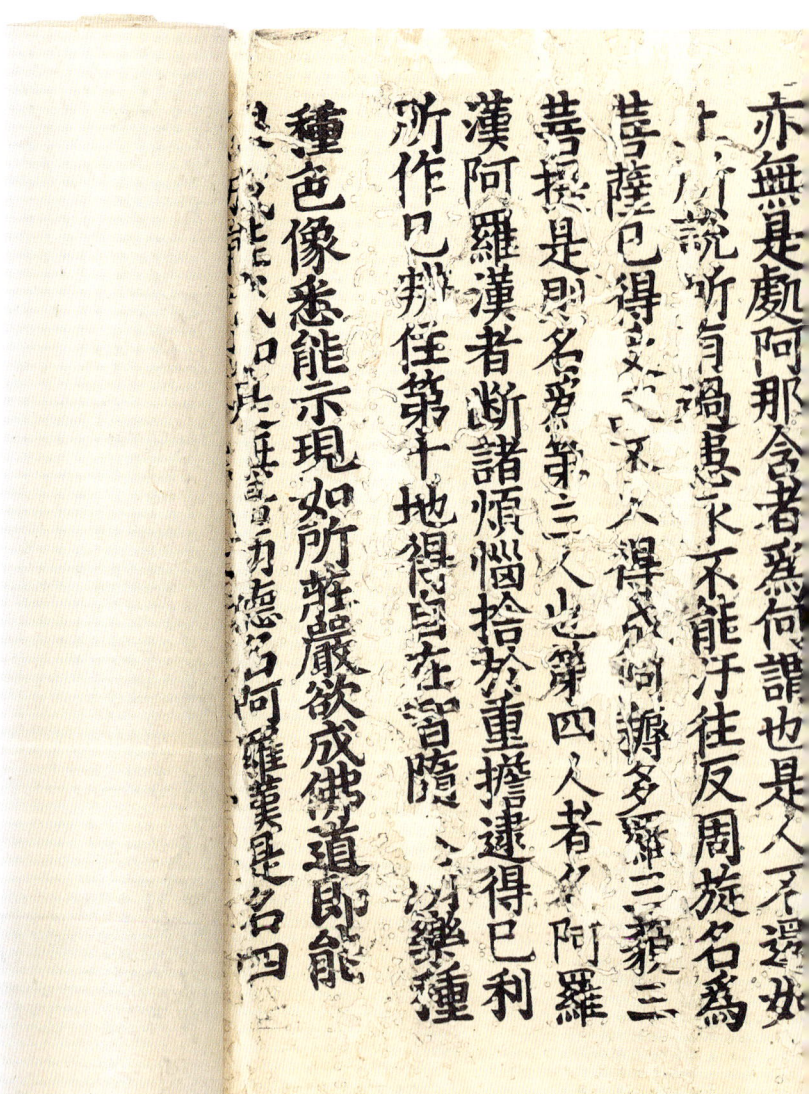

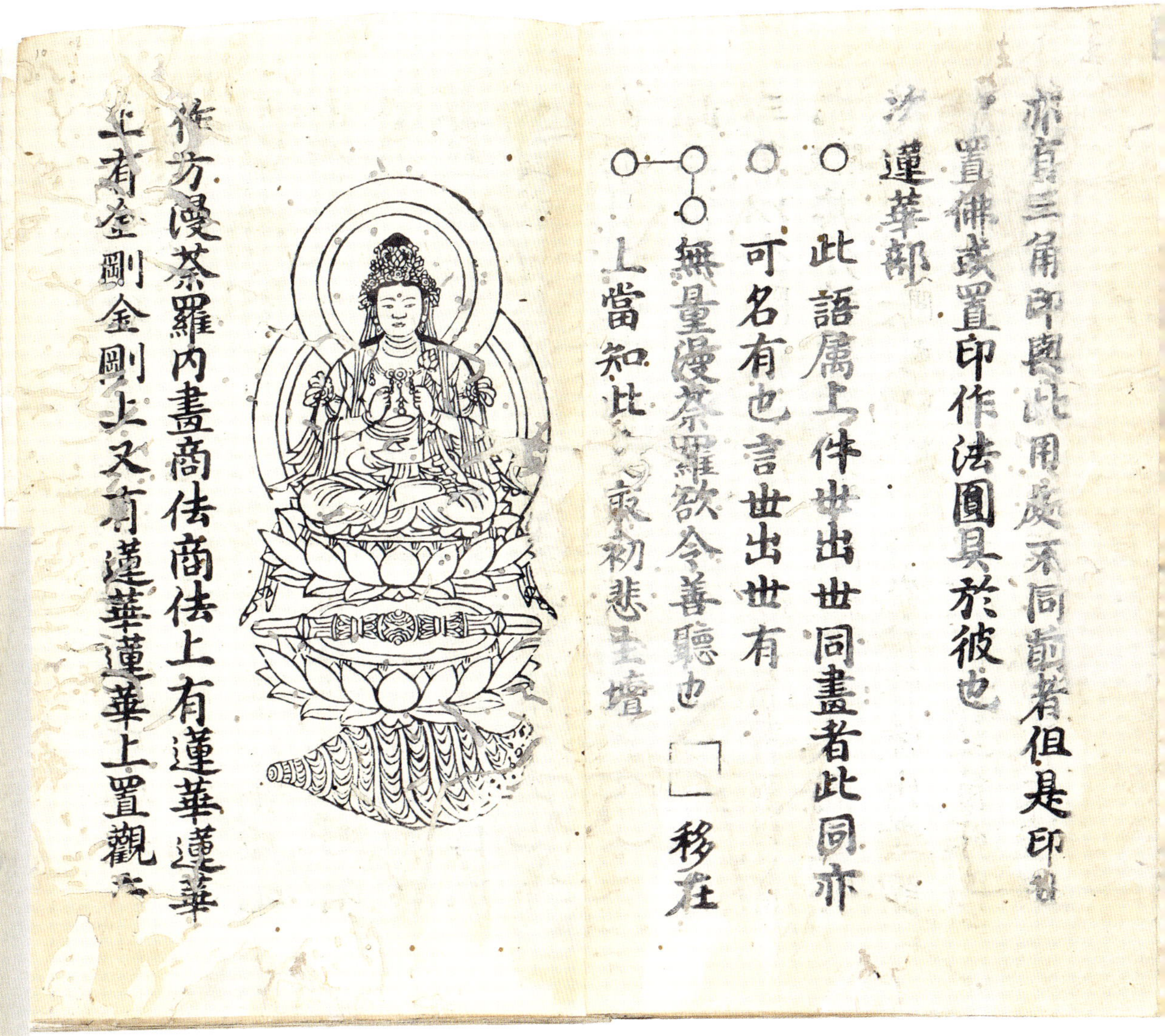

依方漫荼羅內畫商佉商佉上有蓮華蓮華
上有金剛金剛上又有蓮華蓮華上置觀…

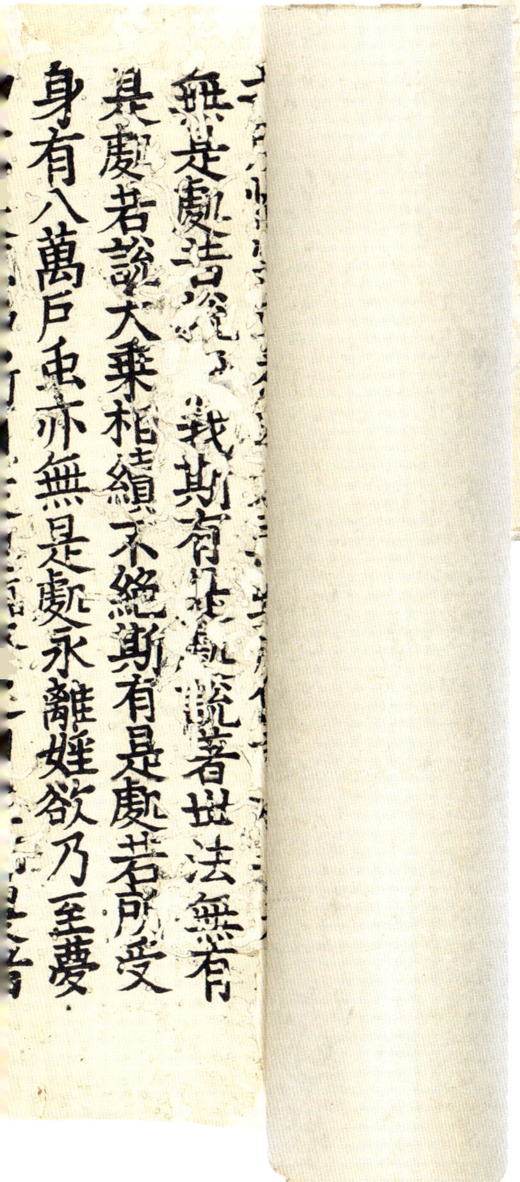

沙蓮華部
此語屬上伴世出世同畫者此同亦
可名有也言世出世有
無量漫荼羅欲令善聽也
當知比之…東初悲王壇
移在

亦有三角印與此用處不同前者但是印
置佛處置印作法圓具於彼也

身有八萬戶虫亦無是處永離婬欲乃至慶
無是處說大乘柏績不絕斷有是處所受
具處若談…我其有…說著出法無有

10 Two early printed books from the Kornicki collection.
ABOVE *Daibirushana jōbutsukyō sho*, 1278, printed at the
Kongōbuji on Mt Kōya, Japan. This was the first Japanese
edition of a commentary on the Mahāvairocana Tantra
by Yi Xing (683–727), a monk of the Tang dynasty. LEFT
*Daihan nehangyō*, thirteenth/fourteenth century, Japan.
This is a Japanese edition of the Mahāparinirvāṇa Sūtra,
a text on the death of the Buddha. Kornicki 1; Kornicki 2.

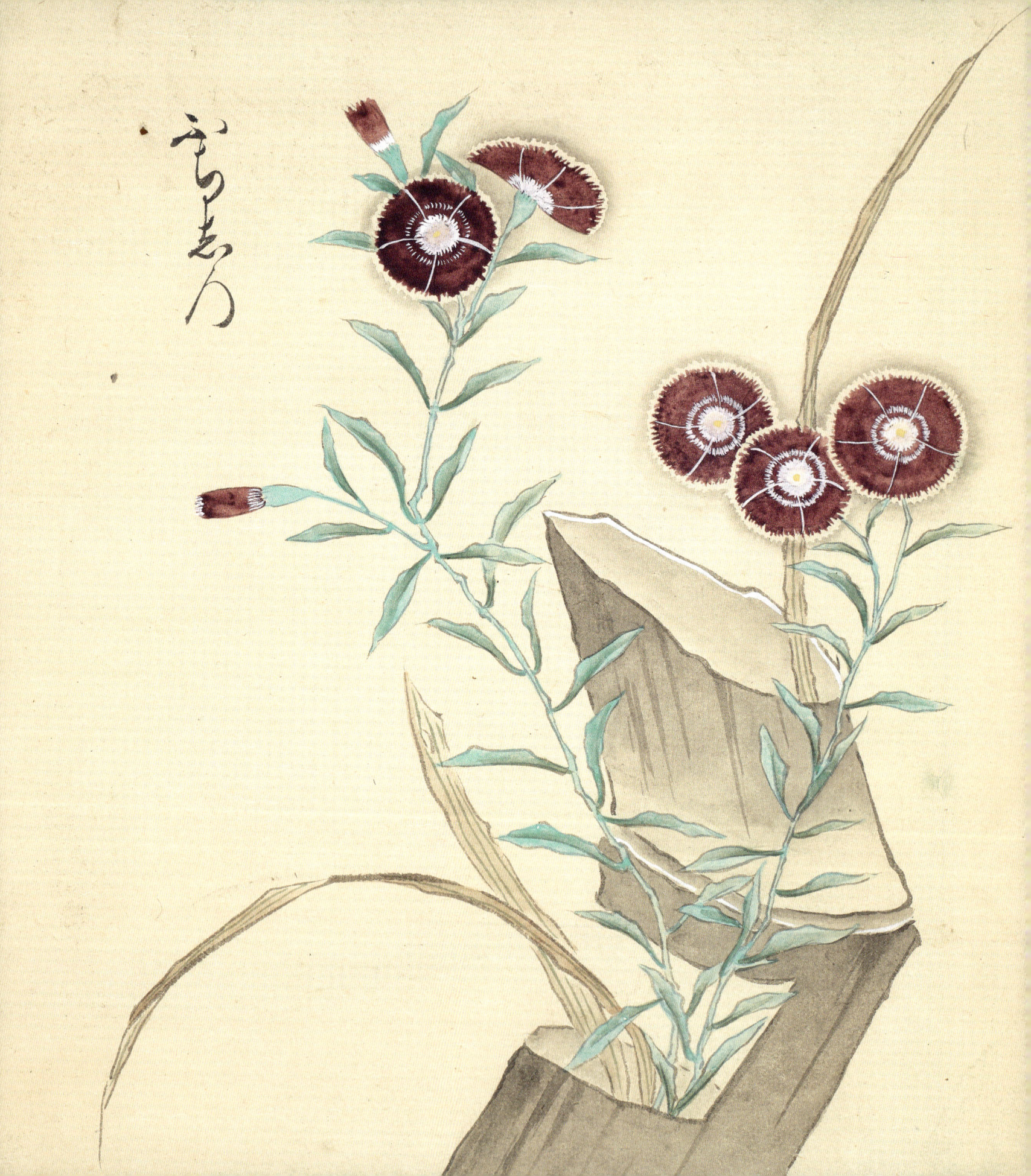

1

# Early encounters with Japan: the first Japanese books to reach Europe

PETER KORNICKI

正月中

二月小

三月大

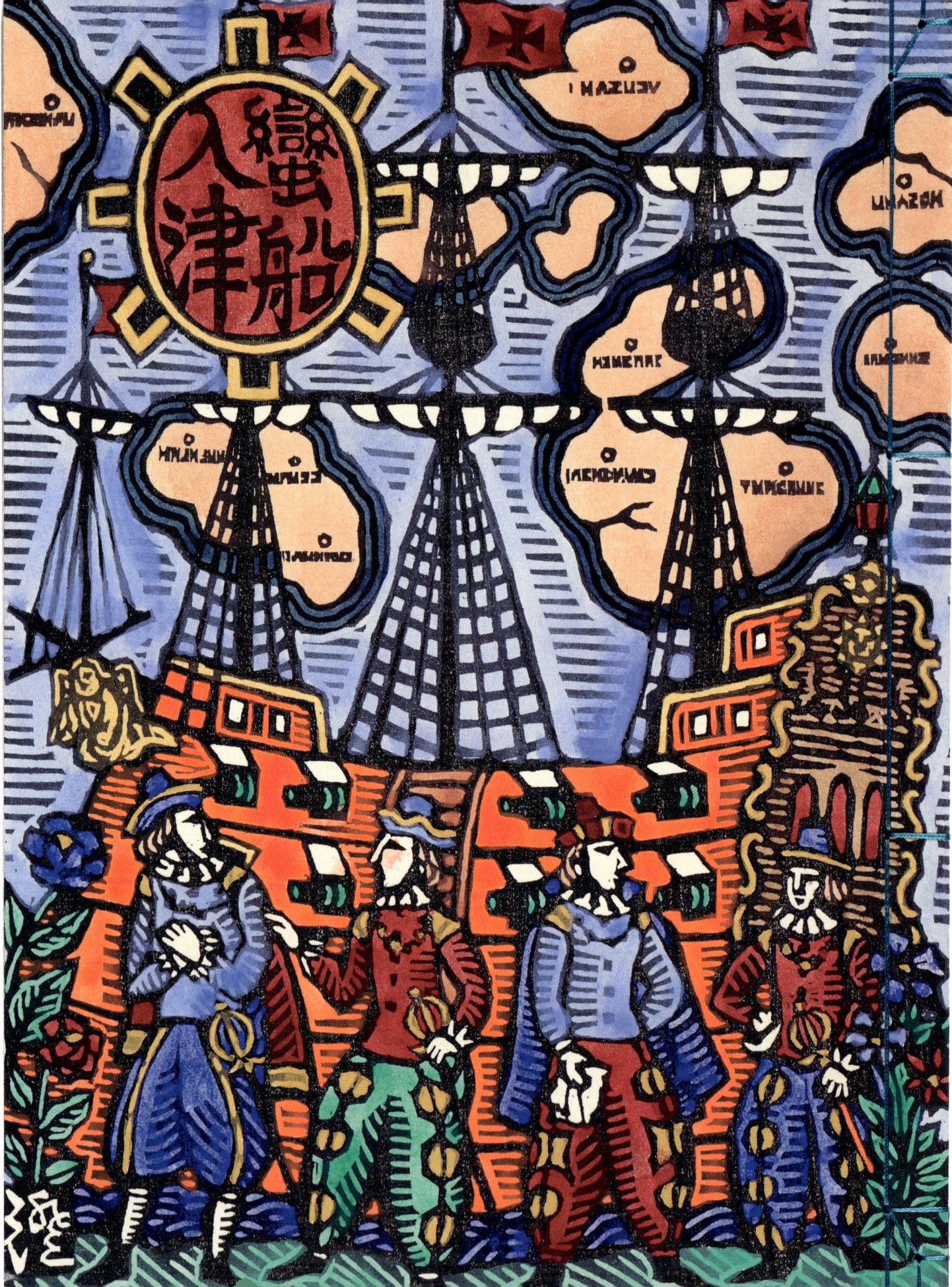

WHEN THE BODLEIAN LIBRARY accessioned its first Japanese books in the seventeenth century, there was not one person in England who could read them. And they were to remain unread and disregarded for centuries. Who collected these books and why, and how did they reach England? How did they end up in the Bodleian, and why did it take so long for anybody to show an interest in them?

Europeans first came into direct contact with Japan in 1543, and merchants and missionaries were soon active on the islands of Japan (FIG. 11). Most of them were Portuguese, Spanish or Italian by origin, but in 1600 the first Englishman arrived. He was William Adams (1564–1620) and he reached Japan as the navigator of a Dutch ship. In time he came to enjoy the favour of the shogun Tokugawa Ieyasu, and he turned this to good use, helping first the Dutch East India Company and then his fellow countrymen in the English East India Company to gain permission to trade in Japan.

Between 1614 and 1619 Adams made a number of trading voyages from Japan to Cochin-China (Vietnam) and elsewhere, and kept logbooks of these voyages (FIG. 12). The last of these ends abruptly on 22 August 1619, when Adams was off the coast of Taiwan on his way back to Japan. The following year, on 16 May, hours before his death, Adams drew up his will – appointing as his executors Richard Cocks (1565–1624), head of the East India Company's trading station in Japan, and his colleague William Eaton. He left Cocks 'all my seacards [charts] … and my best cattane [*katana* is Japanese for sword]' and Eaton 'all my books and sea instruments that I have'.[1]

Whether the logbooks formed part of his estate and were sent back by Cocks or Eaton or had already been sent back to England by Adams before his death is not known, but they found their way into the hands of Sir Henry Savile (1549–1622), the Warden of Merton College, Oxford. How Savile came by them is unclear but, as one of the translators of the King James Bible, he was a colleague of the Archbishop of Canterbury, George Abbot, whose brother Maurice was a founder member

11 Handpainted cover of Kawakami Sumio, *Bansen Nyūshin*, 1969. European merchants are shown arriving on Japanese shores. Nipponica 1002.

2     The 20 dayd being friday we went about on bifsined to
trim our fip but on lym was bad that wee could do nothing
wee fayrt to tary till other weder buied
this day fayr weder the wind at n Eſt

### 4

3     The 21 being saturdayd here cam a nobell man to Cetouodou
fled from the wauls in Nabu this nand was          we dayd
I heard that the Emperor had got the victory of the wou I
was glad to hear this day we went about to make a pounsd
and other bifsinds in trimmy our clost this day wee a barke fo
Rojima wth my letters this day very fayr weder the wind Est

4     The 22 being sonday wee went about our bifsinds in
trimming our fip this day verri fayr weder the wind
at S W E wet S wst

5     The 23 being monday we still went about to trim
our fip the wind nothereli foull weder

6     The 24 being tuesdayd we still did Calk our fip in
and wth out this Day we set Carpenters a worke to make a
pounp this day it was wethergloud weder but the wind not so
                                                 all most

7     The 25 wth in our fip the Carpenters wook was doon
both sids wth out bord wee neer dom this dayd the
rayn did hinder our wook the wind was no rayny weder
being wednesdayd Et

8     The 26 dayd we begann to tak in balloſt and still Calkynd
wth in E wth out but at noond wee wher aboue not Coueld
to woork but wold haue thee hued wth was goon to
Siam but I had mony and wth hout this
day was fowr dayd the wind at n nwst foull
weder wth rayny

9     The 27 dayd the boothsann Cam to me in the bohalfe
of the Coumpani for their other I told them it was
not dou to them before they Cam to Siam at wt place god sending
to remember if wo ſtay long in Siam I would pay them and after I could not no would not
4 mony wayes but if they had donriget doon them I would mak them wt
raiſd ahebaſt but if they had donriget doon them I would mak them wt
mony wt satisfaction I should be apoynted by the Juſtis of Jappan and
bsids ſtand to ther vppon to satisfi them I would giue them a byll of my
ſelf wayes hand but they would not ſtand to the Juſtis of Jappan
goon but would ſtand ther demand or wee go forwaird in the
               voyage but returne Et

12 Logbook kept by William Adams, 20–27 January 1615, during his voyage to Siam (Thailand). This page records an enforced stay in the Riu Kiu Islands as his junk had sprung a leak (Chinese hostility meant it was impossible to land in China). Alongside difficulties in obtaining the necessaries for repairing his ship, and then the sailors demanding their wages in advance, Adams reports relief at the news of the 'Emperor's' victory during the siege of Osaka. He is referring to the Shogun Toyotomi Hideyori, the effective ruler of Japan at that time. MS. Saville 48, fol. 4r.

of the East India Company. Maurice could have passed the logbooks on to him. Savile donated them to his friend Thomas Bodley, making these logbooks the Bodleian's first acquisition that came from Japan.

By 1620 the Bodleian possessed books in several 'exotic languages', including Chinese, 'Mexican', 'Brazilian' and Arabic. Thomas James, the first librarian, mentioned them in the Latin preface he wrote to the printed Bodleian catalogue of 1620, adding that, 'if not at present, then in the future they will be of benefit to the British state and letters, since matters so demand and the trade of our people in those remoter regions is growing day by day'.[2] He may not have known it, but British traders were already operating in Japan and within a decade the first Japanese books were to reach the Bodleian.

In June 1613 the first English ship reached Japan and anchored at the port of Hirado, on an island off the coast of north-western Kyushu where the Dutch East India Company already had a trading station. The ship was the *Clove*, one of the three ships comprising the eighth voyage of the East India Company. John Saris (*c*.1580–1643) was in command of the expedition, and he brought with him letters and gifts from King James I in the hope of establishing a trading relationship with Japan. After conferring with Adams, Saris made a formal request to Tokugawa Ieyasu for permission to trade in Japan. Ieyasu was by this time living in retirement in Sunpu (Shizuoka) while the incumbent shogun, his son Hidetada, ruled from Edo (Tokyo). Ieyasu still wielded power, however, and he granted permission for the East India Company to trade in Japan. This was embodied in a 'vermilion-seal

document' (*shuinjō*), a permit containing a vermilion impression of Ieyasu's seal, which was taken back to England as proof of the right to trade in Japan. By 1680 this document had reached the Bodleian Library, possibly via the Abbots again, for George was an Oxford man, but it was only in 1985 that it was recognized for what it is (FIG. 13).[3]

Having accomplished his mission, Saris left for England in December 1613. He took 'divers of their books' back with him, which were seen by clergyman–publisher Samuel Purchas. Purchas was aware that they were printed, but commented that 'the pictures in their books are not comparable to the art in ours'. He seems not to have been offended by the pictures, but in December 1614 the East India Company was appalled by 'certain lascivious books and pictures brought home' by Saris and had them burnt. It does not follow, however, that all the books bought home by Saris were erotic in content. Purchas, who would surely have been offended by erotica, may well have seen other books. We shall probably never know.[4]

### RICHARD COCKS IN JAPAN

Saris left Richard Cocks in charge of the Hirado Factory with seven other Englishmen, to work there and in sub-factories in Osaka, Sakai and Edo (these closed down in 1616). Cocks and his colleagues remained in Japan until 1623, when the Hirado Factory was closed because of poor trading

13 *Shuinjō* ('vermilion-seal document'), 1613. This permit, authenticated by the seal of the shogun Tokugawa Ieyasu, grants merchants from the English East India Company the right to trade with the Tokugawa state and establish a trading post on Japanese soil. MS. Jap. b.2.

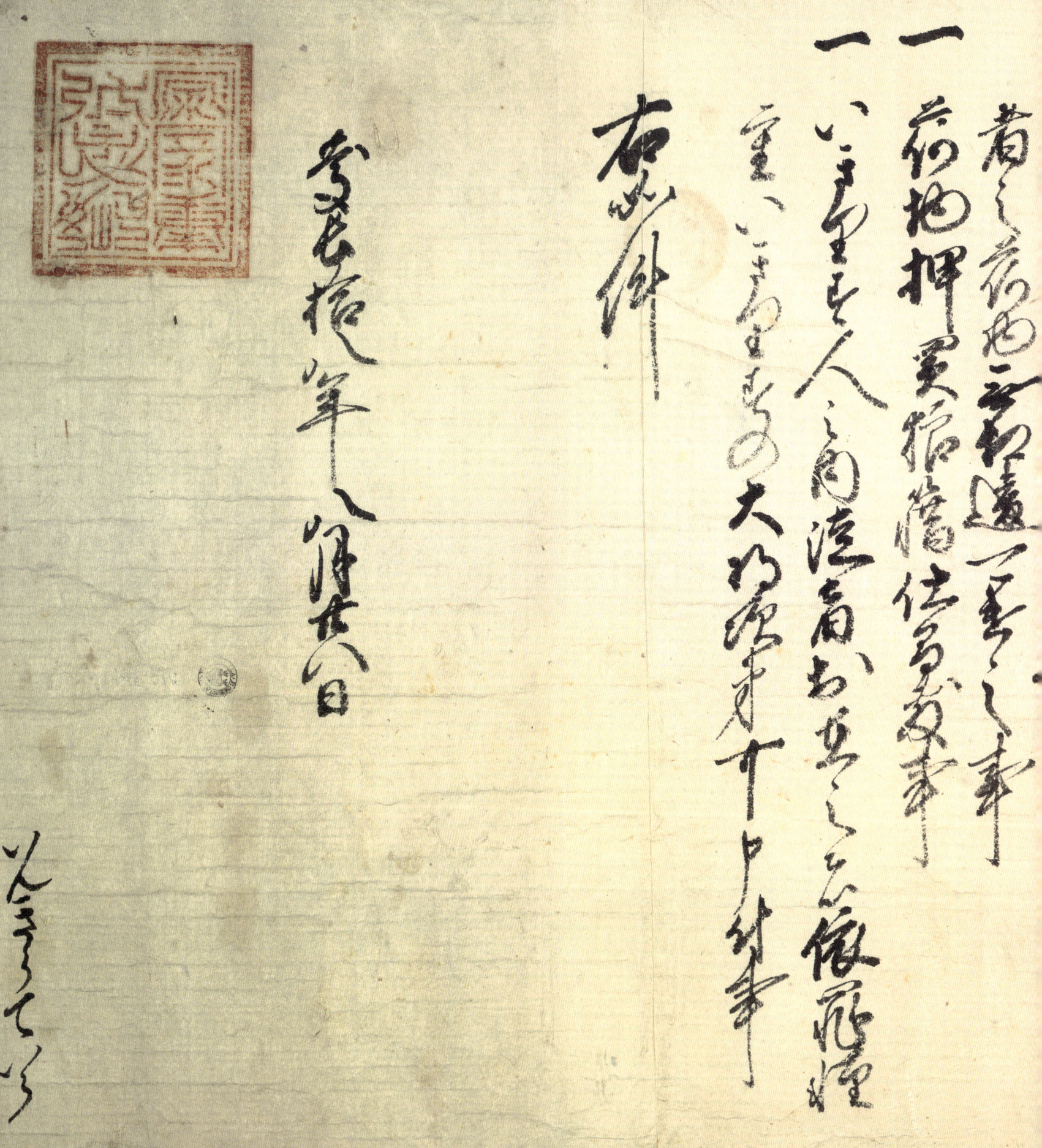

一、荷物押買狼藉仕間敷事

一、里々百姓〻之荷物等の大小
　　荷物拾ヶ所可申事

右如件

　　慶長拾年八月日

一、高麗とも日本へ渡海を
船乗高麗方より渡海仕
付て渡海仕候儀遠路に付て渡海仕

一、船中へ荷物を渡し候
付て荷物を渡し候事　　見様に

一、日本へ何を添え渡し候
遠き難風帆柱縄付て浦々に売

一、沖船を永屋敷に家を立て
船沖を永屋敷に売買に仕両国に付て候儀

一、高麗とも日本へ渡海を
付与え人に付候事　渡海仕候儀

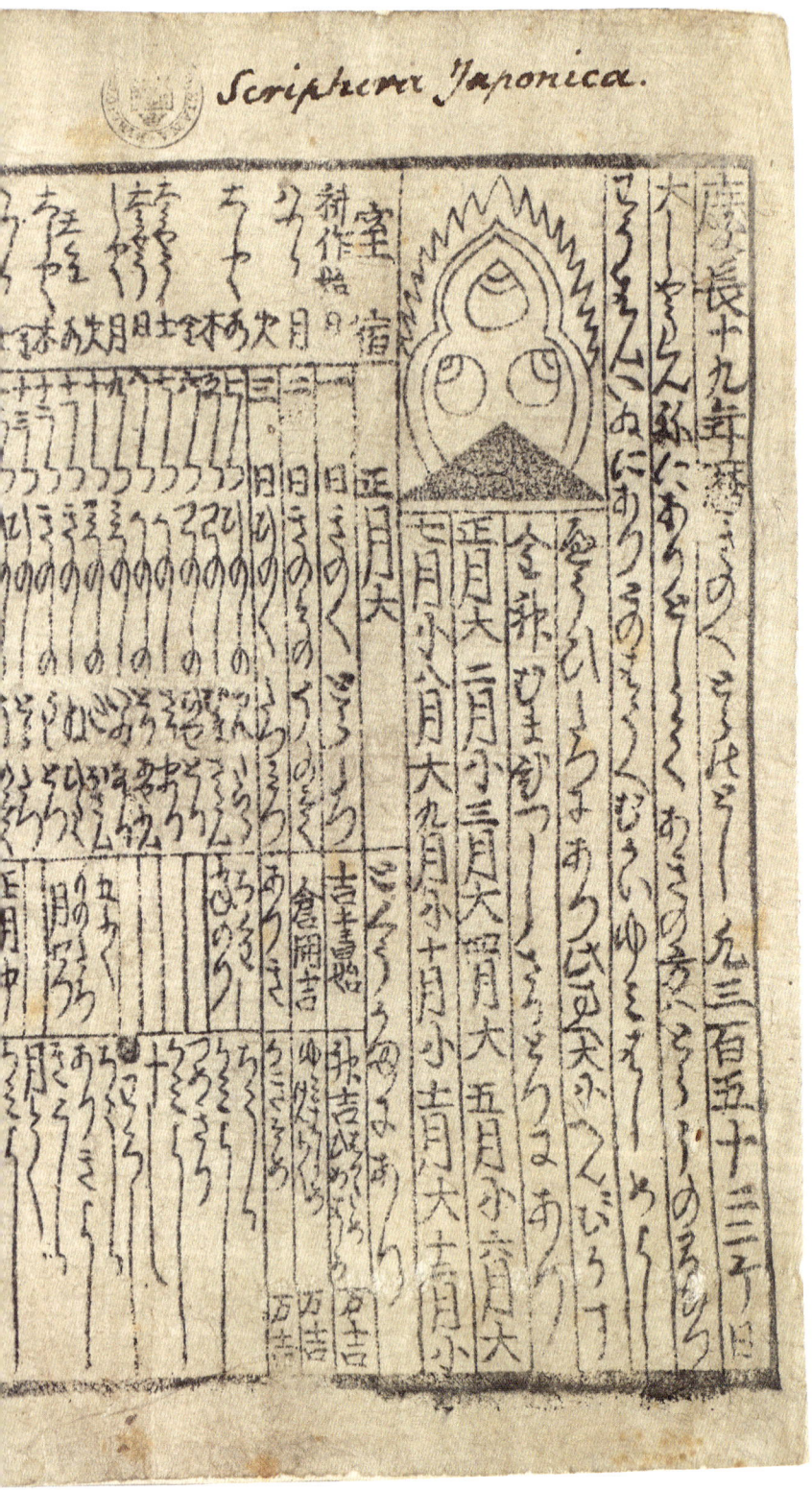

returns. Sadly, Cocks died on the voyage home. In 1673 the East India Company sent their ship *Return* to Japan to request a renewal of trading privileges, but were rebuffed.[5] The first English engagement with Japan thus lasted for less than a quarter of century, and contacts were not resumed until the nineteenth century. Brief though this first engagement was, it nevertheless resulted in the Bodleian's first acquisitions of Japanese books.

Richard Cocks had a lot to occupy him in Hirado as he tried to find a market for English broadcloth, but he had intellectual tastes and took an interest in Japanese books.[6] He surely cannot have known that printing had first been undertaken in Japan in the eighth century, that books had been printed with woodblocks for centuries, or that commercial publishing and typography were new developments when he arrived in Japan in 1613. In fact, he may have been surprised to find printing practised at all, but his diaries and letters testify to his purchase of the latest products of the nascent Japanese publishing industry. The first purchases Cocks made were of some woodblock-printed almanacs for the year 1614, printed towards the end of 1613. On 10 December 1614 he sent almanacs to four of his correspondents, so he had clearly acquired at least four copies by this time. Who were these four correspondents, what did Cocks say about his gifts, and what became of them?

The first recipients were the Merchant Adventurers at Middelburg in Holland. Cocks wrote:

14 Woodblock-printed almanac for the year 1614. Pen inscriptions, in a seventeenth-century hand, read *Scriptura Japonica* and (on the reverse) 'Specimen of Japanese printing'. Nipponica 379.

'Inclozed I send your Wor'[ship]s a Japan almanack whereby yow may see their order of printing lettrs & carectors, & how they devide the yere into 12 monethes.' Cocks had been a freeman of the Company of Merchant Adventurers of London earlier in his career, and this letter suggests that he was keeping in touch with some of his former colleagues active in Holland. To John Saris, newly returned to England, he wrote: 'I did thinke to have sent you a Japan almanacke in another letter to the same effect as this, dated the fifth and twentieth ultimo [25 November] and sent by the *Sea Adventure* by way of Syam, but forgot to put it in, yet now commeth here inclosed.' Saris had taken some Japanese books home with him, as we have seen, so Cocks knew that he had an interest in Japanese books. Writing to Sir Thomas Wilson in London**,** Cocks says: 'Herinclozed I send yow a Japan almenack, whereby yow may see their order of printing figures and carectors.' Between 1603 and 1608 Cocks had been trading at Bayonne and sending information to Wilson, who was Secretary to Robert Cecil (1563–1612), the first Earl of Salisbury.[7] The final recipient was Lord Salisbury in London, to whom Cocks wrote: 'Herinclozed I send your Lor' a muster or memorial of the names of most p'[ar]te of the greate princes and lordes of Japan … Herew'thall cometh a Japan almanack, whereby your Lor' may see their printing.' Since Cocks describes Wilson as 'Secretary to the Right Honor'ble the Earle of Salisbury, Lord High Treasurer of England', it seems that he was unaware that the first earl, who held this office, had died on 24 May 1612 and had been succeeded by his son.[8]

What do these letters tell us? Firstly, it seems from his letter to Saris that Cocks had the almanacs in his hands by the end of November 1614. If, as seems likely, he had acquired them not long before, then he did so when they were nearing the end of their usefulness – possibly they had even been remaindered. Since Cocks was in Hirado at this time, he must have acquired them there. It may seem surprising that books were being traded in a place as remote as Hirado, but in the early seventeenth century Hirado was no backwater. In addition to the English and Dutch traders there was also a community of Chinese merchants, and Japanese merchants came to acquire valuable goods from overseas.[9]

Secondly, Cocks clearly had some idea of the contents of these almanacs. At this stage of his sojourn in Japan he must have depended entirely upon interpreters. In time he learnt some spoken Japanese, but it is doubtful if he ever learnt much of the written language. Thirdly, the letters demonstrate that Cocks' motive for sending the almanacs to his correspondents (Saris apart) was to provide proof that printing was practised in Japan, and that in Japan the year was divided into twelve months. Cocks, it seems, set a lot of store by the practice of printing, perhaps to show that Japan was comparable with England and therefore a worthy trading partner.

Thanks to Cocks' purchases, two textually identical copies of the 1614 almanac arrived in England and are now preserved in the Bodleian (FIGS 14 & 15). One of them carries at the beginning the penned inscription *Scriptura Japonica* (Japanese writing), and on the binding 'Specimen of Japanese printing'. Both inscriptions are in seventeenth-century hands, but they are not the hand of Cocks. The other copy contains a later inscription reading

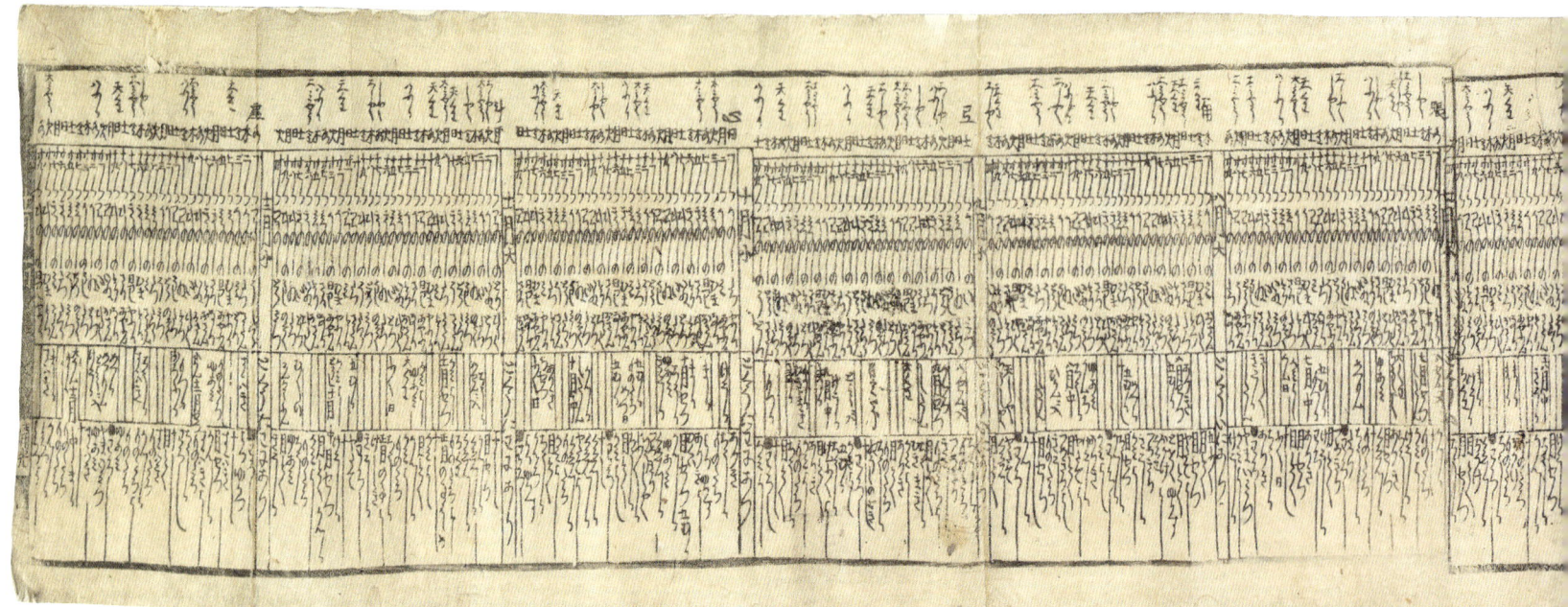

15 (& PAGE 24) Woodblock-printed almanac for the year 1614. One of four calendars sent back to England by Richard Cocks. Nipponica 466.

'Japanese almanac for 1614'.[10] Most likely these were the copies sent to Wilson and Salisbury.

The almanacs each consist of a single long sheet, printed with two woodblocks. The text is mostly in syllabic letters (*hiragana*) and contains few logographic characters apart from numerals; at the end there is a date, 'first of the eleventh month [1613]', and the name Kiyomitsu. They contain the term *keko* to denote a day on which acupuncture or the taking of animal life is to be avoided, which is only found in calendars printed in Kyoto and Nara. For each day of the year the almanac provides information about the hexagenary cycle, the day of the week, and the level of good fortune it would bring. Woodblock-printed almanacs like this have a long history in Japan, with the oldest extant examples dating from the fourteenth century. Inevitably, very few copies of printed almanacs have survived, for most were discarded at the end of the year. These

two are, in fact, the only known surviving copies of any almanac for 1614.[11]

What about the 'muster or memorial' sent to Salisbury? This can now be identified as a manuscript in the Bodleian which is written in an early seventeenth-century hand (FIG. 16). The damaged heading describes it as 'A breefe Catalogue or Illust[ratio]n of the ... Revenewes of all the nobles of Japon'. The hand of the heading closely matches that of Tempest Peacock, an employee of the East India Company; the list itself is in a different hand. The superscription on the other side, 'Revenewes Of all the kings of Japan', is in the hand of Cocks. In all, seventy-two daimyo (feudal lords) are listed by title and territorial income. Some of the information was clearly taken from official documents, but the sterling exchange rate is hopelessly wrong and exaggerates the apparent wealth of the daimyo.[12]

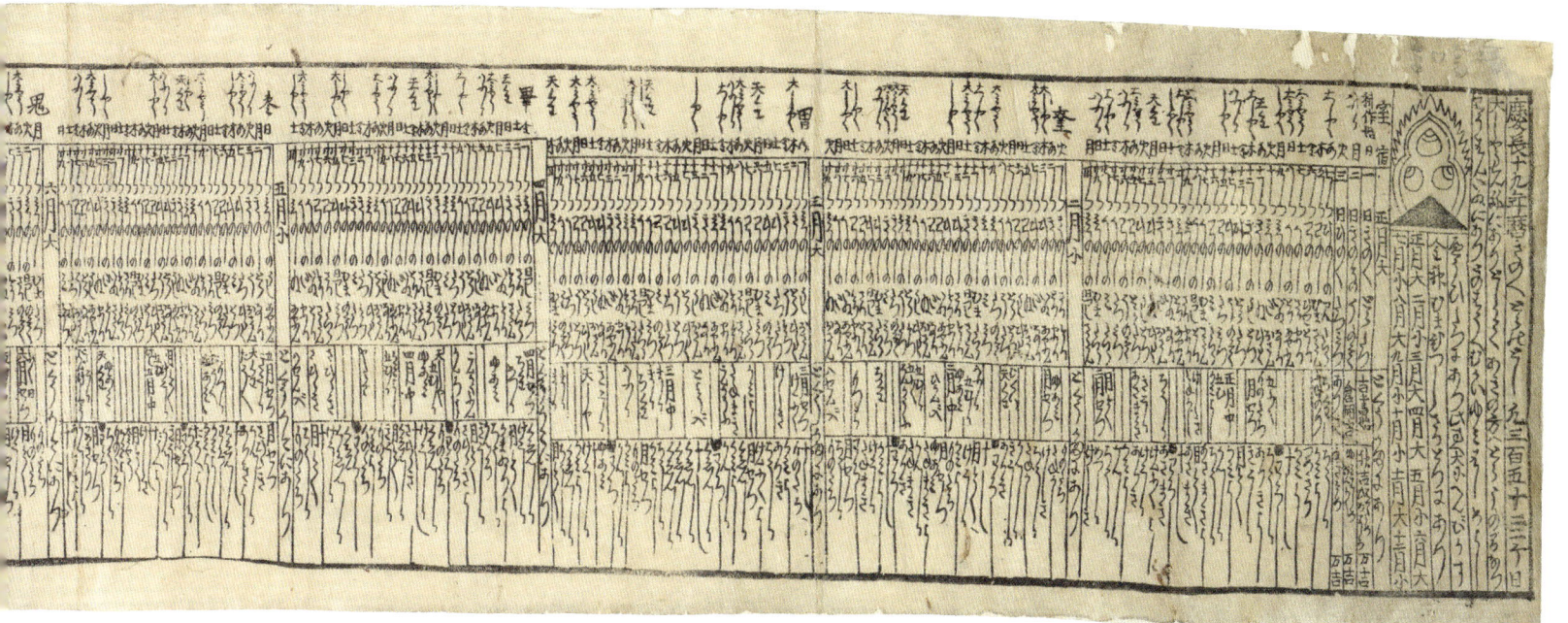

The muster and one of the almanacs, along with two of Cocks' letters, were sent by Thomas Wilson to King James in March 1619. 'This long scrole of fine paper', he explained, 'is their carracters & manner of printing, & is one of their annuall almanacks … The other paper … is a relation of the greatnes of the states and revenewes of all the nobles under the Emp'r of Japan, most of them equalling or exceeding the revenews of most of the greatest princes of Christendome.' The king was unimpressed, and declared Cocks' account of Japan the 'loudest lies'.[13]

One of the almanacs eventually entered the Bodleian as part of the donation made by Archbishop William Laud in the years 1635–45. It is not clear when the other one, with the two inscriptions, entered the Library, but they are both included in Edward Bernard's catalogue of the books and manuscripts of England and Ireland

(1697). The muster was given to the Ashmolean Museum in 1683 and was transferred to the Bodleian in 1860.[14]

The almanacs were not the only Japanese books Cocks bought. When he was in Kyoto in 1616, he wrote in his diary that he bought '54 Japon bookes printed, of their antiquities & cronicles from their first begyning'. This was a copy of *Azuma kagami* (*Mirror of the East*), a history of the Kamakura shogunate from 1180 to 1266, which had recently been printed with movable type. Four volumes of this edition are now preserved in Cambridge University Library, and two are in the library of Trinity College, Dublin. They all contain brief explanations written in Cocks' hand, which indicate that he had some idea of the contents and that he knew that Japanese books began at the opposite end from European books.[15]

A breefe Catalogue or Illust a of t Reueneweß of all the nobleß of Japon
the Emperour and his w ßome few other petty Lordß rated
by the numberß of Cokeß of ryce diſtribeð euery Cokeß of ryce being
in valen 7 18 6 8 ſterlinge mij the number of Giueß reſpect unto Japon
vis diuided being . 66 .

| | | Cokeß | | | | Cokeß |
|---|---|---|---|---|---|---|
| Imprimis | Mattßedayre figgenna Cammæ. | 1302700 | 51. | yammazakke Sammanouskr. | | 003500 |
| 2 | Tannaka chriſtoungooena Cammæ. | 0302000 | 52. | Cooyde woouKro. | | 0050200 |
| 3 | Crooday echrhegenna Cammæ. | 0490000 | 53. | Camme moſſaſhre donno. | | 0038000 |
| 4 | Hackangawa ſhruorina Cammæ. | 0070470 | 54. | Cooyde yamatto. | | 0009200 |
| 5 | Farema ſkooreoCo n. | 0056000 | 55. | Towrre dewa | | 0030000 |
| 6 | Tannaka Iſſona Cammæ. | 0020000 | 56. | Sattakre donna | | 0380000 |
| 7 | Foowloo ſhmmaſhinnano na Cammæ. | 0350000 | 57. | maydaſhreigen na Cammæ. | | 2000000 |
| 8 | Shimmana Cammæ. | 0116970 | 58. | Foolougſhema na Try. | | 0700000 |
| 9 | Cattoofrigona Cammæ | 0519900 | 59. | Moowre donna. | | 0500000 |
| 10 | Faſhbay EchrheWna Cammæ. | 0399599 | 60. | momgame donna. | | 0500000 |
| 11 | Krnoſta yemonna Tay. | 0030000 | 61. | Catta frigona Cammæ. | | 0670000 |
| 12 | Mowrreeſh na Cammæ. | 0019000 | 62. | Maſſamme donno. | | 0700000 |
| 13 | Faſheba Sanſeymon. | 0817500 | 63. | Shimaſſh donno. | | 0800000 |
| 14 | Faſheba Soymon na Tay. | 0498200 | 64. | Imra donno. | | 0060000 |
| 15 | Aſſanakrrno Cammæ. | 0374200 | 65. | Arrima donno. | | 0060000 |
| 16 | Mattſſodayre Langattano Cammæ. | 0310000 | 66. | Figgrnna Cammæ Ferando. | | 0060000 |
| 17 | Catto Sammanowſkrr. | 0186700 | 67. | tera Shimana Cammæ Caratts | | 0120000 |
| 18 | Fachiſka Awwoohocammæ. | 0191500 | 68. | Cownda mma na Cammæ. | | 0120000 |
| 19 | Mattßodayre Tooſana Cammæ. | 0202600 | 69. | Calſa Sammæ. | | 0400000 |
| 20 | Sakkown no Fooyyr. | 0171800 | 70. | Cownda Hemoo. | | 0120000 |
| 21 | Awwa Sakkoown. | 0030030 | 71. | Todo Hemona Cammæ. | | 0360000 |
| 22 | Catto Sayyrmon. | 0040011 | 72. | Mattrdayre Shimmoſſa. | | 030000 |
| 23 | Taggema na Cammæ. | 0026706 | | | | |
| 24 | Camma moowre Iſſoomona Cammæ. | 0032000 | | | | |
| 25 | Mangwithr. | 0016000 | | | | |
| 26 | Shoſhema Sayyrmon. | 0030250 | | | | |
| 27 | Tackenanga foyyrm. | 0050689 | | | | |
| 28 | Shoſſema moo foyry. | 0004700 | | | | |
| 29 | Wooſhema mangoſeger | 0007500 | | | | |
| 30 | Tarkrnatta Yangona Cammæ. | 0016000 | | | | |
| 31 | Catto frrnay. | 0030600 | | | | |
| 32 | Cattoyoza frro. | 0004000 | | | | |
| 33 | Tacklaugry Langatto. | 0010000 | | | | |
| 34 | Farema naykrr. | 0005000 | | | | |
| 35 | Farrewo Krmmontes. | 0010000 | | | | |
| 36 | yrwammæ. | 0006800 | | | | |
| 37 | nannomaa krwko. | 0004000 | | | | |
| 38 | Krmmowtes. | 0005000 | | | | |
| 39 | Farrema dayſhoo. | 0045900 | | | | |
| 40 | Langafona Cammæ | | | | | |

## THE NOH TEXTS DONATED BY ROBERT VINEY

Bernard's catalogue reveals that there were other Japanese books in the Bodleian by 1697 – a uniform set of three books containing the texts of Noh plays for chanting (FIG. 17). Since these were donated to the Bodleian in 1629, they were the first Japanese books to enter the Library, pre-dating the arrival of the almanacs. One of the three books contains an inscription reading: *Liber Bibliothecae Bodleianae ex dono Roberti Viney in artibus magister ex Aula Magdal. Nov. 10 1629* (Book of the Bodleian Library, given by Robert Viney, Master of Arts of Magdalen Hall). Robert Viney (1607–1687)

16 LEFT Sheet entitled 'A breefe Catalogue or illust[ratio]n of the … Revenewes of all the nobles of Japon', 1614. The document lists seventy-two daimyo (feudal lords). This 'muster' (list) was sent back to England by Richard Cocks; it was recently identified in the Bodleian Library. MS. Ashmole 1787.

17 BELOW & OVERLEAF Covers of *Yashima*, *Yatatekamo* and *Jinen Koji*, all undated. These are the chanting texts (*utaibon*) of Noh plays. Donated to the Bodleian in 1629, these were the first Japanese books to enter the collection. Nipponica 131–133.

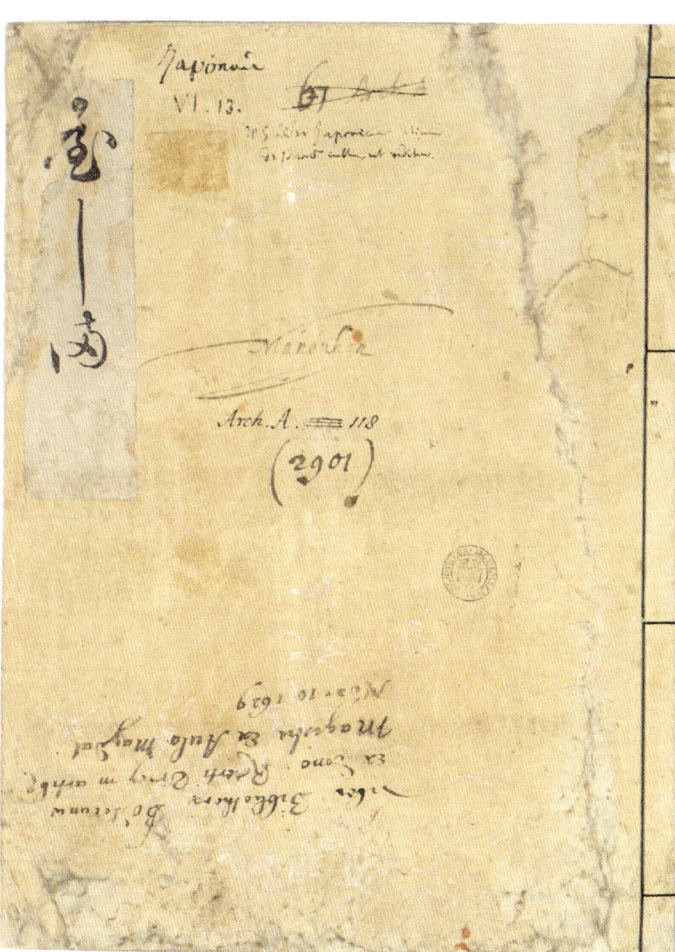

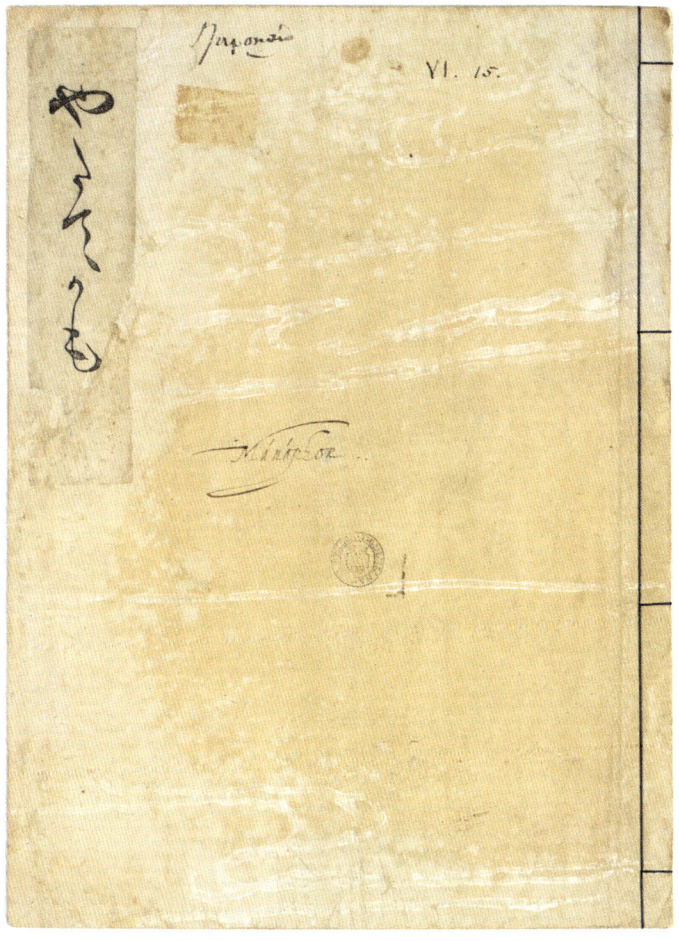

matriculated at Magdalen Hall (Hertford College) in 1622, took his MA in 1628, and in 1652 became rector of Barnack in Northamptonshire.[16] He never left England, so how did he come by these books? His mother Susan was the sister of John Jourdain (*c.* 1572–1619), who joined the East India Company in 1607, served as Chief Factor at Bantam (Banten near Serang, at the western end of Java) and returned to England in 1617. Jourdain was estranged from his wife and son, so Susan was the executrix and chief beneficiary of his will.

There were in fact originally at least four of these Noh texts in the possession of the Viney

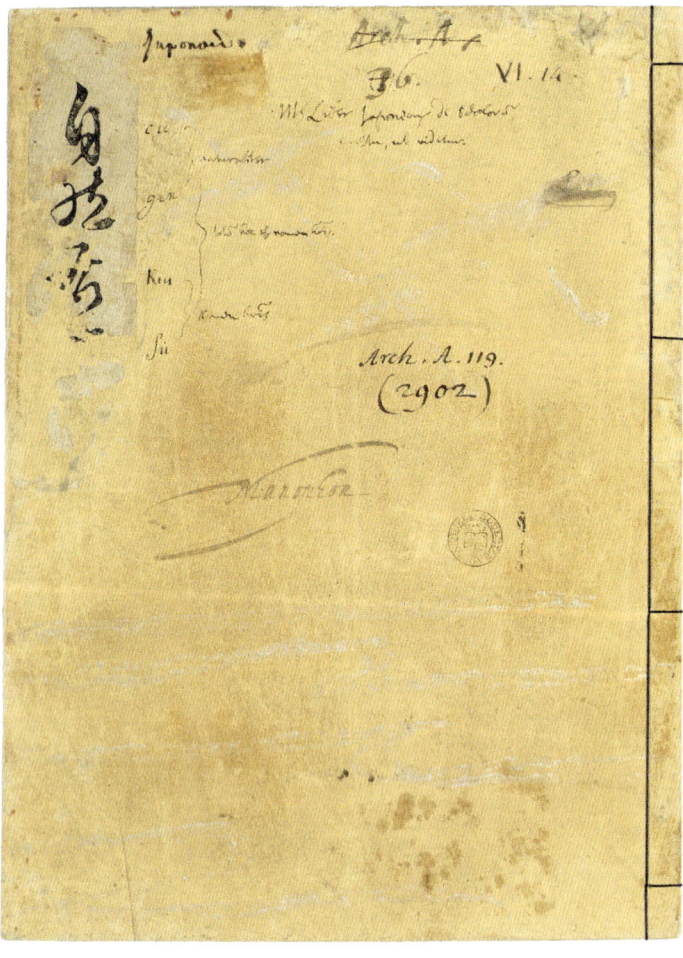

family. Robert's fourth son, David (*c.* 1652–1720), donated one to his Cambridge college, Sidney Sussex; since the undated inscription in this volume describes him as an MA, the donation must have been made some time after 1679.[17] We will probably never know if Robert Viney simply overlooked this fourth book, or if he kept it as a souvenir that his son could see no sense in retaining. At any rate, this book clearly belongs with the others.

The three Bodleian volumes are titled *Yashima*, *Jinen Koji* and *Yatatekamo*, and the Cambridge one *Kiyotsune*. They each contain the text of a Noh play, with diacritics to assist chanters.[18] In *Yashima* a travelling monk spends the night on the island of Yashima and encounters the ghost of Minamoto no Yoshitsune, who tells him the story of the battle that took place there in the twelfth century; *Jinen Koji* concerns a Buddhist preacher who saves a young person from a slave dealer, while in *Yatatekamo* a provincial Shinto priest goes up to the capital and worships at the Kamo shrine, encountering two mysterious women who tell him about the history of the shrine. In *Kiyotsune*, the eponymous hero returns to his wife as a ghost after his suicide.

These texts were printed typographically. In the last decade of the sixteenth century, typography reached Japan from two directions. Jesuit missionaries brought a printing press to Japan in 1590 and began printing doctrinal and other works in Latin, Portuguese, romanized Japanese and even Japanese script. At around the same time, Japanese armies which had invaded Korea brought back a printing press used for Korean typography, which anticipated Gutenberg by several centuries, and in 1593 a

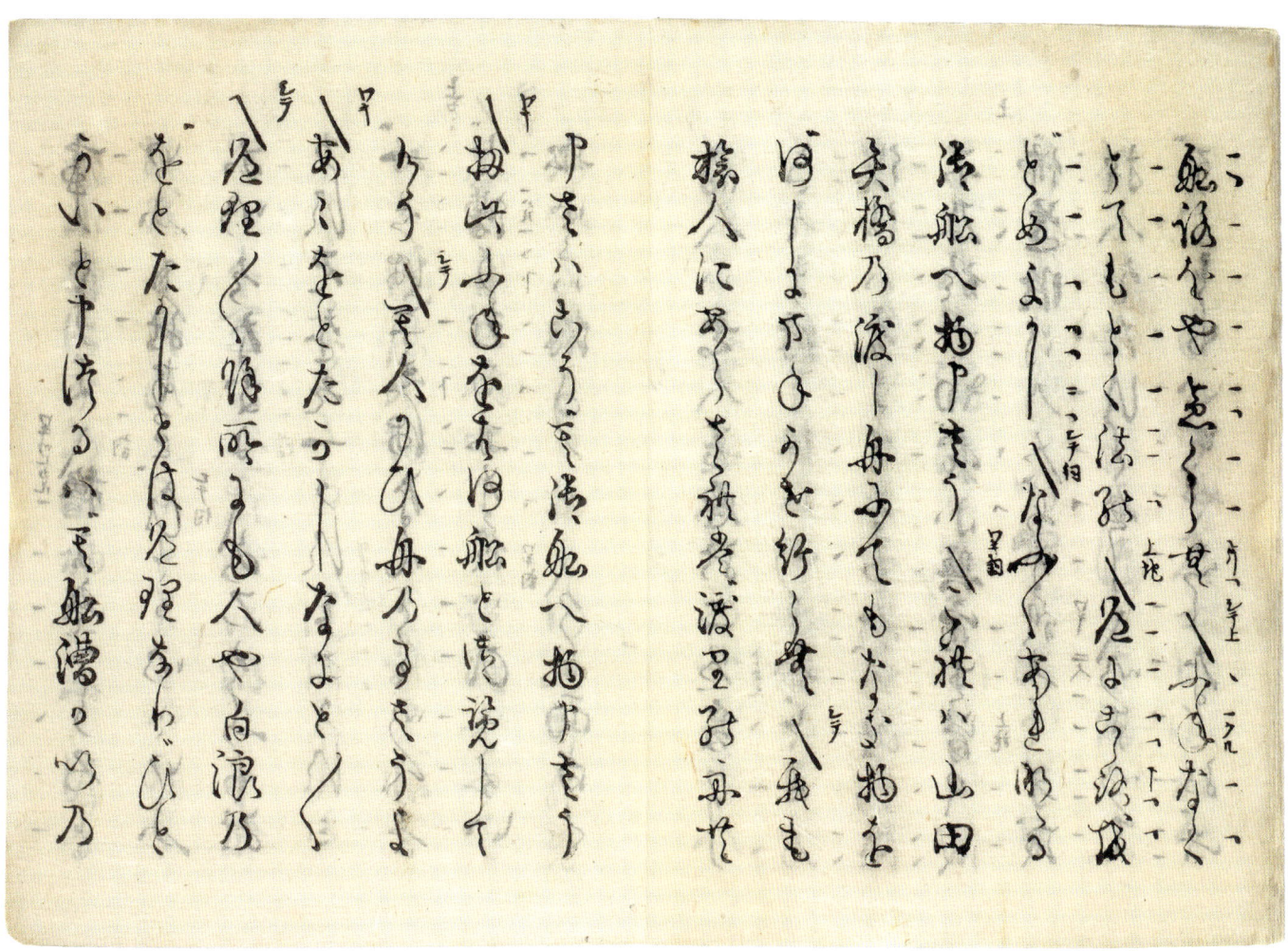

18 Opening pages of part 5 of *Jinen Koji* (see FIG. 17, OPPOSITE). In this part of the play, the eponymous Jinen-Koji calls out to a group of human traffickers, who have just left the shore on a boat. Dialogue ensues between them, and Jinen-Koji succeeds in detaining the boat. Nipponica 131  133.

classical Chinese text was printed using this type. Both traditions contributed to a boom in movable-type printing in Japan. In the first decade of the seventeenth century, the merchant Suminokura Soan and the calligrapher Hon'ami Kōetsu collaborated to produce a series of exquisitely designed books in Saga, then a village to the west of Kyoto. Known as *sagabon*, they are characterized by type reproducing a flowing cursive script and with abundant ligatures to reproduce the appearance of elegant calligraphy; woodblock-printed illustrations added visual appeal, and the covers were decorated with mica (see chapter 4).[19]

These Saga imprints include many different undated editions of a 100-volume set of Noh plays, some furnished with coloured papers or luxurious covers, some with 'butterfly' binding, and some with standard thread binding. The four books that passed through the hands of Robert Viney all have covers decorated with mica, several of them with a design showing three cranes in flight, but the texts are printed on plain white paper and have thread-sewn binding.[20]

All four books have the word 'Manophon' written on their front covers in an English hand with large flourishes. In the 1697 catalogue, 'Manophon' was taken to be a name – spelt this way in Roman letters, it is indeed a name found in what is now Thailand and Laos, and it is certainly true that Cocks met merchants from Siam, where the East India Company maintained another trading station. However, no such name appears in any of the documents relating to the East India Company's activities in East Asia. What is more, if the books reached Viney by way of John Jourdain, as suggested above, then it is hard to see why an Englishman should have written such a name on the cover.

It is more likely that an interpretation first put forward by Professor Yamanaka Reiko is correct. She suggested that the word Manophon is in fact a representation of the Japanese word *mai-no-hon* ('dance book'), which refers to the performing art known as Kōwakamai. *Mai-no-hon* were books which presented Kōwakamai texts as reading matter, and some of them contained the notation used by chanters. It is perfectly possible, then, that Noh texts were mistaken for Kōwakamai texts. Kōwakamai texts were well known to the Jesuits in Japan; the library of the Jesuit College in Macao possessed in 1616 a Japanese book described in the catalogue as a *mai-no-hon*, so the term may have been in common use, at least among foreigners. How, then, might *mai-no-hon* have become *manophon*? Europeans consistently used *f* to represent Japanese syllables beginning with an *h*, as in *mono-no-fon* for *mono-no-hon* (book), and it is not surprising that an English writer would opt for *ph* instead. The loss of the *i* in *mai* is probably simply due to a failure to transcribe the sounds accurately.[21]

How then could Jourdain have come by these books? He did not visit Japan, but he met Cocks in 1612 and probably again in 1614, when the ship carrying Cocks and Saris to Japan stopped at Bantam. Several letters from Cocks to Jourdain survive, and in a letter to the East India Company of 10 February 1615 Jourdain states that he had recently received letters from Cocks, so there can be no doubt that they kept up a correspondence. Given that Cocks knew Jourdain, and that he himself had seen Noh plays performed in Hirado in 1613, it is possible that he bought these books when in Kyoto in 1616 and sent them to Jourdain. Alternatively, Richard Wickham, who was working there in 1616, might have bought them – he was also a book collector and in 1616 he was in correspondence with Jourdain, who wrote to thank him for 'the things you sent'. After Jourdain's death in 1619, the books would then have come into the possession of Susan Viney, who died in 1622. Robert Viney came of age in 1628 and, evidently having no interest in these exotic books, he promptly donated them to the Bodleian.[22]

19 Portrait of Thomas Hyde (1636–1703) by an unknown artist. Hyde was an English Orientalist who in 1665 became librarian-in-chief of the Bodleian. The portrait shows a Chinese scroll in Hyde's right hand. LP 183.

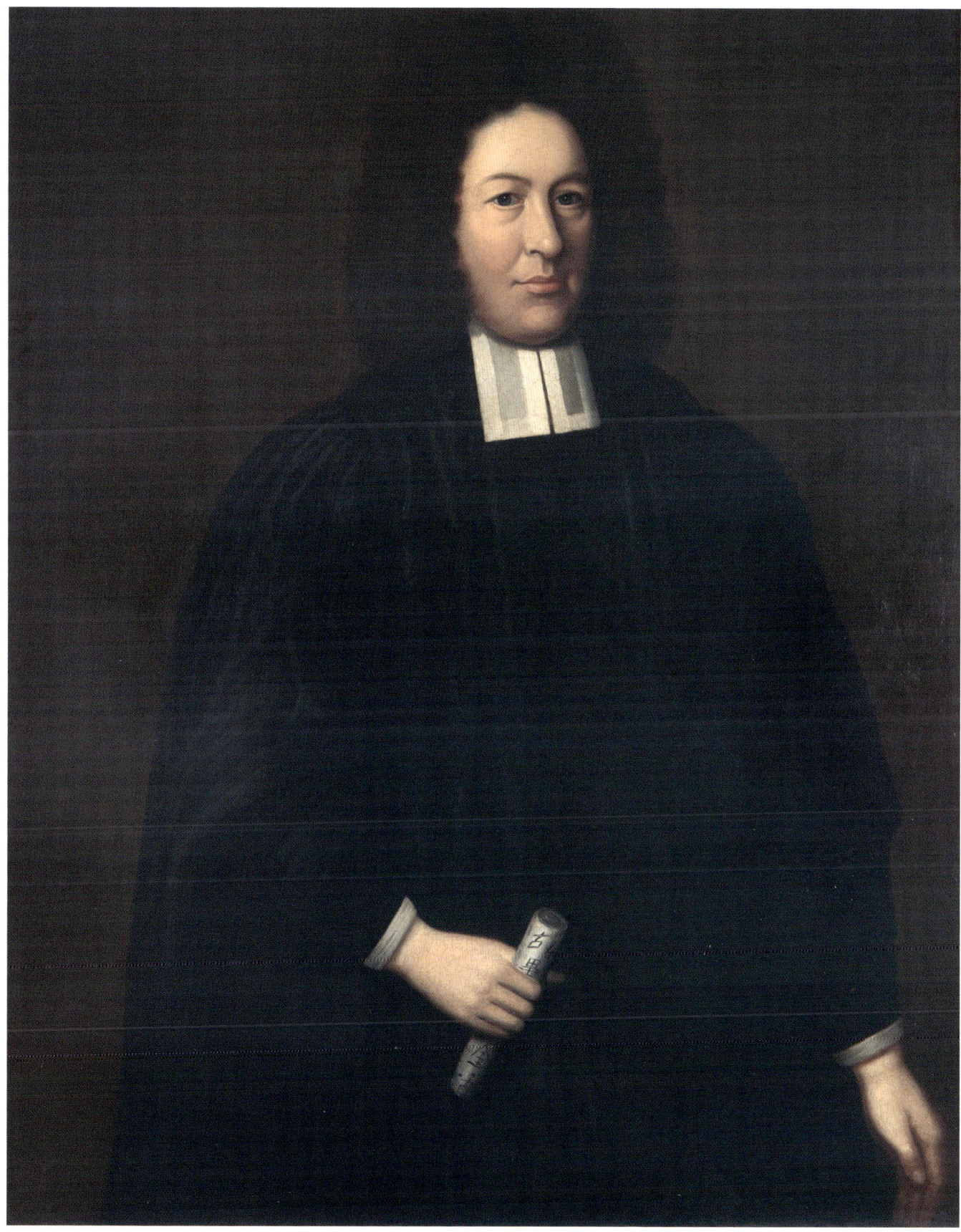

The three playbooks in the Bodleian contain some other interesting inscriptions. On the covers of *Yatatekamo* and *Jinen Koji*, a seventeenth-century hand has written *MS liber Japonicus de idolorum cultu, ut videtur* (Japanese manuscript book, concerning the worship of idols, as it appears); the same appears on the cover of *Yashima*, with the addition of the word *etiam* (also). In the case of *Jinen koji*, the same person has written, next to the four characters of the title, explanations in Latin: *Naturaliter* / [???] *hoc est nomen hominis* / *Nomen hominis* (Naturally / [???] this is the name of a person / name of a person), while a different hand has added the Chinese pronunciations of those characters. Although the writer has misinterpreted the title, the first two characters are indeed usually translated as 'nature', so this was by no means guesswork. The person responsible for the transcriptions and for these errors is Shen Fuzong (*c.*1658–1691), a Catholic convert who had been brought to Europe by the Flemish Jesuit Philippe Couplet. He spent some time at the Bodleian in 1687 working with Thomas Hyde (1636–1703), an Orientalist who became Bodley's Librarian in 1665 (FIG. 19).

Shen examined the Chinese books in the Library, giving Roman transcriptions of the titles and, since he could speak Latin, telling Hyde what the books were about, albeit sometimes incorrectly.[23] He it was, then, who provided the Roman transcriptions of the pronunciation of the characters forming the title of *Jinen Koji* in his southern Chinese dialect, while Hyde wrote down in Latin what Shen said about the meanings of the characters and the contents of the books. Shen would, of course, have been unable to read the

books since they were mostly in Japanese script, and only one of them had a title written in Chinese characters. Shen may well have shared Jesuit suppositions about heathen Japanese practices and misinformed Hyde about the nature of these three books; in a letter, he referred to Buddhist temples as the temples of 'idolators'. Hyde later compiled a catalogue of the 'Chinese' books in the Library in which he described the three Noh texts as 'books about the cult of idols in the Japanese language' and referred to the 'name Manophon' on the cover. It is clear, then, that this was the source of the information in the 1697 catalogue.[24]

These three books also have inscriptions in French, reading *Livre Japonais* and in one case also *Sur les Rois et idoles* (on their kings and idols). Again, it is clear that the person who wrote this had no idea of the contents and it is most likely that this was Philippe Couplet himself, who accompanied Shen to Oxford.

## THE BODLEIAN LIBRARY AND JAPANESE BOOKS IN EUROPE

At this point, it is worth considering two final pieces of evidence relating to Cocks' book-collecting in Japan. First, in 1620 he wrote to Sir Thomas Wilson, 'I send yow hearinclosed a blind profesie'. 'Blind prophecy' seems to have

20 RIGHT (& PAGE 22) Japanese botanical manuscripts ended up in the possession of successive Sherardian professors of botany at Oxford. Illustration from MS. Sherard 256, fol. 2r.

21 OVERLEAF Books originally acquired in 1700 by Dutch collector Nicolaes Witsen. The botanical paintings and captions were executed in Japan and later bound in Europe. In places Latin or Dutch names were added in pencil.

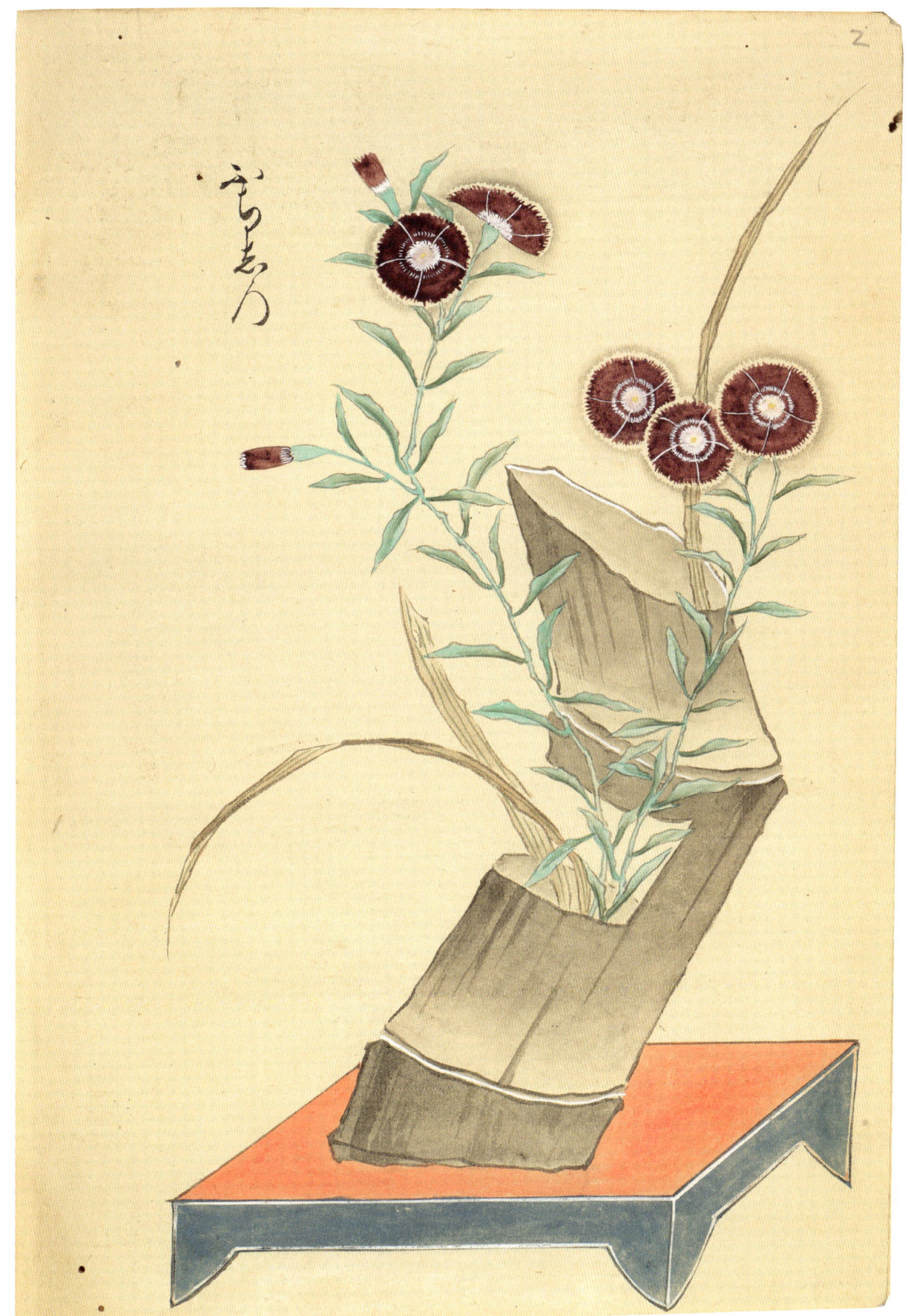

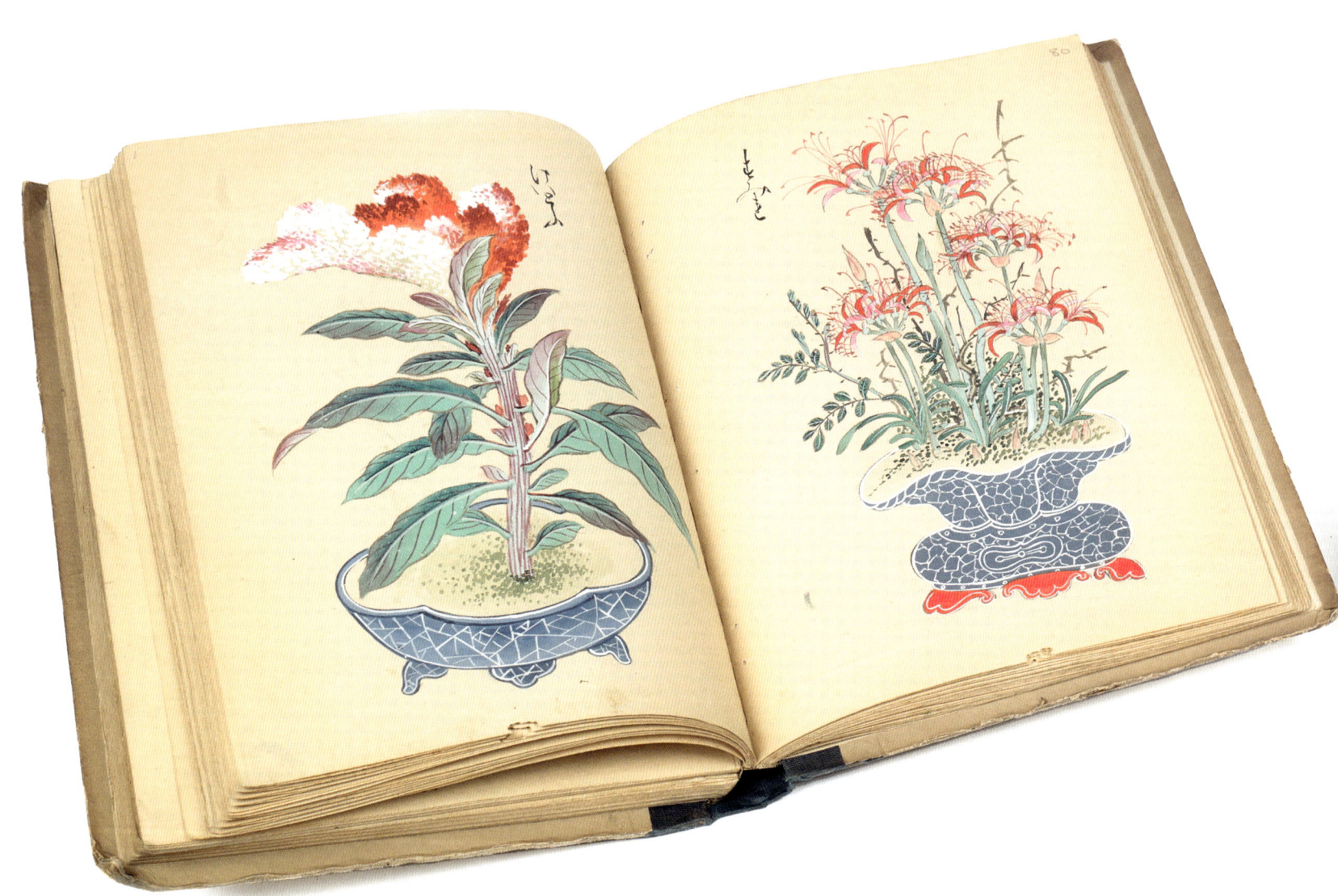

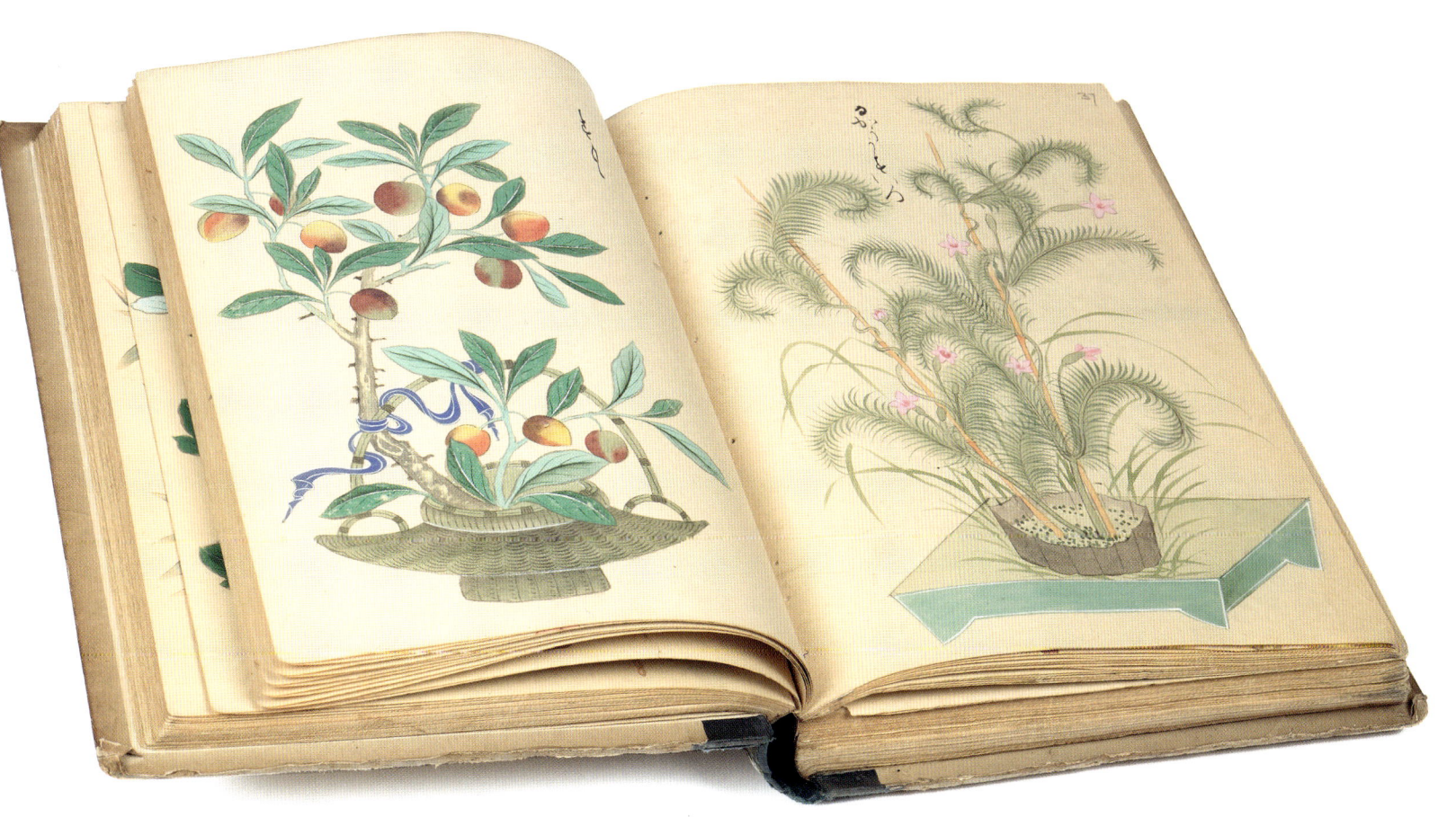

been a contemporary catchphrase: it appears in *Hall's Chronicle* (1548) and George Puttenham's *The Arte of English Poesie* (1589), in the sense of 'false prophecy'. Cocks is probably referring to a printed fortune from a Shinto shrine or Buddhist temple.[25] Second, in a letter written in 1639, East India Company chaplain Patrick Copland states that he had visited Nagasaki, adding that, 'These I had of Capt. Cox, our Cape-merchant [i.e., head merchant], a Popish catechism imprinted in Naugesack [Nagasaki], in the Italian letter, and Japan tongue, which catechism I have now in my study.' Copland, who was a Presbyterian, joined as chaplain on the Company's tenth voyage in 1612. On reaching Bantam the ships remained there for a while; one of them, the *Hosiander*, sailed on to Japan in 1615 with Copland on board. Cocks met him, for he mentions him in his diary.[26] It appears from Copland's account that Cocks had acquired a book printed by the Jesuits, which seems to have been a Japanese text in Roman script. Most of the publications of the Jesuits in Japan were destroyed during the suppression of Christianity later in the seventeenth century and very few works survive, often just one or two copies. In his 1639 letter, did Copland mean a work bearing the title 'catechism'? In that case, it must have been one of the works that do not survive. If not, there is just a chance that Copland's 'catechism' is one of the surviving Jesuit publications from Japan in the Bodleian Library (see chapter 5).

Were these various books which are now held in the Bodleian Library actually the first Japanese books to reach Europe? The only other possible sources of Japanese books in Europe were the missionaries of various nationalities, the Portuguese merchants and, from 1600 onwards, the Dutch merchants operating in Japan. By these various routes it is certain that Chinese books reached Europe well before 1629. The Escorial monastery in Madrid, for example, acquired a handful in 1573; they had originally been collected by a Portuguese missionary who had worked in Macao for twelve years. Dutch merchants were also bringing books back, and as early as 1605 the leading bookseller of Amsterdam printed a catalogue of the Chinese books he had in stock.[27] To date, however, only two Japanese books have been identified that can be conclusively shown to have reached Europe before the Viney donation of 1629. One is the Cambridge copy of *Azuma kagami*, which contains an inscription showing that it belonged to William Chidley of the Queen's College, Oxford, on 26 January 1626. The other is a copy of *Rakuyōshū*, a dictionary of Chinese characters used in Japan which was compiled by the Jesuits and which was donated to Leiden University Library in 1605. Apart from this, however, none of the early Japanese imprints in Leiden were acquired before the eighteenth century. It is hard to believe that members of the Dutch East India Company were unaware of the demand for exotic books in Amsterdam, or made no effort to test the market for Japanese books, yet no such books have come to light.

Later in the seventeenth century, Japanese books did begin to reach Amsterdam from the Dutch East India Company's base in Japan and a few of these, like many of the Chinese books, eventually found their way to Oxford. Most of the Japanese books seem to have first belonged to Nicolaes Witsen (1641–1717), a long-serving mayor of Amsterdam and administrator of the Dutch East India

Company, and then to Andreas Müller (1630–1694), a German sinologist. A collection of Müller's writings published in 1695 includes a dedication to Witsen, dated 1680, in which Müller thanks him for the gift of various Chinese and Japanese books.[28] Witsen's books and other possessions were auctioned in 1728, and among them were six large volumes of botanical illustrations which Witsen had received from Japan in 1700 (FIGS 20 & 21). They were acquired at auction by the German botanist Johann Dillenius, who in 1734 became the first holder of the Sherardian professorship of botany at Oxford. Dillenius's books, in turn, were acquired by Humphrey Sibthorp and his son John, who both succeeded Dillenius to the chair of botany, and these six volumes now form part of the John Sibthorp collection in the Department of Plant Sciences.[29] What became of the other Japanese books in the collections of Witsen and Müller is unknown.

Witsen did not know either Chinese or Japanese, but Müller made progress with both. By contrast, it can safely be said that nobody in England could even begin to read the books that Cocks had sent back. Cocks was probably well aware of this, but much the same was true of the Chinese books which ended up in seventeenth-century England. So why send them at all? Let us consider this question first in relation to Cocks and then his recipients.

Cocks was unusual among seventeenth-century traders in Japan in that he took an interest in Japanese books, although Richard Wickham also seems to have been a collector.[30] Cocks' curiosity may have been aroused by learning something of Japan before he left England. He must surely have heard of the presence in London of two Japanese youths called Cosmus and Damian in the years 1588–91, and he may have come across some of the other sources of information available at the time, either in England or during his long residence in Bayonne.[31]

Cocks clearly expected his correspondents to be interested in the books he sent, and this suggests that he was aware of growing European interest in East Asian scripts and print. Rumours about the Chinese script had circulated for centuries, and in 1570 the first European book to contain Chinese characters was printed in Coimbra – this book also contained renderings of those words in *hiragana* (Japanese phonetic lettering system), with their meanings but not their pronunciation. In 1586, Blaise de Vigenère (1523–1596) included in his *Traicté des chiffres* (*Treatise on Numbers*) a table of the *hiragana* together with some numerals (FIG. 22) – he muddled the pronunciations but got the numerals right, and was aware that Japanese was written vertically from right to left. A very similar table appeared in Claude Duret's 1613 *Thrésor de l'histoire des langues de cest univers* (*Treasury of the History of the Languages of the World*) with the same errors.[32] These examples demonstrate that Japanese writing, too, was beginning to attract the curious.

East Asian scripts in print were also proving of interest. An echo of this can be found in a partial copy of *Mengzi* (*Mencius*) preserved in New College Library. On the back cover a seventeenth-century hand has written: 'Mr Grimes. I have sent you a booke printed in the language of Chyna to shew you the form of theyre print, which Language noe man cann understand but them selves.'

The identity of neither the writer not the recipient is known, but the writer evidently thinks that Mr Grimes will be interested to see a printed Chinese book. As we have seen, Richard Cocks made precisely the same point when sending copies of the almanac to his correspondents, and so did Sir Thomas Wilson when presenting one to King James. Another preacher employed by the East India Company, Arthur Hatch (1593–*c.* 1639), who was in Japan from 1621 to 1622, was struck by the antiquity of both the written language and Japanese printing. As he wrote in a letter to Samuel Purchas, 'They have the use of writing and printing, and have had the space of many yeeres, no man knows certainly how long.'[33]

The Japanese collection in the Bodleian Library is remarkable for documenting the brief period in

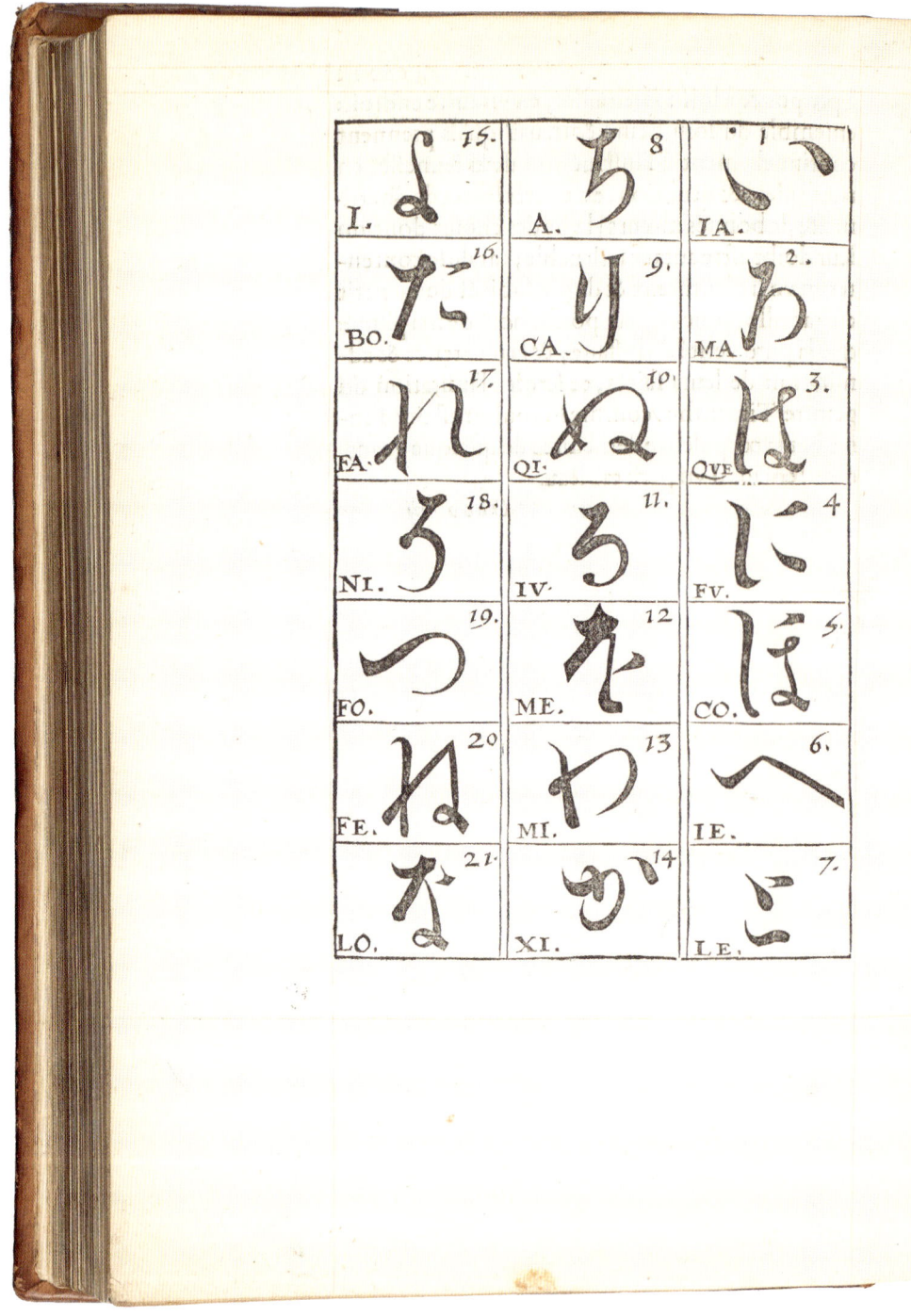

22 Plate CCCXXX from Blaise de Vigenère, *Traicté des chiffres*, 1586. The table shows various letter combinations and Roman numerals, alongside the counterpart *hiragana* (Japanese phonetic lettering system). Douce B 490.

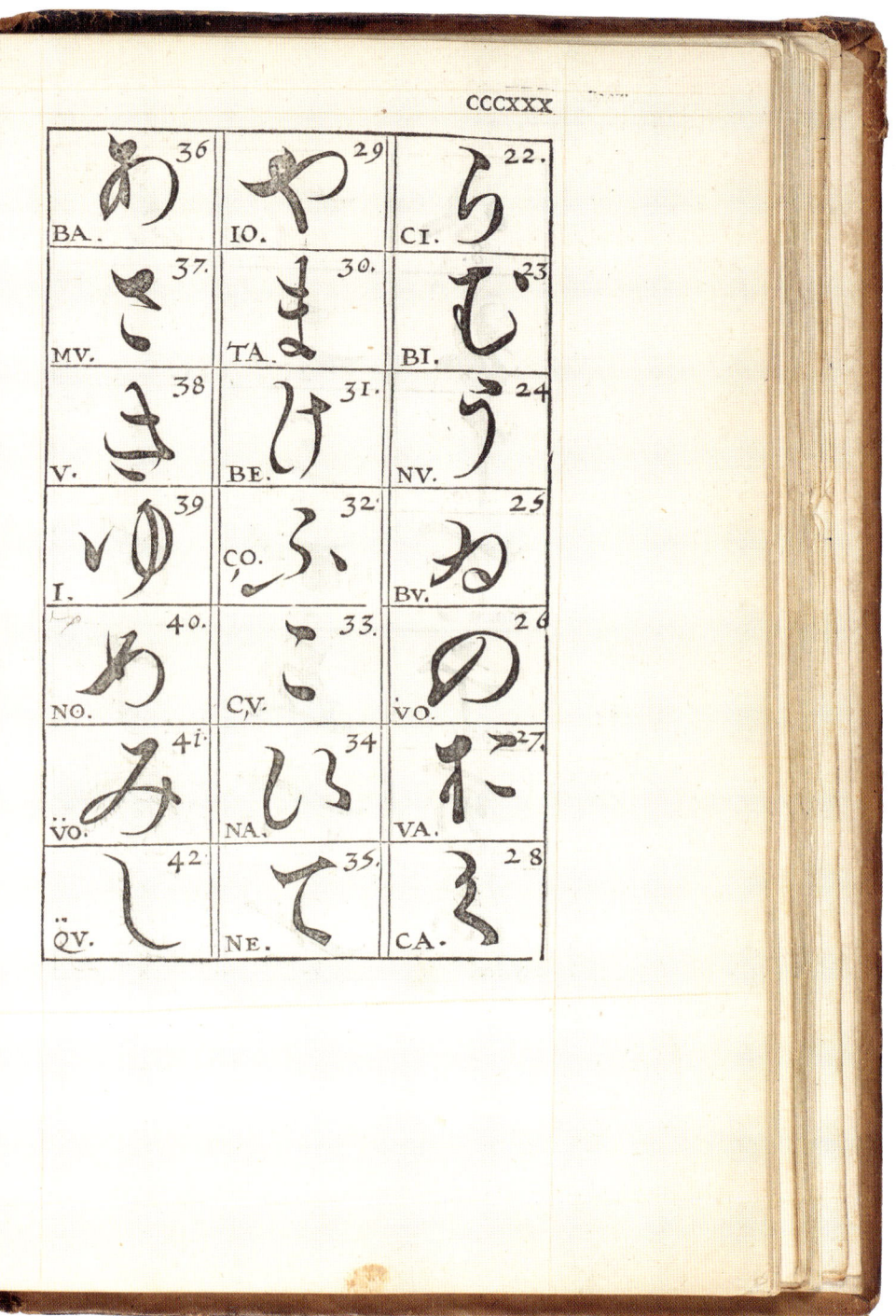

the seventeenth century when English traders were active in Japan, but it also reflects contemporary interest in Japanese writing and printing. Cocks' contacts in England may well have been intrigued by the books he sent back, but they were unable to read them and could only treat them as curiosities, and this is doubtless why they were all eventually donated to the Bodleian. In the end, the passing interest aroused by these books went no further, while the contemporary interest in Arabic, on the other hand, led to the establishment of chairs of Arabic in Oxford and Cambridge in the seventeenth century. There were, after all, few direct contacts between England and Japan after 1623, nor were there any obvious religious, intellectual or mercantile benefits to be had. Consequently, it was to take another couple of centuries before the Japanese and Chinese books could even be catalogued, let alone read.[34]

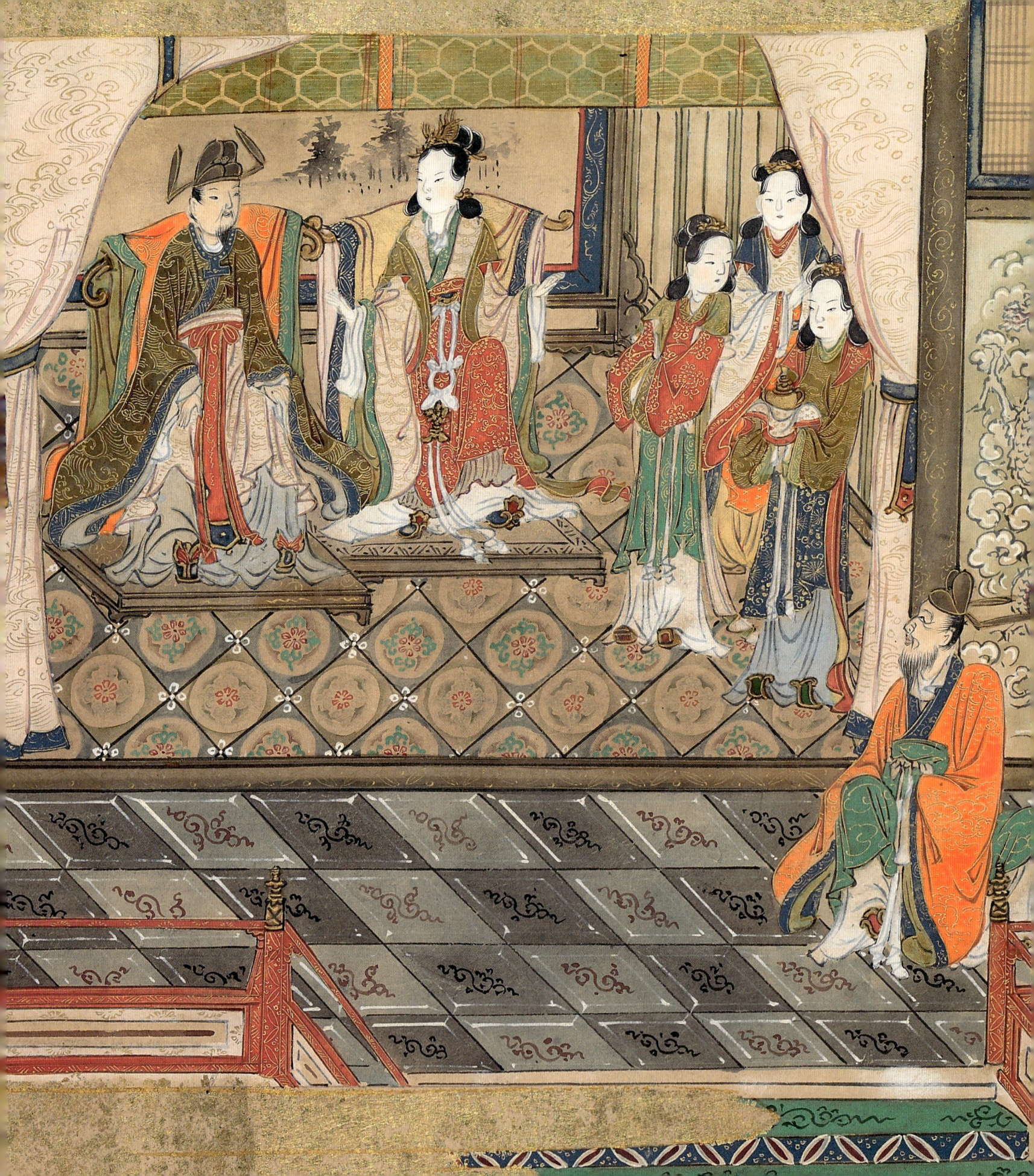

2

# The gilded library: bridal treasuries, illustrated manuscripts and *The Song of Everlasting Sorrow*

MELISSA McCORMICK

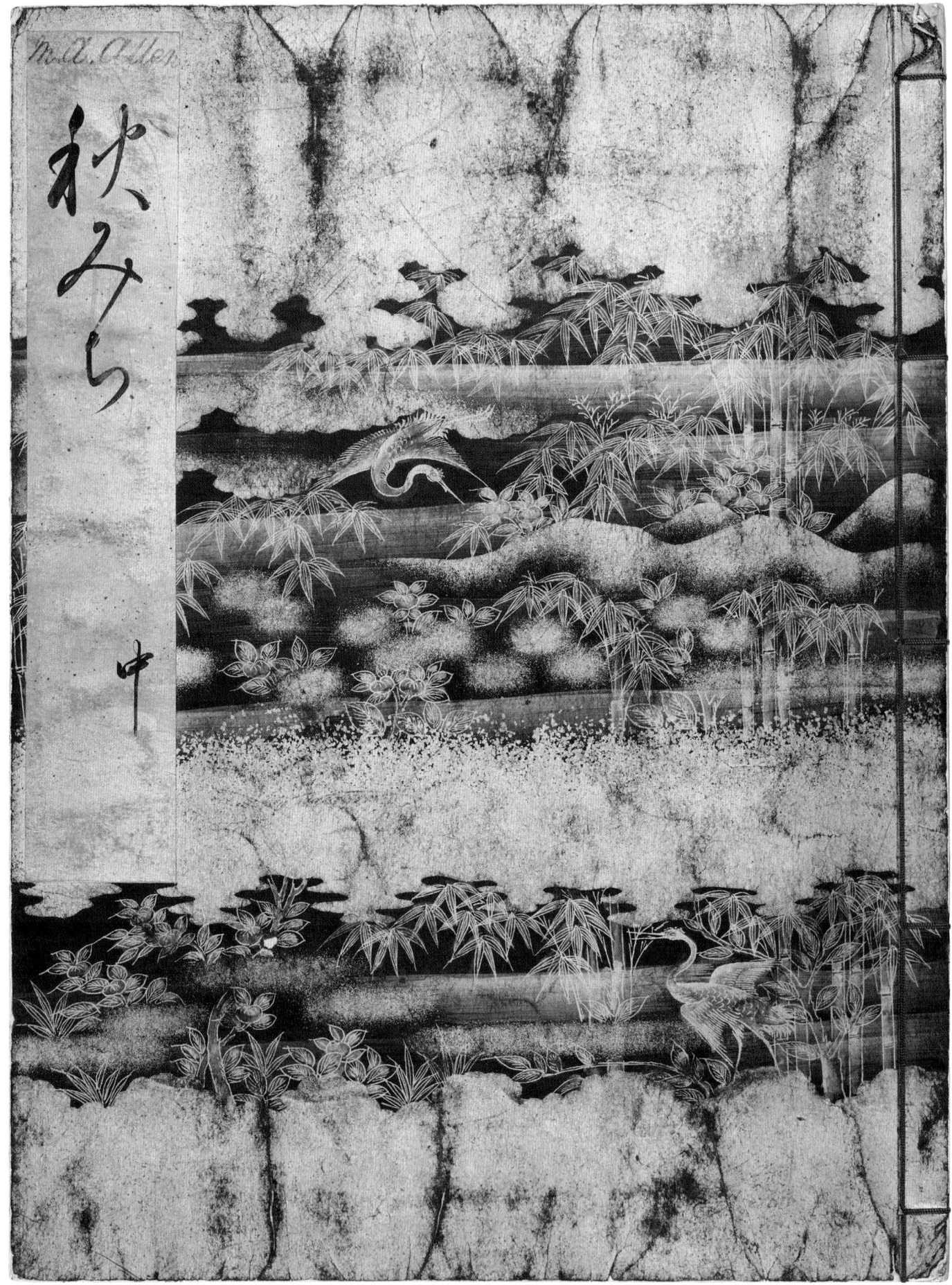

秋みら

中

THE RICHLY ILLUSTRATED NARRATIVES in both book and scroll formats in the Bodleian Library represent an efflorescence of handcrafted manuscript-making from the Edo period (1615–1868). Early modern Japanese decorated manuscripts preserve long-standing traditions of textual and pictorial storytelling, book binding and textual illumination. For this reason, they might seem to be historical outliers in what has come to be known as the 'age of print'. The importance of the new print culture of the Edo period of course should not be underestimated; the overwhelming numbers of printed books and their mass distribution resulted in nothing short of a knowledge revolution.[1] Nevertheless, the relative lack of attention to manuscripts of the seventeenth century is striking. Peter Kornicki has attempted to redress this situation by exploring why manuscripts persisted in the face of print alternatives and posited convincing suggestions ranging from the practical to the aesthetic.[2] Meanwhile, Julie Nelson Davis and Linda Chance have called into question the traditional divide between manuscript and print itself.[3] They argue compellingly that, because calligraphic forms of handwriting were employed to create the xylography of *printed* books in Edo Japan, 'printing became a vehicle for manuscript'.[4] While these scholars have largely focused on textual examples, it is also true that in the seventeenth century, deluxe, *illustrated* manuscripts not only persisted but flourished, in larger numbers than ever before. The aim of this chapter is to introduce several of these illustrated manuscripts in the Bodleian Collection – and to delve deeply into one, *The Song of Everlasting Sorrow* – to understand the reasons behind the burst of such creative manuscript energy in this era of typographic culture.

The Bodleian collection offers important examples of the early modern boom in illustrated manuscripts: codices with indigo-dyed paper covers embellished with finely wrought pictorial motifs in gold (FIG. 23); handscrolls with calligraphy elegantly brushed on papers that have been prepared with gold underdrawings and designs; manuscripts in large and small formats embellished

23 *The Tale of Akimichi*, illustrated manuscript, eighteenth century. Vol. 2 of an original three-volume set. Cover: indigo ground, gold paint designs. MS. Jap. d.65.

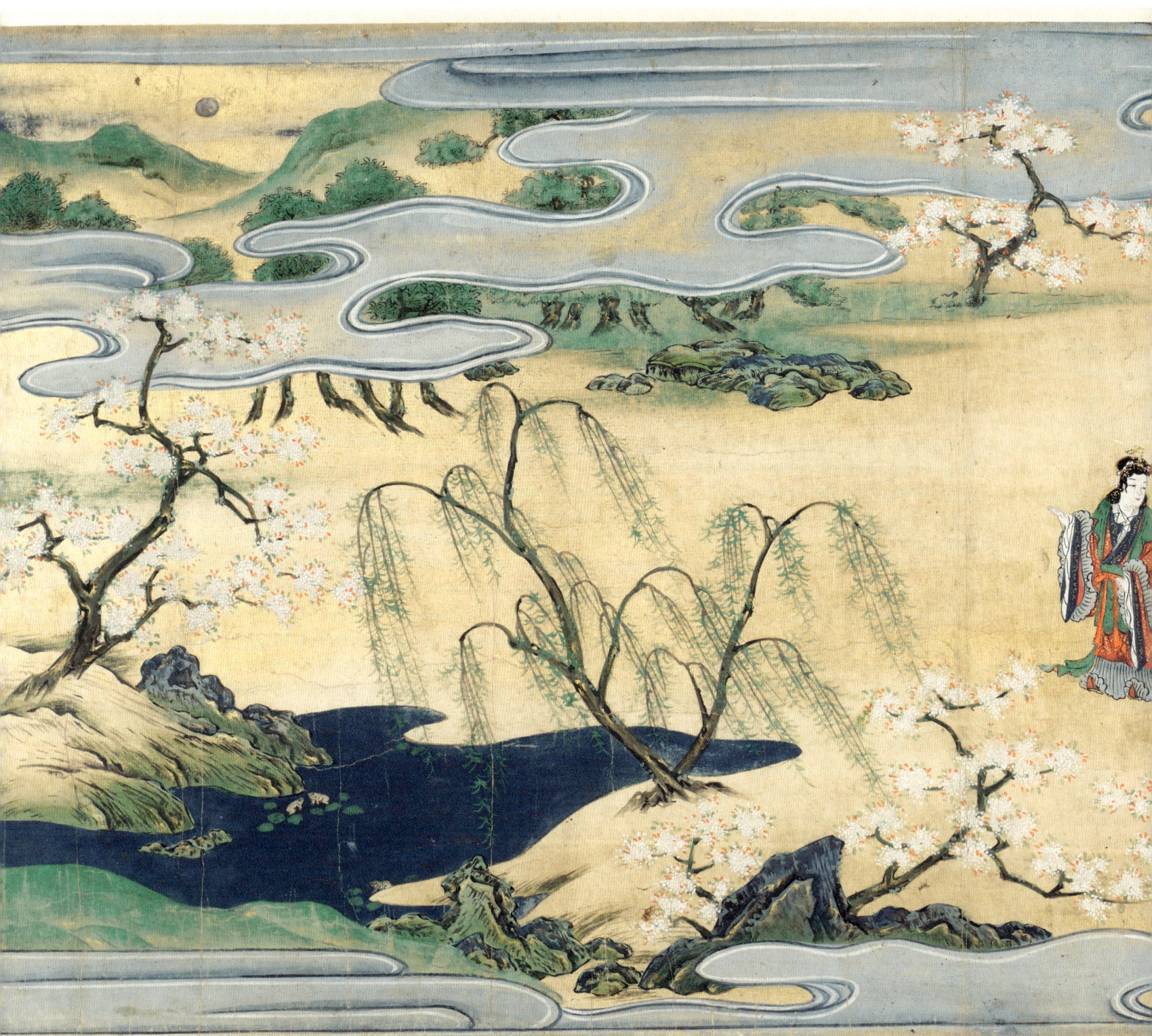

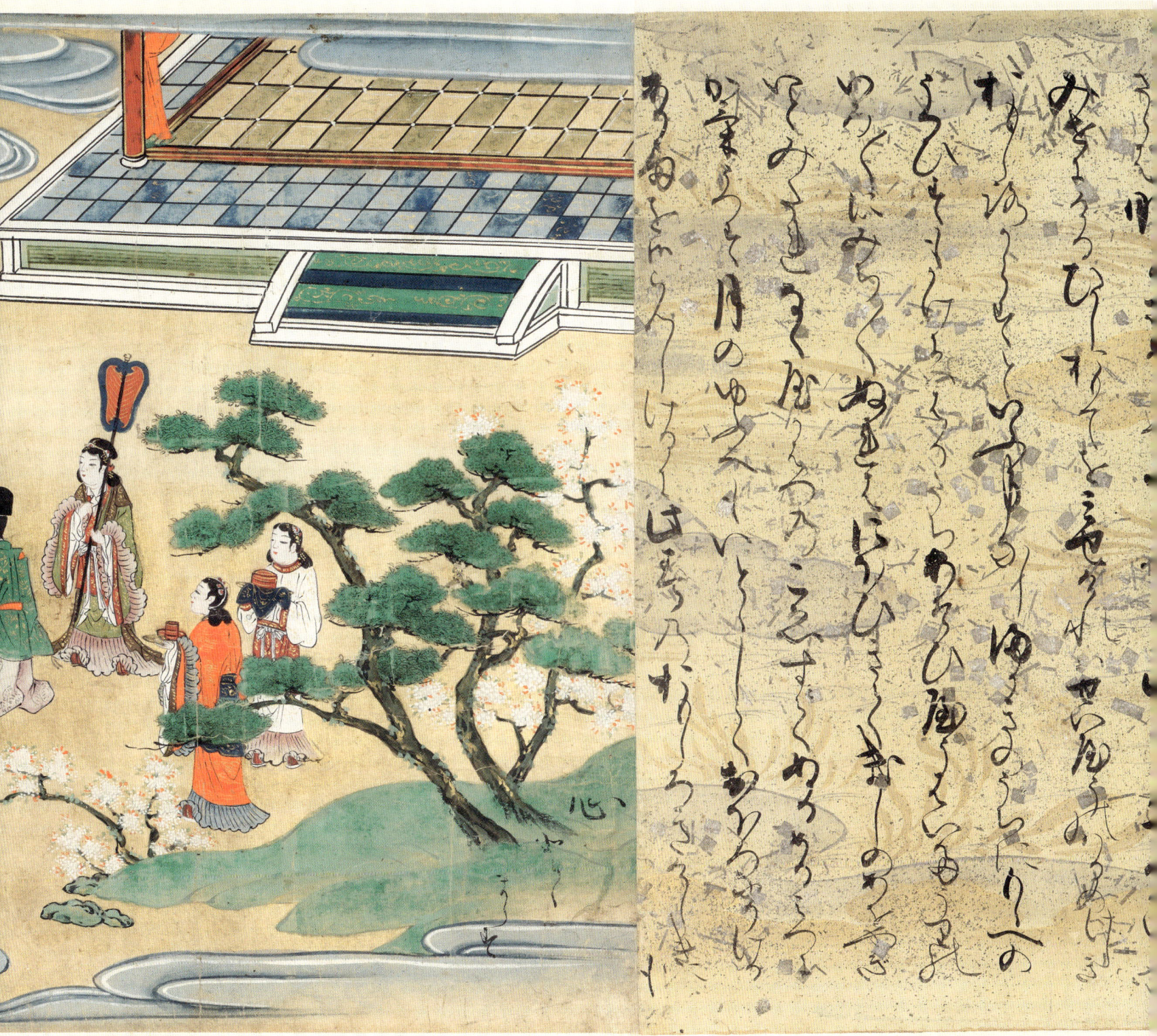

心ゆか

ましく

with hand-drawn and painted illustrations executed in rich mineral pigments and gold that draw from a familiar visual language of traditional narrative art. One jewel in the crown of the collection is *The Legend of Urashima Tarō* (FIG. 24), the famous story about the fisherman Urashima Tarō, who is whisked away to a magnificent underwater paradisal realm by the enchanting Otohime, only to return to his village to find that thousands of years have mysteriously passed.[5] In addition to vibrant polychrome paintings with elegant touches of gold paint, the scroll offers a rare early modern example of calligraphy papers dyed in rich colours and decorated with cut and scattered silver and gold, reminiscent of the apex of Heian-period (794–1185) paper decoration. Encountering such an object, the question as to why such manuscripts persisted in the face of print may seem obvious. Clearly the cultural associations that accompany the ancient handscroll format, the work's materiality of precious metals and mineral pigments, and the visual and haptic experience it offers, place it in an altogether different category to a print version of this story. While printed books clearly offer many desirable traits – efficiency of production and distribution, lower costs, ease of use – the value of illustrated manuscripts lies equally in their role as social objects, rather than solely as books to be read.

The vast majority of Edo-period illustrated manuscripts that survive today in large numbers around the world, however, are conceptualized as reading

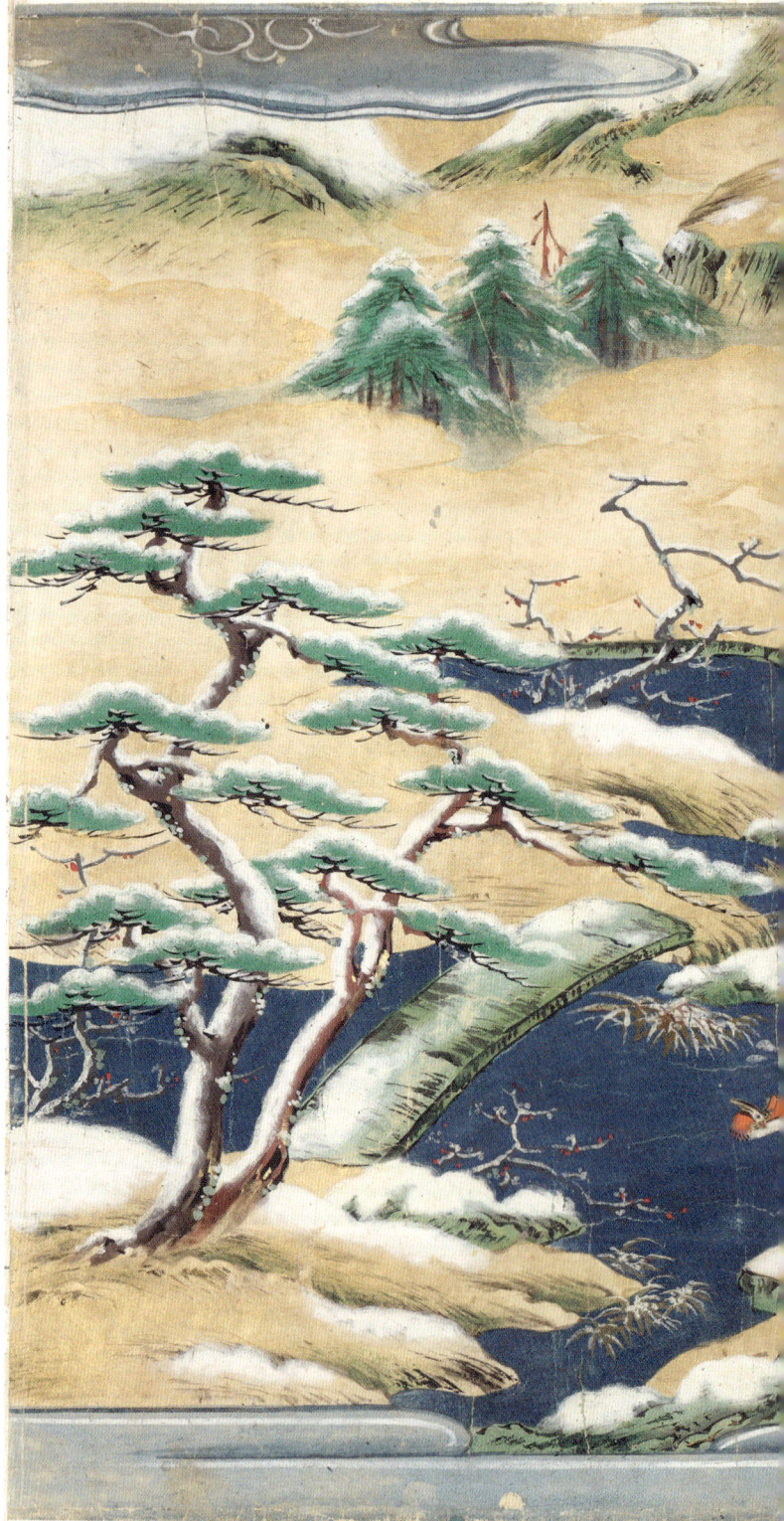

24 PREVIOUS SPREAD & RIGHT *The Legend of Urashima Tarō.* One handscroll, ink, colours, gold and silver on paper, seventeenth century. Otohime shows the fisherman Urashima Tarō the sumptuous gardens of the four seasons (spring to winter, right to left) in the paradisal realm where she resides. MS. Jap. c.4 (R).

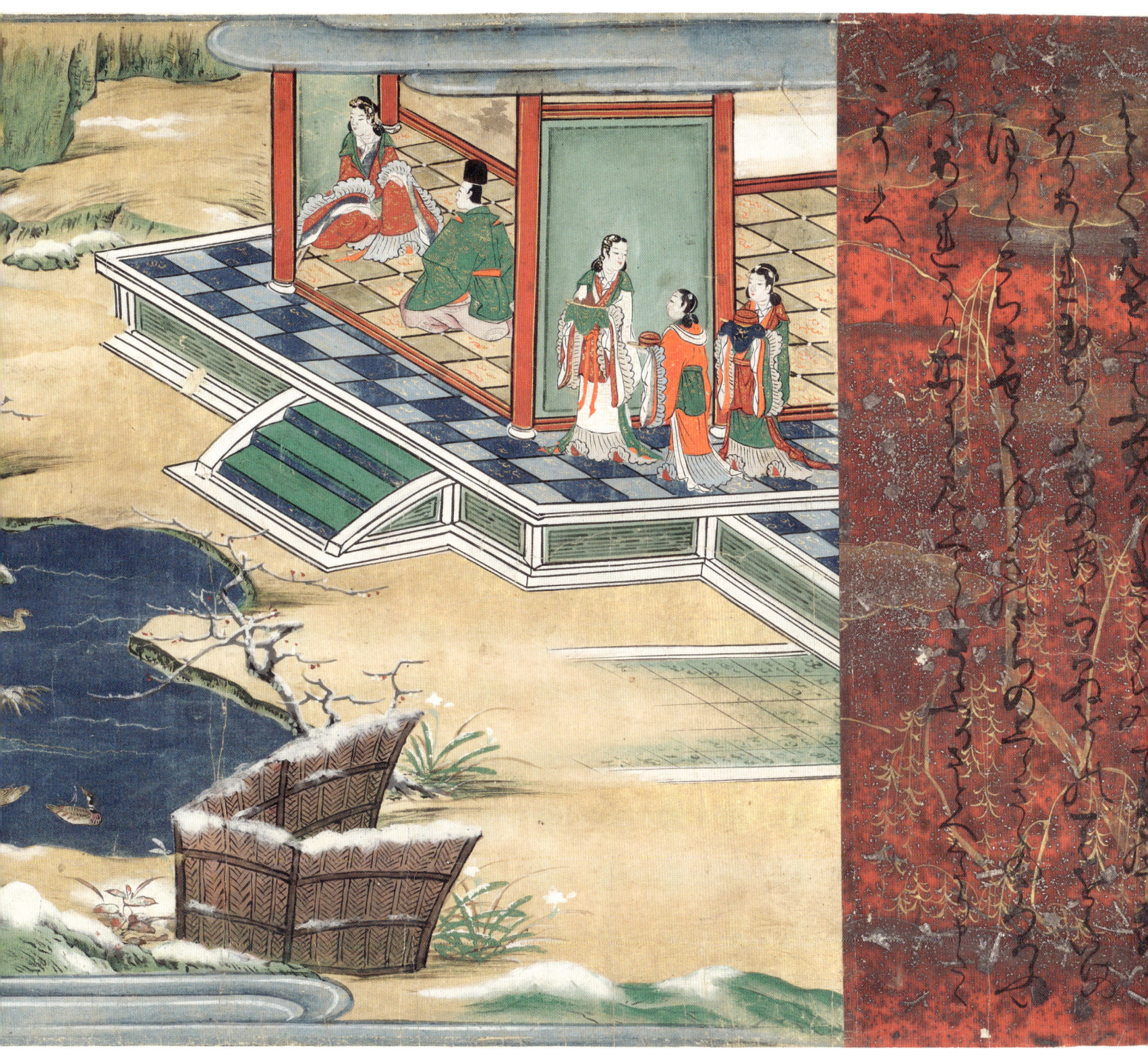

ゑ

materials. Early modern Japanese manuscripts and scrolls are commonly housed, for example, in library collections. Alongside the Bodleian, two other important examples are the Chester Beatty Library in Dublin and the Spencer Collection of the New York Public Library in New York City. There, Japanese books and scrolls are catalogued alongside reading materials from vastly different time periods and parts of the world. Naturally in a library or a museum context, manuscripts have tended to be viewed as singular literary works and storytelling artefacts, interpreted primarily in isolation from their other social functions. There is value, however, in imagining such Japanese books and scrolls as more than singular – as originally being parts of larger household libraries with significant extra readerly social functions. In fact, it could be argued that many of the richly decorated books and scrolls that survive today were created or purchased to function as presentation items. As such they were integral parts of a feudal system that turned on gift-giving and reciprocity. Their value derives equally from the painstaking labour, pictorial and textual knowledge, and artisanal expertise that went into their production, and that bestowed prestige upon those associated with them. It was precisely because of this materiality, something that printed texts could only attempt to emulate representationally, that such opulent manuscripts came into being and continued to be produced in large numbers throughout the eighteenth century.

On the other hand, it should be emphasized that these manuscripts were created in dialogue with printed texts. As stated by Davis and Chance (noted at the beginning of this chapter), it is important to avoid the longstanding default understanding of a fundamental ontological opposition between print and manuscript, and an attendant discourse of print triumphalism. The examples in this chapter demonstrate that the Edo period witnessed a new phenomenon of handwritten texts and hand-painted illustrated manuscripts that were based entirely on printed books. Therefore, rather than a natural and linear evolution from manuscript to print, leading to greater efficiency and accessibility, there was in fact more of a dialogue between the two. Moreover, it could be argued that the eventual decrease in lavishly illustrated books and scrolls aligns with changes in the wider social structures – namely the demise of the Tokugawa feudal system that had long required their production – rather than a replacement by print alternatives.

## BRIDAL BOOKS AND THE TROUSSEAU

One social phenomenon that appeared with new systematicity and that coincided with the increased production of deluxe books and scroll manuscripts during the Edo period was the bridal trousseau of household items (*konrei chōdo*, or *konrei dōgu*).[6] Amassing household items for an impending marriage was a centuries-old practice, but the trousseau, and marriage processions, reached new heights of ceremonial splendour under the Tokugawa shogun. The occasion of a marital union offered an unrivalled opportunity to express shogunal power and prestige, and may be considered under the rubric of political diplomacy.[7] As such, the Tokugawa shogun set a high standard for the grandeur of the trousseau and the public spectacle of the wedding procession, from the early years of the shogunate as the regime consolidated power to the end of the era in the nineteenth century. The bride's ornate palanquin attended by a massive entourage of dignitaries, and the trousseau of hundreds of items in several large, decorated crates emblazoned with family crests, were both paraded through the streets before thousands of onlookers.[8]

The pomp and political manoeuvering of nuptial ceremonies were not limited to sovereigns and shogun alone. With roughly two hundred and seventy daimyo governing over their respective domains (*han*) throughout the archipelago, the forging of political alliances through conjugal unions was a common occurrence. Marriages arranged autonomously between daimyo families, however, posed a potential threat to Tokugawa supremacy, and thus official permission from the shogunate began to be required. At the same time, strategic marriages between daughters of Tokugawa shogun (biological and adopted) to members of the three Tokugawa branch families (*gosanke*) and the various daimyo in the *bakuhan* domanial system became an important means of maintaining the delicate balance of power among these groups. The weddings of Tokugawa daughters thus provided not only opportunities for public spectacle, but for internal displays of fealty to the regime by subordinate feudal lords. The many daimyo of the realm were regularly ordered to recognize Tokugawa marriages by contributing precious objects to the array of household items in shogunal daughters' trousseaus – including books and scrolls.

Records of marriage preparations and ceremonies from this period contain meticulous inventories of items received from daimyo for the trousseau, and include the specific titles of gifted manuscripts. Examples abound, but the trousseau for the wedding that took place in 1729 between the shogunal daughter Takehime (1705–1772) and Shimazu Tsugutoyo (1702–1760), daimyo of the Satsuma domain, represents one on a large scale. For this marriage, arranged by the bride's adopted father, the eighth Tokugawa Shogun Yoshimune (1684–1751), all two hundred and seventy daimyo of the realm were ordered to contribute gifts.[9] Gifted books include the kind of titles one would expect for a bride of Takehime's status: volumes of classical *waka* poetry collections such as the *Kokinshū* (*Anthology of Waka Ancient and Modern*), and the *Hyakunin isshu* (*One Hundred Poems by One Hundred Poets*), and stories with plots centered on aristocratic courtship and imperial lineage such as *The Tale of Genji* (*Genji mongatari*), *The Tale of Sagoromo* (*Sagoromo monogatari*), and *Tales of Flowering Fortunes* (*Eiga monogatari*). As recent scholarship has demonstrated, however, military tales and histories – subject matter rarely associated with women and the bridal trousseau – were equally, if not more, prevalent among trousseaus for brides from military families or those marrying into such lineages.[10] Brides who married into households of the warrior class, even those who descended from courtly nobility, would receive nuptial libraries replete with literature that focused on warrior identity and told tales of martial valour, political legitimacy, and wifely fidelity and sacrifice.

The books in the trousseau thus suggest their role in a process of acculturation by the bride, entering a new milieu in which she would be responsible for sustaining a family's legacy for future generations. It makes sense then, that in some of these cases, the books and other objects for a bride of aristocratic, non-military heritage were not gathered by her own family as a dowry, but were furnished by the warrior household into which she was marrying.[11] In 1752, for example, when the daimyo of the Owari domain, Tokugawa Munechika (1733–1800) married Takagimi (later known as Tenryōin, 1730–1778), a noblewoman from the aristocratic Konoe family, the trousseau included a 51-volume set of *Mirror of the East* (*Azuma kagami*), a massive history of the Kamakura shogunate compiled in the thirteenth century and written in *kanbun*, Japanized classical Chinese, as well as a 40-volume set and index of the historical epic *The Chronicle of Great Peace* (*Taiheiki*, late fourteenth century), which ultimately legitimizes the centralized rule of a warrior government.[12]

Given the number of elite marriage ceremonies that must have occurred, and for which only a fraction of documents and inventories survive, the amount of goods produced and purchased for trousseaus during this period must have been immense. Even among the numerous trousseau objects that have survived in physical form and are now housed in museums and private collections, not a single set of 'bridal household items' (*konrei dōgu*) remains totally intact. When not handed down in families as heirlooms or property, objects were frequently dispersed piecemeal; they were gifted to loyal attendants, for example, or sold to commercial shops and dealers.[13] With the widespread dispersal of trousseau items produced on a massive scale, including books and scrolls, it seems safe to suggest that many, if not most, of the

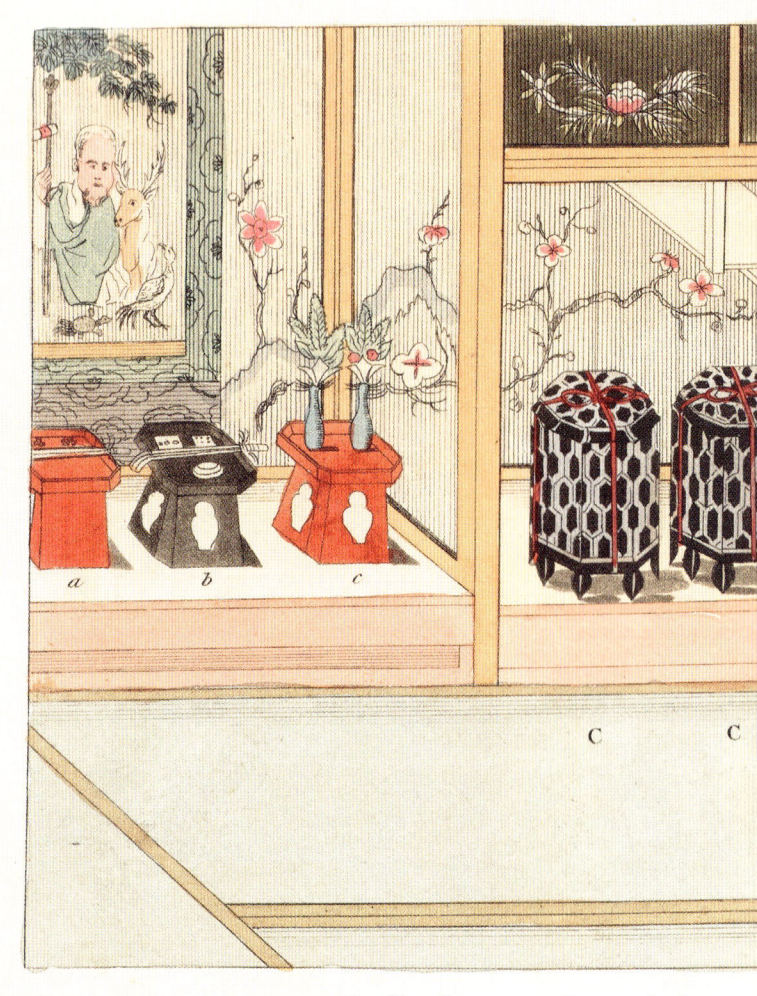

1. & 2. Two horses to hang clothes up

gorgeously decorated manuscripts now in libraries and museums outside of Japan were originally created for nuptial libraries.[14] This would hold true even if their subject matter might seem unappealing to young women according to standard assumptions about readership. Thus, understanding such manuscripts as literature for the trousseau has the potential to disrupt conventional notions

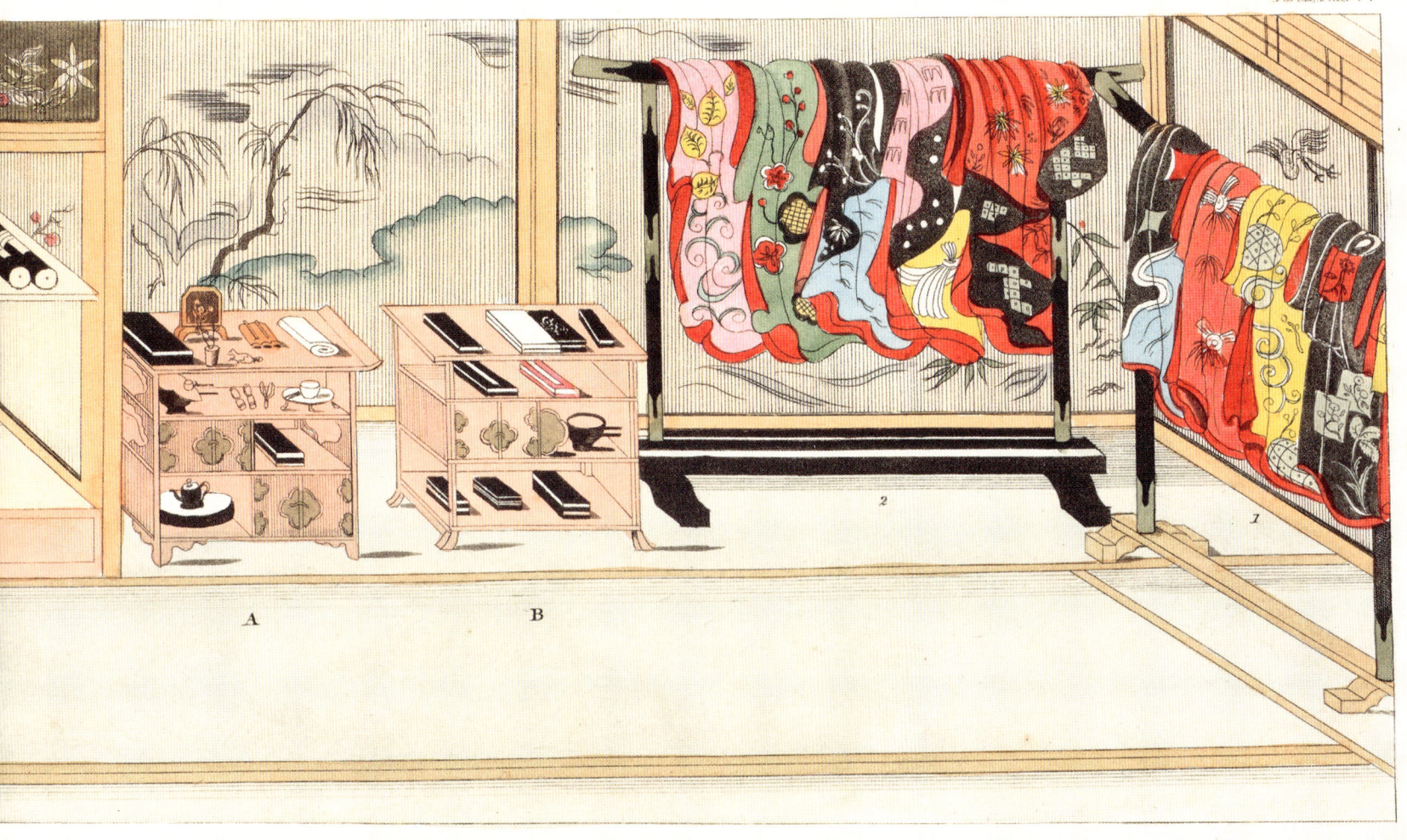

A. The Mizoesi.   B. The Koerodana.   C.C. Two boxes with shells.   a. The Fikiwatasi.   b. The Tekaké.   c. The Sousous.

about gendered categories of literary genres. As will be seen below, the inclusion of narratives usually understood to be mournful, for example, or simply exalting martial valour, could have taken pride of place in the bridal trousseau, leading to new interpretations of such texts and making the category of bridal books (*yomeiribon*) more capacious. Accepting a wider range of reading materials as

25 From Isaac Titsingh and Frederic Shoberl's *Illustrations of Japan: Consisting of Private Memoirs and Anecdotes of the Reigning Dynasty of the Djogouns, or Sovereigns of Japan.* Printed for R. Ackermann, London, 1822. Douce T subt. 7. ABOVE Plate showing the display of bridal trousseau items in a wealthy commoner class household, *c.*1750. OVERLEAF Illustration of the three marriage ceremony display shelves, including the *shodana* (the 'text shelf') designated for books, scrolls and albums.

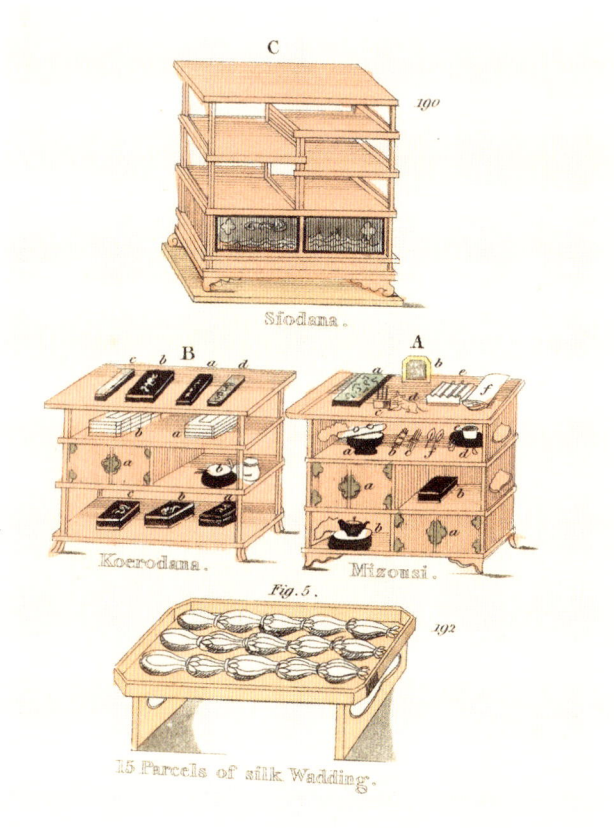

of Japan, based on the most popular Japanese marriage ceremony guide of the Edo period for wealthy merchants and townspeople (FIG. 25), provides some sense of the aspirational wedding preparation and ceremony rooms intended to augur good fortune.[16] Here, belongings prepared for the bride, from a pair of matching lacquer containers of poetry-inscribed seashells to an array of patterned robes, are displayed alongside auspicious symbols, such as the hanging scroll of the god of longevity in the alcove. Literary texts and writing materials were a focal point during nuptial ceremonies and celebrations, as they were presented on standardized display shelves (seen near the centre of FIG. 25).[17] The so-called 'text shelf' (sho-dana, or siodana in Titsingh's text) was one of the three most important pieces of marriage display furniture in a bride's trousseau (LEFT). It typically contained four shelves in a split-level arrangement above compartments fronted by sliding panels.[18] It was customary to place books, scrolls, albums and lacquered boxes of poetry sheets, for example, on these shelves – a mere sampling of the library prepared for the bride's entry into the groom's household. An extant example of a wedding bookshelf from a Tokugawa marriage that took place in 1814 (FIG. 26) suggests the greater degree of grandeur demanded for shogunal marriages. The shimmering, 'pear-skin' (nashiji) surface of this lacquered bookshelf acts

having been made for trousseaus can add nuance to how extant manuscripts might have been intended to communicate specific values, while more fully accounting for the expectations of women as new brides in establishing the ethical foundation of a household in the early modern period.[15]

No matter the subject matter of gifted bridal books, however, their exterior material presentation needed to accord with a visual environment of pure felicitation. In fact, the symbolic environments of nuptial ceremonies in the Edo period were methodically engineered to exclude traces of inauspiciousness, resulting in rooms saturated with imagery of longevity, fecundity and enduring unions. A plate from Isaac Titsingh's Illustrations

26 Lacquer (maki-e) bookcase with Aoi crest. This bookcase formed part of the trousseau of Katahime, sister of Toyohime of the Kishū Tokugawa family, who married the 11th shogun, Tokugawa Ienari. Katahime married the 10th lord of Sendai, Date Narimune, in 1814. Hayashibara Museum of Art.

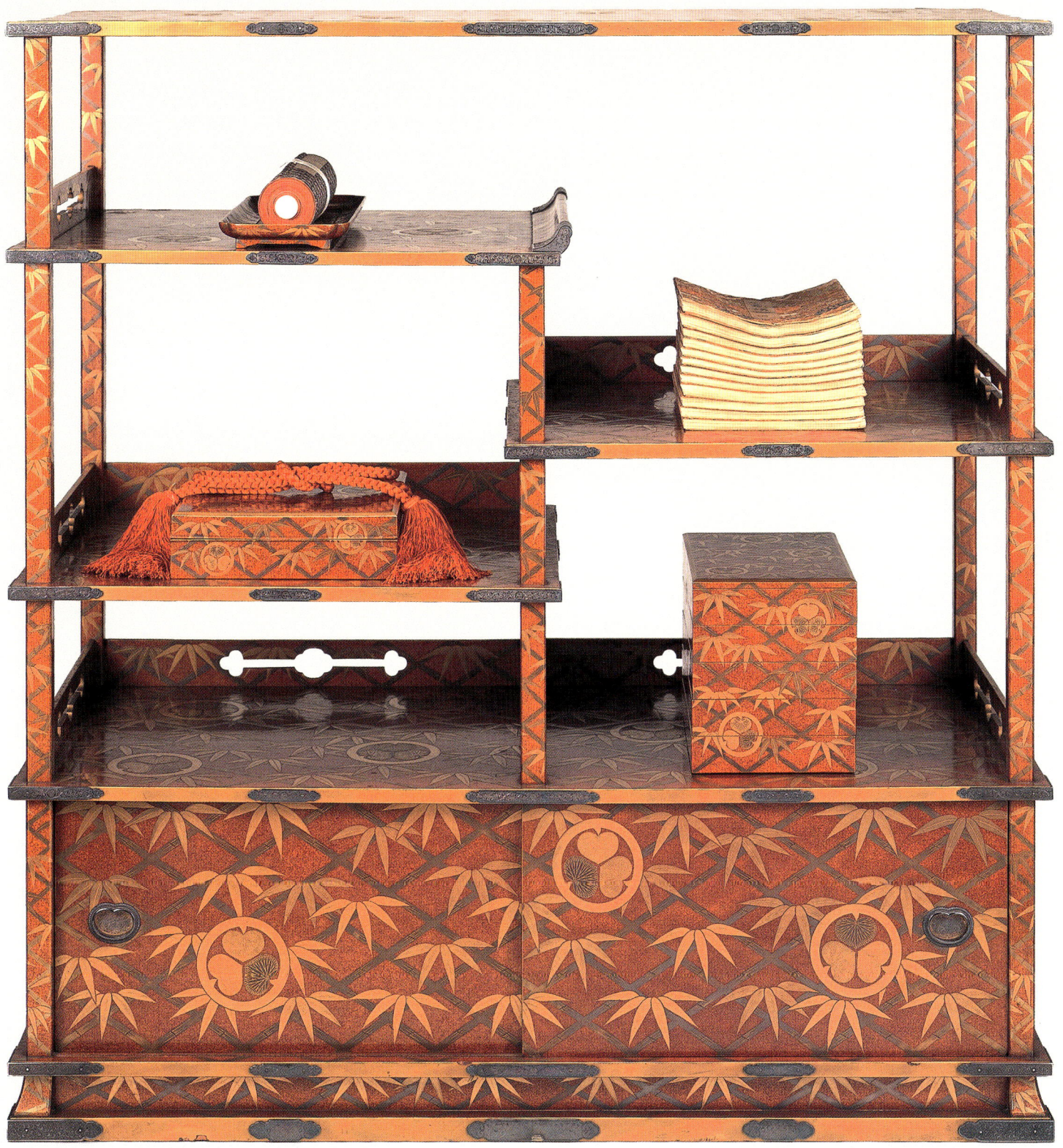

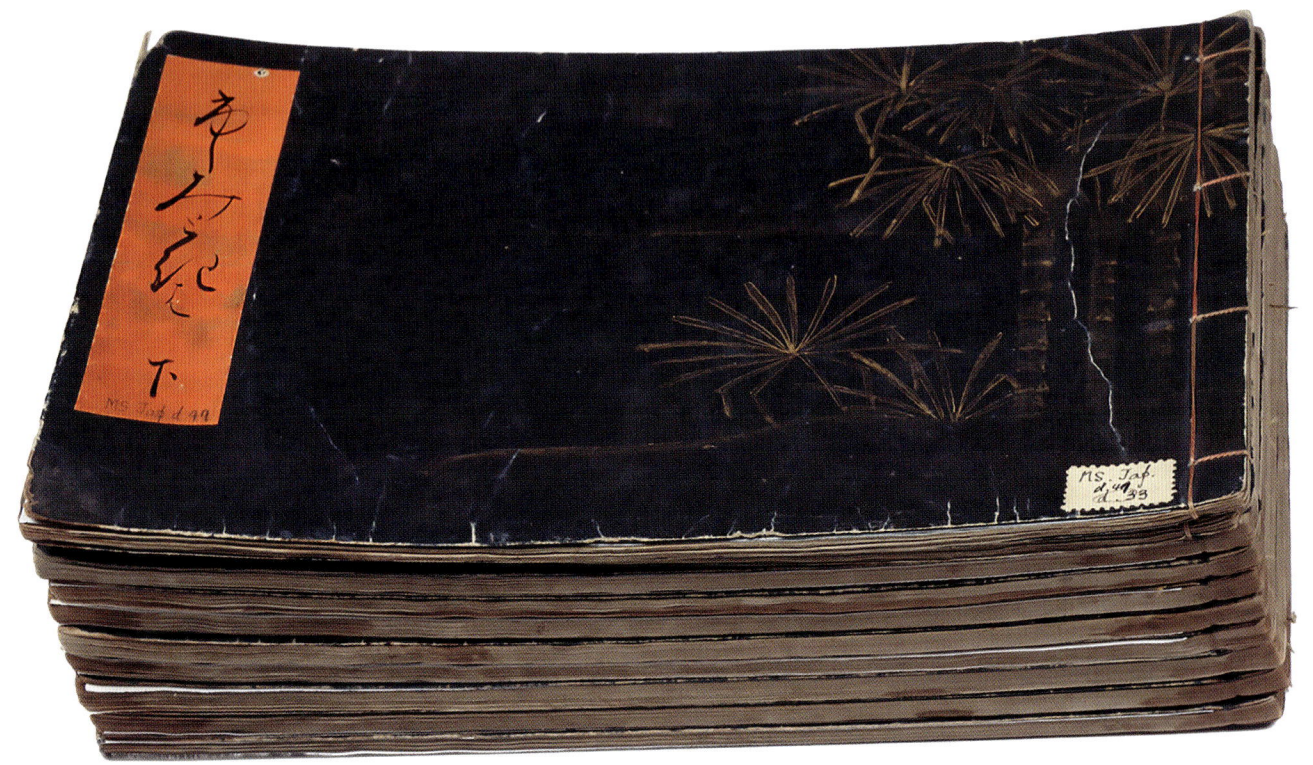

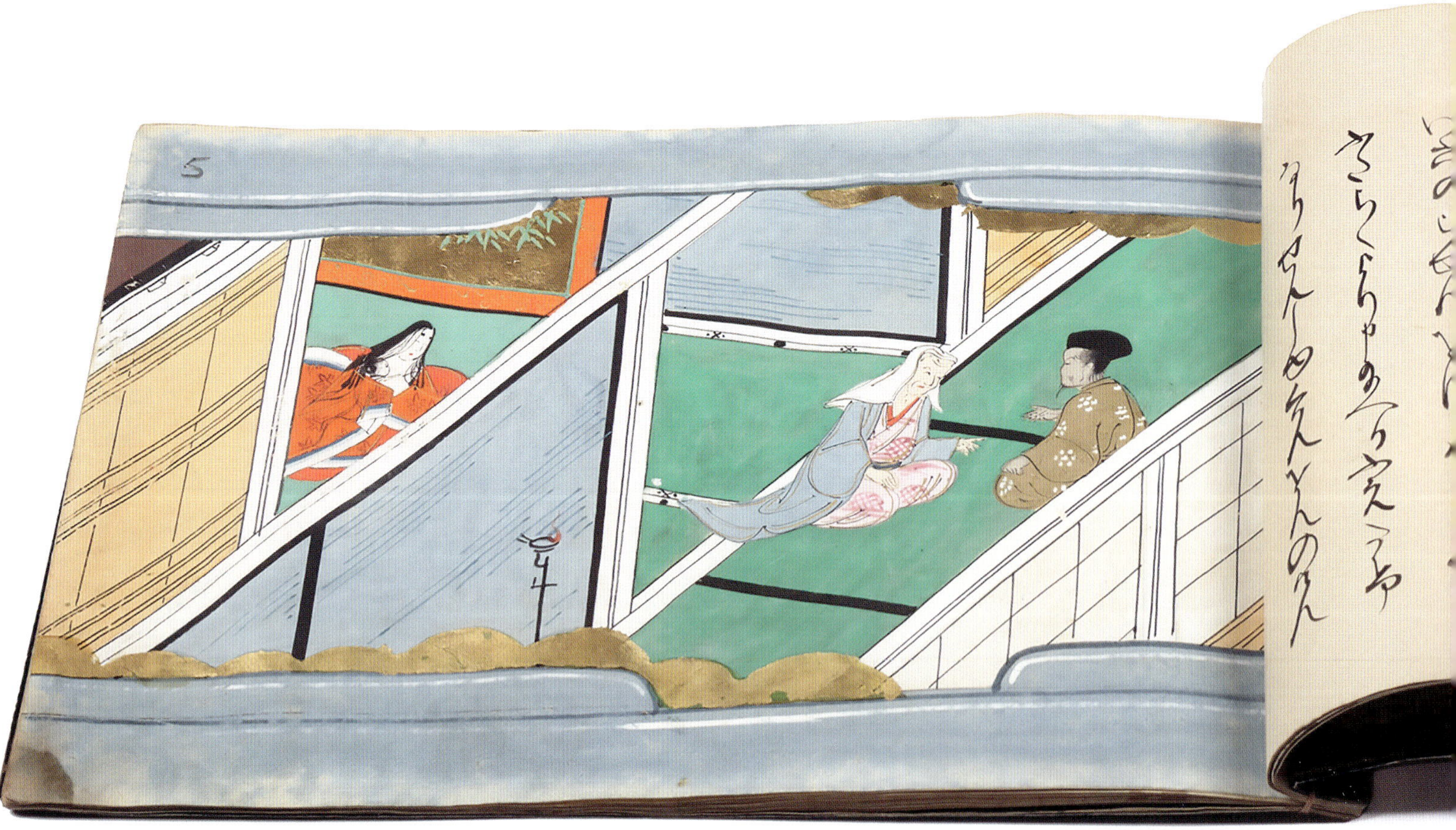

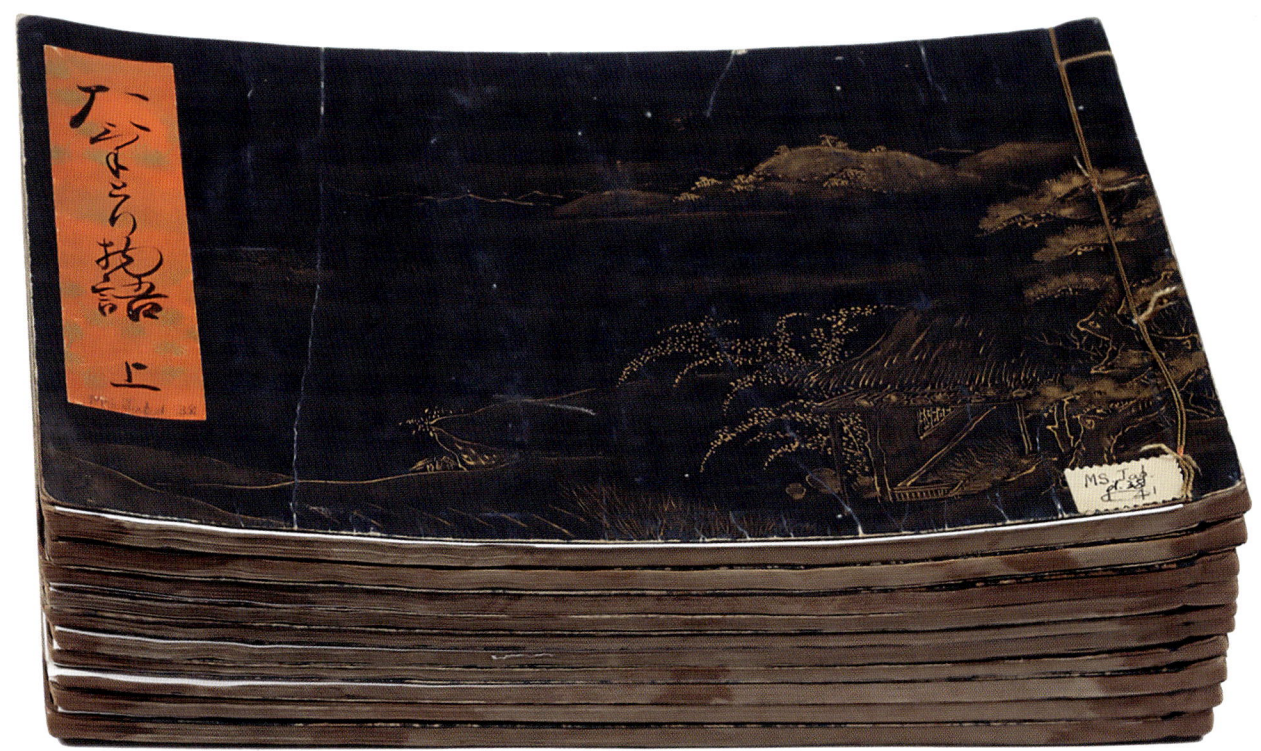

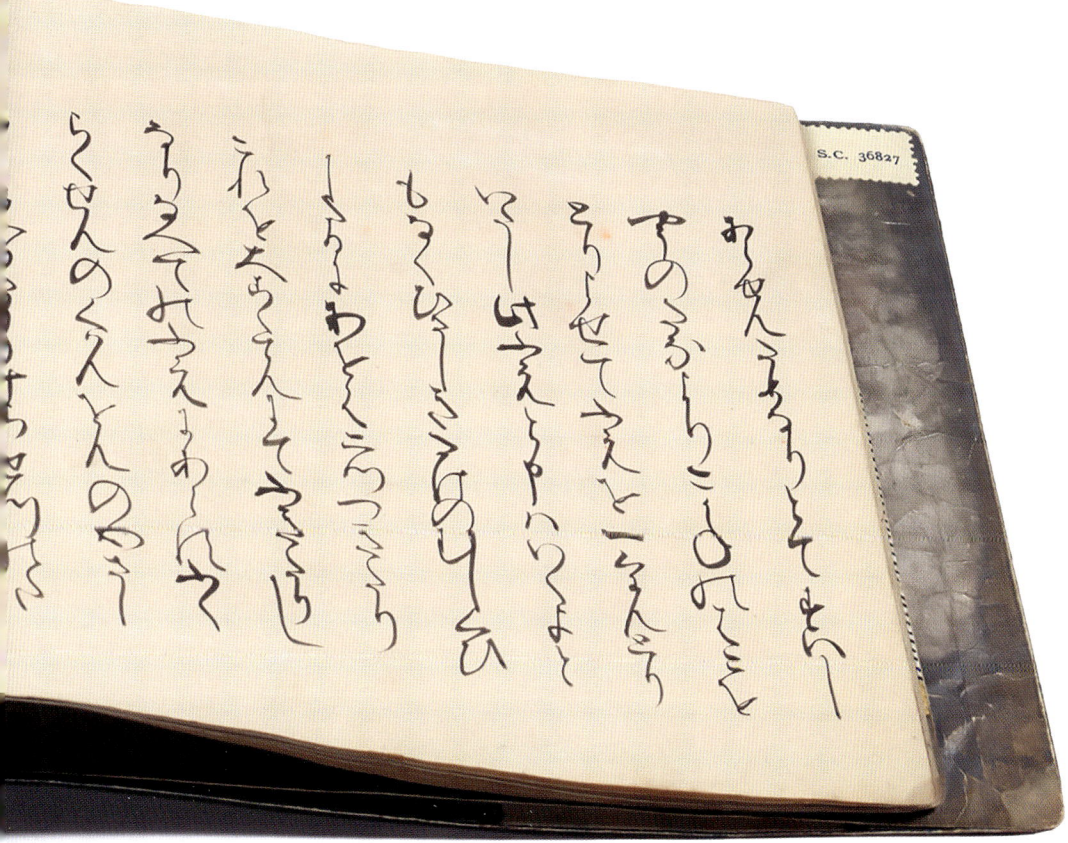

27 Group of *Nara e-hon* (Nara picture books), from a seventeenth-century series comprising twenty-one volumes. The books consist of *Otogizōshi* (popular short stories). The finely illustrated pages, in ink, colour pigment and gold, are bound in gold-decorated indigo-blue Japanese paper covers and silver-decorated endleaves. The nine books shown are: *Aoba monogatari* (MS. Jap. d.30), *Bunshō* (MS. Jap. d.48, 49, 50), *Fushimi Tokiwa* (MS. Jap. d.46, 47), *Hachikazuki* (MS. Jap. d.43, 44, 45), *Ibuki* (MS. Jap. d.31, 32), *Kowata Kitsune* (MS. Jap. d.33, 34), *Sagoromo* (MS. Jap. d.35, 36, 37), *Taketori monogatari* (MS. Jap. d.38, 39, 40), *Tamamitsu* (MS. Jap. d.41, 42).

as the ground for an auspicious motif of young bamboo. The bamboo plant, symbol of vitality and prosperity, is superimposed over a diamond-shaped lattice, and overlayed with the striking circular crest of the Tokugawa family – three heart-shaped leaves of the *aoi* plant – proclaiming the bride's lineage. The books and scrolls for such a display were first and foremost intended to instantiate auspiciousness, and employed visual and material symbolism to suggest a felicitous union and future lineal prosperity.

Many of the manuscripts in the Bodleian would have sat comfortably within the most elite trousseau or daimyo household library, saturated as they are with auspicious symbolism, from their external decorated covers to their narrative content, which tends to centre on felicitous bonds between men and women. Even the somewhat less opulent works, such as the group of nine pictures books (*Nara e-hon*) (FIG. 27), might have been made with trousseau and wedding libraries in mind, as Ishikawa Tōru and others have suggested.[19] Delphine Mulard, in her meticulous and insightful study of *The Tale of Bunshō* (*Bunshō sōshi*) and Edo-period manuscripts, justly urges caution in categorizing such tales as part of a trousseau.[20] Mulard notes the absence of all but the most canonical book titles in elite wedding inventories, and the lack of wedding records for families of lower social strata. It seems likely, however, that the power of what might be called a 'daimyo trousseau aesthetics' extended beyond the most rarified households and paved the way for an abundance of new commercial enterprises and shops selling and making manuscripts that catered to wealthy merchants for their own wedding

ceremonies and felicitous library needs.[21] Moreover, it should be noted that an anthology of medieval short stories published in the eighteenth century that became the basis for many *Nara e-hon* was originally titled *The Felicitous Wedding Companion Library* (*Shūgen otogi bunko*) and was sold and advertised alongside didactic and practical guides for women.[22] The original understanding of these stories as having once been part of a felicitous nuptial library tends to be overlooked, but it is clear that the ethos of the trousseau library extended beyond the elite echelon of society.[23]

To bring more clarity to this issue and the relationships between printed books and hand-written manuscripts in this era, the remainder of this chapter focuses on two manuscripts of *The Song of Everlasting Sorrow* (*Chōgonka*) and what their formats, materiality and content can tell us about their possible role in launching a woman's married life in a new household. Two illustrated examples of this work in the Bodleian collection, in codex and scroll format, demonstrate how *The Song of Everlasting Sorrow*, East Asia's most famous tragic love story, was interpreted among certain members of Tokugawa society, and how it could be deemed appropriate for a marriage library.

## A TRAGIC STORY FOR AN AUSPICIOUS BEGINNING

An epic poem composed by the Tang dynasty Chinese poet Bai Juyi (772–846), *Song of Everlasting Sorrow* became one of the most well-known and frequently illustrated literary works of Chinese origin in Japan. The famously tragic story relates the Chinese emperor Xuanzong's excessive affection for the beautiful Yang Guifei (719–756) and his

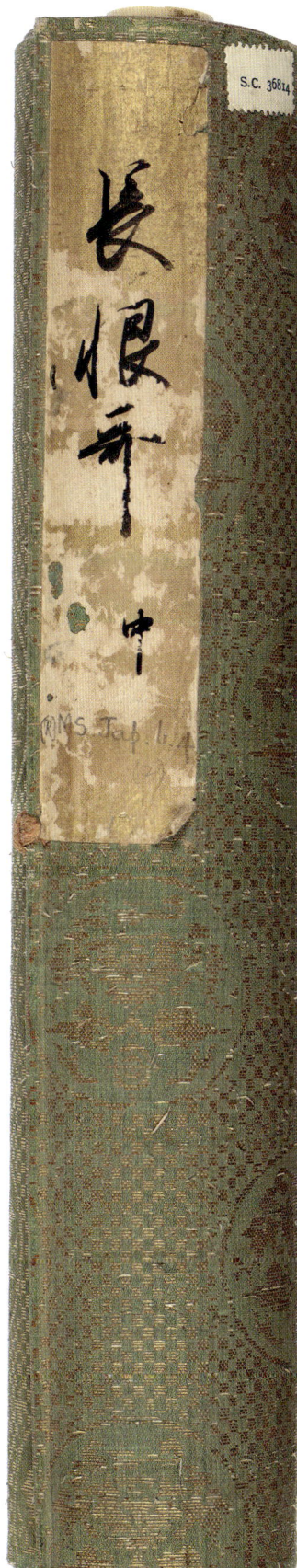
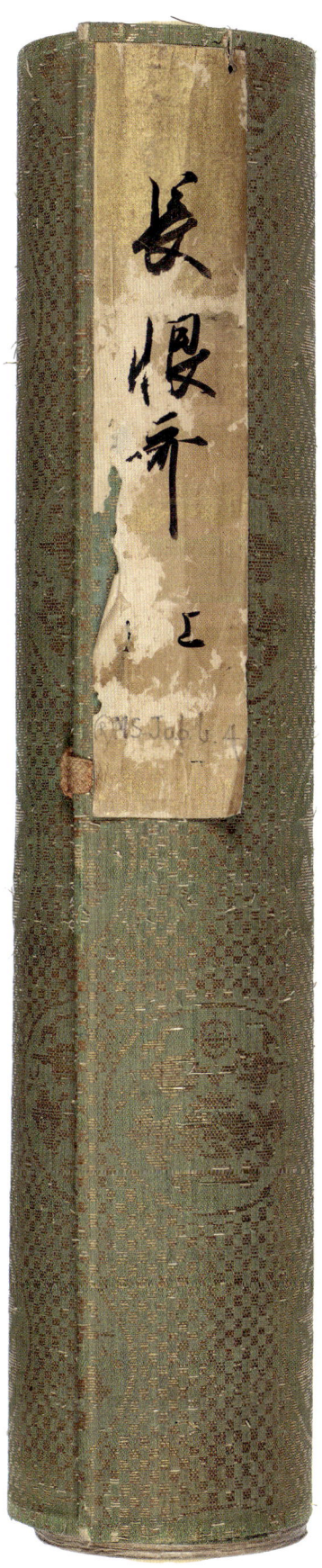

28 *The Song of Everlasting Sorrow* (*Chōgonka*) by Bai Juyi (742–846); *The Tale of Yang Guifei* (*Yōkihi monogatari*) by Asai Ryōi (1612–1691), seventeenth century. Two handscrolls: ink, colours and gold on paper. Vols 1 and 2 of an original three-scroll set. MS. Jap. b.4 (R).

29 OVERLEAF *The Song of Everlasting Sorrow* (*Chōgonka*) by Bai Juyi (742–846); *The Tale of Yang Guifei* (*Yōkihi monogatari*) by Asai Ryōi (1612–1691), seventeenth century. Three thread-bound volumes: ink, colours and gold on paper. Covers: indigo ground, gold paint design. MS. Jap. d.14–16.

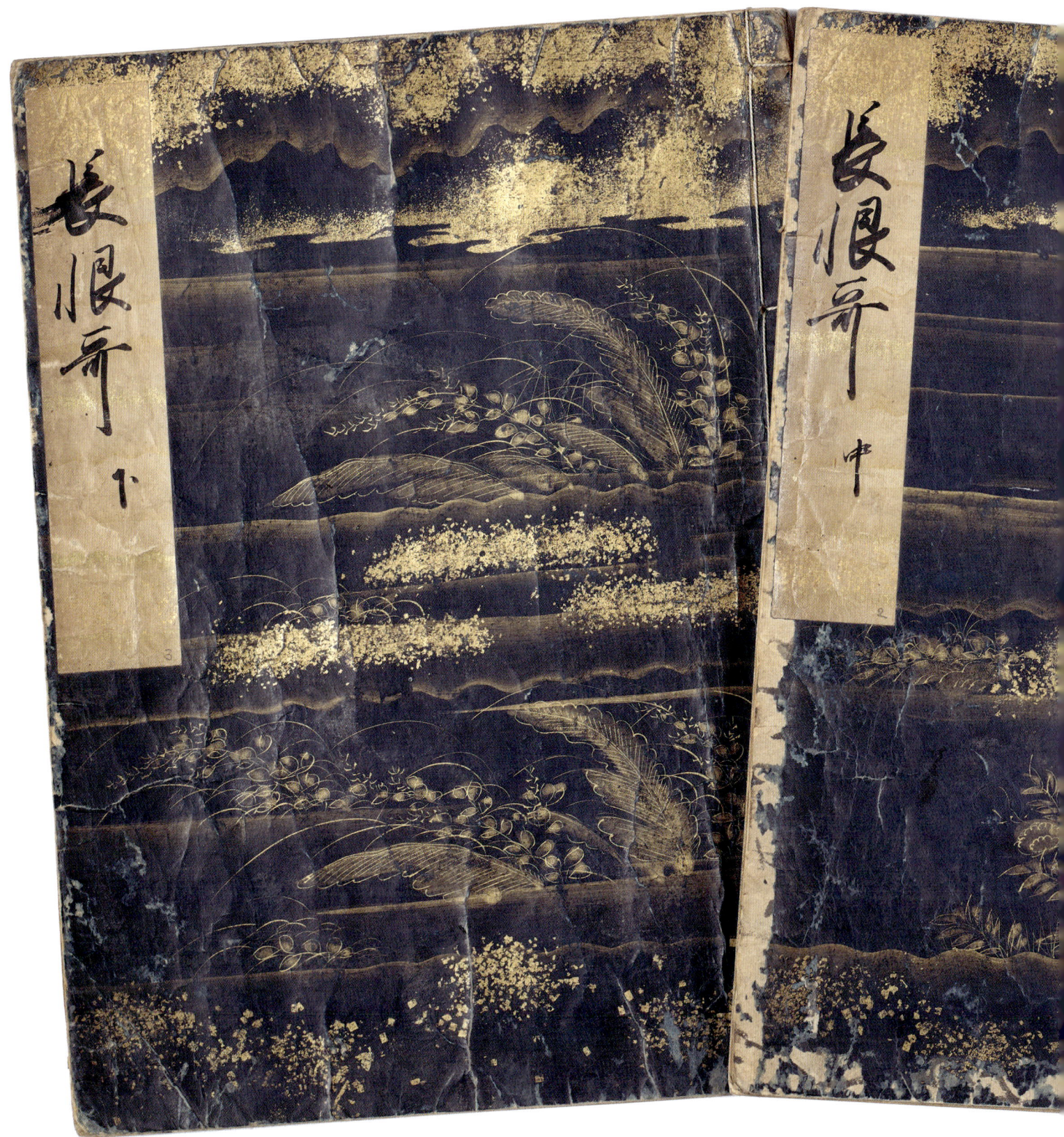

長恨歌　下

長恨歌　中

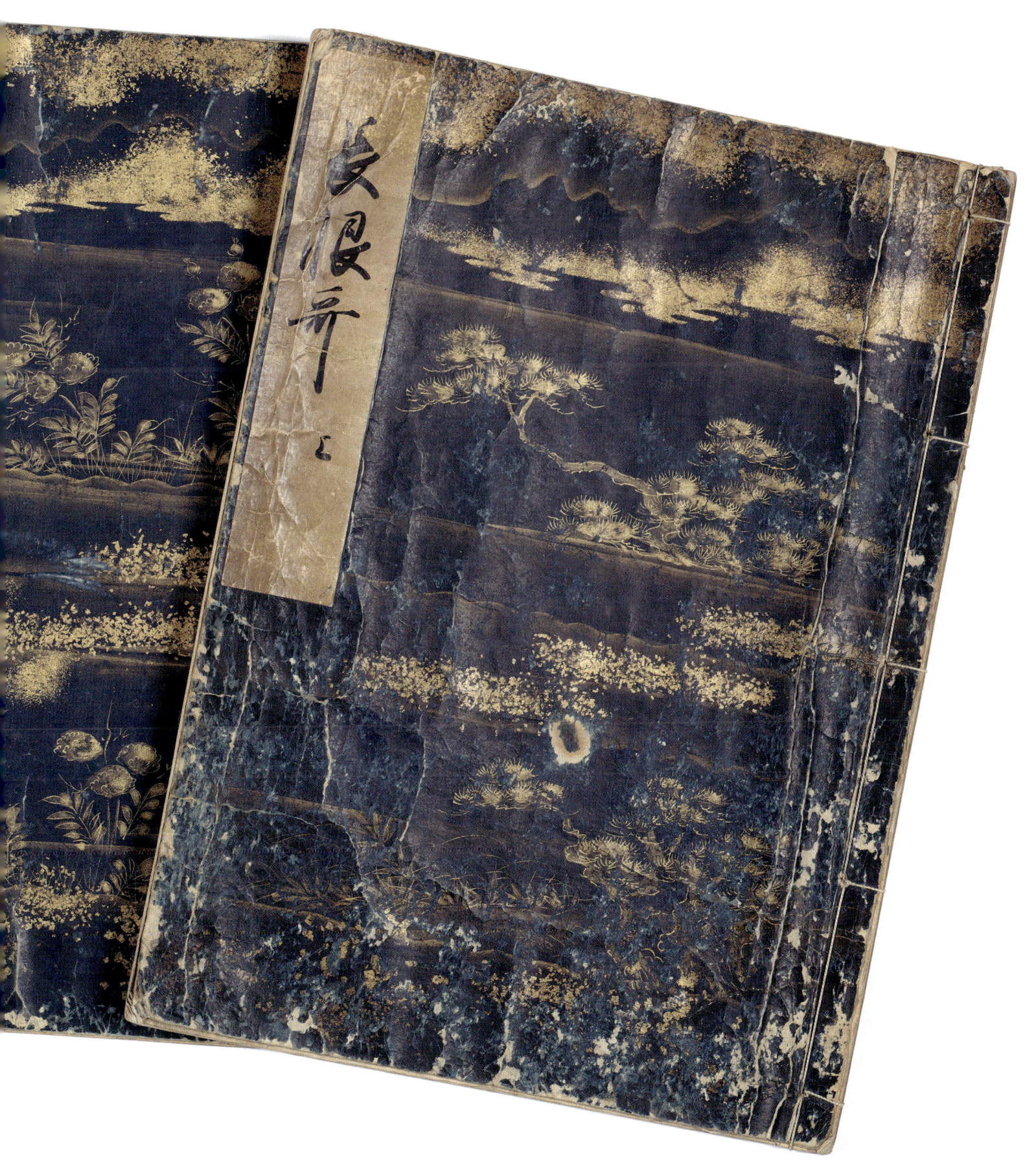

profound grief after she is put to death following the rebellion of An Lu Shan (703–757), for which she and her brother Yang Guozhong (?–756) were blamed. The work enthralled readers with its elegant classical Chinese language and memorable poetic imagery, and its dramatic themes of eternal romantic bonds, tragic death, political intrigue and violence. Because the poem explained the events behind the decline of one of the greatest dynasties in history, it served as a cautionary tale for later governments and political regimes across East Asia. Over the centuries in Japan the ballad was a consistent source of literary and artistic inspiration, shaping countless works of poetry and prose, and a wealth of paintings. The bulk of existing artistic works date from the Edo period, such as a spectacular set of handscrolls by Kano Sansetsu (1590–1651) in the Chester Beatty Library, and numerous hanging scrolls, fans and folding screens.[24] Unlike most of these works, however, the Bodleian manuscripts do not illustrate the original Chinese ballad per se. Although the cover titles on both manuscripts (FIGS 28 & 29) say *Chōgonka* (i.e. *Song of Everlasting Sorrow*), they actually reproduce the contents of a popular three-volume woodblock printed version of the ballad (FIGS 31, 32, 33) with commentary, in Japanese, called *The Tale of Yang Guifei* (*Yōkihi monogatari*, 1658–1672) by the writer Asai Ryōi (1612–1691).[25] Both works thus represent

30 *The Song of Everlasting Sorrow* (*Chōgonka*) by Bai Juyi (742–846); *The Tale of Yang Guifei* (*Yōkihi monogatari*) by Asai Ryōi (1612–1691), seventeenth century. Scroll One, Painting Two: Emperor Xuanzong seated alongside Yang Guifei in the imperial palace. MS. Jap. b.4 (R).

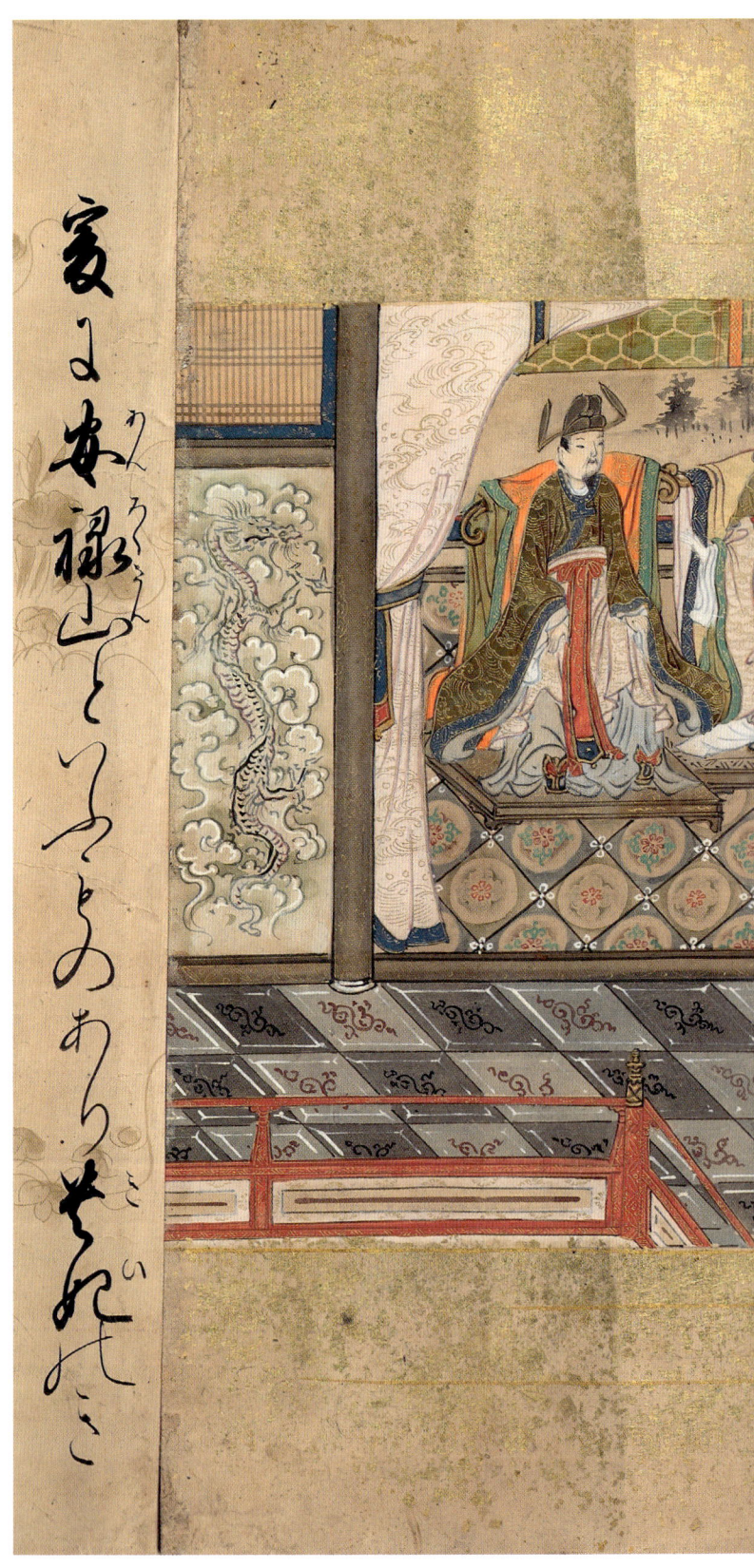

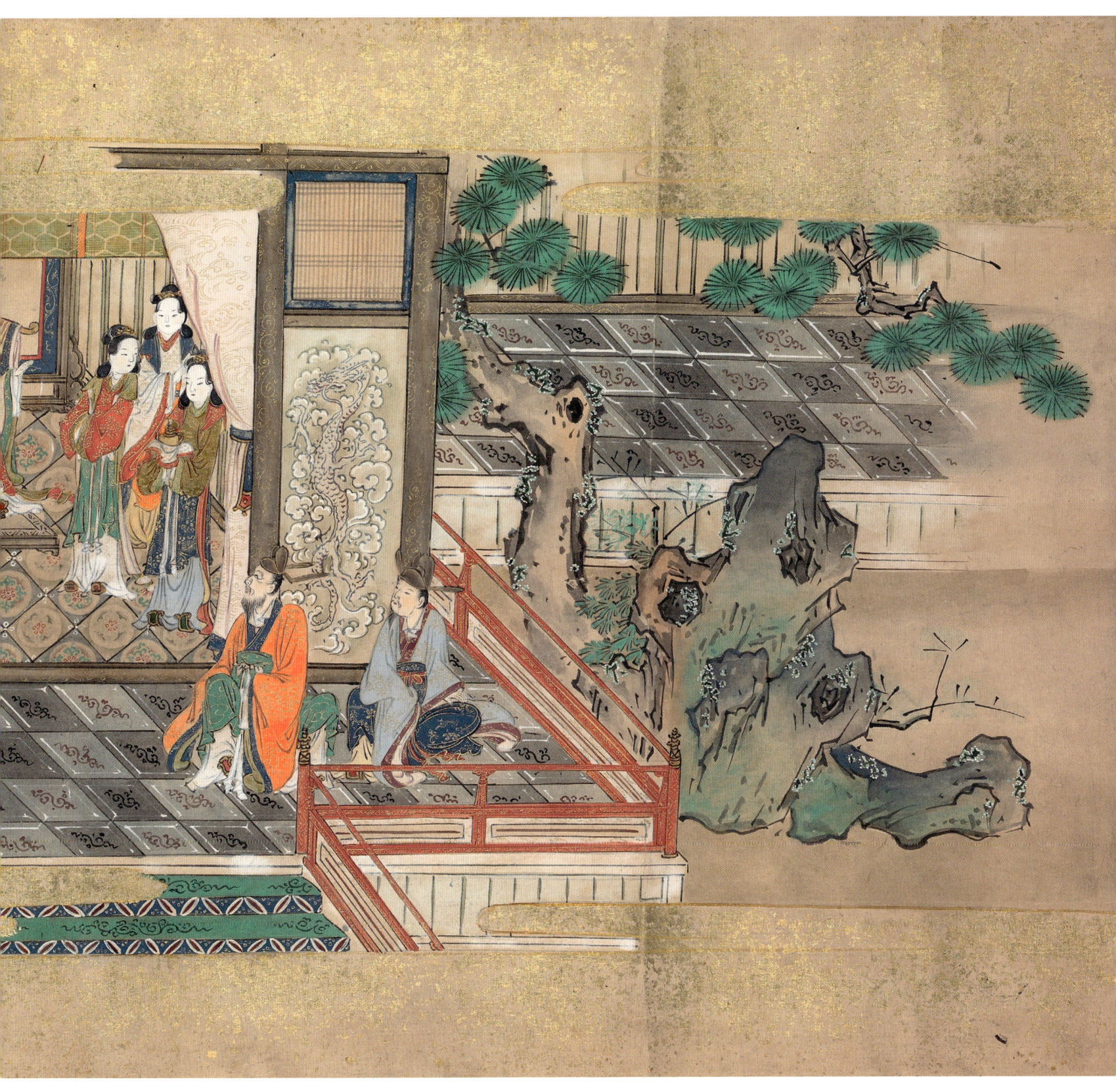

an important example of a printed book, and an educational text at that, being used as a direct model for deluxe illustrated manuscripts.[26]

Looking only at the outside of the Bodleian's *Song of Everlasting Sorrow* in the handscroll format (FIG. 28) – a prestige format with connotations of august libraries of scroll collections of the past – one might assume that a canonical text awaits inside to be unrolled. The mounting is richly decorated, beginning with an olive-green silk and gold brocade in a checkerboard and circular crest pattern, with brown silk cords, ivory rollers, and title labels of paper decorated with designs of clouds in gold paint and scattered gold.[27] Opening the scroll, the opulence continues: elaborately decorated papers with golden underdrawings serve as the ground for elegant calligraphy and richly illuminated paintings (see FIG. 30). The codex version in the collection is similarly extravagant (see FIG. 29).[28] Dark-blue dyed covers form the ground for an evocative golden landscape of vine-wrapped pines and young bamboo, framed by clouds and mist bands in evocative shapes that are rendered in varying techniques of gold application, from drawn horizontal lines to scattered pieces of cut gold leaf. The inside covers of the books are stamped with chrysanthemum designs in gold, scattered between gold mists and cut gold, while underdrawings (both pictorial motifs in gold, and stamped designs in silver) appear throughout the book beneath the calligraphy. Even if these works were used or created as gifts or items for a bridal trousseau, why invest in such lavish materiality and craftsmanship to reproduce an educational primer like *The Tale of Yang Guifei*, which was readily available as a printed book?

One answer is the straightforward appeal of *The Tale of Yang Guifei* as a commentary, which for certain readers existed as a stand-in for the original ballad. Readers in seventeenth-century Japan of course engaged with Bai Juyi's poem in classical Chinese on its own, with its one hundred and twenty lines of verse, each seven characters long, structured as pairs of complementary couplets. But the annotated versions that translated the Chinese verse into Japanese served an important role in mediating the epic poem. In his commentary, Ryōi added a vivid introduction, followed by the full poem and line-by-line explanations, etymologies and historical context. To do so, he relied on an earlier commentary by Kiyohara Nobukata (1475–1550), but he made even that explanatory text easier to read by employing the Japanese phonetic *kana* script.[29] Ryōi also illustrated his commentary with a total of fifteen pictures. The resulting three-volume book was the only text a reader needed to learn the Chinese classic ballad and to become familiar with its language. Even more importantly, as we shall see, this set of printed volumes provided for Edo-period readers a moral framework in which to understand the significance and relevance of the poem. Moreover, Ryōi gave the didactic commentary a title that sounds like an interesting story: *The Tale of Yang Guifei* suggests a hybrid narrative-commentary. Most importantly, however, it seems that Ryōi's text could have essentially replaced Bai Juyi's ballad in much the same way that Michael Emmerich has argued the eleventh-century *Tale of Genji* was 'replaced' by a particular printed offshoot in nineteenth-century Japan.[30]

What was Bai Juyi's original Chinese language ballad being replaced with in the Bodleian

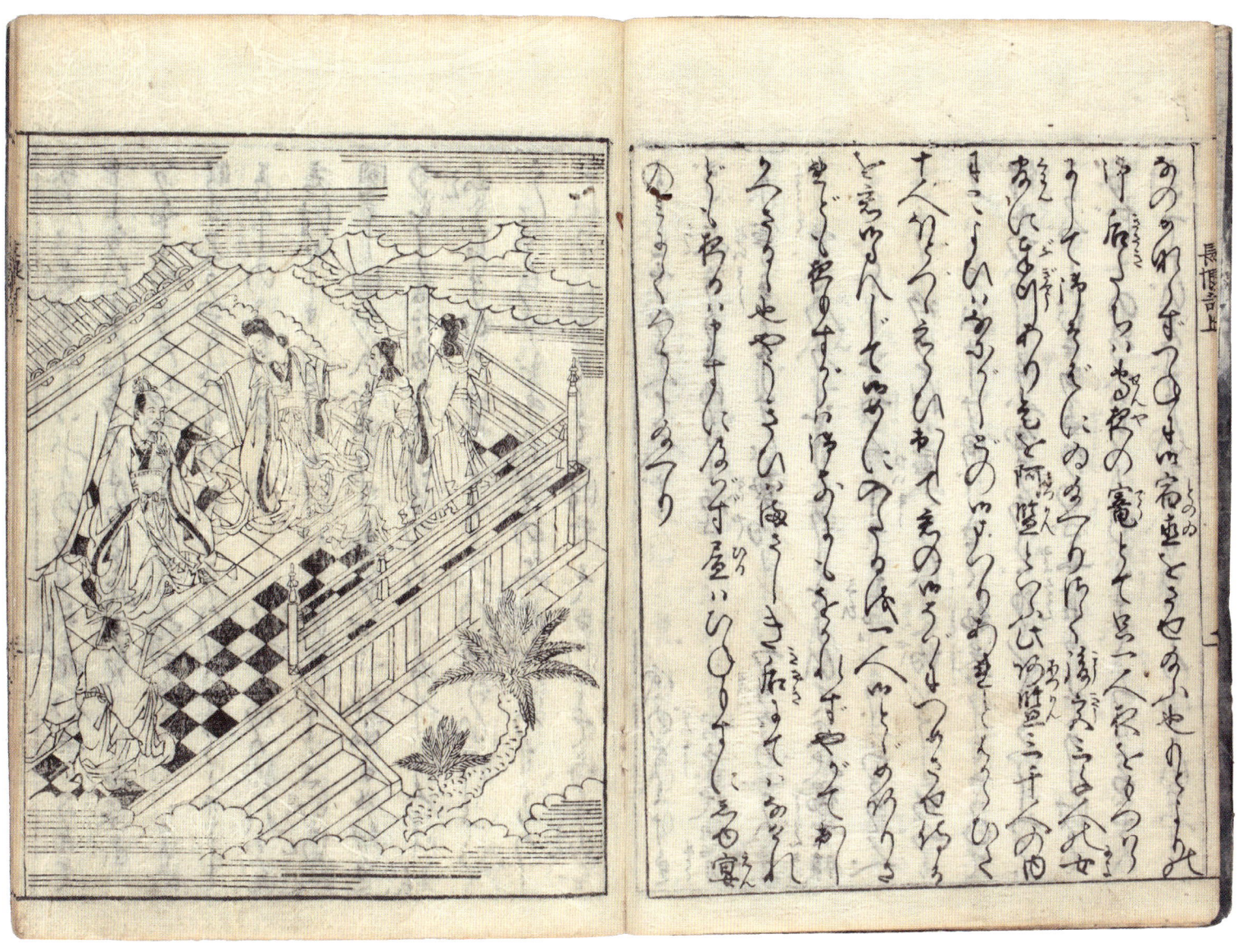

あのねすつてい宿虫ととせのふやのとそれ
ゆうちらいゆ能の竃とて足一人衣とそつり
うゆて満そゆとにぬるよゆにく溝えろほ人収女
おにまりよりも去と阿野よ及此やゆ腔三十人の田
まこにいいより一ぢのゆらりめ去とそらいく
大人切てゆひよいれて去ののゆろくいよつる又好
ところゆんへーて当いのてろてい人とーゆひり
せとろ当めのちゆりとよろてとよりやさて却
うろ去してゆくよいはるうときいめより
どようやさひ海ろーきめていゆて
どさ取いいすにならずそ田敷
のこまよくりいーろてり

長恨章上

manuscripts? Ryōi's printed commentary of Bai
Juyi's ballad, which the Bodleian manuscripts
illustrate, in many ways interprets the *Song of
Everlasting Sorrow* as a cautionary tale focusing on
the pitfalls of lust and the misdeeds of Yang Guifei
as a root cause of dynastic downfall. Take the first
three illustrations in the popular printed book
version, for example, which depict Emperor Xuanzong's excessive preoccupation with the beautiful
Yang Guifei (FIG. 31), the antics in the palace of

31 *The Tale of Yang Guifei (Yōkihi monogatari)*, 1658–72
by Asai Ryōi (1612–1691). Edo period printed book.
Emperor Xuanzong seated alongside Yang Guifei in the
imperial palace.

the future rebel, An Lushan (FIG. 32), and the clash between An Lushan and Yang Guifei's elder bother Yang Guozhong that led to the violent rebellion (FIG. 33). These three original scenes illustrate the introduction to Ryōi's commentary. In this inaugural position, they shape the reader's experience as a paratext and function as a prelude to the annotated and illustrated ballad by Bai Juyi that follows. In this capacity they set an admonitory tone. The three episodes emphasize the causal relationship between the emperor's lustful preoccupations and his neglect of government and the mayhem that follows, with each scene building upon the next.

The Bodleian manuscripts follow the printed versions closely in text and image, while adjusting for the horizontal format and adding to the reading and viewing experience with rich colouration and the tactility of mineral pigments and gold. The first scene of Xuanzong and Yang Guifei in the

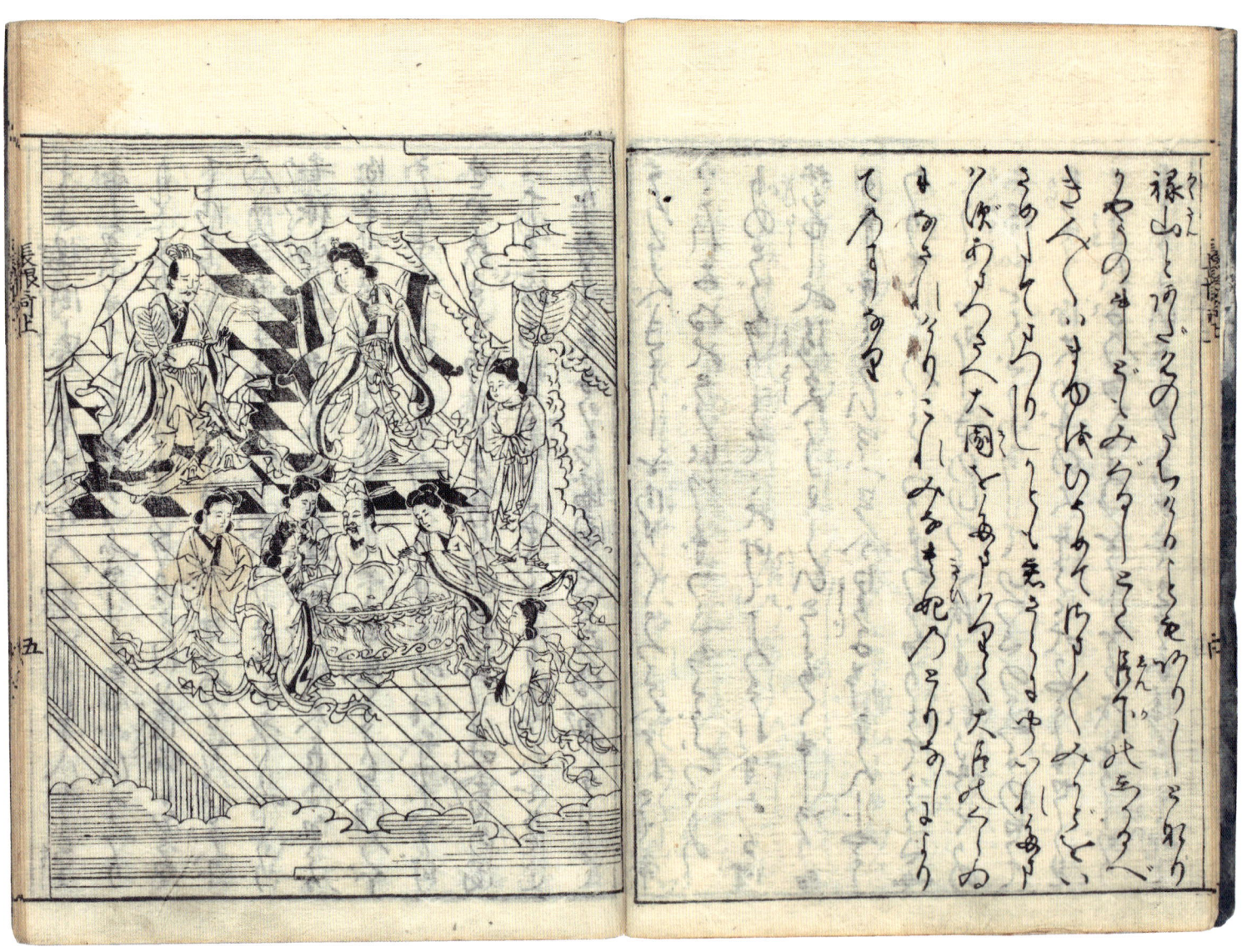

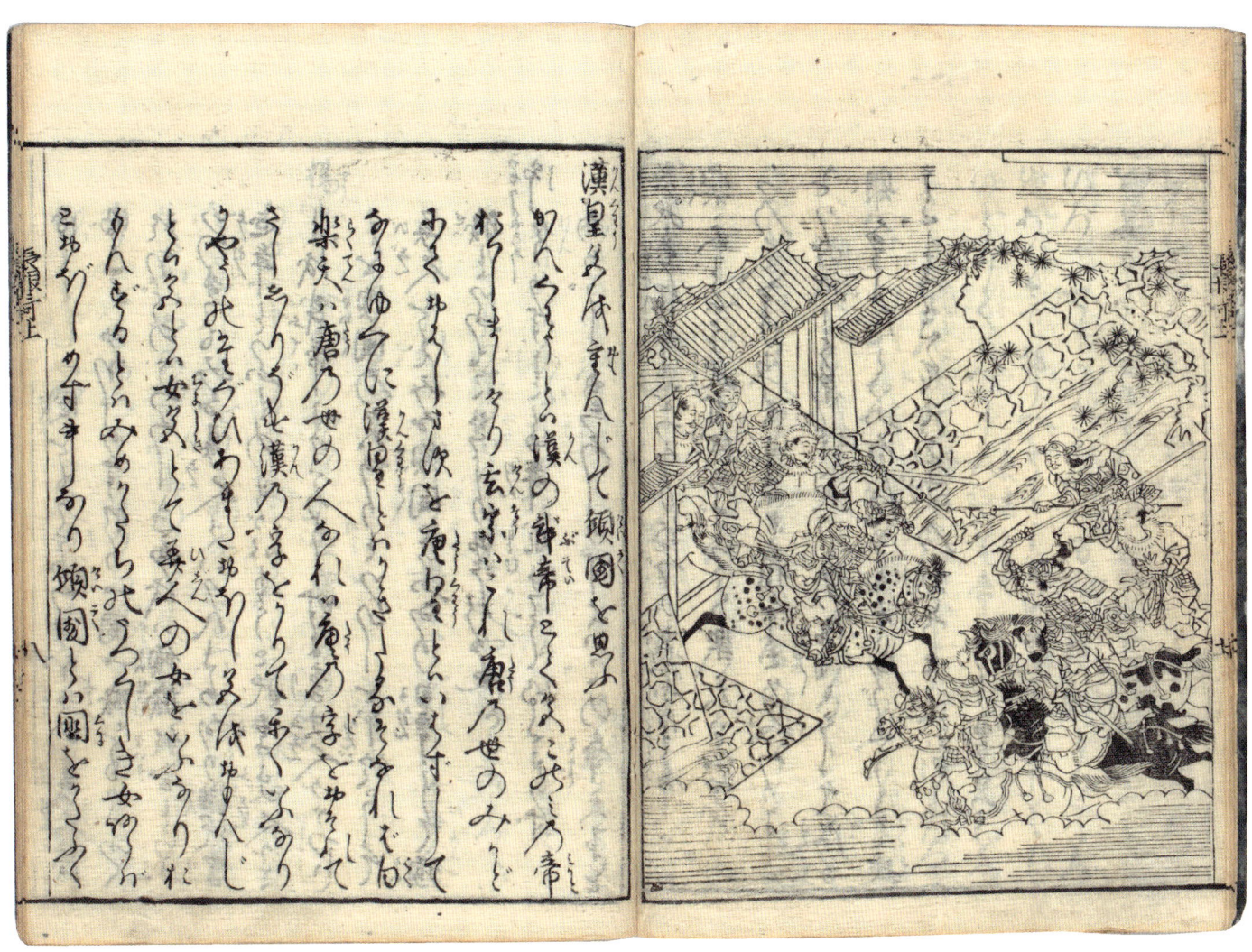

32 *The Tale of Yang Guifei* (*Yōkihi monogatari*), 1658–72 by Asai Ryōi (1612–1691). Edo period printed book. Emperor Xuanzong seated alongside Yang Guifei in the imperial palace with An Lushan in the bath.

33 *The Tale of Yang Guifei* (*Yōkihi monogatari*), 1658–72 by Asai Ryōi (1612–1691). Edo period printed book. The clash between An Lushan and Yang Guifei's elder brother, Yang Guozhong.

palace, for example (see FIG. 30), situates them in gorgeous surroundings, above colourful tiled floors, wearing elaborately patterned gold-inflected robes, and attended to by three elegantly outfitted serving ladies. Reading the handscroll from right to left, the calligraphic text immediately preceding the image to the right explains that 'even though Yang Guifei was not an official empress, she occupied the emperor's nights and his days, as they lost themselves in wine-filled revelry'. Yang Guifei is shown sitting atop a throne-like chair as though she is the empress, while Xuanzong sits gazing in her direction, transfixed. Two male courtiers

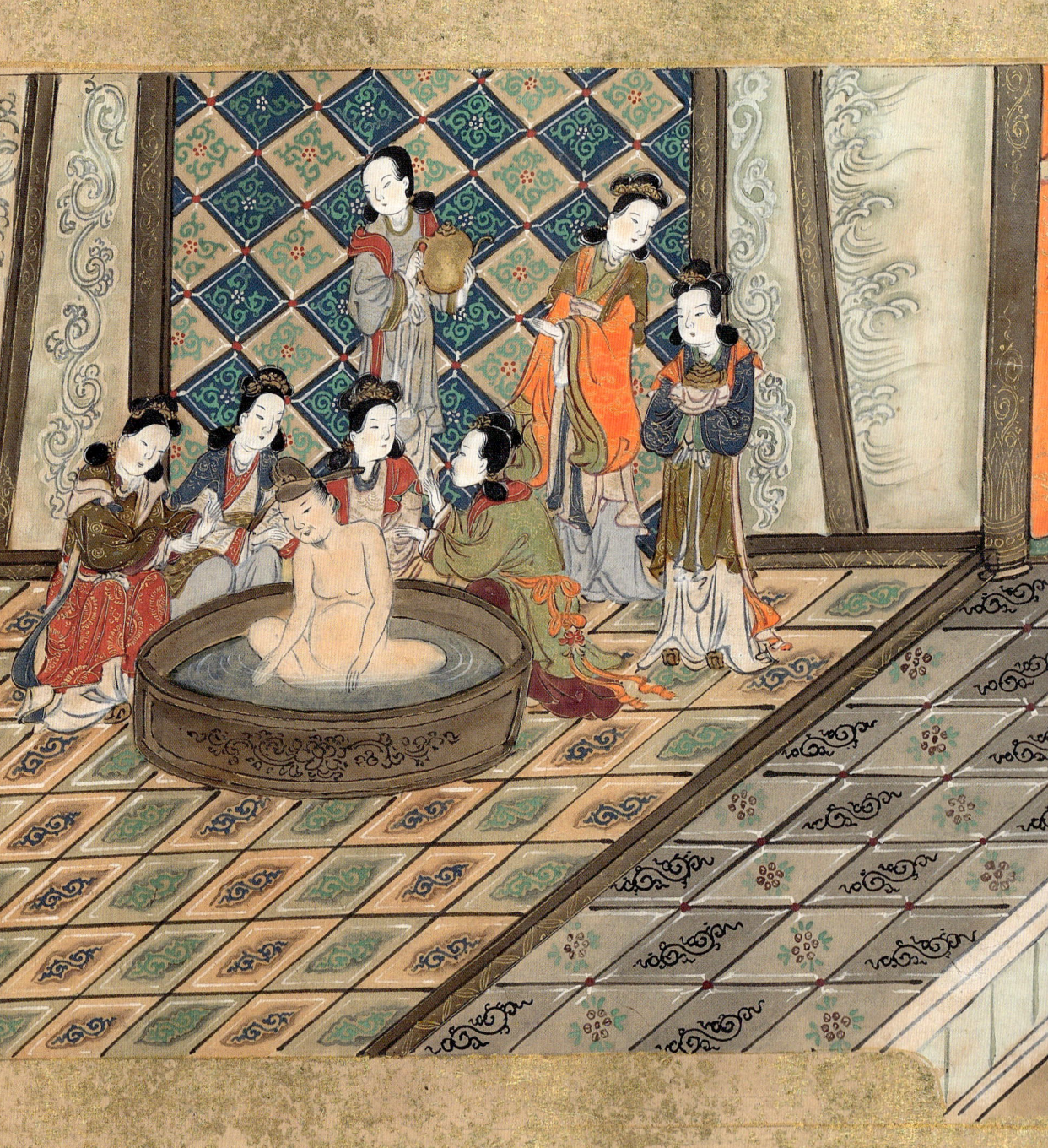

また楊国忠として
きんの兄わらぎん

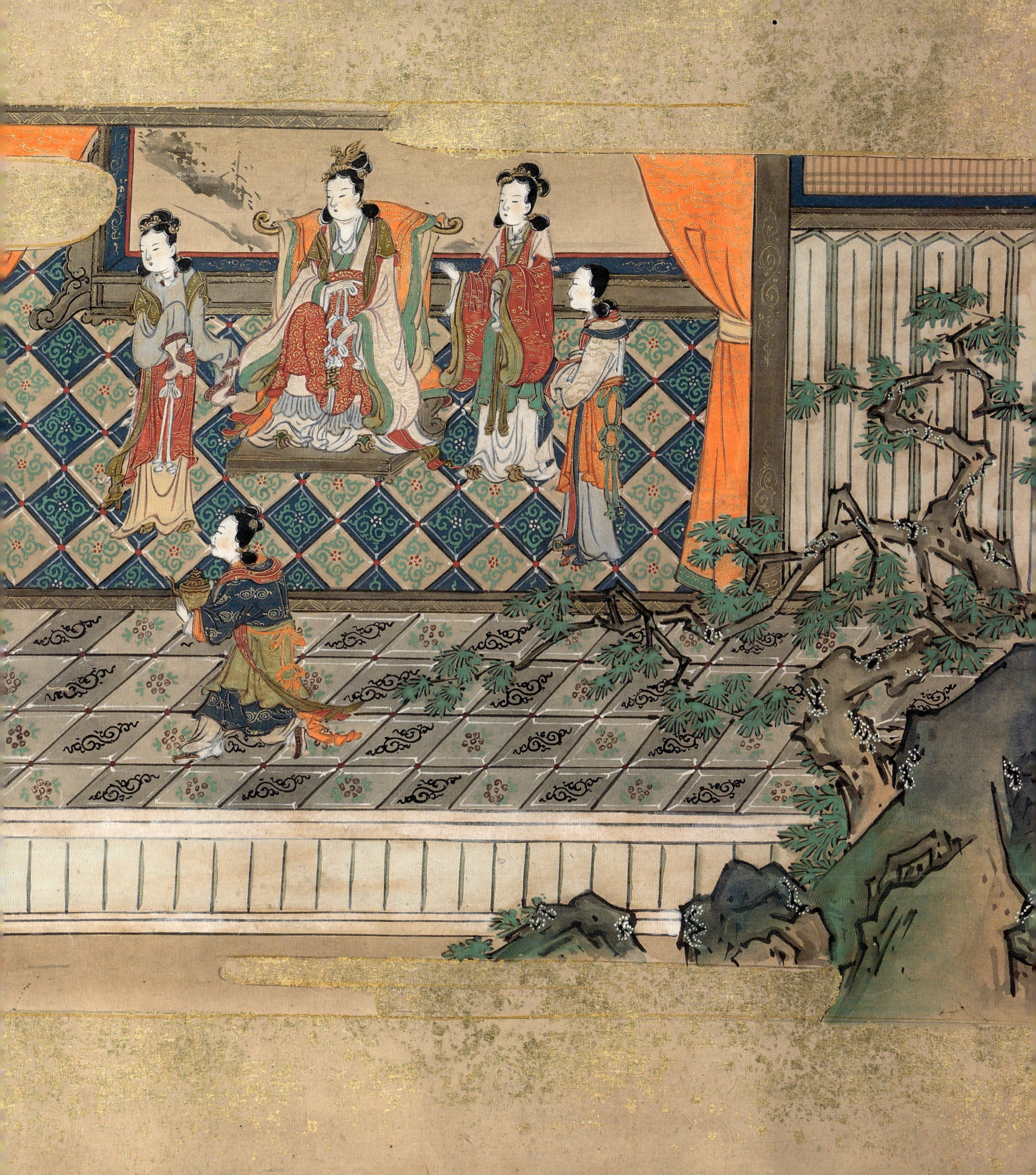

appear on the veranda, perhaps urging the sovereign to return to his duties, while Yang Guifei bends both hands at the wrists in a gesture that seems to urge the emperor to stay. The serving lady to the right, holding a golden wine ewer, perhaps hints at the bacchanalian existence described in the text.

Drawing on legends about the questionable immoral behaviour of these characters, the next painting illustrated in Ryōi's introduction depicts how An Lushan, a warrior of Turkish and Sogdian origins, and future rebel against the court, ingratiated himself into the palace. As legend apparently had it, Yang Guifei legally adopted An Lushan and also took him as her lover. Ryōi's commentary prominently features a related and unexpected anecdote. The episode consists of a mock birth in the women's quarters, as seen in the printed version (FIG. 32), as well as the Bodleian handscroll (FIG. 34) and painted codex (FIG. 35), depicting a naked An Lushan seated in the hot water tub used during childbirth. Both Emperor Xuanzong and Yang Guifei were susceptible to An Lushan's manipulation, and both are shown in the Bodleian's painted book version watching his antics in the bath. The handscroll painting of the same episode (see FIG. 34), on the other hand, may absolve the sovereign somewhat by excluding him from the image. There Yang Guifei

eyes the naked man on her own, evoking their rumoured illicit relationship which, in some accounts, helped incite the rebellion. The Bodleian codex version (see FIG. 35) may also implicate the woman, or it may allude to legendary rifts between Yang Guifei and Xuanzong; it shows the emperor pointing a seemingly accusatory finger in her direction, as she demurely tilts her head. In this way, the manuscripts introduce entirely new material from the commentary before the reader even begins reading the ballad. As a result, they strike a different tone to that of the faithful illustrations of Bai Juyi's text, like Kano Sansetsu's painted rendition, which as Shane McCausland has described, emphasizes romance and the profound bond between the couple, and following the tenor of the ballad, 'avoids directly casting aspersions on Yang Guifei's character'.[31]

Another example of the emphasis on Yang Guifei's misdeeds and eventual comeuppance is the surprisingly explicit image of Yang Guifei's corpse. In the Bodleian's codex manuscript, the portion of the ballad that deals directly with her death and the emperor's reaction is illustrated across four scenes that take place as the emperor flees the capital under siege by An Lushan. In the first scene, Yang Guifei is led away by the faction of the imperial army that demands her death as retribution for the sins of her relatives. In the second the emperor,

34 PREVIOUS SPREAD *The Song of Everlasting Sorrow (Chōgonka)* by Bai Juyi (742–846); *The Tale of Yang Guifei (Yōkihi monogatari)* by Asai Ryōi (1612–1691), seventeenth century. Scroll One, Painting Three: Yang Guifei in the imperial palace with An Lushan in the bath. MS. Jap. b.4 (R).

35 *The Song of Everlasting Sorrow (Chōgonka)* by Bai Juyi (742–846); *The Tale of Yang Guifei (Yōkihi monogatari)* by Asai Ryōi (1612–1691), seventeenth century, Vol. 1. Emperor Xuanzong and Yang Guifei with An Lushan in the bath. MS. Jap. d.14.

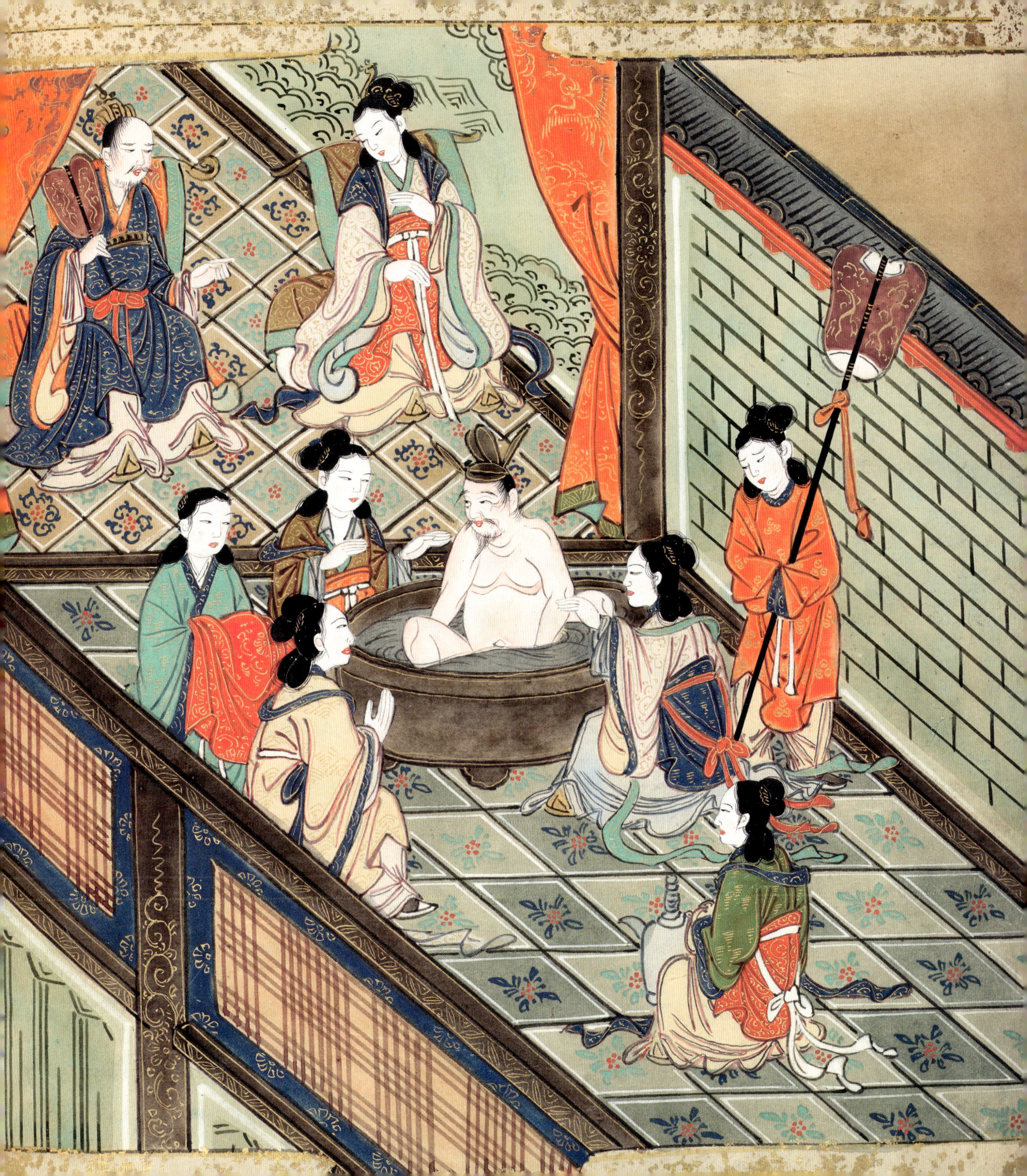

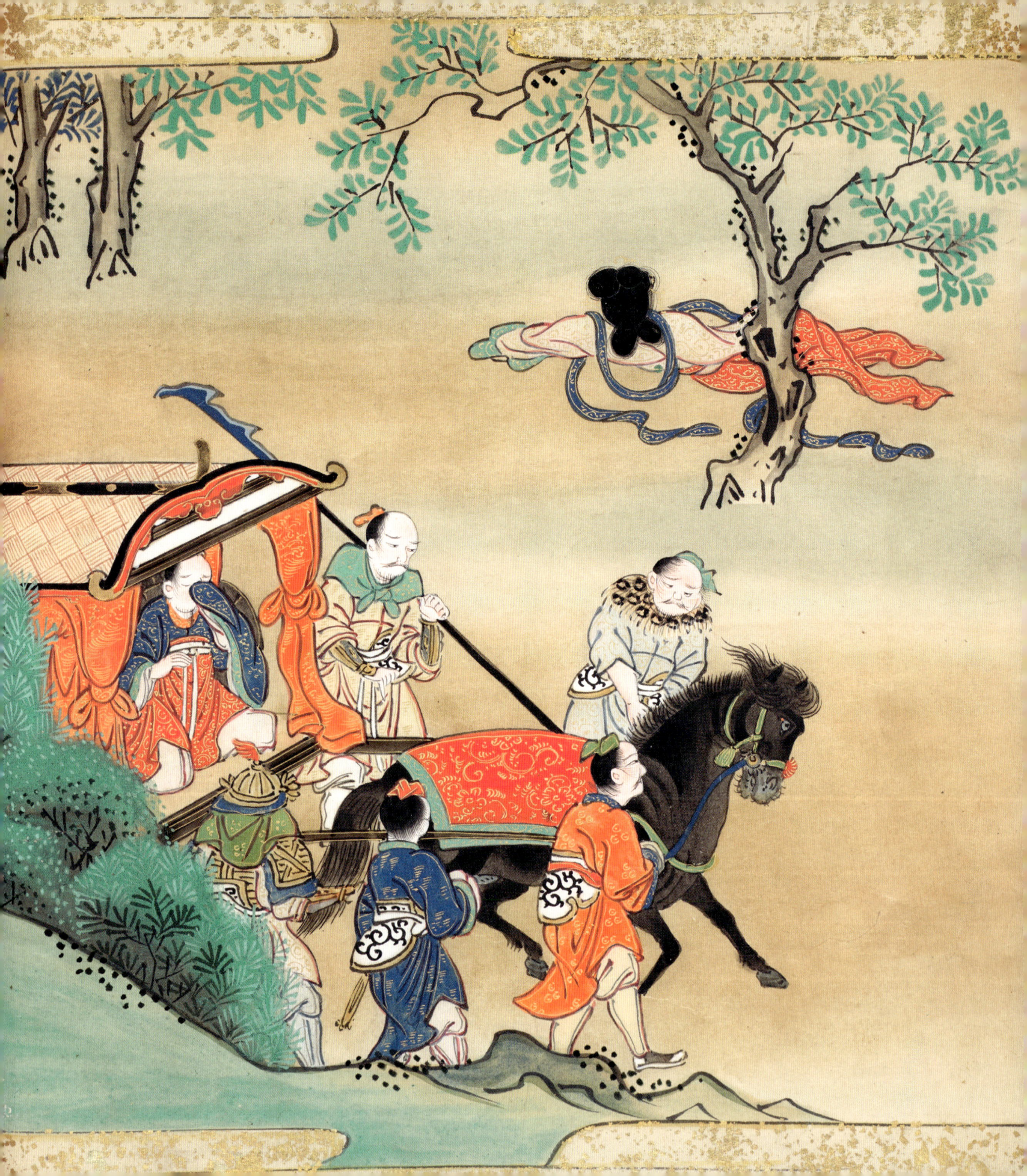

having been unable to protect his love, turns around in his carriage and sees her corpse, while in the third he journeys in the vicinity of Shu. The final scene shows the emperor on his return to the capital, passing the site of Yang Guifei's death, where he lingers. Seeing no trace of her presence, he lets his horse bring him home.

Ryōi's commentary, with its admonitory tone, allots a great deal of space to explaining the demand for Yang Guifei's execution – no doubt in anticipation of readers who would question a sovereign's powerlessness to save his lover, and who might therefore question the depth of his feeling. Significantly, the illustrations for Ryōi's *The Tale of Yang Guifei* commentary veer from the tradition of *Song of Everlasting Sorrow* paintings in scrolls, screens and fans by explicitly illustrating the line from Bai Juyi's poem that describes the situation after her strangulation:

> Our lord and ruler covered his face,
>     unable to protect her;
> He looked around, and blood and tears
>     were flowing there together.[32]

The explanation that follows each line of the poem in Ryōi's commentary of the Bodleian manuscripts mentions how some accounts say Yang Guifei was hanged from a pear tree in front of a Buddhist hall by a silken cord given to her by the emperor. The Bodleian's codex manuscript illustration (FIG. 36) depicts Yang Guifei's limp body

36 *The Song of Everlasting Sorrow* (*Chōgonka*) by Bai Juyi (742–846); *The Tale of Yang Guifei* (*Yōkihi monogatari*) by Asai Ryōi (1612–1691), seventeenth century, Vol. 2. Emperor Xuanzong viewing the corpse of Yang Guifei. MS. Jap. d.15.

outstretched, turned away from the viewer, at the base of a tree. Her flowing blue scarf circles around her chest and shoulders suggestive of a noose and the famous act of strangulation, while her head appears at an odd angle, seemingly raised. In the lower left corner, the emperor covers his face, as in the poem, seated in a carriage that is turned around from the usual leftward facing direction found in most illustrations. This perspective makes his view of Yang Gueifei's body inescapable, forcing him to see the body and the 'blood and tears … flowing there together'.

The handscroll in the Bodleian includes this scene as well (FIG. 37) – but, perhaps during a later remounting, the painting was removed from its correct chronological sequence in Scroll Two, and now, surprisingly, is the very first painting in Scroll One.[33] The image of Yang Gueifei's dead body (or more precisely her robes as a signifier of the body beneath the tree) appears after a short first section of text. This text preceding the image, to its immediate right in the scroll (p. 84), explains how the emperor's passion for his other concubines had cooled, and various gentlemen offered him their daughters, but there was 'no woman beautiful enough to win his heart'. The painting was inserted precisely at this spot in the scroll by cutting the paper of the first section of text at an unnatural spot, mid-sentence. The image of Yang Guifei's lifeless body (p. 83) now bisects the two-character phrase 'beautiful woman' (美 p. 84, 人 p. 82). Whether intentional or not, the result is uncanny for a work that pontificates about the behavior of China's most famous femme fatale, who, as the poem states, possessed 'a beauty that could topple a dynasty'. The Bodleian handscroll image of Yang

なりつき、驪山の花清宮とて、小雨小

とさわりく、女御天衣みんのさめ
にて温泉のゆ湯をまいらせて女房

さらにもさきてとんがんくも
さ小御かるすゆ一人しくして

て法方とりてうちをういあり
又して云ひ女といひもるゝを

のましろうこそことてしてよる
ふみ人とくいあらさしてありて

さんといひますくさんじてこれ
さんといひ、弘農の楊玄琰もそのたりみ

もとめつくそりつうつるとひて
よこしまのうちのこれよ父うをゆ

わくなくそよ玄宗の御けよ寧ありて
すふきいまくしゆくりけんそう里

帝このゆうとすめうとして父の
楊玄琰らくくしようくして賣て

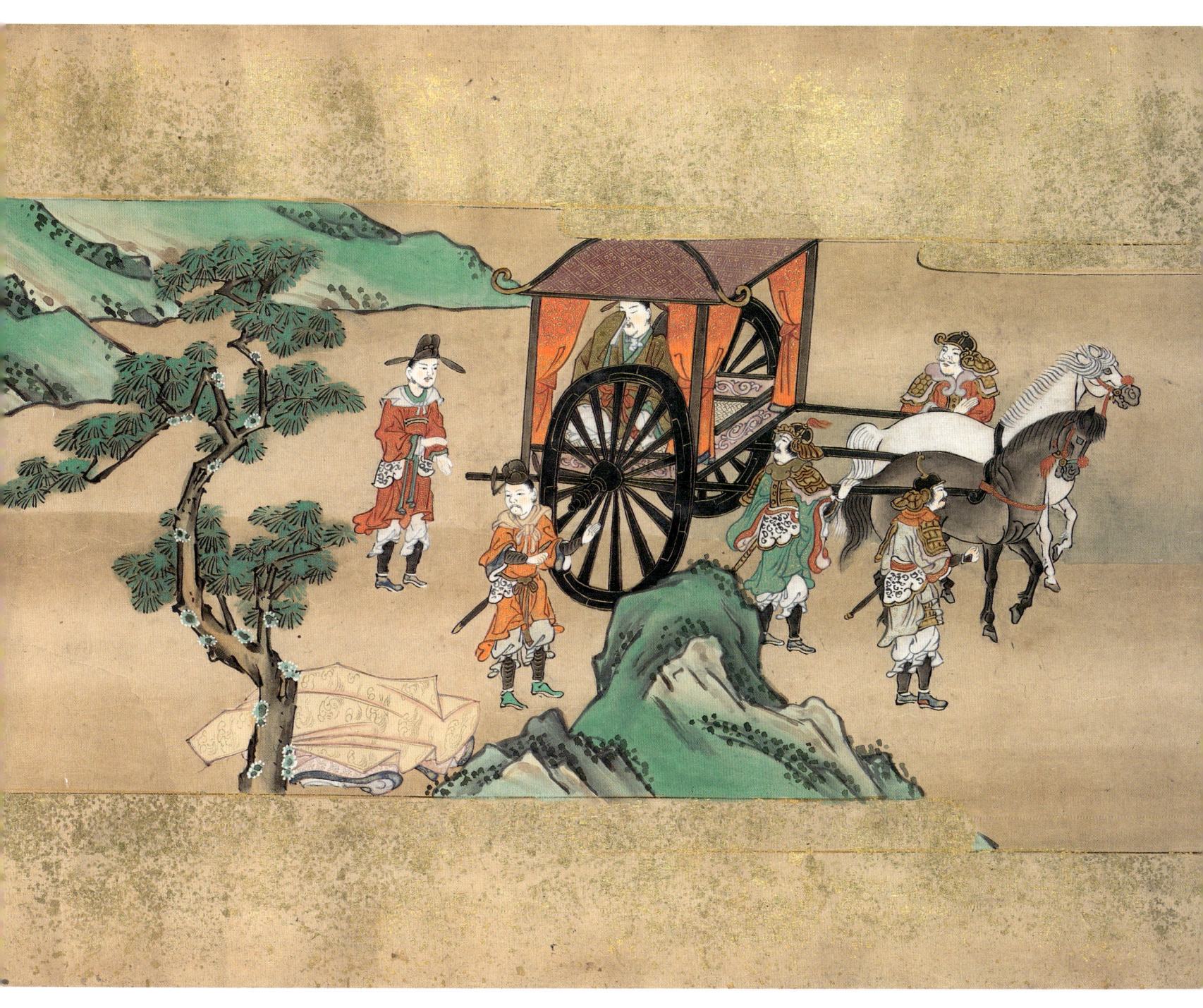

此長恨歌といふは唐乃玄宗皇帝御

位にましまして十年久しくををさめ

たまひしかひなくさかりなる

よく國をおさめ民をはぐくみ

を御心ゆるすことをなかりしを

きはめて色をおもんじそのをき

をうつはたれ給をにこれを次ぎ

りうへもなく元歌皇后武帝妃として

らうたけさ元歌皇后武帝妃として

てらりんうへこ楊貴人わつてて

せのありさ君の御てわびうつり

そこまうかにことをきをわる竜

うくをとろくゆろやうにも

下大ほうしとをへくられあから

しこしみのひとりまふりとて

妾

Guifei's body is less graphic than the codex or print version of this scene, since it does not show the woman's head or thin scarf that evokes her strangulation or hanging. Its placement here, however, at the start of the reading or viewing experience, suggests a preliminary overarching admonition, or even a kind of *memento mori*, as the scene also stages the emperor's contemplation of her corpse from his carriage.

Despite the death and seemingly tragic romance at its centre, *Song of Everlasting Sorrow* was not a taboo subject for bridal trousseaus. Bai Juyi's ballad was multifaceted enough to allow for a selective focus on certain images for illustration – paintings could focus solely on scenes of rebellion to urge political savvy and wise rulership, or they could feature episodes of the emperor and Yang Guifei's pleasure-filled life in the palace to create an atmosphere of courtly splendour, while images depicting the ruler's devotion and lifelong mourning of his lover could reflect a poignant romantic ideal. As Muraki Keiko has deftly shown, *Chōgonka* paintings and the many related printed books and commentaries produced in the Edo period often added auspicious motifs to text and image to create a felicitous tone.[34] They could

expand upon, for example, a famous line in the ballad that linked the birth of daughters to a family's fortune.

Muraki has also unearthed an exceptionally detailed historical example of how Yōwain (1638–1711), a woman originally from the nobility but married to the daimyo of the Satsuma domain, Shimazu Mitsuhisa (1616–1695), sought out a small-format folding screen of *Song of Everlasting Sorrow* for a bridal trousseau in 1701.[35] The then sixty-three-year-old Yōwain explains in a letter to her elder brother in Kyoto that she got the idea for commissioning a *Chōgonka* screen from reading Bai Juyi's ballad, and that she wishes for the painting to be displayed at the wedding 'site of the ceremonial felicitations' (*shūgen no za*), where she herself would not be present. Muraki suggests that this represents a new phase in the reception and rehabilitation of Yang Guifei's image, when a *Chōgonka* screen could be viewed as purely auspicious, appropriate imagery for sending a blessing for the marriage bonds, lineal abundance, longevity and good fortune.

The striking image of Yang Guifei's lifeless body might thus seems out of place, but as readers of the ballad know, the beautiful maiden does not stay inanimate for long. In the climax of the work, Emperor Xuanzong employs a Daoist wizard to seek his love in the afterworld. The messenger sent by the emperor does indeed find her, residing in the mountain of the immortals, Penglai (FIG. 38). Even in this paradisal realm, however, the woman mourns her lost love:

37 PREVIOUS SPREAD & LEFT *The Song of Everlasting Sorrow* (*Chōgonka*) by Bai Juyi (742–846); *The Tale of Yang Guifei* (*Yōkihi monogatari*) by Asai Ryōi (1612–1691), seventeenth century. Scroll One, Painting One, in which Emperor Xuanzong views the corpse of Yang Guifei. MS. Jap. b.4 (R).

Broken forever, the love that was shared
    in the Court of Shining Light,
Now days and the months pass but slowly
    in the Palace of Penglai.[36]

Yang Guifei is recuperated in moralistic terms by the end of Bai Juyi's poem, when she expresses her undying bond to the emperor, which is also how Ryōi's commentary ends. The commentary further elevates Yang Guifei by concluding with two separate images of the immortalized woman, seated in a regal manner, as the emperor's messenger kneels before her (FIG. 39). In its explanatory notes to the lines of the *Song of Everlasting Sorrow* cited above, describing Yang Guifei's lonely existence in the realm of the immortals, Ryōi's commentary introduces readers to a legend in which Yang Guifei is revealed to be the deity of the Atsuta Shrine in Japan.[37] The deity took the form of the beautiful maiden Yang Guifei to seduce emperor Xuangzong, thereby distracting him from attacking Japan: 'During the reign of Xuanzong, the realm was so calm and subdued, that the emperor set his sights on conquering Japan. Learning of his plan, the deity of Atsuta Shrine manifested as Yang Guifei and incited unrest in China to save Japan.'[38]

This retelling of events upends the entire *Song of Everlasting Sorrow* narrative. It removes any reason for regret over lost love, as Yang Gueifei is transformed into a native deity, and a national heroine, powerful enough to overturn the greatest of dynasties on behalf of Japan. One would be hard pressed to find a more appropriate role model for a bride, both loyal and self-sacrificing, under the Neo-Confucian moralist dictates espoused by the Tokugawa regime.

In this light, the deluxe manuscripts of Ryōi's commentary in the Bodleian collection could have *literally* replaced Bai Juyi's ballad on the bridal bookshelf or in various cultural contexts of display in the Edo period. Significantly, both handscroll and codex manuscripts have a dual identity – bearing only the title *Chōgonka* on their exterior mountings, these objects would have proudly announced a household's ownership of an important classical work, while at the same time disguising the more didactic content of Ryōi's *Tale of Yang Guifei* commentary inside. The *Chōgonka* title and manuscript covers are thus the public-facing sides of manuscripts that, between the covers, take a more complex stance toward the story's characters, especially Yang Guifei, moving from reproachful to celebratory as she becomes an incarnation of a Japanese deity.

## THE INTERPRETIVE LENS OF THE HOUSEHOLD LIBRARY

When it comes to the wedding trousseaus of the Tokugawa, elite daimyo and even wealthy commoners, it is important to understand the figure of the bride as a multifaceted persona. She was not only an individual whose readership and use of the gifted books would have been a central concern in their selection, but also a representative of both her natal family and the new household,

38 *The Song of Everlasting Sorrow* (*Chōgonka*) by Bai Juyi (742–846); *The Tale of Yang Guifei* (*Yōkihi monogatari*) by Asai Ryōi (1612–1691), seventeenth century, Vol. 3. The messenger sent by emperor Xuanzong finds Yang Guifei residing in the realm of the immortals. MS. Jap. d.16.

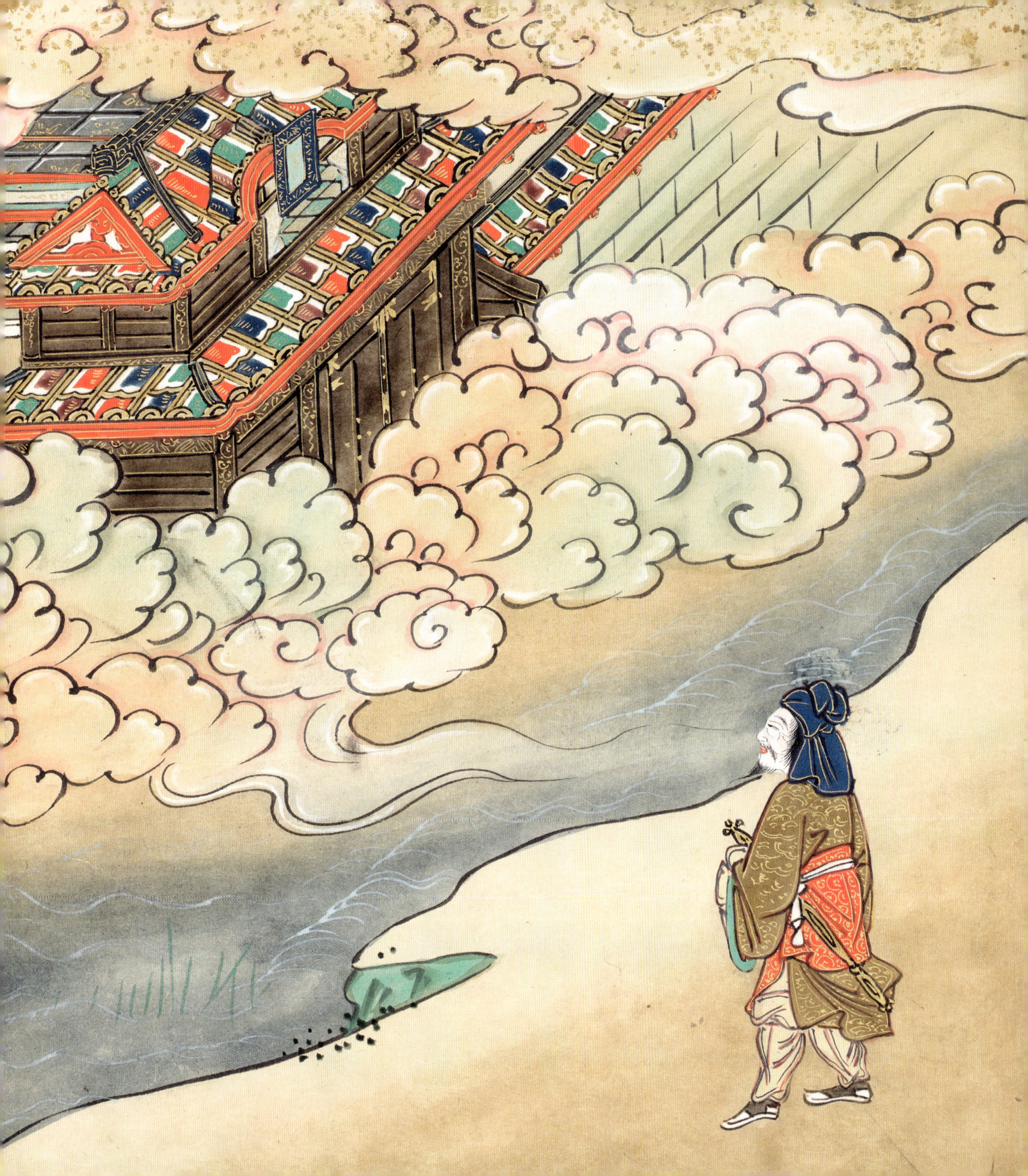

with a status and privilege that separated her from the numerous attendants in her service. Twenty-first-century notions of weddings and marriage customs do not align neatly with the concept of the bride and the character of the trousseau in the Edo period. Even the English terms 'bride' and 'bridal' pose problems, given their present-day associations with contemporary conventions of femininity and connotations of individual actors and independent marital households. The word for a newly married woman in Edo-period Japan is *yome* (嫁). Rooted in the idea of a woman joining the household to attend to its rituals, it conveys the sense of a corporate house and lineage. This should be kept in mind when considering the objects of historical trousseau, including manuscripts made and purchased for brides, but also for the men in the house and the children to be educated in the future.

Keeping the social function of the bridal or household library in mind, the cause of the decrease in manuscript numbers toward the end of the Edo period would seem to lie beyond a simple demand for printed alternatives. The material necessities of daimyo obligation, emulated by the commoner class and which generated such massive numbers of trousseau artefacts, gradually came to a halt with the end of the Tokugawa regime in 1868. The gilded libraries that were both spectacular and scholastic eventually dispersed in fragmented form to libraries around the world. It thus bears exploring the collective identity that such books and scrolls may have possessed as objects created for a household library. Doing so imbues the individual works of literature and their illustrations with an extra-literary social dimension and a new interpretive lens through which to understand these timeworn tales.

39 *The Song of Everlasting Sorrow* (*Chōgonka*) by Bai Juyi (742–846); *The Tale of Yang Guifei* (*Yōkihi monogatari*) by Asai Ryōi (1612–1691), seventeenth century, Vol. 3. Emperor Xuanzong and Yang Guifei in the palace. MS. Jap. d.16.

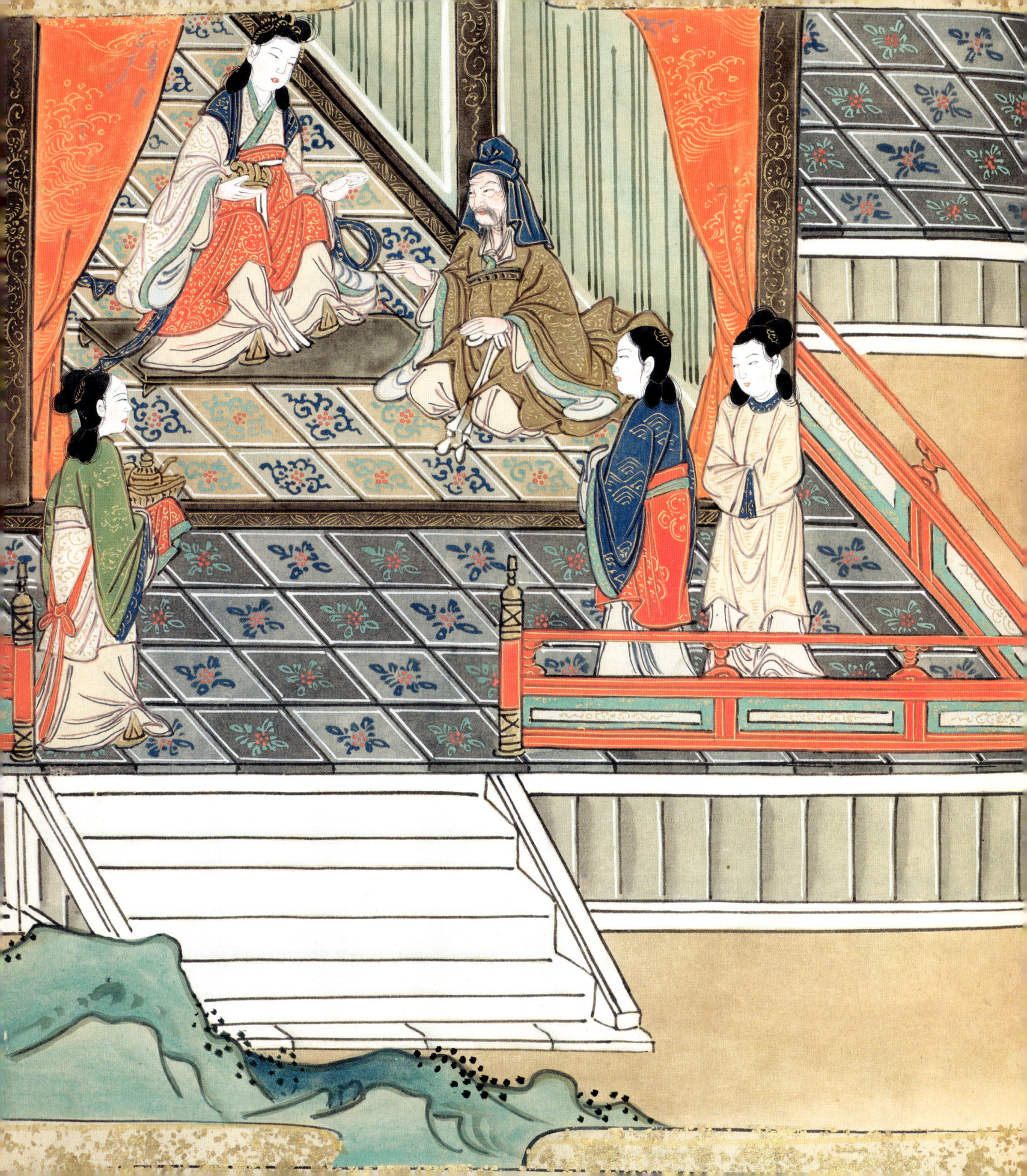

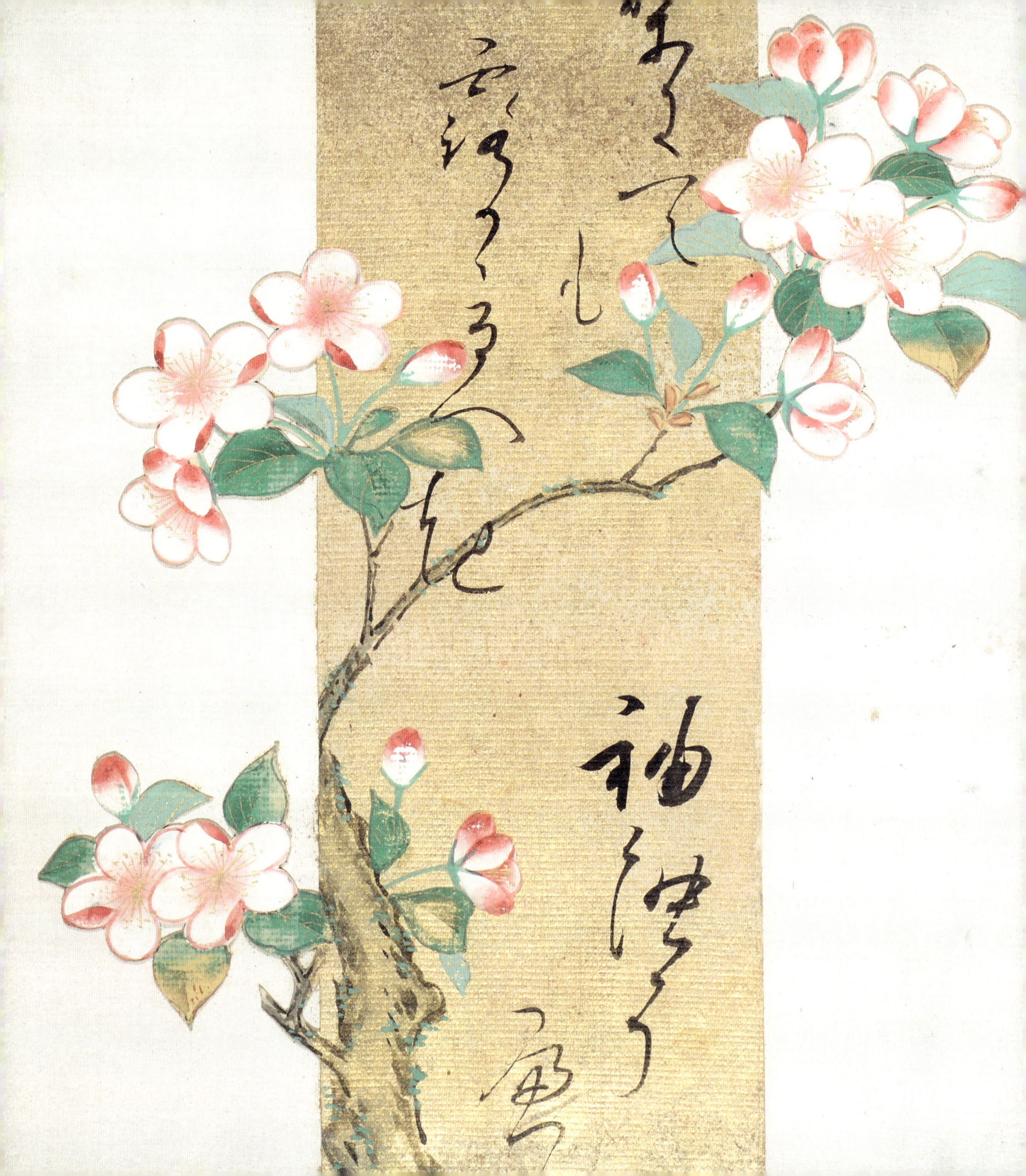

# *Scenes of the Four Seasons* and Teika's *Ten Styles*: two suites, two views

EDWARD KAMENS

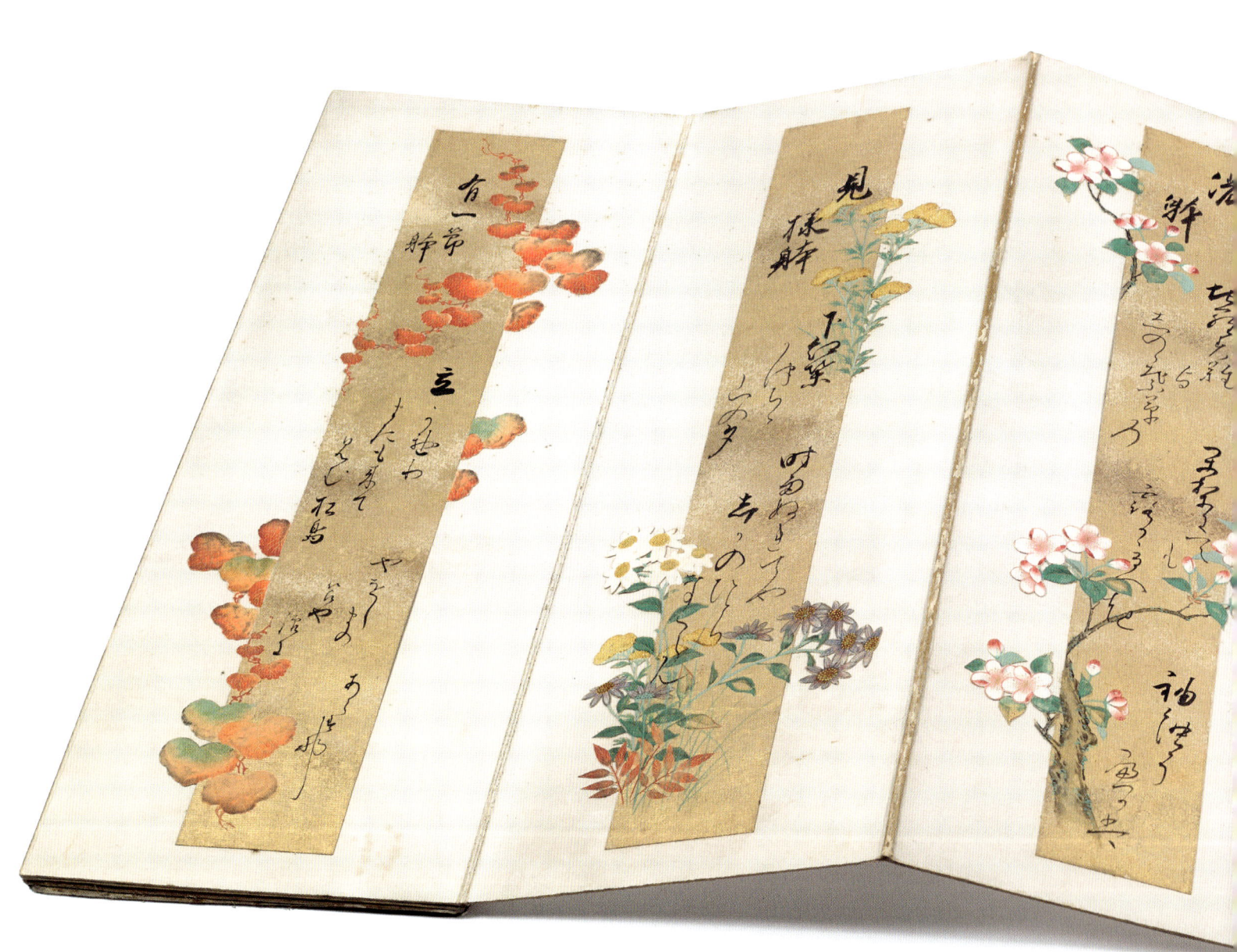

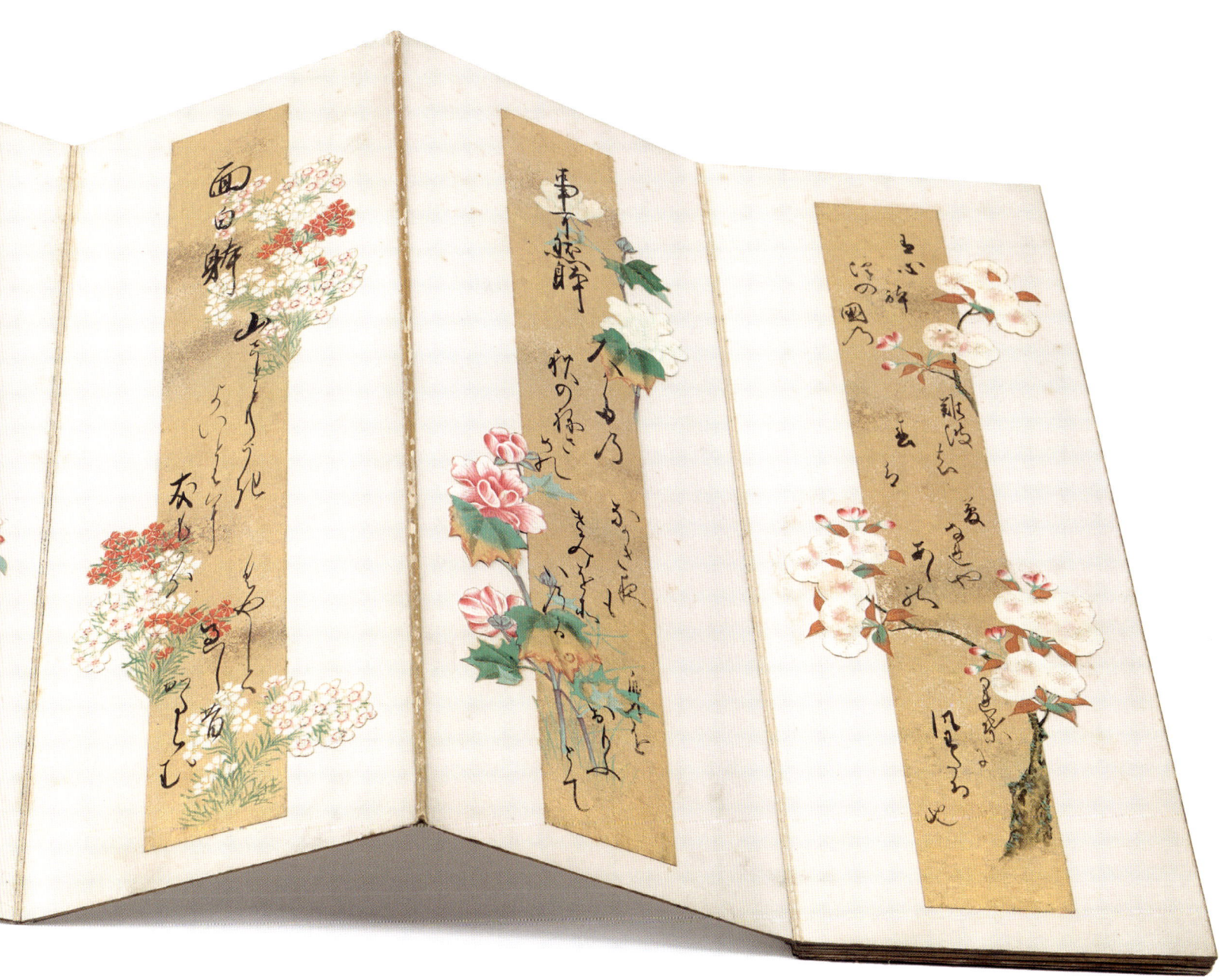

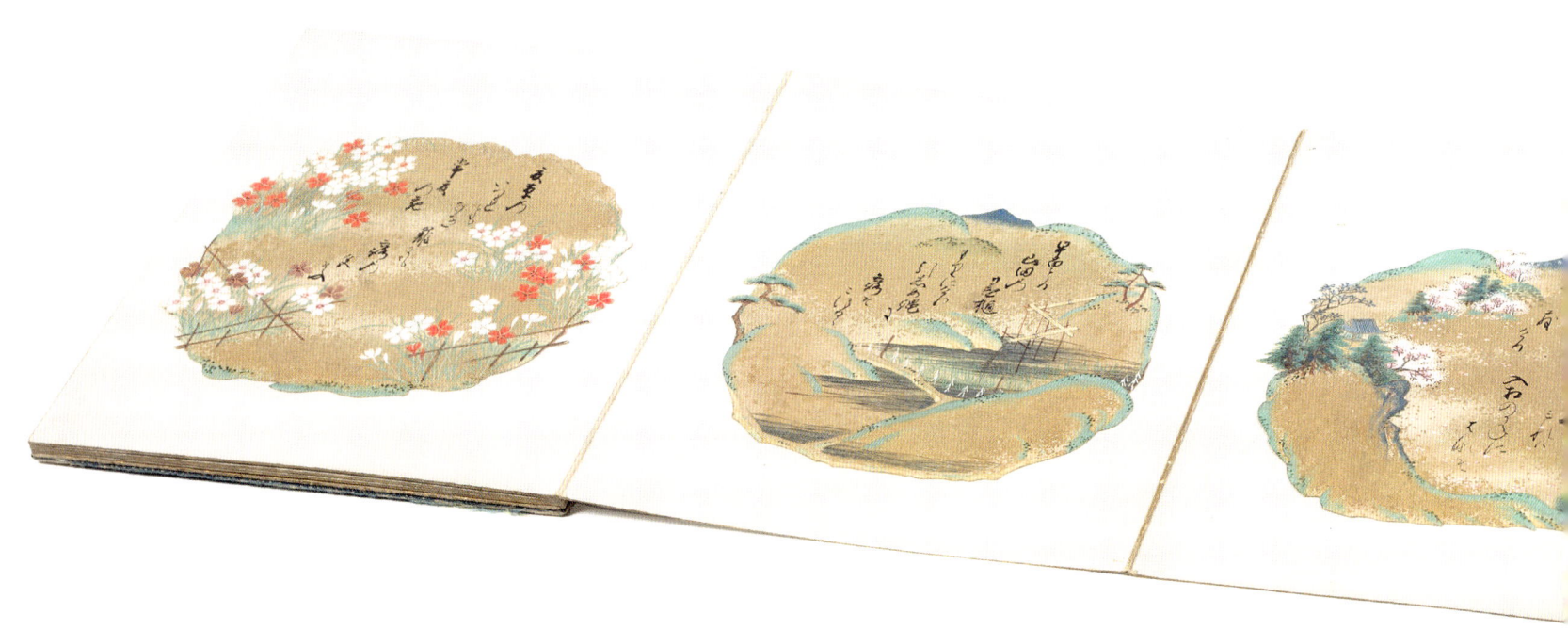

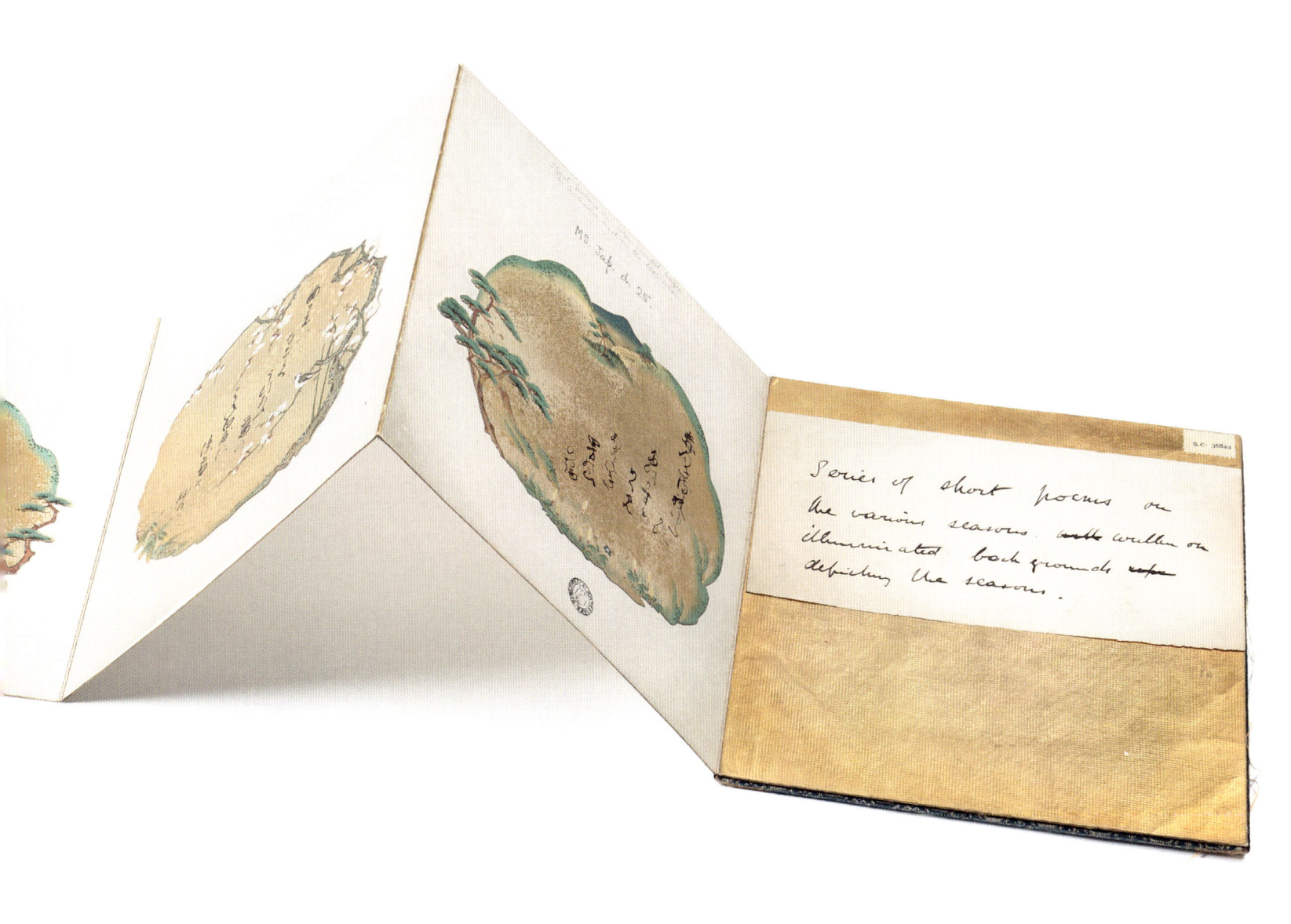

Series of short poems on the various seasons. ~~both~~ written on illuminated backgrounds ~~repre~~ depicting the seasons.

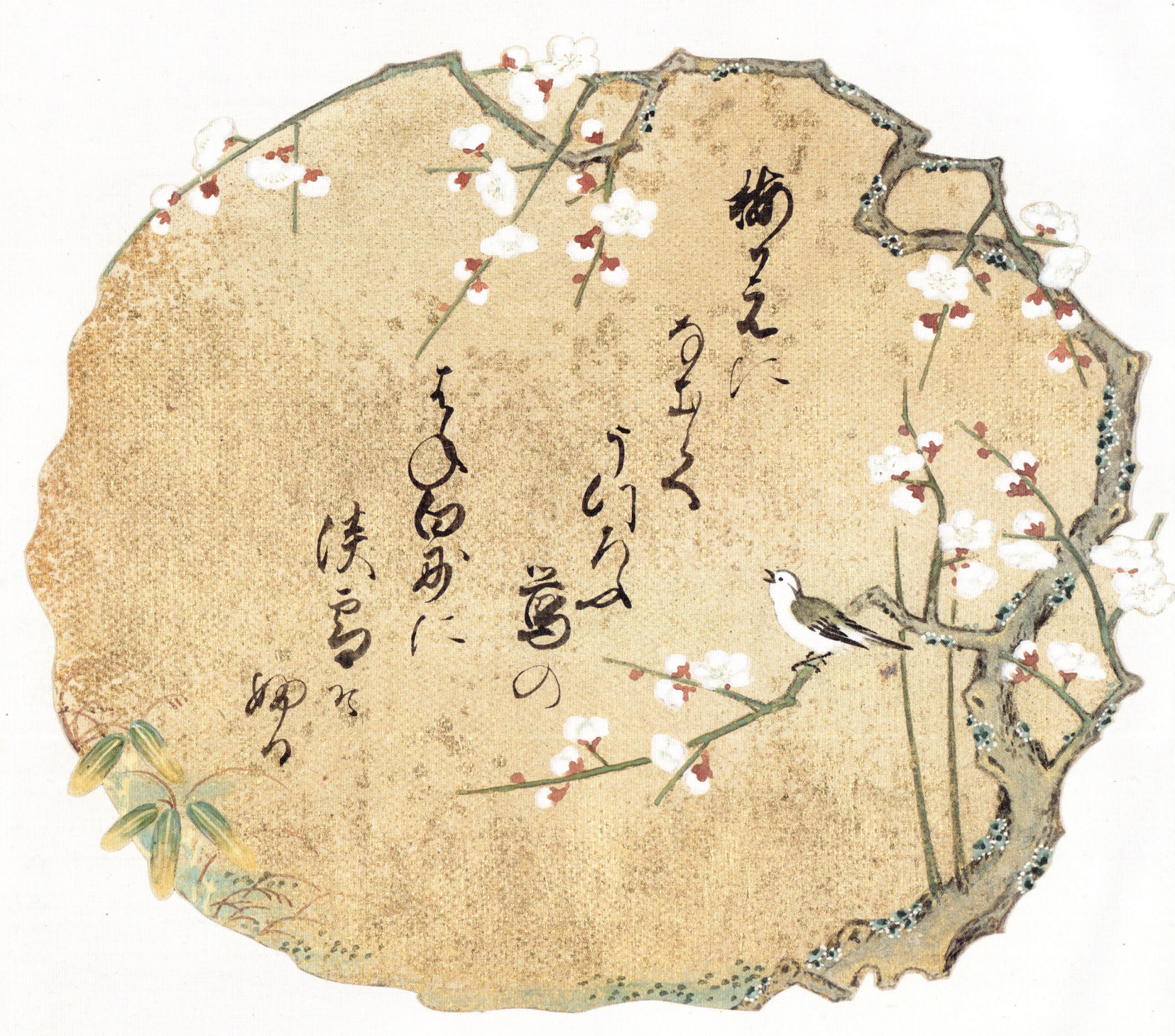

TWO FOLDED BOOKS in the Bodleian, both dating from the early to mid-seventeenth century, contain sets of attractively decorated pictorial designs and hand-brushed texts that graciously invite the viewer to respond to their formal and aesthetic features (FIGS 40 & 41). Given their modest scale, designed as it would seem for hand-held viewing, they suggest an ambience of some intimacy and informality. They appear to be made for pleasurable perusal, not for intense study nor for excessively minute analysis.

These two books are roughly similar in scale and form, with their contents mounted on each section of their fairly thick and sturdy paper boards, bound in the accordion-like mode most commonly referred to in Japanese as *orijō* (sometimes called a 'leporello' or 'concertina' in Euro-American contexts). But a closer look suggests that they present an interesting case of similarity and difference in the use of related materials in this format. The content of one (see FIG. 43) consists of ten rectangular poetry cards (*tanzaku*), mounted together with cut-paper ornaments (*kirigami*) placed around, and in some places overlapping, the surfaces of the cards. The other (see FIG. 44) reverses this arrangement, consisting of roundels that are themselves formed as *kirigami*.

## THE TWO SUITES

In the *tanzaku* album, one poem per *tanzaku* is inscribed in texts that meander through an arrangement of floral and arboreal *kirigami* shapes. We see blossoms, flowers on stalks, colourful leaves and drooping branches, as befits the subject matter of the poems. In the other, each *kirigami* roundel itself represents an imaginary space – suggesting an orb that has been flattened to two dimensions – in which appear miniaturized landscapes with floral, arboreal and, in some cases, additional

40 PAGES 92–3 *Teika's Ten Styles*, mid-seventeenth century (?). Ink, pigments and gold leaf on paper. This folded album (*orijō*) consists of rectangular poetry cards, painted and inscribed with poetry. MS. Jap. b.1.

41 PREVIOUS SPREAD & LEFT *Scenes from Nature in the Four Seasons*, seventeenth century. Ink, pigments and gold leaf on paper. This folded album (*orijō*) consists of painted roundels inscribed with poetry. MS. Jap. d.25.

architectural and avian forms. Here again the poem scripts meander across this imaginary space, in arrangements that guide the reader's eye from right to left (as is conventional in East Asian writing). For the most part the texts read horizontally, in contrast to the vertical arrangements of the *tanzaku* poem inscriptions. By these means, in two somewhat different manners, the poem texts are blended into the visual analogues, accents and counterpoints of the pictorial components of both sets.

It seems that one distinctive hand inscribed all the poems in each book – a different hand appearing in each. As we will see, these hands were not those of the creators of the poems but were reproducing them from other pre-existing sources. We can assume that the selection of the poems in each case was the prompt for these visual renderings (rather than the other way around) – but that does not mean that the viewer more readily gives attention to one or the other. What emerges in each of the books, through the combination of these elements, is a thematically coherent and co-ordinated programme. In their respective formats and their similar engagements with floral and other natural themes in the pictorial and text registers, both books engage with long-standing Japanese visual and literary conventions. In so doing, they recapitulate familiar practices and strategies for the reproduction of iconographic elements and canonical texts – in this case, these comprise readily recognizable emblems of nature and the seasons along with poems that work with those emblems as their central figures.

This chapter treats the content of these two folding books as 'suites', with divergent content but similar underlying conceptions. The term 'suite' is not a technical term of common use in the discussion of such artefacts (although such sets are not uncommon in Japanese culture, from the pre-modern to the contemporary); nor does 'suite' have a cognate term in Japanese art history or book history vocabularies.[1] It is used here to suggest a structural analogy to something like such suites as George Frideric Handel's *Water Music* or Gustav Holst's *The Planets* – that is, a grouping of parts that share certain characteristics of theme or occasion and form a coherent programme of variations, with the addition here of the consistent shapes and ornamentations that are the constitutive parts of these books.

In the case of the *tanzaku* album – known by the title of its textual content as *Teika's Ten Styles* (*Teika jittei* or *jittai*) – the programme offers a selection of classical poems (*waka*) from a larger collection which was compiled, we believe, in the thirteenth century or later. It was almost certainly *not* compiled by the great poet Teika (Fujiwara no Teika or Sadaie, 1162–1241), from whom its name is derived. Despite questions about origins and authenticity, *Ten Styles* is prominent in the *waka* tradition in part because of the fame and lasting importance of its putative compiler and the dominance of his descendants in the transmission of the art and practice of classical poetry. The full compilation, from which the poems in the Bodleian album are extracted, serves as an exemplary and didactic amplification of the ten ideal 'styles' (*tei*) in a treatise known as the *Maigetsushō* (*Notes for Monthly Consideration*). Similar image/text renderings of it (as well as text-only reproductions) are found in other collections (see below).

In the other book, *Scenes from Nature in the Four Seasons*, a similar selection of ten *waka* has been assembled. Although the canonical sources for each of the poems in this suite can be identified, no single text can be indicated as an obvious model or source for the group of ten. Renderings of suites of floral emblems of the season – in paintings and other visual media, and in many genres of literary text, especially in poetry in various styles and forms across the ages – are common in Japanese cultural productions and traditions, yet the precise configuration in the Bodleian *Four Seasons* may be unique.

More broadly, one might say that Japanese artefacts – from paintings to ceramics – which combine what we conventionally identify as 'text and image' are ubiquitous, just as they are in many cultures and in many different historical periods. There are many ways to appreciate them, not all of which necessitate painstaking analysis; a more casual viewing may be what is most in keeping with their inherent character. But another, equally plausible, approach might entail a close reading of their visual and textual elements, to elucidate the interactions and jointly produced effects (or signifying and communicative functions) of the components of such artefacts – the workings of their identifiable parts *and* their composed, coherent programmes. This chapter offers two such readings or views; one might be called 'transmedial', the other 'intermedial'.

'Transmedial' here refers to the backstory of the text content – the poems – in these folded books and their amalgamation in their visual programmes. The poems have travelled through various media, starting out from their known

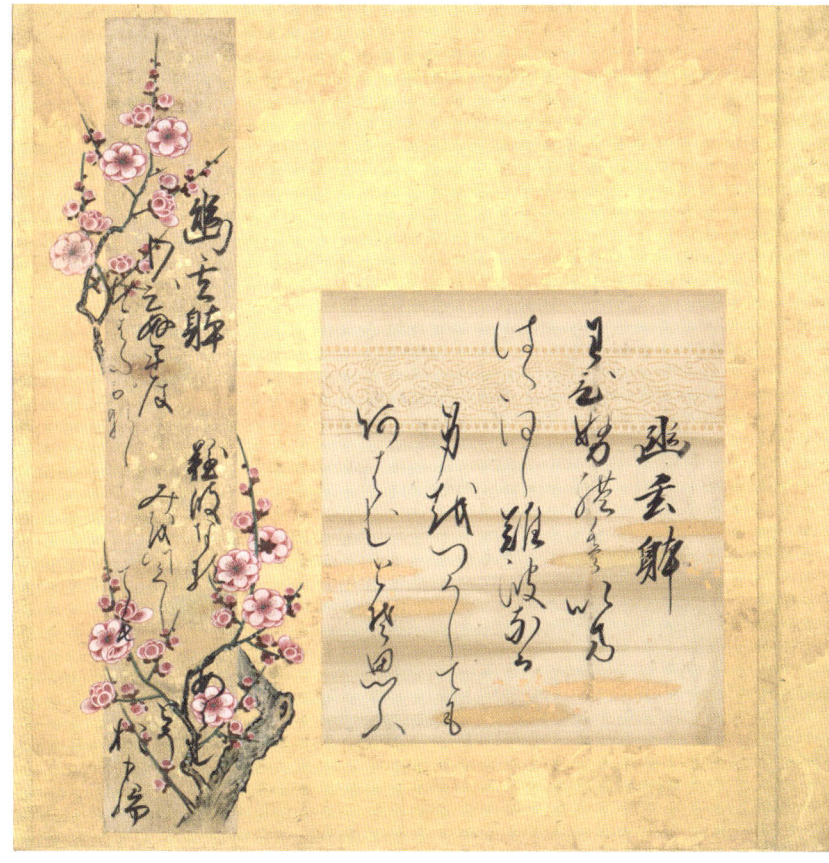

42 Poetry cards in *Teika's Ten Styles of Japanese Poetry*, early eighteenth century. Ink and colour on paper. Metropolitan Museum of Art, New York.

or assumed points of origin in an assortment of disparate moments of composition; then, at one or more stages, they have come together into organized settings. As amalgamated entities they have continued to time-travel up to the point at which the makers of these 'suites' treated them as we now find them. Meanwhile, the individual poems in each set continued their own movement along many other pathways of reappearance and re-use. Along this trajectory in time and space, we can assume – and in the case of some of the individual poems we can show – that the Bodleian folding books are not the first settings, nor their assemblage the first instances, in which these poems (and possibly these very poem-sets) have become part of a visual programme. In short, they have moved from medium to medium; these books are but two points along that trajectory of ongoing transfer and flow. We also know that each poem began its travels as *words*, uttered and/or inscribed for communication and preservation, even if we cannot pinpoint or re-visit that moment or locus of origin. This is the most significant sense in which their backstory or their experience (if we think of them as time-travellers) is transmedial – they have moved from speech and the written word to a medium that combines the written word with the pictorial. No doubt, as suggested, this has occurred more than once.

The outcome of this process, as evidenced in the artefacts at hand, is 'intermedial'. The reader can turn or flip the pages to encounter a series of compositions that work with the two identifiable media – that of painted picture (here worked as *kirigami*) and word – in concert. What captures the reader's attention may be the whole arrangement presented on each board; or it could be the most readily identifiable or most striking of its pictorial elements, especially since the colours are vivid and the details eye-catching; or it could be the meandering lines of text, shifting from quite bold to rather faint strokes of ink, and which may be perceived as either readable poems (for those able to read such cursive brushwork) or as visual designs, or both. Or perhaps the composition as a whole will occupy the reader's primary attention – or perhaps it will be isolated parts that do

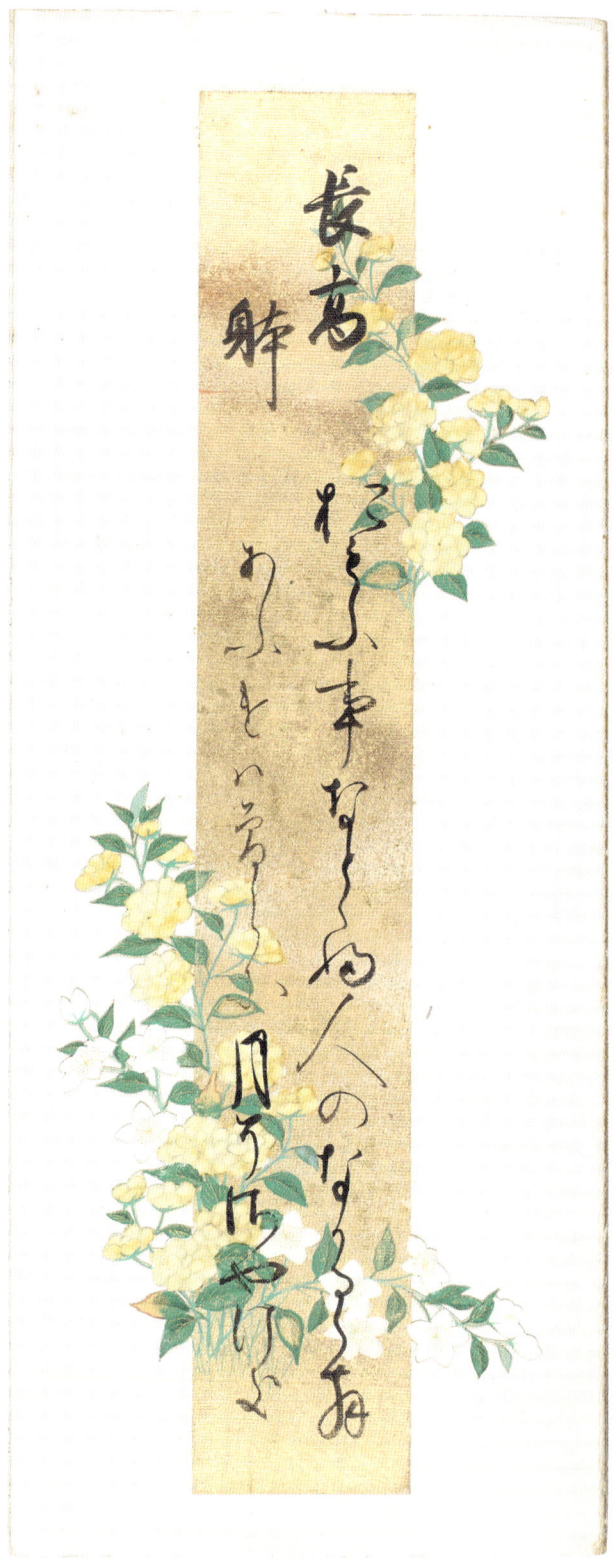

so, in sequence or in simultaneity or oscillation, or perhaps in other modes of sensory perception and cognition that resist any verbal description.

This is no doubt too elaborate and cerebral a description of the pleasurable act of looking at these materials. But the purpose here is to try to account for the particular features of these two artefacts *as such*, while also using them to try to articulate what encounters with such composed, multipart and multimedial artefacts – whether from Japanese sources or others – may entail. In treating them as transmedial and intermedial, we can avoid the ready-to-hand terms 'text and image' and 'image and text' and their implications of juxtaposed dualities, emphasizing instead the joint, oscillating and complementary functions of the elements that make up and display themselves in composed artefacts such as these. While the two books may lend themselves to something like 'close reading' and 'close viewing', they can also serve, as suggested here, as a point of departure for a broader investigation of the nature of (and the work done by) objects of this kind.

## THE TEN STYLES SUITE

In *Ten Styles*, a selection of ten exemplary poems was made from the much more extensive body of poems in the compilation inspired by a passage in *Maigetsushō*, the treatise mentioned above, in which ten major styles of poetic composition, in two hierarchical groupings, are identified in Teika's

first-person 'voice' (perhaps not his own, since the authorship of the treatise is also questionable):

> Those styles I regard as fundamental are the following four of the ten styles that I have designated previously: *the style of mystery and depth, the style of appropriate statement, the style of elegant beauty,* and *the style of deep feeling.* Even among these styles are occasionally to be found poems that have archaic elements, but the general effect is such that their archaic style is not displeasing. After you have developed the ability to compose freely in these gentle and amiable styles, such others as *the lofty style, the style of visual description, the style of clever treatment, the style of novel treatment* and *the style of exquisite detail* are quite easy to learn. *The demon-quelling style* is the one that you will find most difficult to master, but even so, I see no reason why you should not be able to compose in it after you have attained the necessary proficiency … Now among these ten styles there is not one in which the true nature of poetry may be felt more wholly to reside than *the style of deep feeling.*[2]

The absence of illustrative examples in this influential statement of stylistic principles is surely what prompted subsequent practitioners in the art and discipline of *waka* composition to amplify it in compilations of poems grouped as prototypes and models for each 'style'. The version of the resulting *Teika's Ten Styles* text reproduced in a modern printed edition of the *waka* canon (i.e. *Shinpen Kokka Taikan*) is based on a manuscript held in the Imperial Household Ministry. It offers a total of 273 poems, with the number of examples for each style ranging from fifty-eight for the paramount style of 'mystery and depth' to just twelve for the challenging and problematic 'demon-quelling style'.[3]

43 LEFT & FOLLOWING PAGES The ten rectangular poetry cards (*tanzaku*) from *Teika's Ten Styles*, mounted together with cut-paper ornaments (*kirigami*). MS. Jap. b 1.

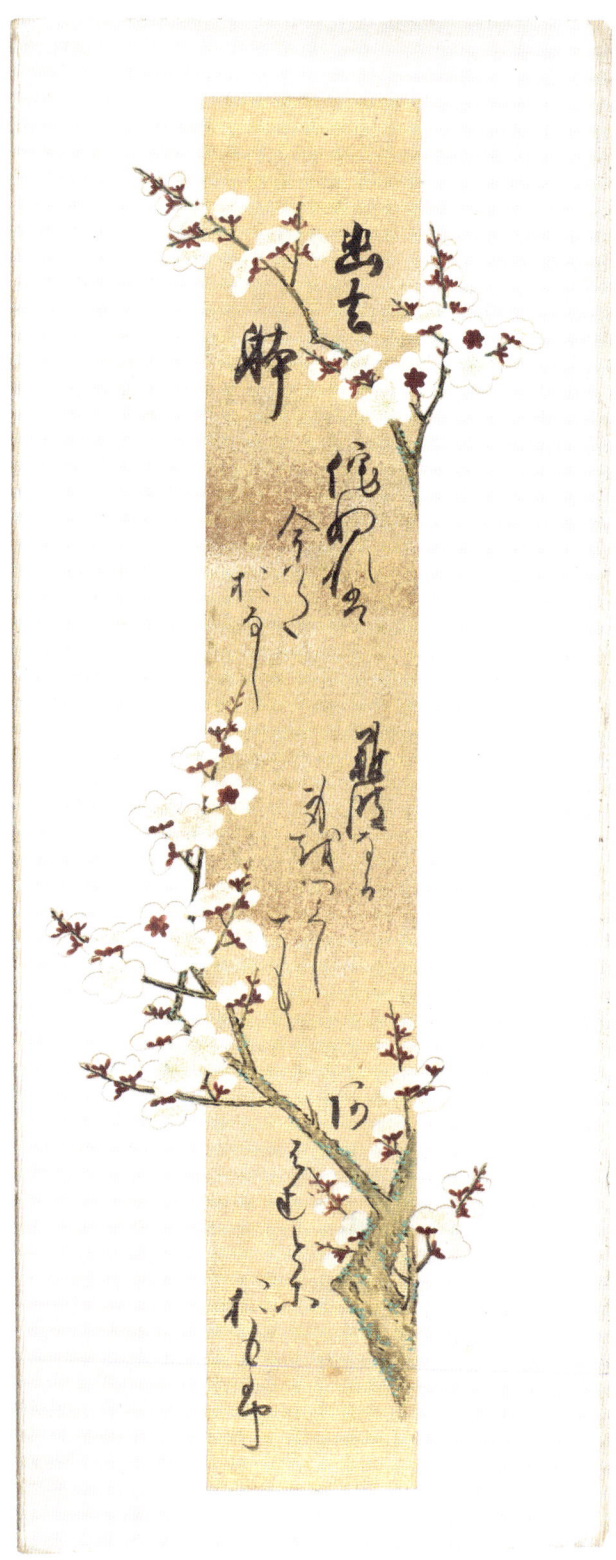

It is of course impossible to know what version the seventeenth-century producers of the Bodleian *Ten Styles* may have consulted, or whether it was a selection made anew from this complete, amplified set of examples. Perhaps, as seems more likely, a ready-made reduced set of ten examples – one for each style – was already established as a group and previously reproduced as such in one medium or another. The latter conjecture is supported, though only partially, by comparison of the Bodleian version with a surprisingly similar rendering in the collection of the Metropolitan Museum of Art, New York (FIG. 42). The Metropolitan version is also an early seventeenth-century production, by unnamed artists, in album format. It offers dual renderings of the selected exemplary poems in pairs, on *shikishi* (square poetry cards) at right and on *tanzaku* (rectangular poetry cards) at left, along with *kirigami* ornaments. The sequence in which the examples of the styles appear differs slightly between these two versions, and the selection of poems is also a close but not perfect match: six of the poems in the Bodleian set exactly match those rendered both ways on each page of the Metropolitan album; the example on the Metropolitan *tanzaku* for the 'style of appropriate treatment' matches the Bodleian's, but the poem on the *shikishi* beside it does not; and neither of the two poems on the Metropolitan album's 'style of visual description' match the one in the Bodleian version.

Brief examination of other (unpublished) renderings of 'Teika's Ten Styles' by calligraphers of the seventeenth and eighteenth centuries likewise reveals the flexibility and fluidity of treatment of this source, as well as its prominence as a subject

for reproduction by accomplished and distinguished calligraphers.[4] In addition, comparison of a
complete manuscript copy of the 'Ten Styles' in the
Date Bunko collection in the Miyagi Prefectural
Library (undated and unattributed),[5] alongside the
Imperial Household Ministry version reproduced
in the *Shinpen Kokka Taikan*, reveals that the
selection of ten examples in the Bodleian as well
as these other various renderings does not by any
means consistently match the poems that appear
as the *first* examples in each grouping. So primary
placement was certainly not the default criterion
for selection.

From these observations we may infer, if nothing
else, that there was no one standard complete or
reduced version of the *Ten Styles* that would have
been likely to serve as the reference or model
for the various artists creating these (and other)
renderings. It was an inviting and readily available
subject and source, and one that bore considerable
prestige, but it could be treated in variable and
shifting manners. In other words, any imagining of
the transmedial process leading to the production
of any given rendering of this work needs to take
into account the possibility of multiple source
texts, previous renderings as models, as well as
other factors shaping each unique occasion of
variant re-creation. As the small sampling of variants surveyed here suggests, any envisioning of this
transmedial process might take the form of two
trajectories or temporal arcs – one that looks back
into the past, starting from the time of the variant
at hand, and another that projects forward in time,
to later ones and potential future renderings. In
this sense, such transmedial phenomena may also
be understood as 'trans-temporal'.

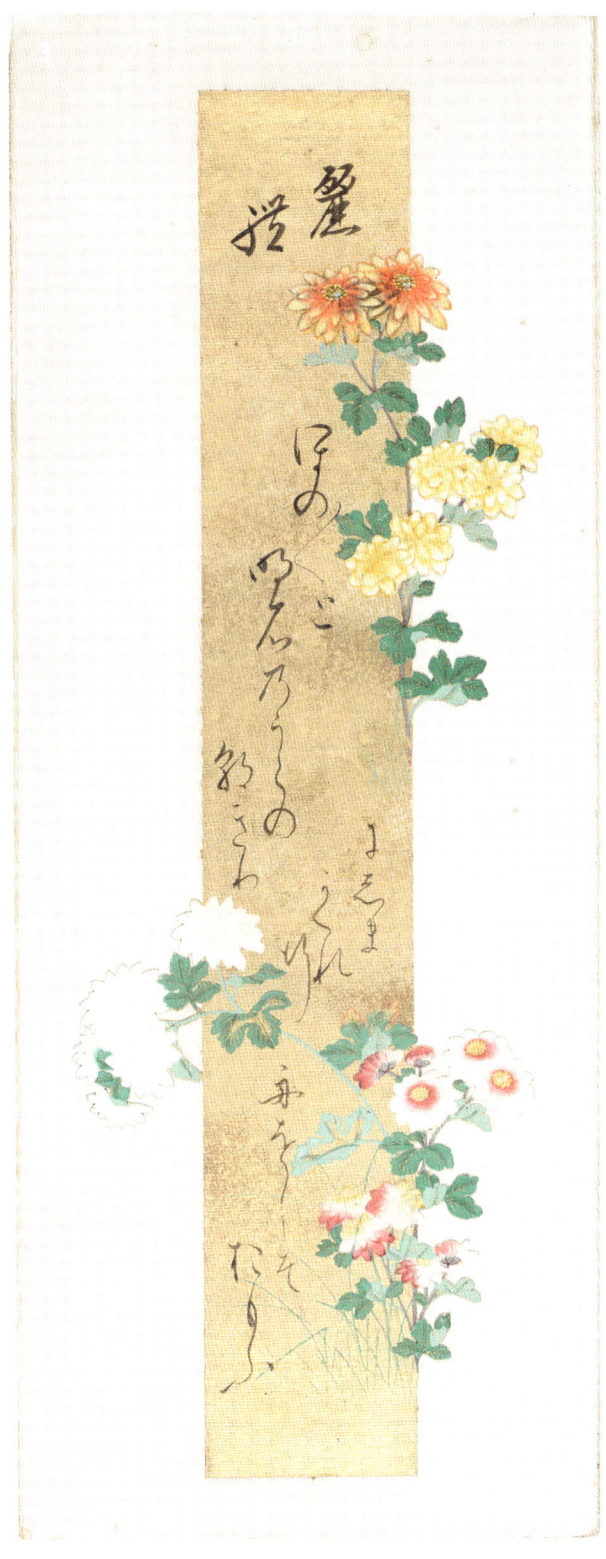

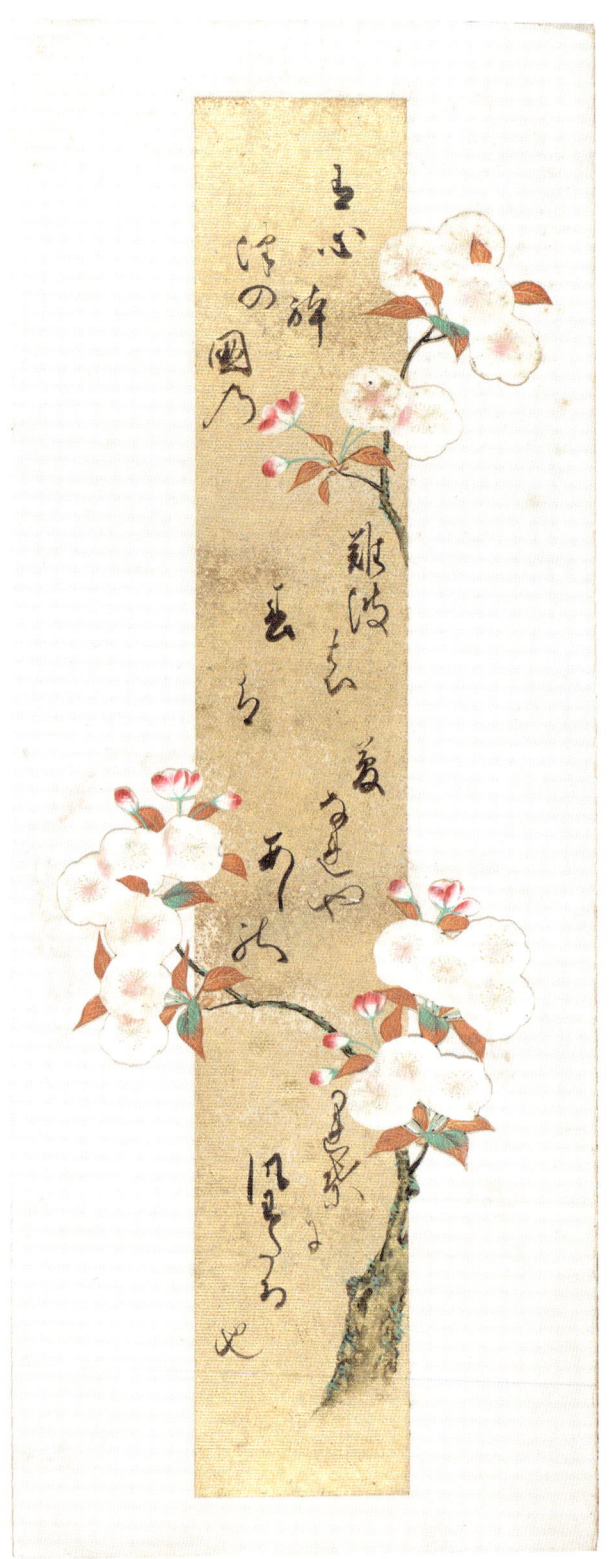

The Bodleian example consists of the following transcriptions and transliterations, which roughly replicate the placement of the names of each of the 'ten styles' in the upper portion of the *tanzaku*. They are followed by the text of each representative poem, reproduced here in modern approximations of the calligrapher's spacing of characters and other orthographic choices. Numbers have been added to correspond to the order in which the ten *tanzaku* appear in the *orijō* (see FIGS 40 & 42).[6]

1 幽玄／躰 侘ぬれは／今はた／おなし／難波なる／
身をつくし／ても／あ／はむとそ／おもふ

**yūgen tei (style of mystery and depth)**
*wabinureba ima hata onaji*
    *Naniwa naru mi wo tsukushite mo awamu to zo*
        *omofu*
travail besets me, so let come what may:
    a Naniwa channel buoy tossed about am I,
        yet will do anything I can to be with you.

2 長高／躰 おもふ事なとゝふ人のなかるらむ／
あふけはそらに月そさやけき

**taketakaki tei (the lofty style)**
*omofu koto nado tofu hito no nakaruramu*
    *afugeba sora ni tsuki zo sayakeki*
no one cares to ask me how I feel
        when I lift my eyes to the sky:
    so luminous, the moon.

3 麗躰 ほの／＼と／明石のうらの／朝きり／にしま／
かくれ／行／舟をしそ／おもふ

**uruwashiki tei (style of elegant beauty)**
*honobono to Akashi no ura no asagiri ni*
    *shimagakure yuku fune wo shi zo omofu*
dimly, dimly in the morning mists over Akashi Bay
    my thoughts follow a boat disappearing
        among islands.

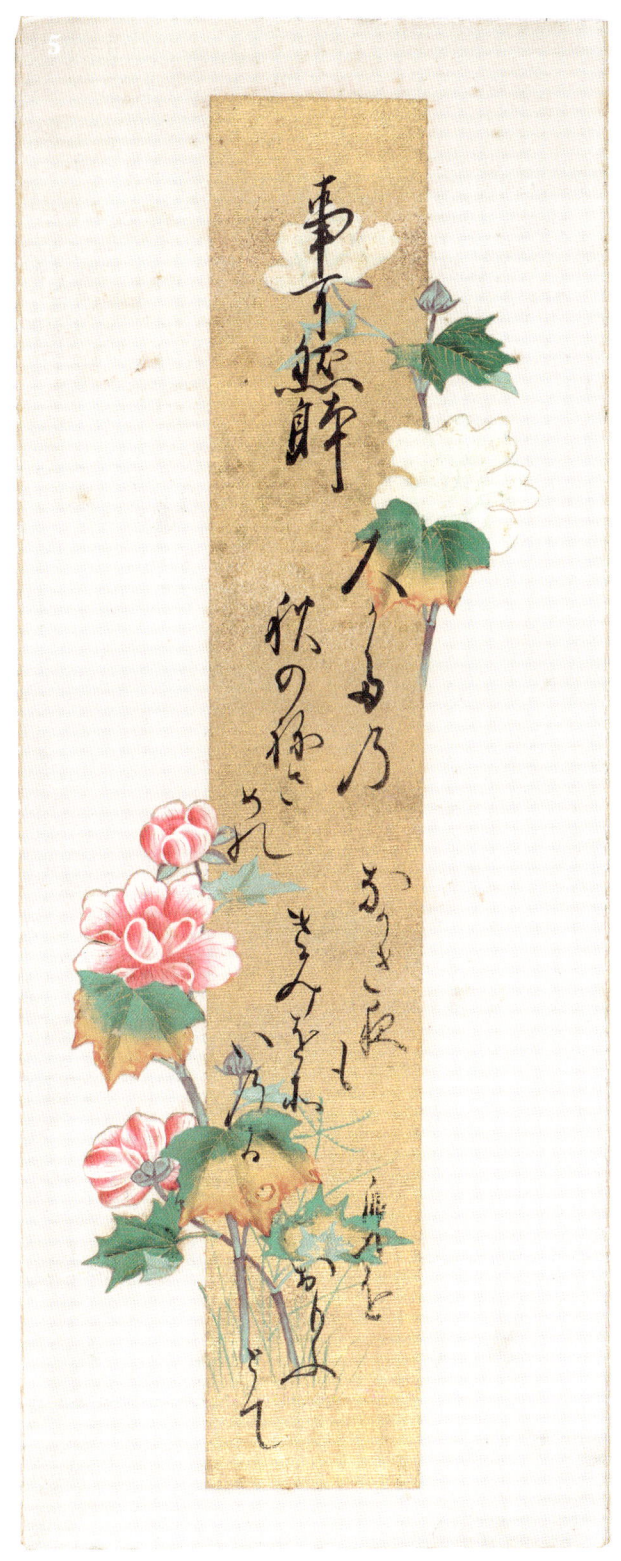

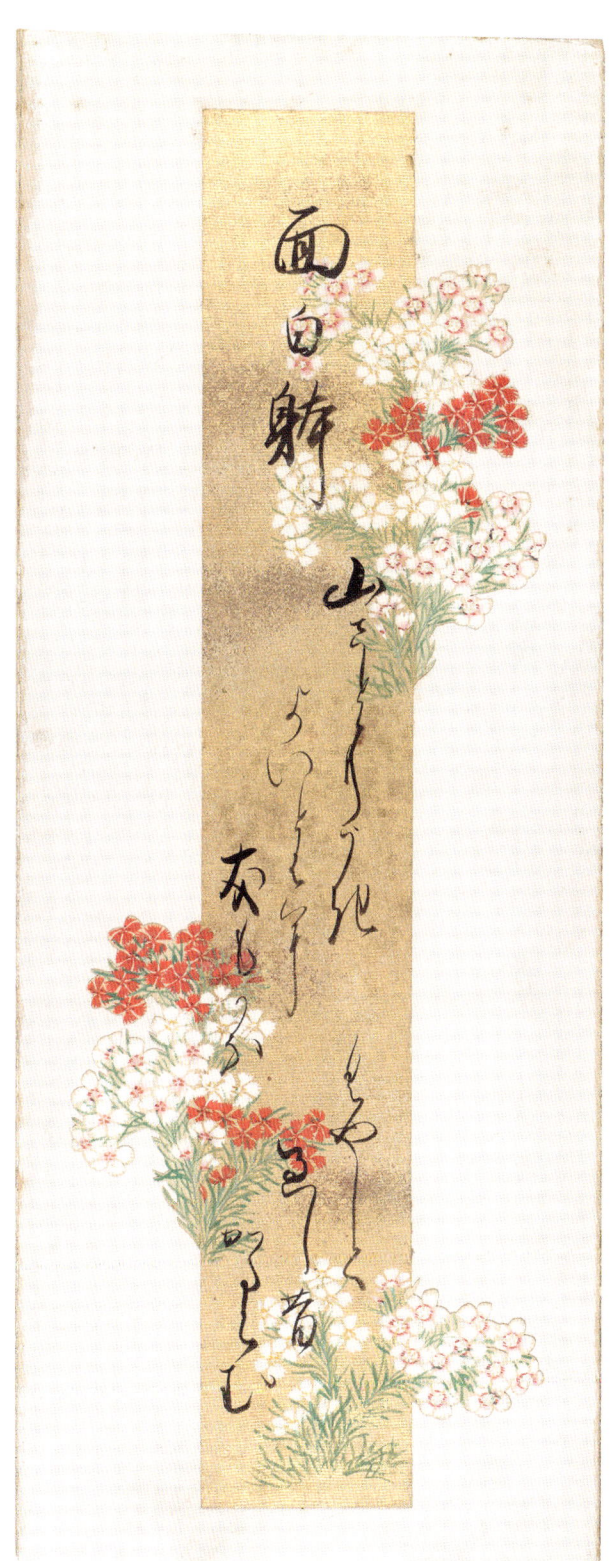

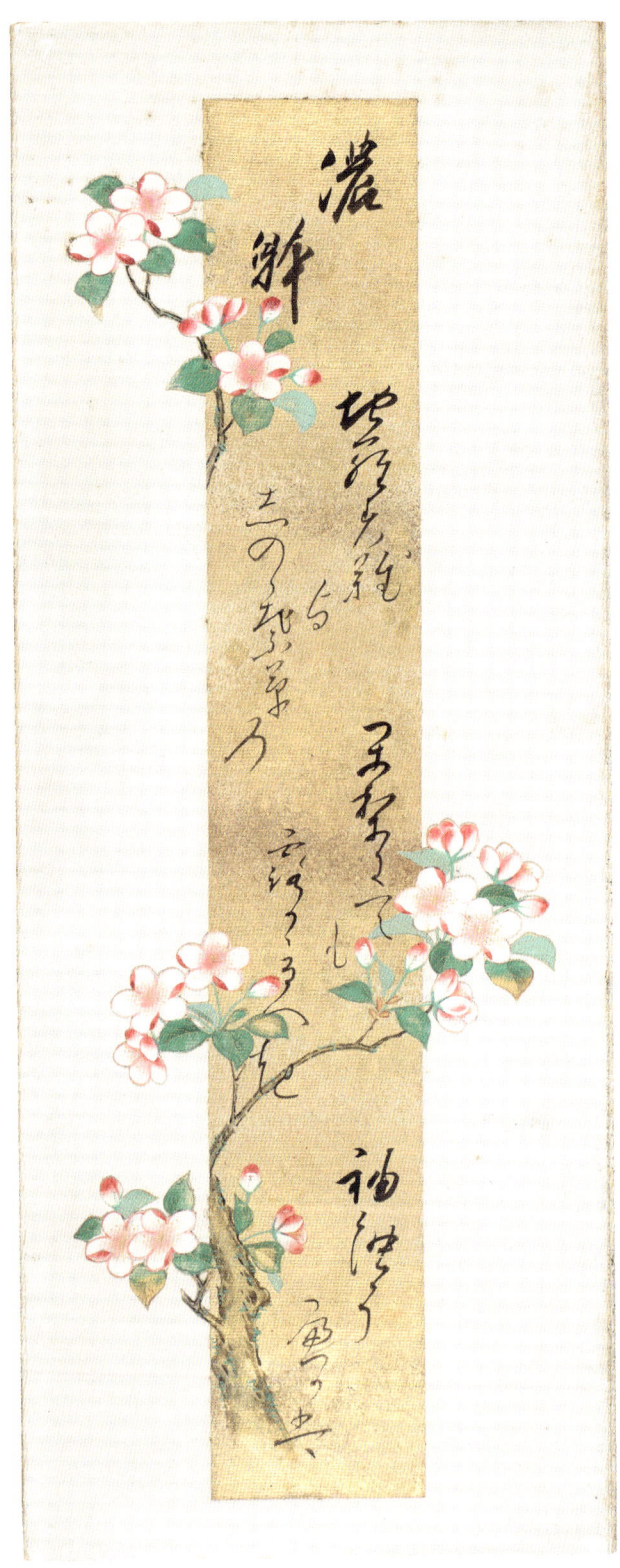

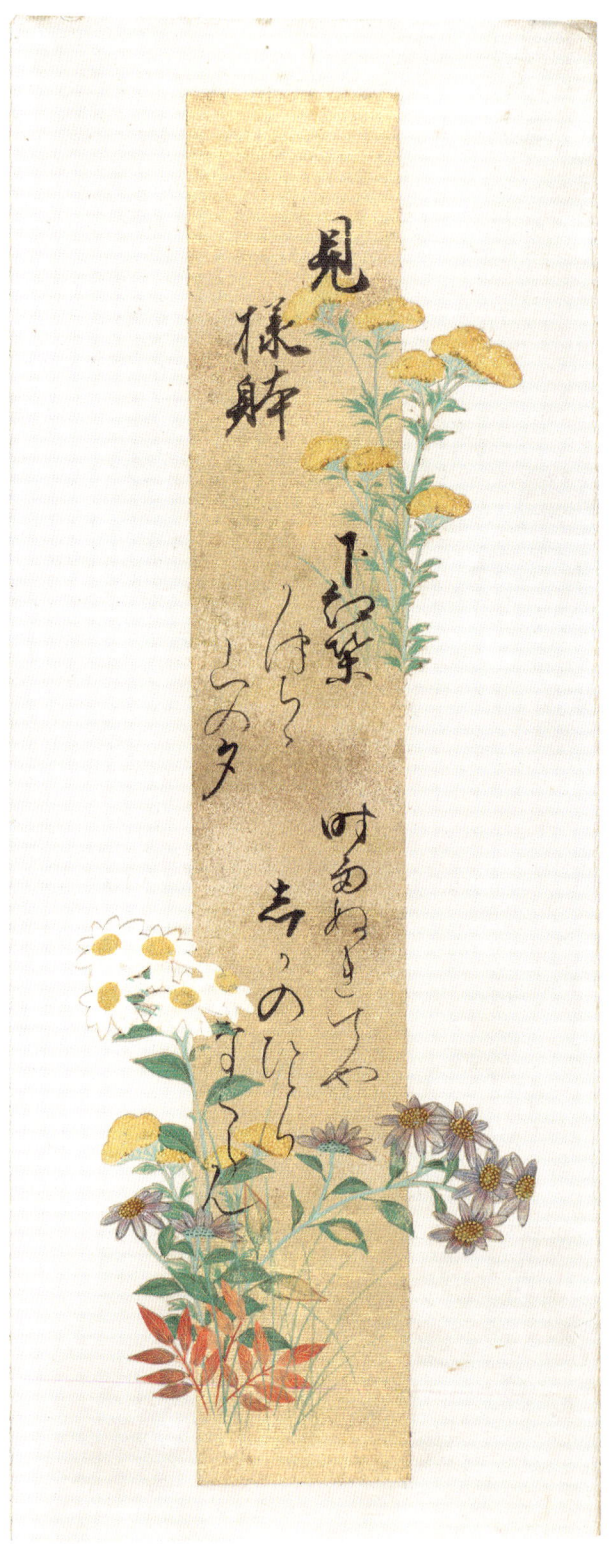

**4** 有心 躰津の国の／難波の／春は／夢／なれや／あしの／かれ葉に／風わたる／也

**ushin tei (style of deep feeling)**

*Tsu no kuni no haru ha yume nare ya*
　　　*ashi no kareha ni kaze wataru nari*

was that spring in Tsu no more than a dream?
　　　the wind rustles withered stalks of marsh reeds.

**5** 事可然躰 大かたの／秋のねさ／めの／なかき夜／も／きみをそ／いのる／身を／おもふ／とて

**koto shikarubeki tei (style of appropriate statement)**

*ohokata no aki no nezame no nagaki yo mo*
　　　*kimi wo zo inoru mi wo omofu tote*

wide awake on a long autumn night – nothing rare,
　　　it passes in prayers for you, my lord,
　　　and thoughts of how blessed am I.

**6** 面白躰 山さとにうき／よいとはむ／友もかな／くやしく／過し昔／かたらむ

**omoshiroki tei (style of clever treatment)**

*yamazato ni ukiyo itowamu tomo mogana*
　　　*kuyashiku sugishi mukashi kataramu*

in this mountain home –
　　　　　oh, for another who hates the floating world!
　　　we then might share memories
　　　　　of our bitter pasts.

**7** 濃躰 ちらすな／よしのゝ葉草／のかりにて／も／露かゝるへき／袖のう／へかは

**komayaka naru tei (style of exquisite detail)**

*chirasu na yo shino no hagusa no kari ni te mo*
　　　*tsuyu kakarubeki sode no uhe ka ha*

scatter it not!
though I cut and gather grasses of longing,
　　　may not the dew that drops from them
　　　be left to rest but briefly on my sleeves?

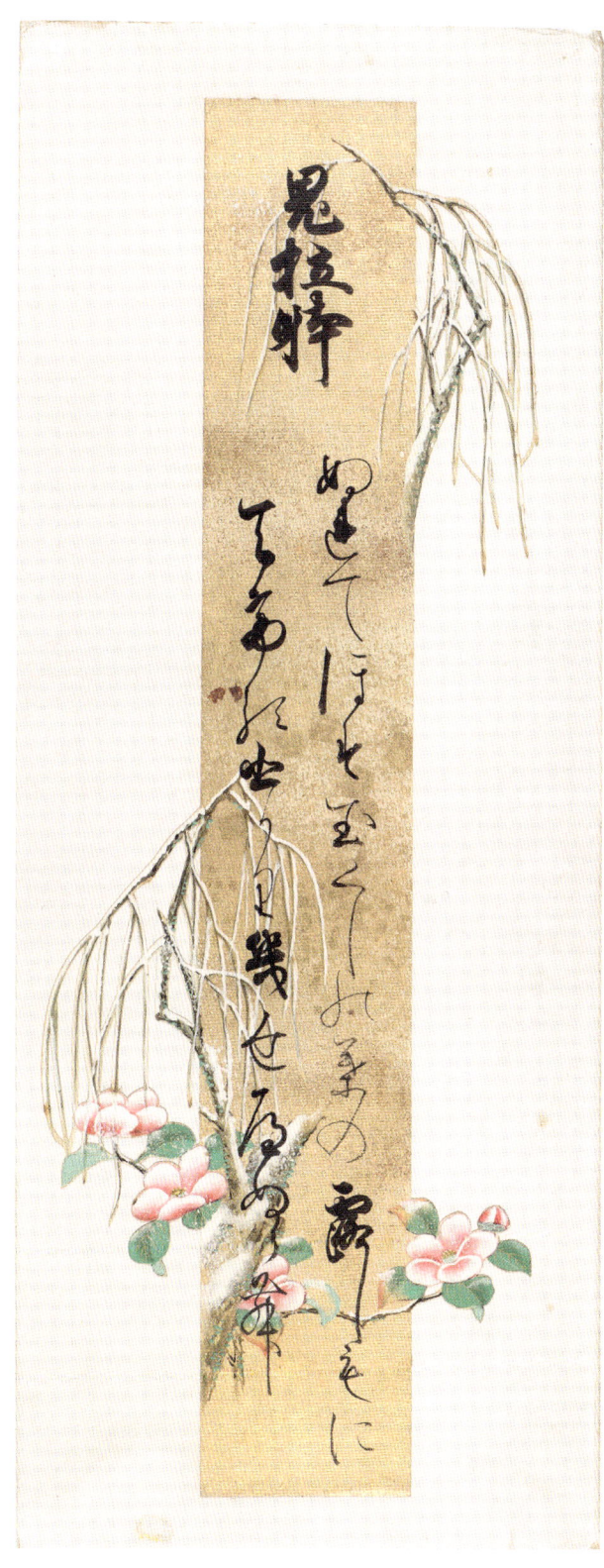

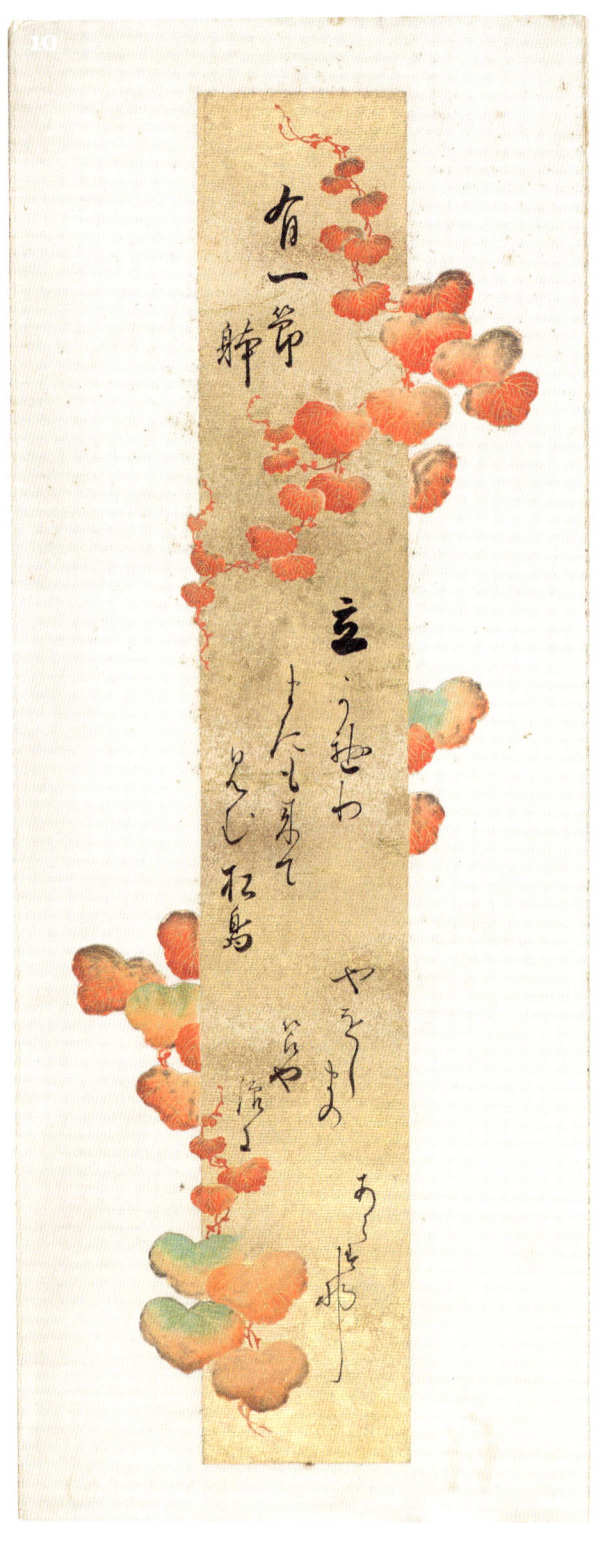

8　見 様躰 下紅葉／かつちる／山の夕／時雨ぬれてや／しかのひとり／なくらん

**miru tei** (style of visual description)
*shita momiji katsu chiru yama no yufushigure*
　　　*nurete ya shika no hitori nakuran*
the most protected of the coloured leaves
　　　are scattering on the mountain
　　as these autumn showers fall;
　　　soaked, perhaps, that lone stag crying out.

9　有一節 躰 立かへり／またも来て／見む松島／やをし／まの／苫や／浪に／あらすな

**hitofushi aru tei** (style of novel treatment)
*tachikaheri mata mo kite mimu*
　　　*Matsushima ya woshima no toma ya*
　　　*nami ni arasu na*
I would return, to see it once again:
　　　so, waves, let you spare the hut
　　on the little island in Pine-Island Bay.

10　鬼拉躰 ぬれてほす玉くしの葉の露しもに／天てるひかり幾世へぬらむ

**kiratsu no tei** (demon-quelling style)
*nurete hosu tamagushi no ha no tsuyu shimo ni*
　　　*amateru hikari iku yo henuramu*
Dew, frost, soaking, then drying,
　　　time and time again
　　　on these leaves of sacred trees –
　　for how many ages have they basked
　　　in the sun's celestial light?

The careful reader may notice that in the Bodleian version, the names of the poets recorded as the originators of these ten poems in readily accessible canonical texts are not included. This is also the case in the above-cited examples of the reduced one-example-per-style treatment of the 'Ten Styles' and also in the full Date Bunko manuscript. However, the Imperial Household Ministry version, as reproduced in the *Shinpen Kokka Taikan*, does include them – as is usually the case in the reproduction of anthologies of most kinds. Their omission may emphasize the poems' own presence and function in this setting as examples of the styles. In other settings – especially in the selective royal court anthologies and many others that adopt their formats – such information, along with additional indications of the pre-selected topic or the known or putative occasion of the poem's making, is almost always included, for various archival purposes and, one might say, to historicizing effect. But that is not the aim of *Ten Styles* in most of its renderings. Their inclusion in the Imperial Household Ministry version might be said to have the effect of introducing a linkage between each poem's implied achievement as a model of a certain 'style', not only as poem *per se* and the capacities and talents of its named maker; that added nuance, however, is not part of the transmedial and intermedial programming of the Bodleian example (nor in others comparable to it.) A list of the poets whose works are displayed in the Bodleian *Ten Styles* follows here, along with titles of the most prominent canonical anthologies in which they appear:[7]

1 Motoyoshi Shinnō (Prince Motoyoshi): *Shūi wakashū* (#766), *Gosen wakashū* 960, *Hyakunin isshu* #20)

2 Daisōjō Jien (Abbot Jien): *Shin kokin wakashū* #1782)

3 Hitomaru (Kakinomoto no Hitomaro): *Kokin wakashū* #409

4 Saigyō (Monk Saigyō): *Shin kokin wakashū* #625

5 Ietaka (Fujiwara no Ietaka): *Shin kokin wakashū* #1760)

6 Saigyō: *Shin kokin wakashū* #1659

7 Shunzei-kyō (Lord Fujiwara no Shunzei): *Shin kokin wakashū* #1111

8 Ietaka: *Shin kokin wakashū* #437

9 Shunzei-kyō; *Shin kokin wakashū* #933

10 Gokyōgoku (Gokyōgoku [Fujiwara no] Yoshitsune): *Shin kokin wakashū* #737

It is not at all surprising that poems from the widely admired and prestigious early thirteenth-century royal anthology *Shin kokin wakashū* (*New Collection of Ancient and Modern Japanese Poems*), attributable to several of its most prominently represented poets (Jien, Saigyō, Ietaka, Shunzei and his son Teika), make up this grouping. It may also be noted that all the poets are male. The *Shin kokin wakashū* and other anthologies in which these poems are to be found of course include poems by women, as well as by many unidentified poets, and the same is true in the full versions of *Teika's Ten Styles*, but poems by named women are in the minority in the vast majority of *waka* anthologies and collections of almost all kinds, regardless of the scale and scope and organizing principles thereof.

One other possibly significant observation to be made is that eight of the ten poems in the Bodleian set are poems that also appear in another selective anthology somewhat more reliably attributable to Teika himself – this is the collection known as *Teika Hachidai shō* (*Teika's Selections of the Anthologies of Eight Eras*).[8] The number of poems included in this anthology differs from one manuscript version to the other. The version in the *Shinpen Kokka Taikan* (also based on a version held in the Imperial Household Ministry) contains 1,809 poems – far more than in the much more limited extent of the *Teika's Ten Styles* texts – so the pattern may not be especially significant, but the association with Teika *per se* as putative compiler may be more so.

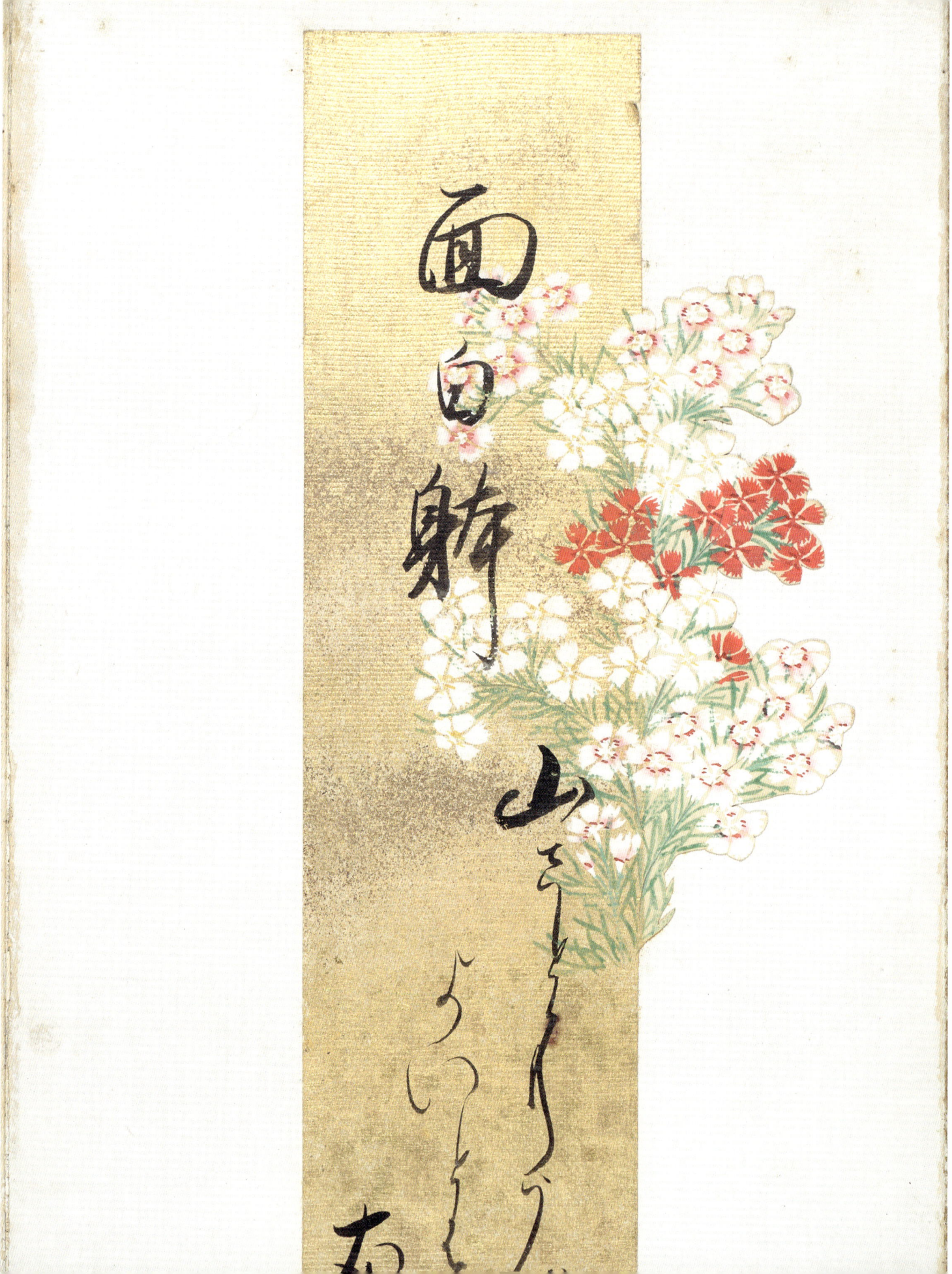

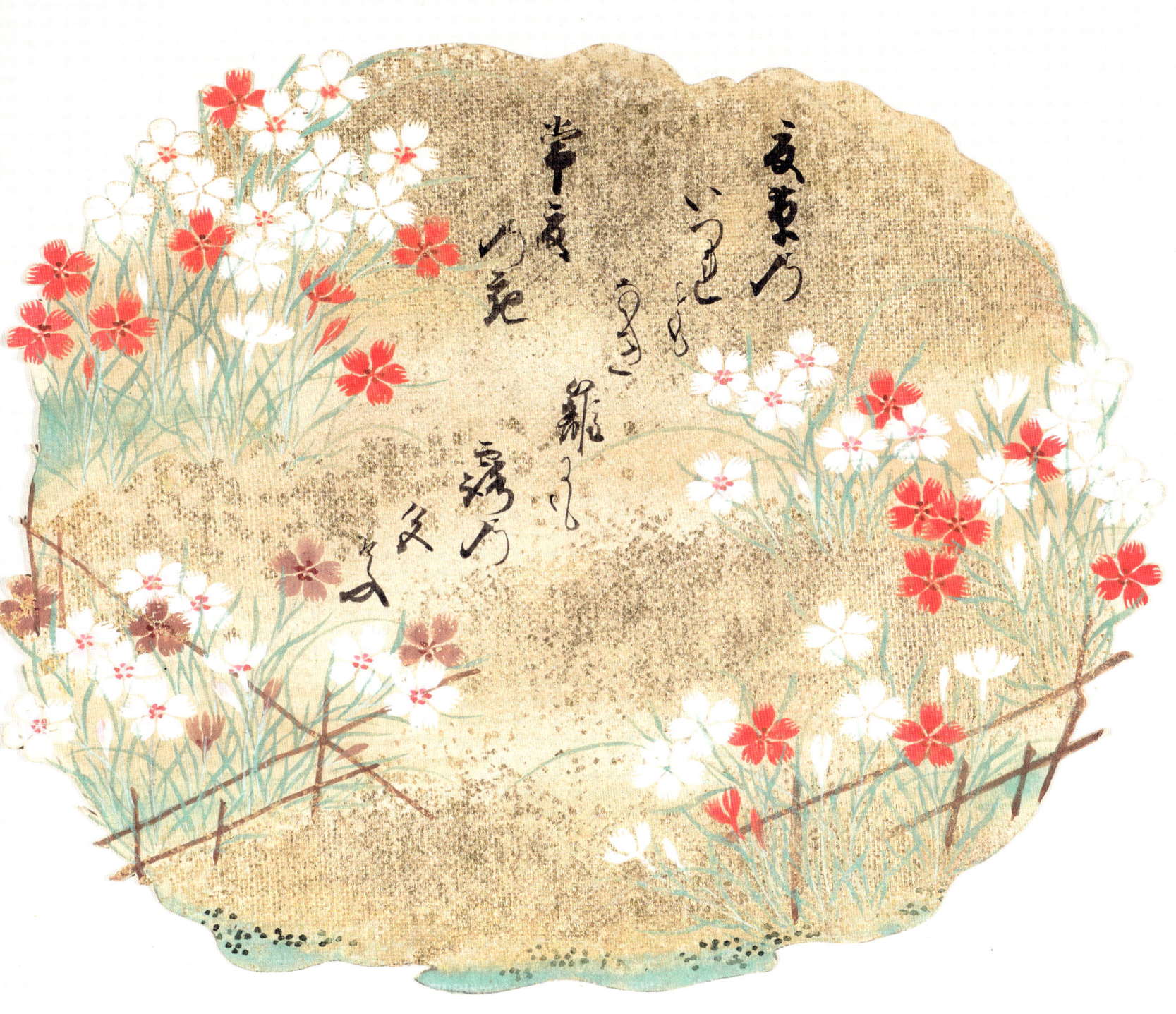

## THE FOUR SEASONS SUITE

With the Bodleian *Four Seasons* there is somewhat less to say, specifically or speculatively, about its transmedial trajectory. But certainly its models are the vast numbers of programmes of poems – quite often (though not always) in intermedial settings – that adopt the temporal framework of the four seasons and select floral, arboreal, avian or other figures as their focus. This particular instance of the rendering of a 'four seasons' programme, in this medium and format, is but one manifestation of the seemingly inexhaustible reproductive capacity of this repertoire of seasonal themes and tropes. Indeed, the four seasons template can be said to be as central to East Asian arts, both literary and visual, as it is in Baroque European painting and music.

In the Japanese setting, there are hosts of precedents in a variety of media. The first selective royal anthology of poetry, the *Kokin wakashū*, opens with six chapters of seasonal poems – two for spring, one for summer, two for autumn, one for winter – and then proceeds through another sixteen chapters on other kinds of topics and themes. This becomes the template for all subsequent royal anthologies, and the same pattern was adopted in many other collections. Though no example of a seasonal landscape painting from the same period (late ninth to early tenth centuries) survives, we know from textual records that a similar allocation of space across six folds of a screen for such seasonal poems was standard, or at least favoured.[9] The 'four seasons' motif in inter-related visual and literary realms might be dismissed as a cliché, were it not so abundantly clear that it was

44 PREVIOUS & FOLLOWING PAGES The ten roundels from *Scenes from Nature in the Four Seasons*, formed as *kirigami*. MS. Jap. d.25.

held in high regard and productively resourced throughout Japanese cultural history.[10]

Such acts of recapitulation have a significance in society and culture that is easily underestimated precisely because of the ubiquitous presence of the familiar. We may take the familiar for granted and it may seem banal, even hackneyed – but it may also serve as a steadying, balancing, recalibrating act for the performer, and its enactment may also be a similarly positive, needs-fulfilling and thus rather satisfying experience for the observer or receiver. This may be more so if there are variations on the basic form and content, simultaneously displaying sameness with and difference from others. This is certainly one of the patterns we see in traditional Japanese cultural productions – cultural producers and performers often aim to ring the changes, to a greater or lesser extent, on received, established materials to satisfy the expectations of their audiences, viewers and consumers.

The cultural producer or programmer who made the selection of ten poems for inscription in the *kirigami* visualizations in the Bodleian *Four Seasons* appears to have operated on this principle, whether deliberately or otherwise. It is entirely possible that the Bodleian artefact is not the first or only time in which this particular set of poems was presented as a group, but no matching works are known at present. The programme as we have it is, in any case, a mix of relatively obscure poems (from collections that suggest an effort to search out the less than utterly familiar) with others that are far more prominent in the *waka* corpus. Along with the *kirigami* rendering of figural elements in the poems, the viewer is provided with a freshened experience of the otherwise comfortably familiar:

1 春のきる袂ゆた／かに／たつかすみ／めくみ／あまねき／四方の山／の端

*haru no kiru tamoto yutaka ni tatsu kasumi*
*megumi amaneki yomo no yama no ha*
spring's sleeves embroidered in rich hues
by these rising mists –
a benediction spreads afar,
to each and every mountain's rim.

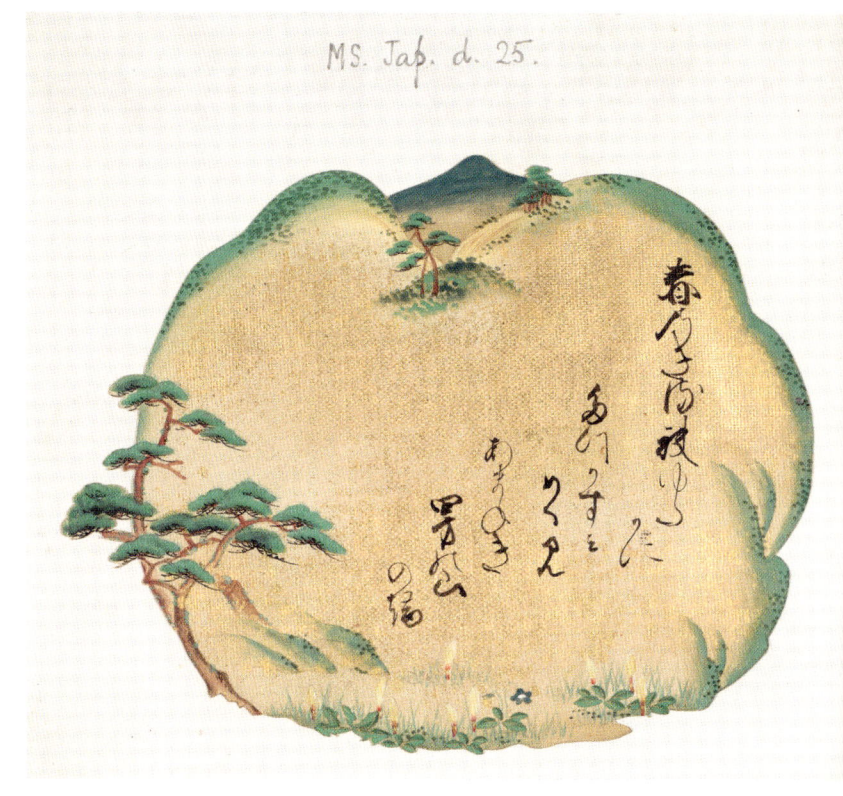

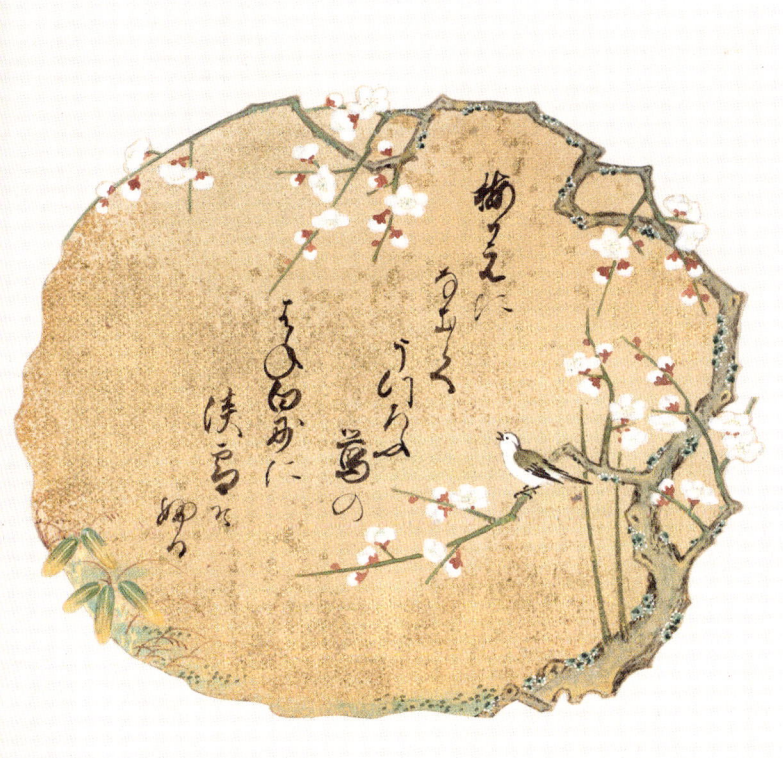

2 梅かえに／なきて／うつろふ／鶯の／はね白妙に／淡雪そ／ふる

*mume ga e ni nakite utsurofu uguisu no hane*
*shirotahe ni awayuki zo furu*
on the wings of a warbler singing on one branch,
then another – thin snow falls,
a linen-white cloak.

3 山寺の春の／夕くれ来て／みれは／入相のかねに／
　はなそ／散ける

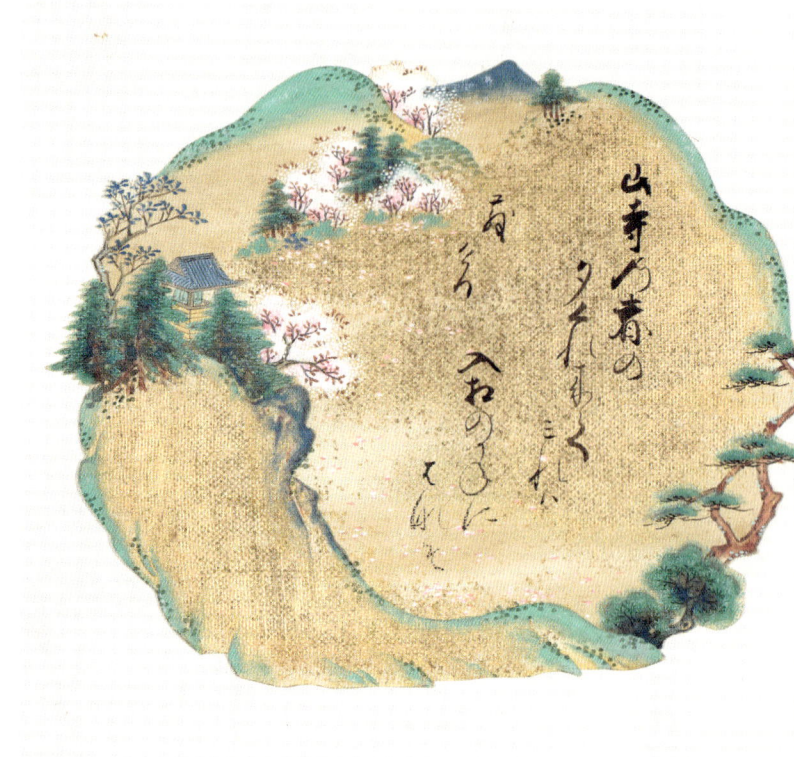

    *yamadera no haru no yufugure kite mireba*
       *iriahi no kane ni hana zo chirikeru*
when I made my way to witness a dusk in spring
    at a mountain temple:
       with the toning of the vesper bell, blossoms fell.

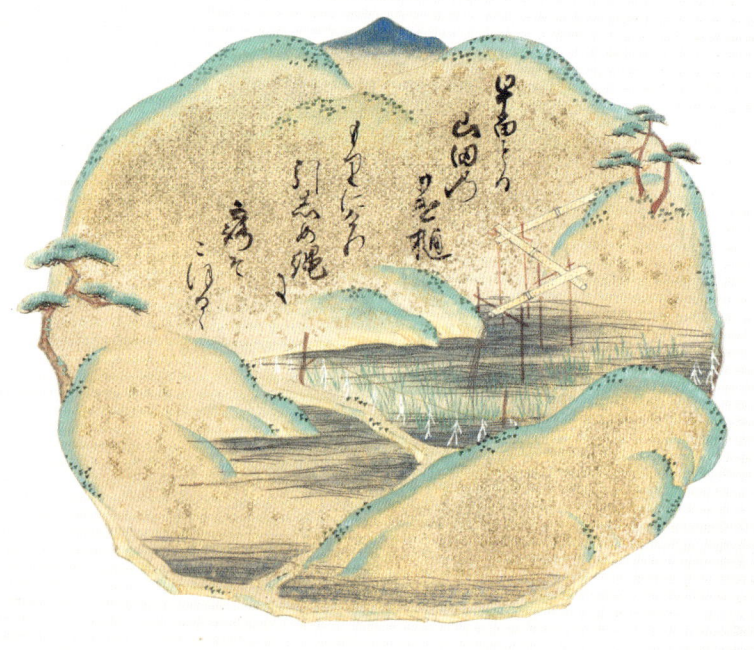

4 早苗とる／山田の／かけ樋／／もりにけ／引しめ縄／に／
　露そ／こほる〻

    *sanahe toru yamada no kakehi morinikeri*
       *hiku shimenawa ni tsuyu so koboruru*
bamboo flumes in mountain fields
    of young seedlings are overflowing,
      for dew drips from cordons strung at their borders.

**5** 夏草の／いつれ／とも／なき／離にも／露の／色／そふ／
常夏の花

*natsukusa no izure to mo naki magaki ni mo*
　　　　*tsuyu no iro sofu tokonatsu no hana*
on a lattice hedge where summer flowers grow
　　　　to baffling profusion, the pinks stand out
　　　　in colours enhanced with dew.

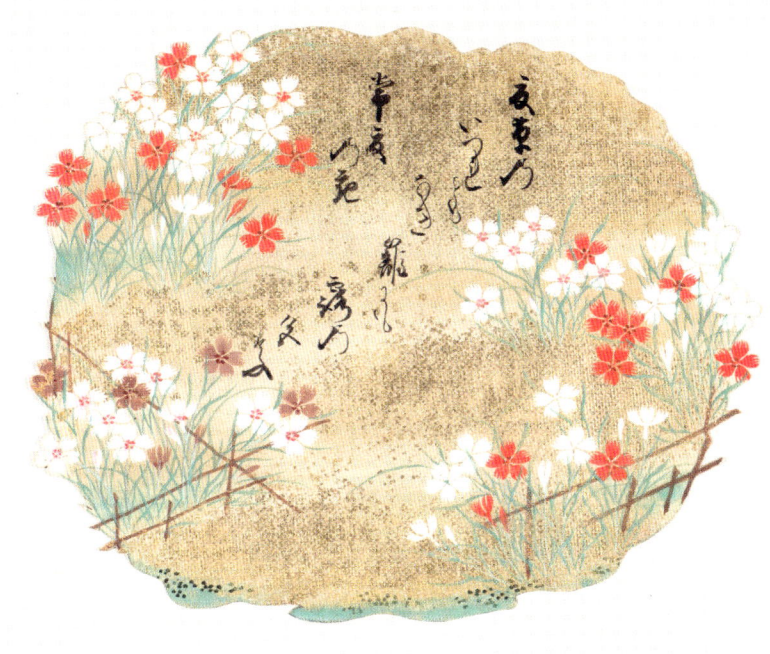

**6** 秋風に山／とひ／こゆる借りかねの／いやとをさかり／雲／
かくれ／つゝ

*akikaze ni yama tobikoyuru karigane no*
　　　　*iya tohozakari*
　　　　*kumogakuretsutu*
wild geese cross the peaks aloft on autumn wind
　　　　and then grow yet more distant,
　　　　drifting out of sight among the clouds.

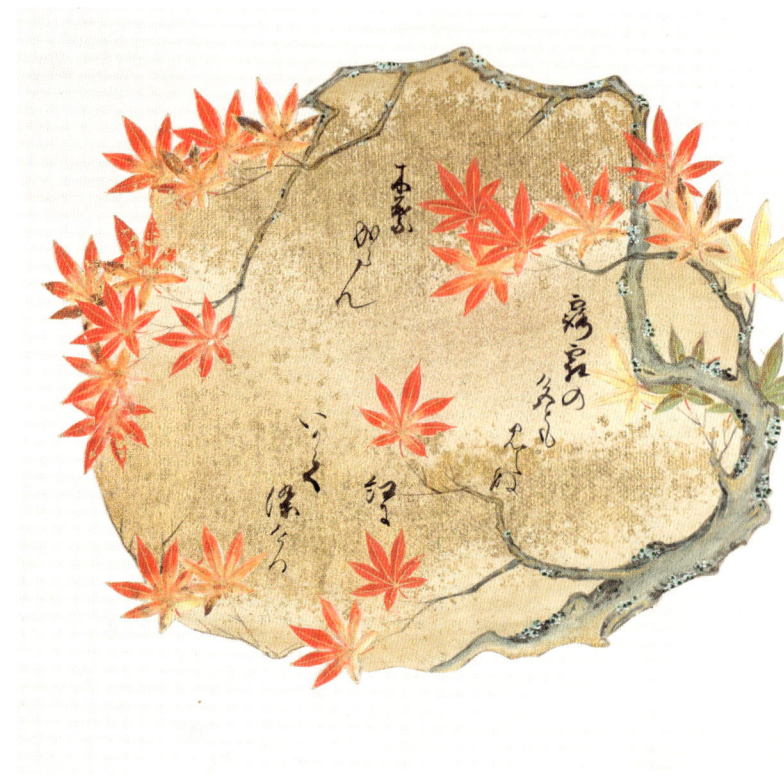

7 露霜の／色とも／見へぬ／紅に／いかて／染ける／
木葉成らん

*tsuyu shimo no iro to mo mienu kurenai ni*
　　　*ikade somekeru ko no ha naruran*
in nothing like the colour of the dew or frost,
　　　　but in scarlet –
　　　how is it that the leaves of these trees
　　　　are dyed like this?

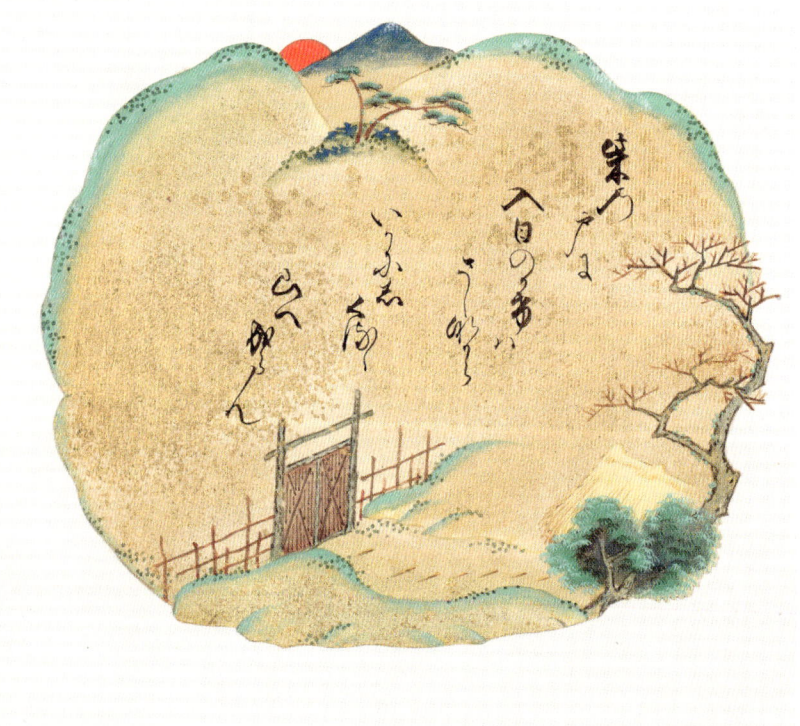

8 柴の／戸に／入日のかけは／さしなから／いかにし／
くるゝ／山へ／成らん

*shiba no to ni irihi no kage ha sashinagara*
　　　*ika ni shigururu yamabe naruran*
the setting sun's rays still light up the brushwood
　　　　doorway,
　　　yet somehow the foothills are now bathed in
　　　　showers.

**9** 水鳥の／青羽は／冬もかれ／ぬとや／芦間さへ／行／池の／面影

*mizudori no aoba ha fuyu mo karenu to ya*
　*ashima sahe yuku ike no omokage*
Have the green leaves not lost all their color now,
　　in winter?
　　Even as the pond freezes, their verdant image
　　remains amongst the reeds.[11]

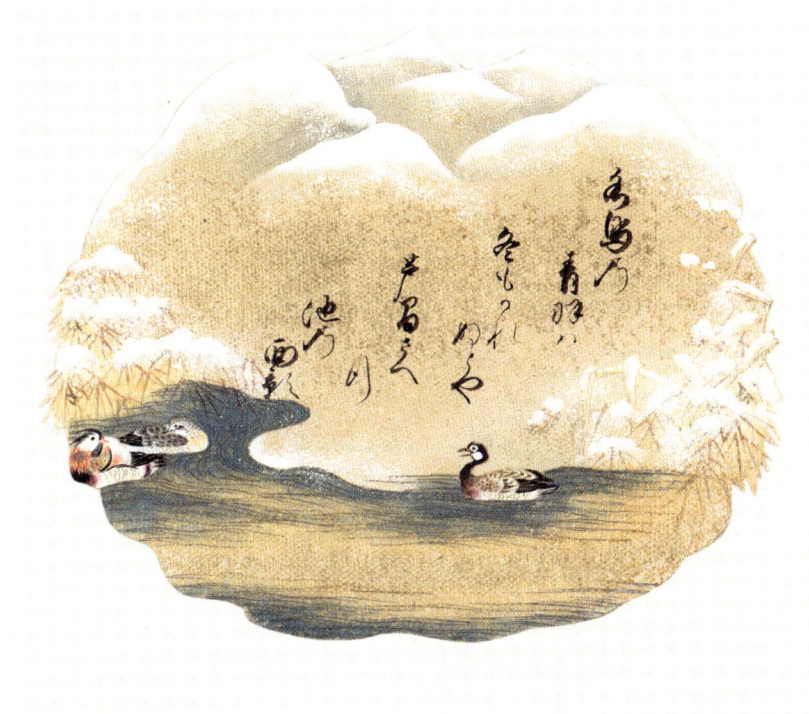

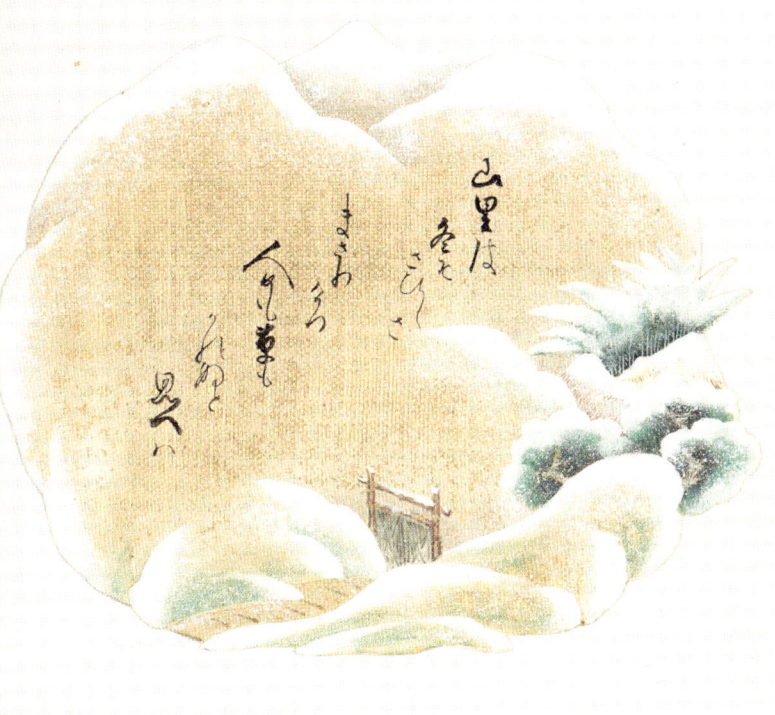

**10** 山里は／冬そ／さひしさ／まさり／けり／人めも草も／かれぬと／思へは

*yamazato ha fuyu zo sabishisa masarikeri*
　*hitome mo kusa mo karenu to omoheba*
loneliness intensifies in a mountain home in winter:
　　this I have come to know
　　as both company and grasses fade away.

The visualizations in the ten roundels containing these poems make explicit what is already apparent in their figural schemes – in some instances, more so than the poems may warrant.[12] But ten is an unusual number for a series on a seasonal theme; twelve, the number of the months, is what we might expect in a programme of this kind. Their number determined (or conveniently matched) the number of panels in pairs of screens on which classical depictions of the seasons were depicted. So, perhaps, the Bodleian is missing two of its original sections. What we have are three spring scenes (1–3), two summer scenes (4–5), two autumn scenes (6–7) and three winter scenes (8–10) – an unusual distribution and thus, perhaps, refreshing in its own way. Once again, the high-profile *Shin kokin wakashū* is the predominant source, but the scope of selection ventures beyond it. As with the *Ten Styles*, none of this metadata is in the work itself. The poems are there, solo and in sequence, to do their work as a seasonal suite – not as celebrations of their makers, nor, for that matter, to emphasize any particular aspect of their previous treatment.[13] The themes that determined the inclusion and treatment of the ten poems are specifically seasonal (with the exception of poem 7, the figural scheme of which is patently autumnal), as the following list of sources (and poets, where named) suggests:

1 Fujiwara no Teika; *Shūi gusō* [his personal anthology] #2090; a poem on the first month of the year, for twelve-month screen honouring the presentation at court of a new consort, in 1229 [*Kangi gannen jūichigatsu nyogo judai onbyōbu waka/ tsukinami onbyōbu jūnijō waka*]
2 *Shin kokin wakashū* #30; Spring Book 1; poet unknown

3 *Shin kokin wakashū* #116; Spring Book 2: Priest Nōin
4 *Shin kokin wakashū* #225; Summer Book: Minamoto no Tsunenobu ['on transplanted seedlings in rice paddies' (*sankei no sanahe to iheru kokoro wo*)]
5 *Shin gosen wakashū* #240; Summer: Naidaijin (i.e. Ichijō Uchizane) ['on pinks drenched in dew' [*kuboku, tsuyu wo obiru*]
6 *Shin kokin wakashū* #498; Autumn Book 2: Hitomaro
7 *Shin shūi wakashū* #1664; Miscellaneous Book 1); Cloistered Prince of the Second Rank Kakuyo
8 *Shin kokin wakashū* #572; Winter: Fujiwara no Kiyosuke
9 *Dairin gushō* #5198; Volume 12, Winter Book 1: Retired Emperor Go-Uda [a poem on 'reeds in the cold pond' from the 'Poetry Gathering in 700 Rounds at the Kameyama Villa] (*Kameyamadono shichi hyakushu*)
10 *Kokin wakashū* #315; Winter; Minamoto no Muneyana

It is worth considering that the selection of poems for the Bodleian's *Four Seasons* was probably guided at least in part by visual sensibilities – that is, with attention to the ways in which they might lend themselves to representation in this particular *kirigami*-roundel format. (This might also be the case, to some extent, in the configuration of the materials in *Ten Styles* as well.) As it happens, the Beinecke Rare Book and Manuscript Library at Yale University possesses a rather similar set of mounted *shikishi* and roundels, bound as an *orijō* with *kirigami* decoration, the content of which is a suite of poems entitled *Flowers and Birds of the Twelve Months* by Fujiwara no Teika. He was commissioned in 1214 to originate this programme and the poems for it, for paintings and inscriptions to be mounted on sliding doors at Ninnaji, a Kyoto monastery; it was reproduced frequently thereafter

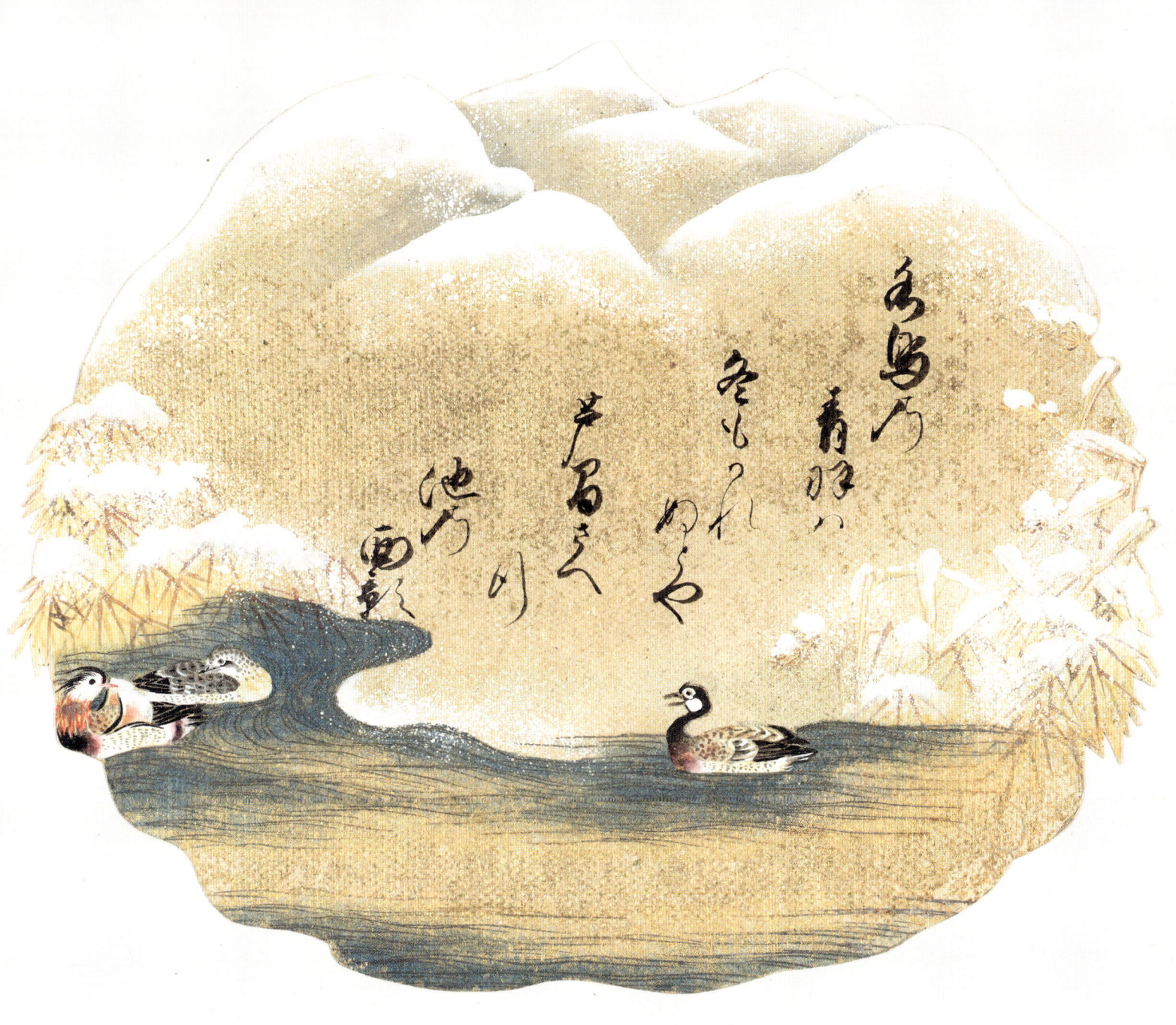

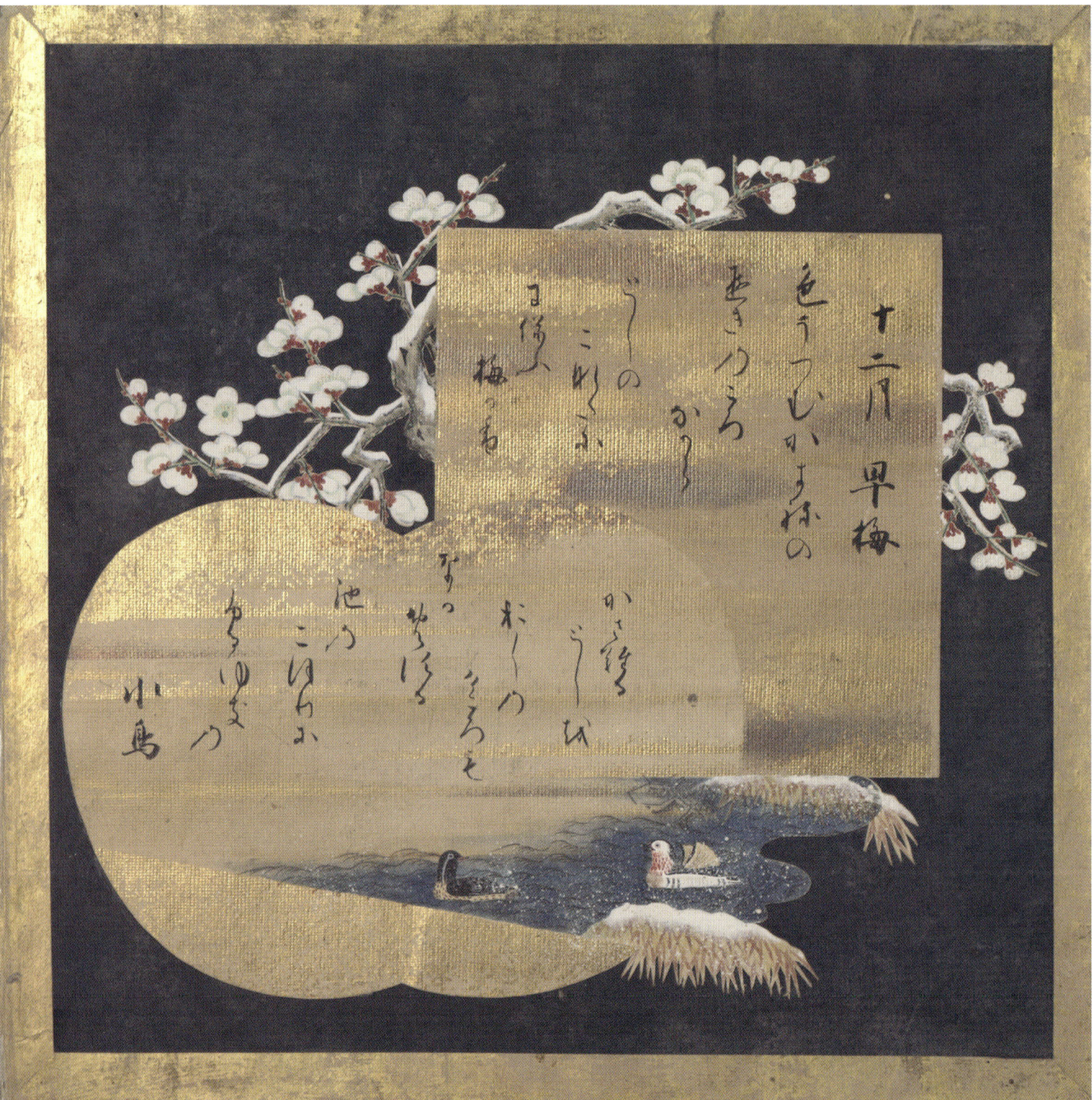

in many media, garnering particular interest in the late seventeenth century.[14] The Beinecke *kirigami orijō* rendering – yet another re-visitation of a familiar subject for intermedial representation – may date from that period, if not somewhat later. In its visual details, it bears strong resemblance to the Bodleian *Four Seasons*. For example, the mandarin duck (*mizudori*) in the Beinecke *orijō* visualization of Teika's poem on that avian emblem of the twelfth (winter) month (FIG. 45) is basically the same as that in the Bodleian visualization of Go-Uda's winter poem (poem 10; see p. 119) – and this is despite the fact that, as explained in note 12, the mandarin duck is not an active subject in the original poem. Indeed, the iconography in this scene is consistent with that in many another rendering of Teika's *Birds and Flowers*, including the corresponding panel in a pair of screens reproducing this subject that was created by the Kyoto painter Yamamoto Soken and a coterie of courtier calligraphers *c.* 1690.[15] Iconography is, of course a code, a visual language that abets identification, orientation and recognition, and which exerts its influence across time. The codes of *waka* practice and production are, and do, much the same.

## BEYOND THE SUITES

Of all the poems found in these two *orijō*, by far the most familiar is Hitomaro's '*Honobono to…* (*Dimly, dimly…*), the third item in the *Ten Styles* and its exemplar of the 'style of elegant beauty'.

45 Winter month visualization from Fujiwara no Teika's *Flowers and Birds of the Twelve Months*, late eighteenth to mid-nineteenth century. Ink and colour on decorated paper squares (*shikishi*). Beinecke Rare Book and Manuscript Library, Yale University.

This is the poem that invariably accompanies any visualization in intermedial programmes that celebrate revered poets *per se*, and in which an image of Hitomaro and the poem itself almost always lead off the sequence or suite. This is true in the many intermedial renderings of the selective series known as *Sanjūrokkasen* (*The Thirty-Six Immortal Poets*), which is itself also transmedial; the poems selected one by one to represent the oeuvre and persona of each poet are, of course, derived from other, prior, collections. Like *Ten Styles* and so many other *waka* series and suites of their kind, the thirty-six immortal poets is a subject that has been rendered again and again since its original conception as a set (by the poet Fujiwara no Kintō in the eleventh century). Again this occurs with variations and rearrangements, though with a very consistent iconography for the imaginary portraits of the poets. The first image and poem encountered in an early eighteenth-century handscroll version, entitled simply *Kokasen* (*Immortal Poets of the Past*), also held in the Bodleian Library, demonstrates the prominence and ubiquity of this poem and portrait pair (FIG. 46). Here, as usual, the poem text hovers near the poet's figure, which faces left, and as always Hitomaro is shown with brush in hand and inkstone at the ready, as if poised to write the poem.

A recent exhibition held at the Musée des Beaux-Arts, Dijon, featured another *kirigami* album version of *Ten Styles* that is held in the collection of the Musée Unter Linden in Colmar, France. Its format closely resembles that of the Bodleian *Four Seasons*, with its gold-tinted roundels and floral decorations, but the poems are inscribed on *tanzaku* – the form used for the same purpose

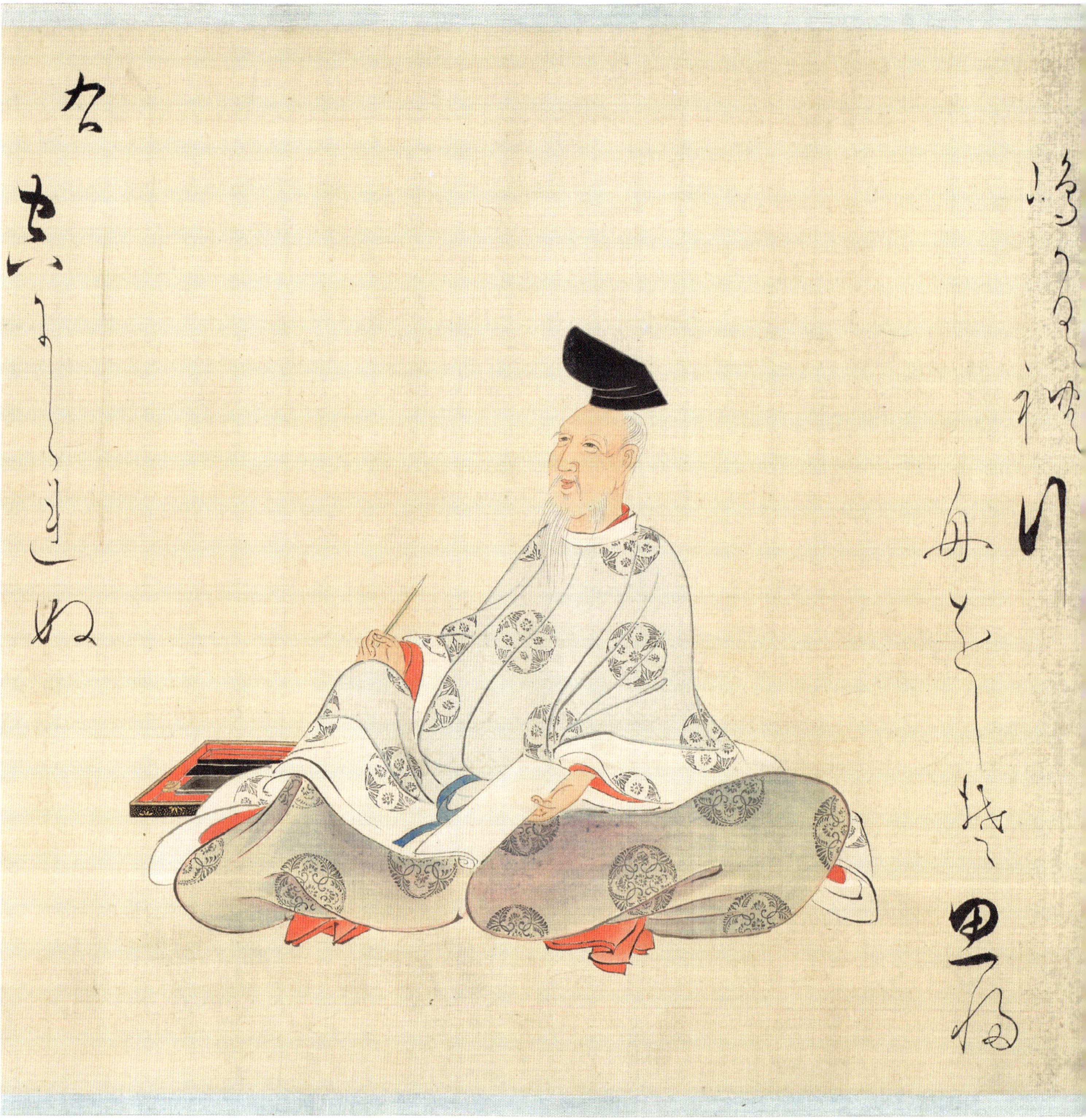

なき数に
君し通ひぬ

鳴る神の　音にのみやは　田植

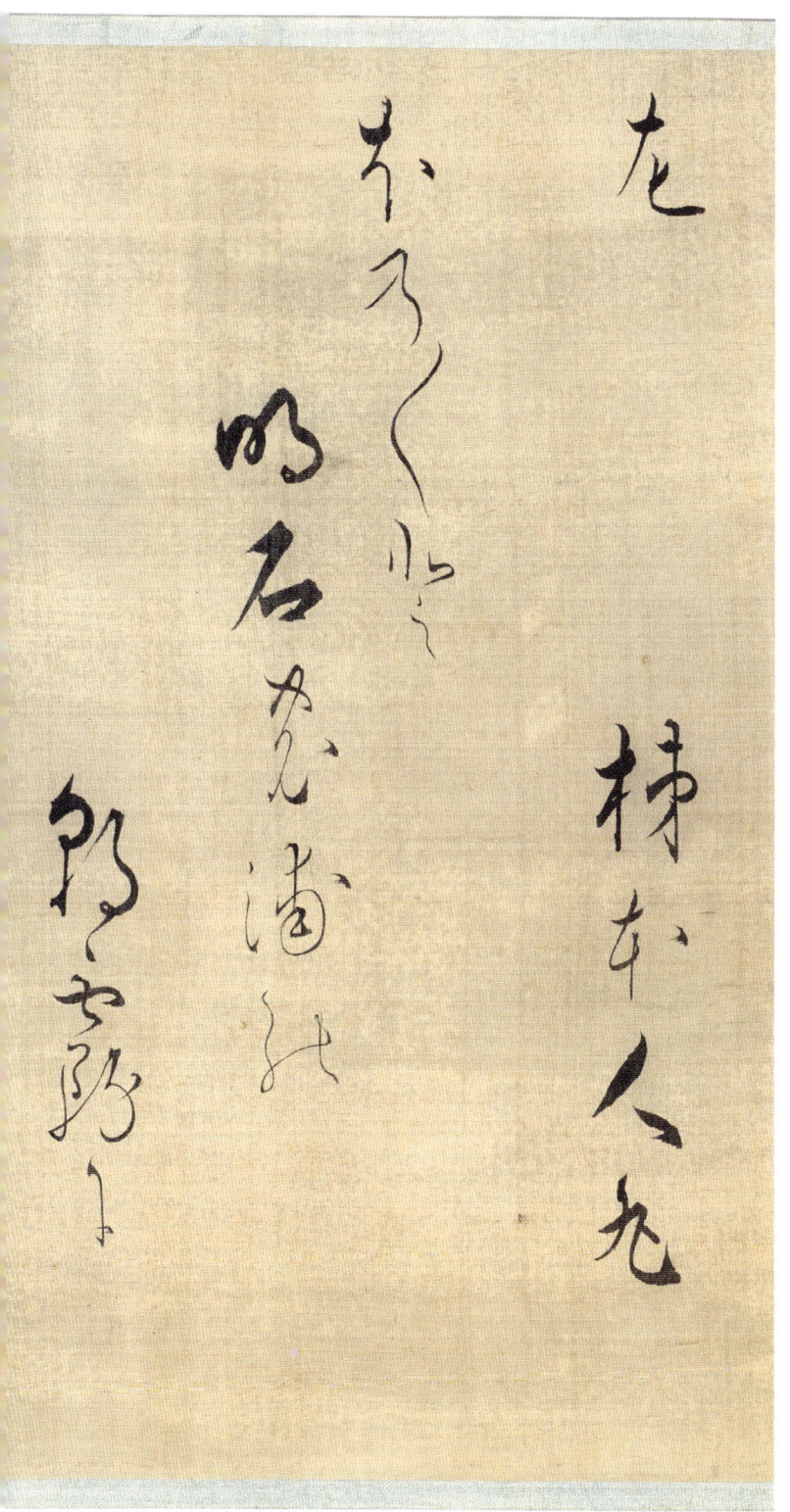

in the Bodleian *Ten Styles*. In other words, the Colmar album combines formal aspects of both of the Bodleian albums. The authors of the Dijon catalogue entry on the Colmar album note that its pictorial style closely resembles that of yet another album, in the Smith-Lesouëf collection in the Bibliothèque nationale de France, and they suggest that both of those albums may come from the same 'atelier'. They further speculate that such works may have been created for patrons among the noble class close to the Kyoto court in the late seventeenth or early eighteenth century, most likely to serve as elegant gifts.[16] Further study of all these albums and the similar works in the Bodleian's Japanese collection and beyond may serve to confirm or refine such conjectures. Such studies may also further our understanding of how transmediality and intermediality work their ways – by means that are readily recognizable, as well as some that are more subtle – in the artefacts examined here and in so many others, whether of Japanese making or otherwise.

46 Kinugawa Morimasa (?–1705), double-page spread from *Kokasen* (*Immortal Poets of the Past*), date unknown. Ink and pigments on silk. MS. Jap. c.7 (R).

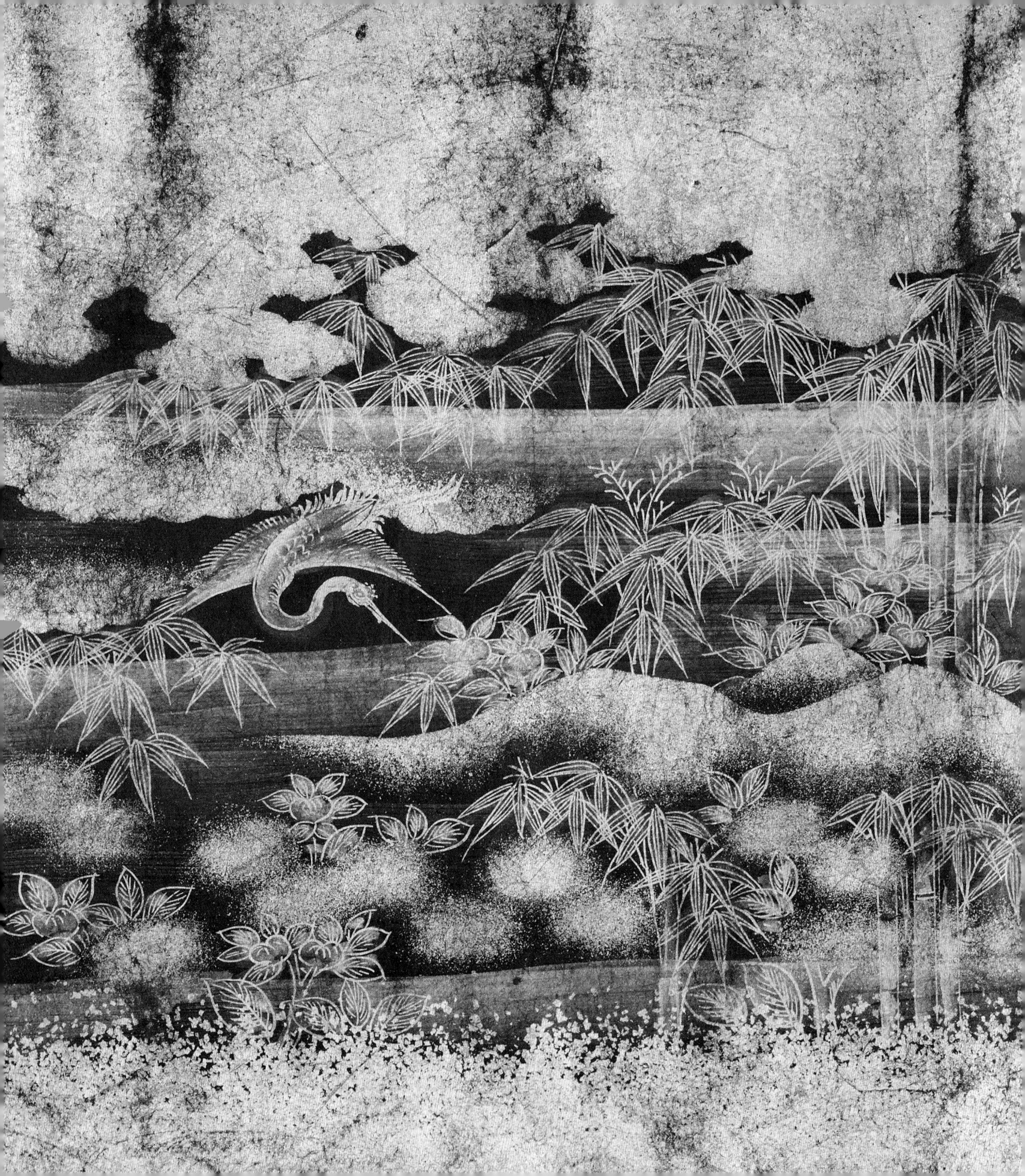

4

# The Japanese book: paper, colour and lustre

## MARINITA STIGLITZ

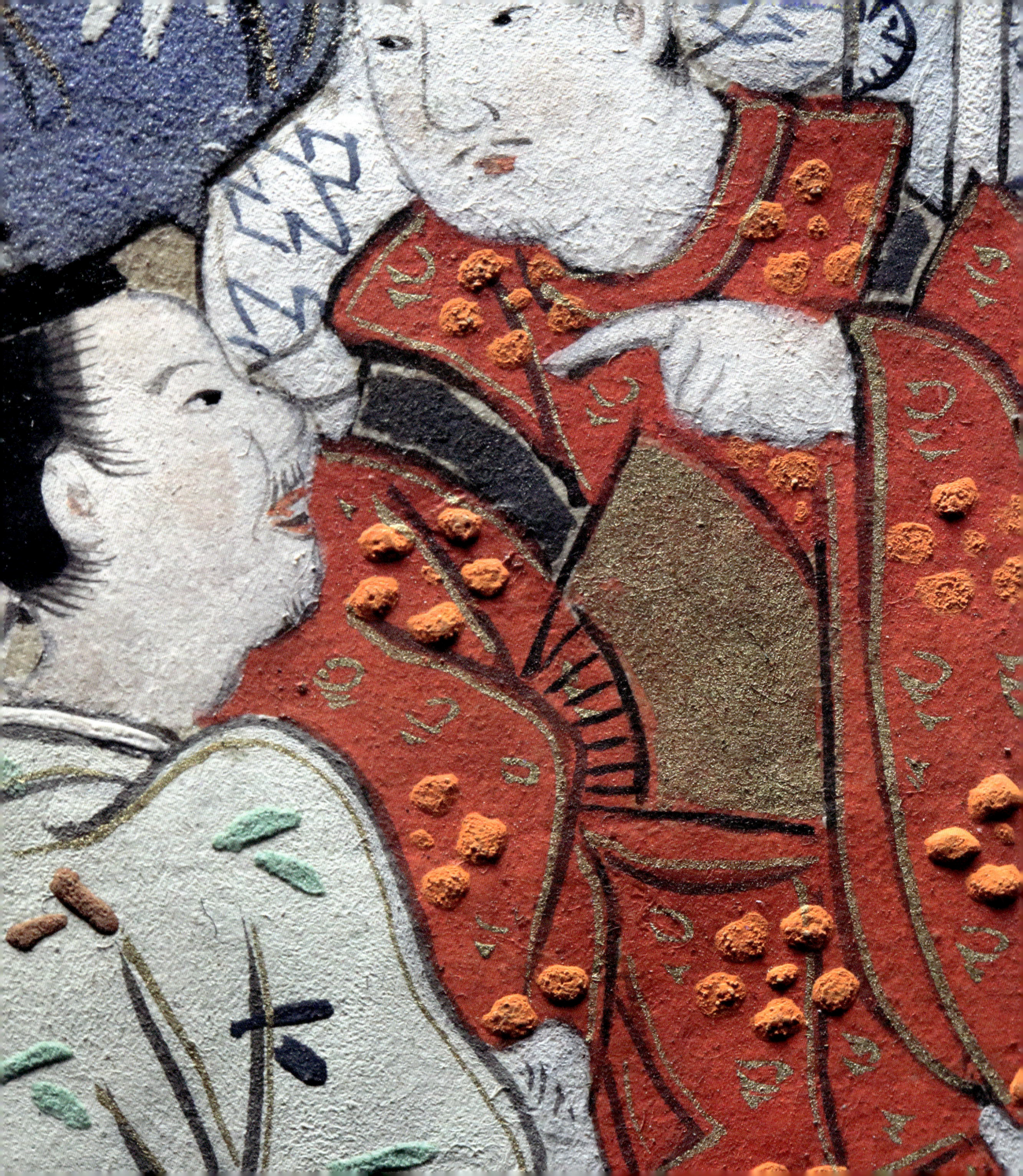

As RECOUNTED in the *Nihon shoki*, one of the oldest chronicles of Japan (compiled in 720), a Buddhist monk named Tamjing arrived in Japan from Koguryŏ, a kingdom of the Korean peninsula, in the spring of 610. He was described as a scholar, well-versed in the five Confucian classics, but also as a craftsman expert in papermaking and the preparation of colours. Whether it be truth or myth, the brief passage in the *Nihon shoki* suggests that knowledge of how to produce paper, and colours, reached Japan from the continent well before the early eighth century. It has shaped textual and pictorial artefacts ever since.[1]

This chapter casts light on the technical aspects that have contributed to the making of printed books and manuscripts, whilst looking at examples from the Bodleian Japanese collection. It considers closely the distinctive characteristics and methods of production of paper and colours, from the raw ingredients selected to the skills involved.

## PAPER

*Washi* (handmade Japanese paper) is closely associated with bookmaking – either used as a substrate for text and images, or turned into a protective cover. Yet this flexible, strong, light and translucent material has many other applications, fully permeating Japanese daily life, from wrapping to making lanterns, fans, umbrellas, kites, dolls, garments, paintings and even elements for interior design in traditional houses (FIG. 47).

Ever since *washi* reached Europe in the seventeenth century – through Dutch merchants, Jesuit missionaries from the Iberian Peninsula, and English merchants from the East India Company – its visual and material qualities have captured the attention of Europeans. For example, the English diarist John Evelyn (1620–1706), on 22 June 1664, wrote about the thin and polished paper of amber colour shown to him by a Jesuit missionary, together with other rarities from China and Japan.[2] The Dutch artist Rembrandt (1606–1669) experimented with Japanese paper to print some of his etchings and, later in the eighteenth century, the German naturalist Engelbert Kaempfer (1651–1716) wrote the first accurate account on Japanese paper and its manufacture, published in his *Amoenitatum Exoticarum* (1712) and posthumously in his *History of Japan* (1727, fig. 48).[3] Largely relying on Kaempfer's work, another medical officer at the Dutch East India Company's trading post in Nagasaki, the Swedish naturalist Carl Peter Thunberg (1743–1828), described Japanese papermaking in his *Flora Iaponica* (1784).[4]

The European attraction to Japanese paper carried on in the nineteenth century. In 1869, the British prime minister William Gladstone prompted Sir Harry Smith Parkes, then ambassador to Japan, to investigate the state of the craft. The outcome was an extensive report, with paper names, manufacturing districts, uses, sizes, prices and actual specimens, which is now divided between the Victoria and Albert Museum, London, and the Royal Botanic Gardens, Kew.[5] Parkes's study is a remarkable record of *washi* technology, fortuitously assembled at a critical time. Soon afterwards, in the mid-1870s, the first mill producing machine-made paper opened the way to the industrialization of papermaking in Japan. Nowadays the old papermaking traditions, passed from one generation to the next, only survive in a few locations.

Papermaking had been practised in many provinces across Japan since the eighth century, and it became a government's concern around 807 with the establishment of a paper mill in the south

47 LEFT TO RIGHT A set of flexible screens from a papermaking mould, the intact bark of *mitsumata* and its white inner layer after cleaning, sheets of *washi* rolled together.

of the imperial capital Kyoto. For a long time, paper was an expensive commodity produced for limited consumption, used primarily within the court and temple environments for Buddhist scriptures and bureaucratic documents, for example. It was not until the early modern period (the seventeenth to the nineteenth centuries) that *washi* became a more widely available commercial commodity, thanks to the establishment of numerous paper mills across the country and various retailers in large urban centres. For instance, shops directories such as *Edo kaimono hitori annai* (1824), a guidebook to shopping in Edo, listed an array of retailers and wholesalers specializing in paper for different

purposes such as writing, calligraphic work, painting and printing.

*Washi* comes in many different sizes, textures and physical properties, depending on the fibres and treatments used in the production process. In the Japanese–Portuguese dictionary *Vocabulario da lingoa de Iapam*, published by the Jesuit mission in Nagasaki in 1603–04, we read entries about a broad range of Japanese papers which are still used today.

A much more extensive list of paper products can be seen in a printed advertisement, possibly late nineteenth century, for the Murata shop in Shin Yoshiwara which lists over forty different

48 OVERLEAF Illustration of the *kōzo* plant, from Engelbert Kaempfer's *History of Japan*, 1728 (first published 1727). Douce K 138.

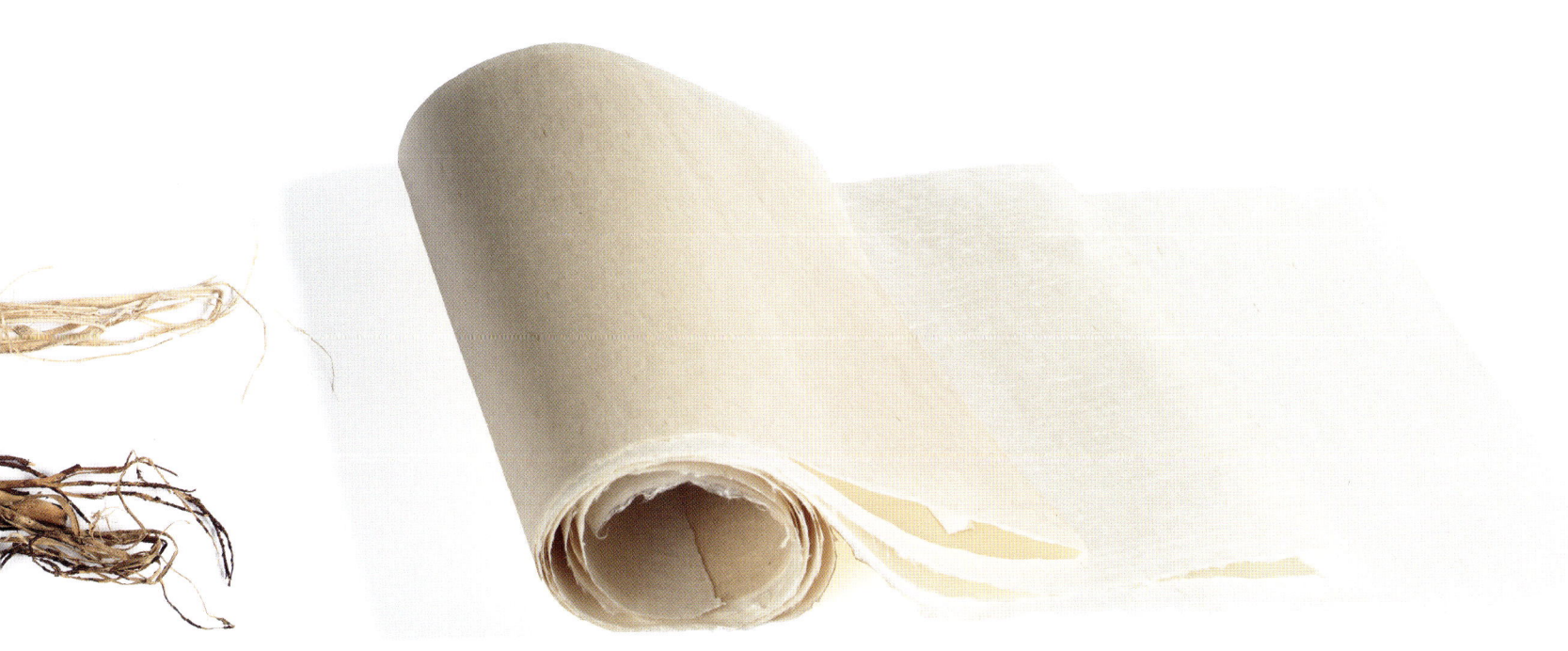

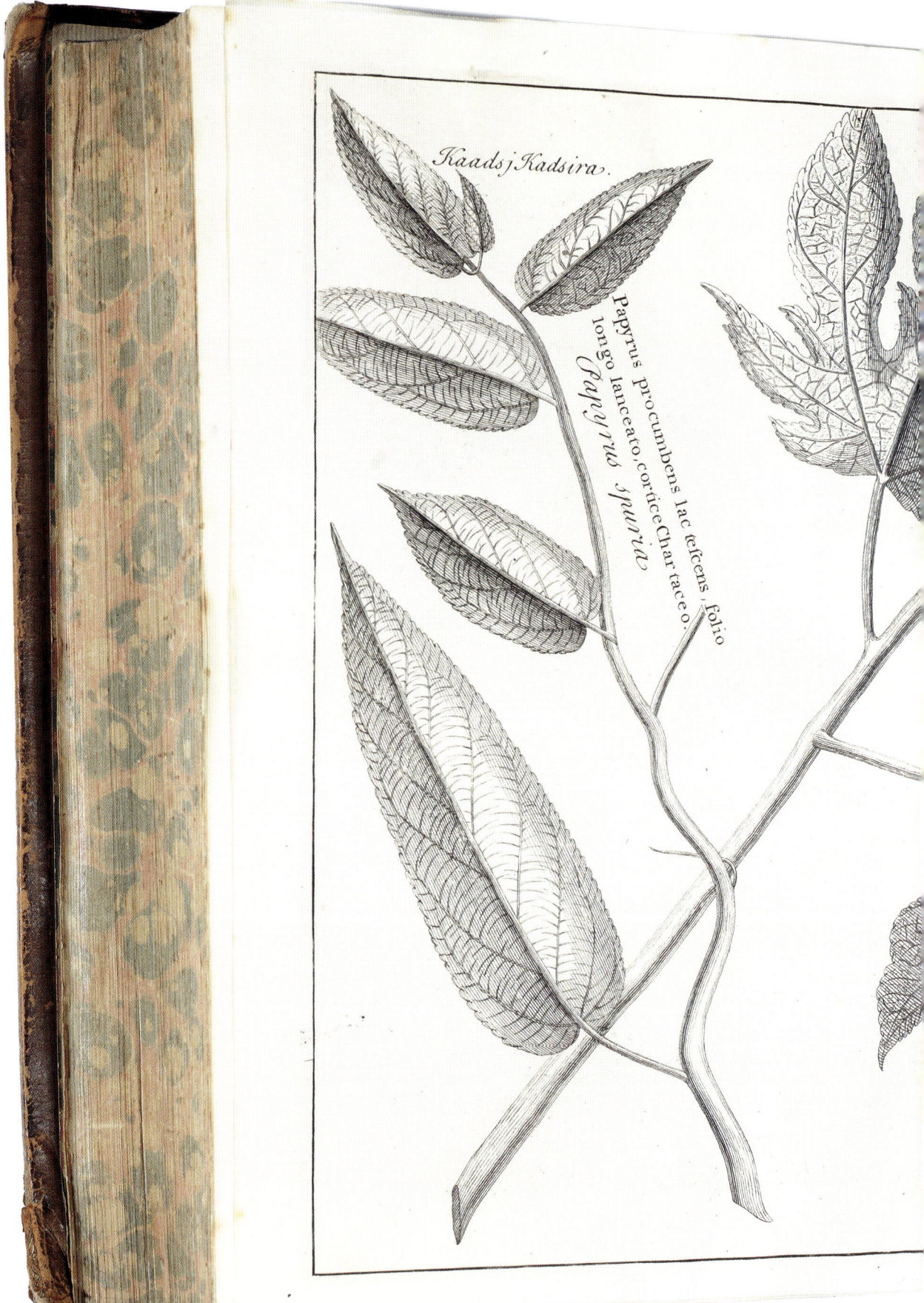

Kaadsj Kadsira.

Papyrus procumbens lac tescens, folio longo lanceato, cortice Chartaceo.
*Papyrus spuria*

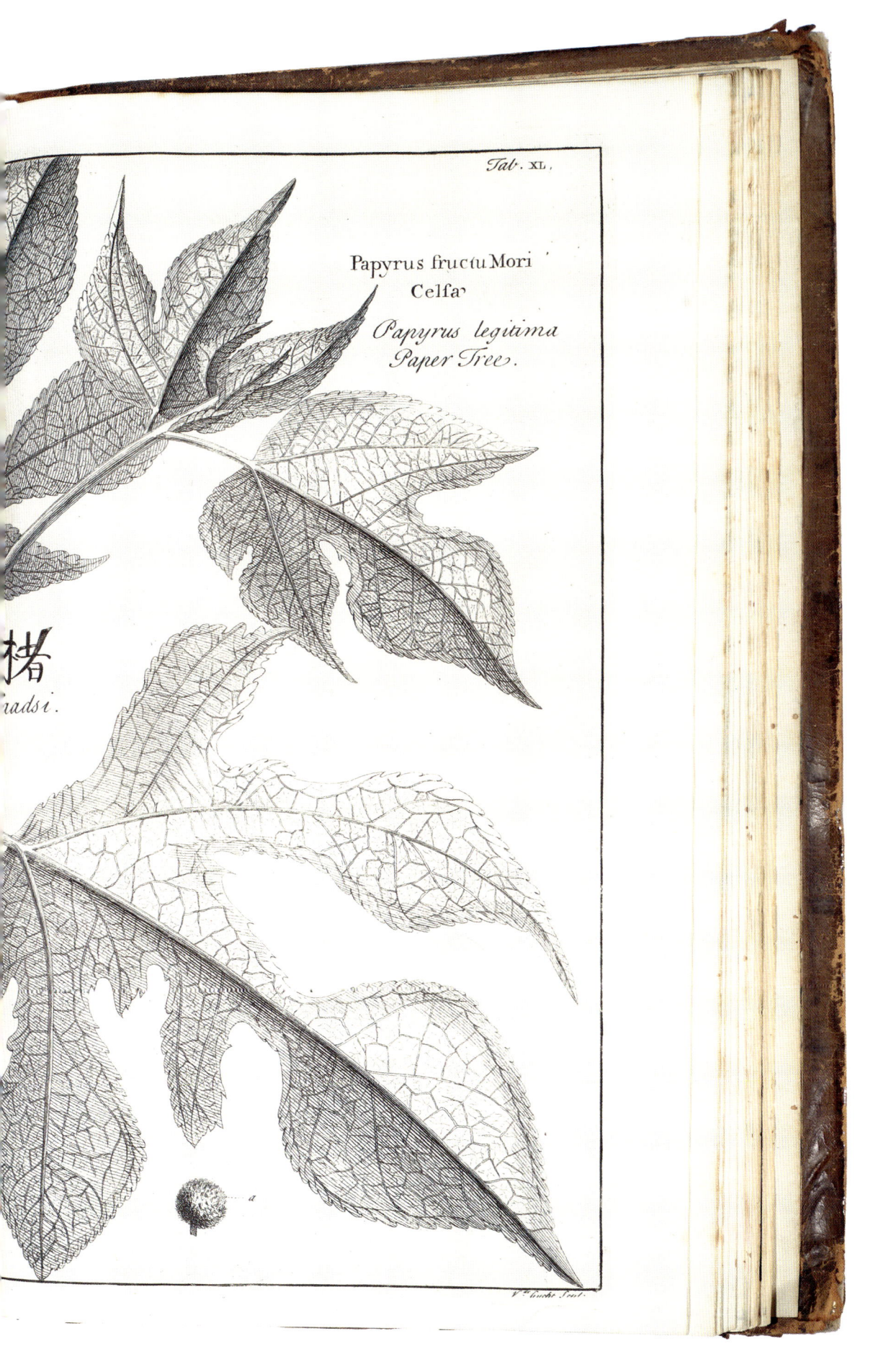

Tab. XL.

Papyrus fructu Mori
Celfa

Papyrus legitima
Paper Tree.

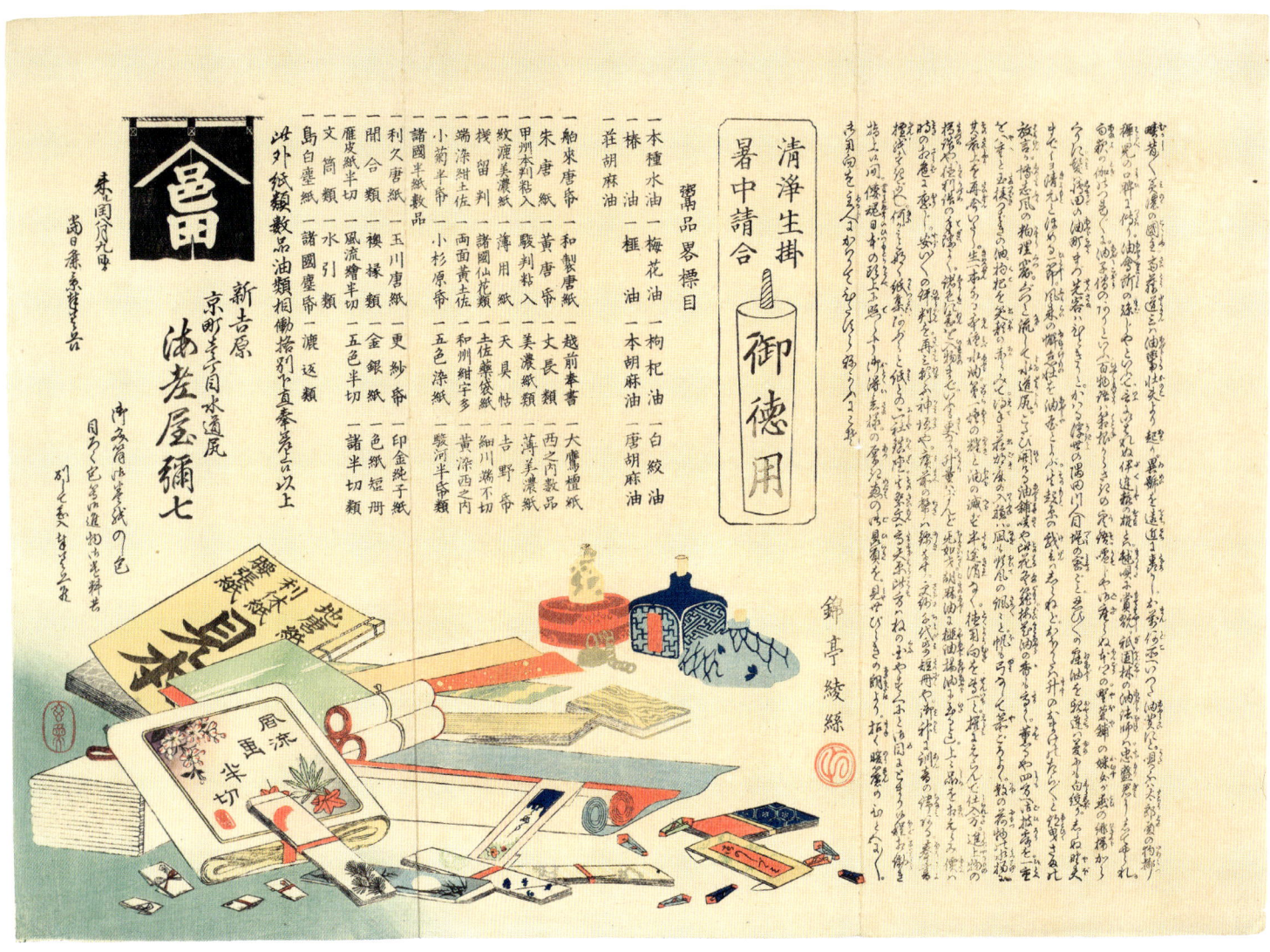

49 Printed advertisement for the Murata shop in Shin Yoshiwara, owned by Ebiya Yoshichi. Possibly late nineteenth century. Over forty different types of paper are listed here. Nipponica 1004.

types of paper, including regional varieties of *washi* and imported products from China (FIG. 49). This document provides us with invaluable information about papers and stationery that were commercially available in Japan during the latter part of the nineteenth century, for example *hōsho*, originating from Echizen, *danshi*, and *sugiharagami* named after Sugihara, Hyogo Prefecture.

Since the eighth century, the most common types of papers used for writing, book production and graphic art were made using an array of locally sourced fibres extracted from *asa* (hemp, or *Cannabis sativa*), *kōzo* (mulberry plants such as *Broussonetia papyrifera* or *Broussonetia kazinoki*) and *gampi* (plants such as *Wikstroemia sikokiana*) (FIG.

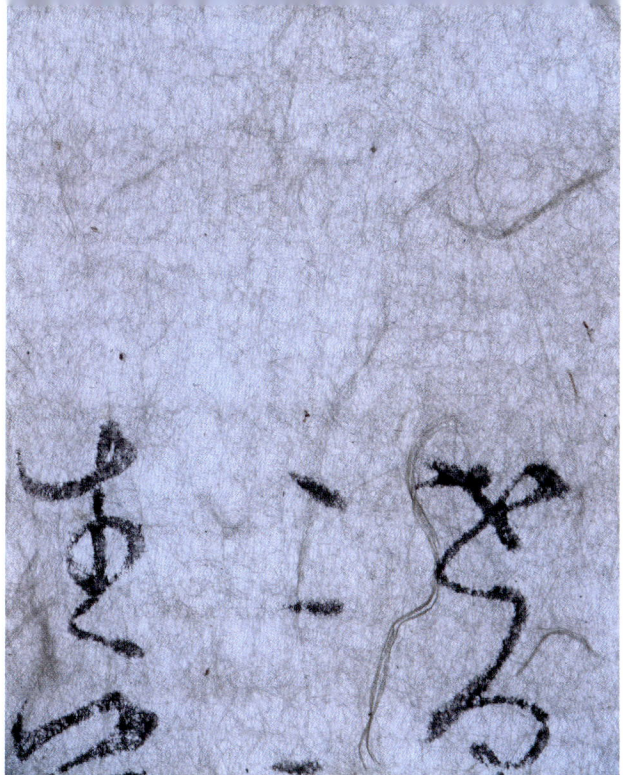
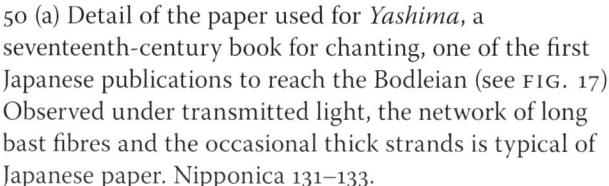
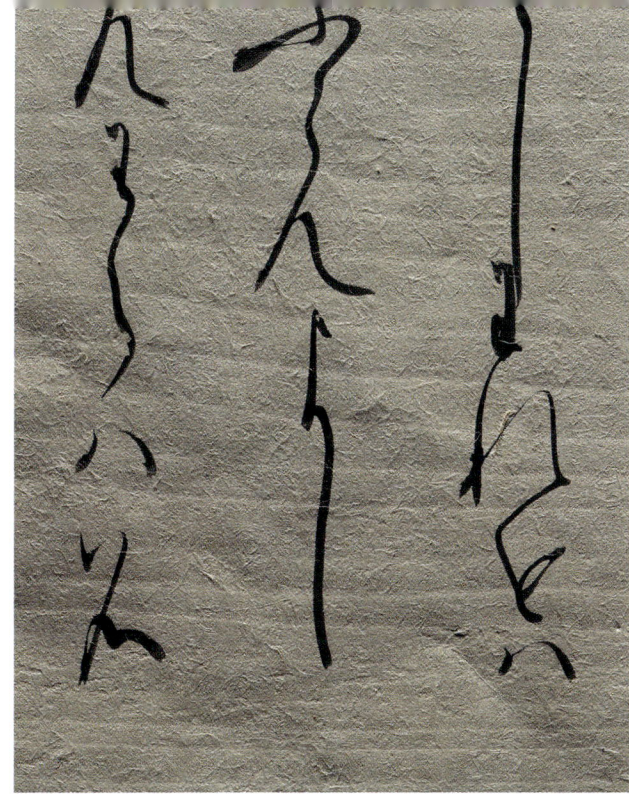

50 (a) Detail of the paper used for *Yashima*, a seventeenth-century book for chanting, one of the first Japanese publications to reach the Bodleian (see FIG. 17). Observed under transmitted light, the network of long bast fibres and the occasional thick strands is typical of Japanese paper. Nipponica 131–133.

50 (b) Detail of the paper used in a painted manuscript entitled *Ibuki*, *c.* seventeenth century. It has the smooth texture and opacity typical of *maniai* paper, made at the time with *gampi* fibres and coloured clay from the Najio area. Woodgrain marks from the board against which the paper dried are evident. MS. Jap. d.31.

50a). Paper produced with the *mitsumata* plant (*Edgeworthia chrysantha*) was introduced much later, at the end of the sixteenth century.

Ordinary types of *kōzo* paper include *Minogami*, made in a variety of thicknesses in the Mino region, and *hanshi*, denoting a paper of small dimensions measuring half the size of other common papers, manufactured in nearly every province from Chikugo to Sekishū and Tosa. *Danshi* and *hōsho* stand out among the prestigious *kōzo* papers. The first is a beautiful paper of considerable thickness, produced in the provinces with a finely wrinkled texture, and the second is a thick and strong paper with a smooth texture produced initially in Echizen and later across the country. *Hōsho* in particular is selected by *ukiyo-e* woodblock printers because it tolerates the repeated friction and rubbing required to produce colourful prints. At the same time, its soft surface is ideal to obtain striking reliefs and impressions; it remains a favourite of artists across the world.

Papers made with *gampi*, such as *torinoko*, are distinguished by a shimmering appearance and smooth texture. *Torinoko* generally has a very uniform surface, as during its making a piece of silk gauze is laid over the papermaking screen. With its exceptional qualities and range, it became the paper of choice amongst the upper classes and famous artists. Another type of *gampi* paper is *maniai*, manufactured in Najio, Hyogo Prefecture, with the addition of local clay of different colours (FIG. 50b). *Maniai* paper presents a distinctive opacity as well as a matt and smooth surface, and was often used for painted manuscripts such as the *Nara e-hon* (see chapter 2).

Despite all these varieties, the basic process of producing paper remained mostly unchanged over the centuries.[6] A number of Japanese primary sources have been used to study the traditional process to produce *washi* and describe the various types of paper. The *Engi shiki* (927), a collection of norms regulating court life, religious ceremonies and the work of the government, includes a full account of the imperial paper mill and other local papers.[7] Before botanists and agronomists began to take the lead in the study of this subject, valuable information about paper and papermaking is often part of diaries, dictionaries and encyclopaedias.[8] The *Yōshū fushi* (1686), a topographical compendium of Yamashiro Province written by physician Kurokawa Dōyū, describes the origin and manufacture of papers made in that province. The first book devoted exclusively to the subject of paper is Kimura Seichiku's *Shifu* (1777), a 'record of papers' which provides exhaustive information concerning the range of papers available at the time. It was followed by *Kamisuki Taigai* (1784), an overview of papermaking by Kizaki Morisue. This illustrated scroll, discovered only in 1940, covers aspects from the figure of the itinerant

papermaker to the advantages of mixing *gampi* and *kōzo*. Subsequently *Kamisuki Chohoki*, a guide to papermaking by wholesale paper dealer Kunisaki Jihee, was published in Osaka in 1798. It describes the manufacture of *Sekishū hanshi* in the Shimane Prefecture, and it is printed on this type of paper. The book's pictures of hard labour show playful details, such as a baby asking his tireless mother 'steam some *mochi* for me to eat instead of steaming *kōzo*'.[9]

From the outset, papermaking was practised from home, often by small-scale farmers during the winter months between the harvesting and the planting seasons, thriving in mountain villages with an abundance of plant fibres and running water. The main fibres used were extracted from hemp, *kōzo*, *gampi*, *mitsumata* and other local plants, which once grew plentifully throughout Japan. The period for papermaking differs slightly according to the geographical area – it usually starts in late November and ends in April. During the winter, the stems of *kōzo* and *mitsumata* are cut back, gathered into bundles to be transported down the mountains, and steamed in large cauldrons of water for a couple of hours; this process enables the removal of the bark from the wooden centre of the stem. The bark is then hung to dry in the winter sun and stored. At this stage the bark is known as black bark (*kuro-kawa*), consisting of a black outer layer, a green middle layer and the white inner layer known as white bark (*shiro-kawa*). The stems of *gampi*, conversely, are cut back in early summer and the bark is immediately stripped with a sickle.

The dried bark is soaked and softened for a day in water, traditionally the river. For the finest papers, the two outer layers are then scraped off

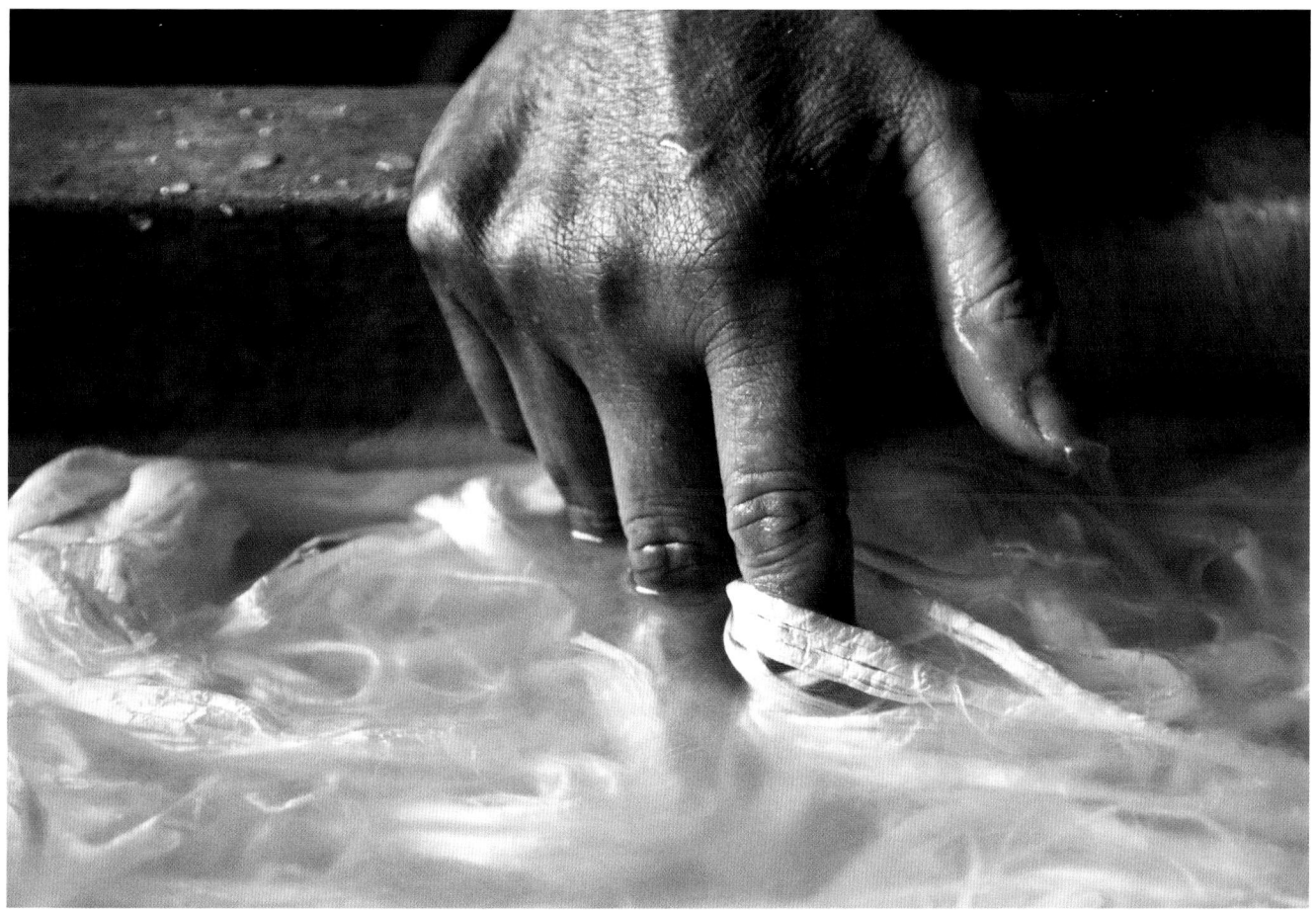

with a sharp knife. The remaining white inner
layer is rinsed thoroughly in the stream before
being dried and bleached in the sun. The white
bark is then cooked with lye, a potassium-rich
alkali made from wood ash, to remove the un-
wanted non-cellulosic material and to soften the
fibres so that they can be separated into strands.
The fibres are then thoroughly rinsed of the alkali
and stream-bleached. Snow-bleaching and sun-
bleaching are the other two methods used which
make the most of the surrounding environment.
The preparation of the fibres continues in a tank

51 *Kōzo* fibres being cleaned by hand in water.
Photograph by Karmen Corak from *Washi, la via
tradizionale*, 2010–11. This series of digital photographs
was printed on Japanese paper made by Hayashi Shinji in
Kurotani, Japan.

of water with the removal by hand of all remaining specks and imperfections (FIG. 51). The clean
fibres are squeezed into the shape of a ball and
hand-beaten with a wooden rod or a mallet to
separate and soften them, preserving intact their
long and slender shape that characterizes Japanese

paper. Eventually this process was undertaken with a mechanized stamping beater and a *naginata* beater, a machine with long bent blades designed to separate the fibres and mix them with water.

The fibres of *kōzo*, with an average length of ten millimetres, are used to produce the strongest papers, whilst the fibres of *gampi*, approximately four millimetres long, make smooth and lustrous papers, and the softer fibres of *mitsumata* are employed for more delicate silky sheets. Besides the fibres, variations in cooking, washing and beating have an impact on the quality of the paper. The fibres are mixed with water in a wooden vat where the sheets of paper are formed on a paper mould (*sugeta*), comprising a flexible screen (*su*) clamped on a lightweight wooden frame (*keta*), commonly suspended from the ceiling to reduce its weight. Its size varies depending on the type of paper being made, local customs and preferences. The screen, originally of reeds, was later made of finely split and bevelled bamboo ribs woven together with silk threads. On the finished sheet, one can see evidence of the mould used in the form of faint 'laid lines' (horizontal lines) and 'chain lines' (vertical lines). The people capable of building the paper mould, like other equipment, play a crucial role in the production of fine paper – very few retain these skills today.

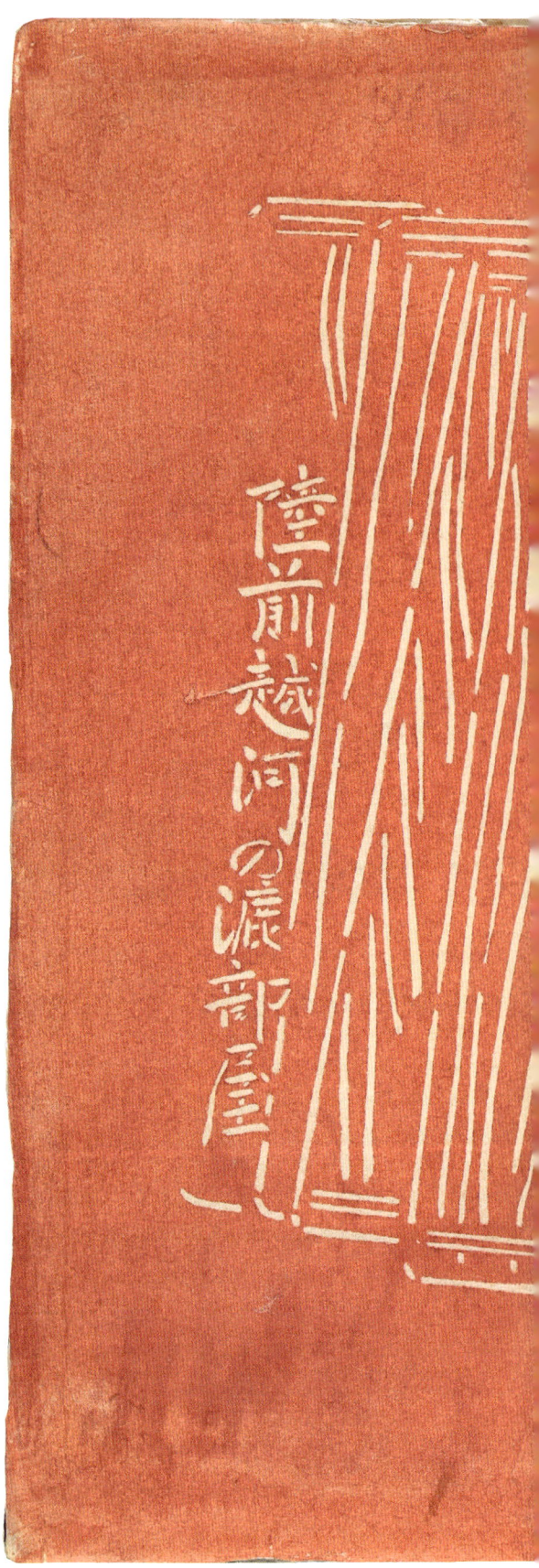

52  Stencilled illustration from Gotō Seikichirō, *Kami no Tabi*, 1964. The illustration depicts a papermaker's workshop. Nipponica 1005.

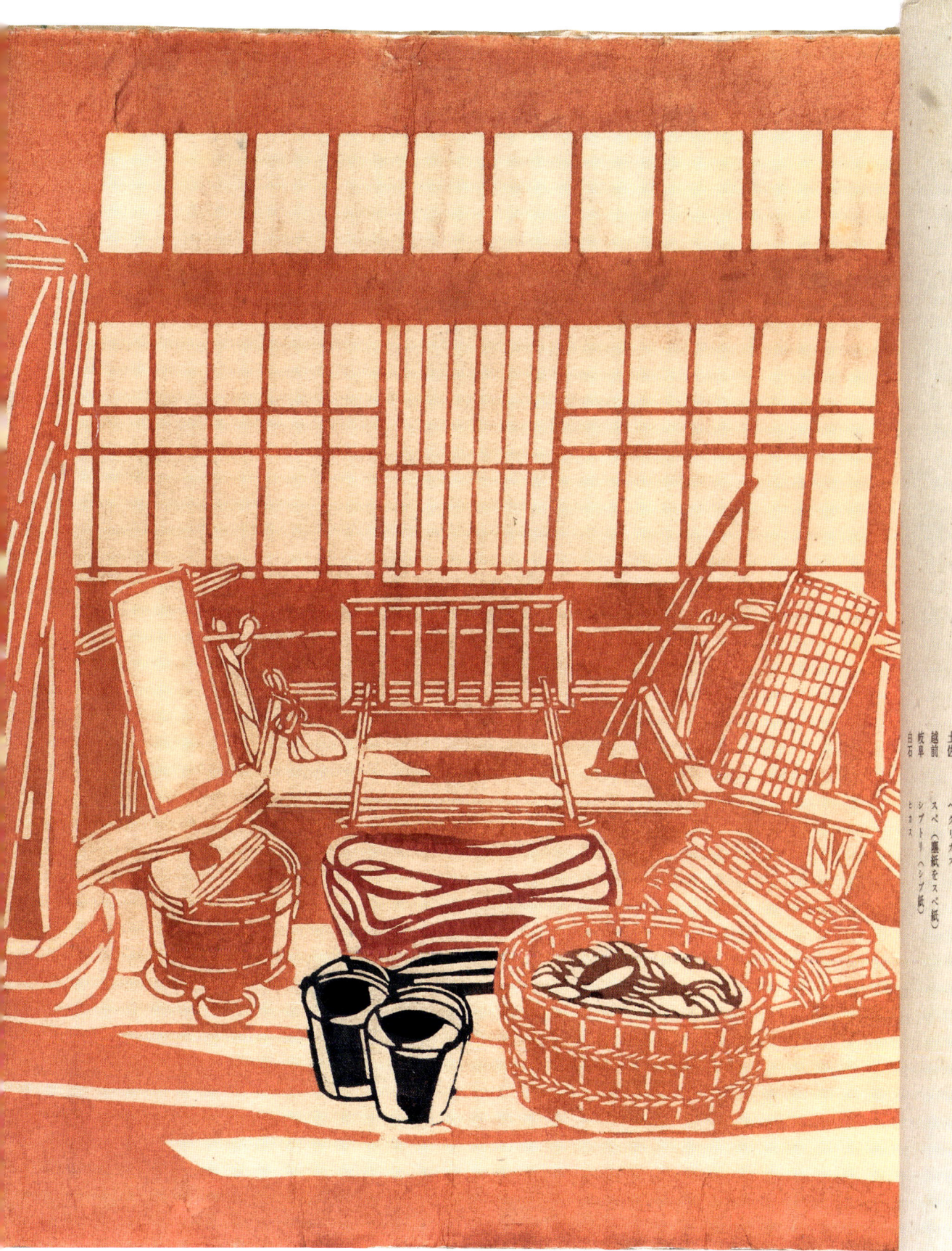

塵紙の製法は打楮（日本の紙・東日本館）玉彫の紙の現を透叩され
と便利です。さらに塵紙は、楮の白皮をとるためには黒皮を取り去
らなければなりません。水に浸けた黒皮をとり出し、小刀で楮の上
皮（黒皮）を剥き取ったものであって、この廃物を利用して漉いた
副産物が塵紙なのです。

楮の剥きかす、すなわち「ヒカス」は各地方により、それぞれつぎ
のような名で呼ばれています。

新潟　　　ソソカワ
島根　　　コカワ
八尾　　　ヒカワ　ヒカス
小川　　　楮カス
土佐　　　ヘグリカス
越前　　　スベ（塵紙をスベ紙）
岐阜　　　シブトヽ（シブ紙）
白石　　　ヒカス

Once the fibres have been mixed with water, making a pulp, the sheet of paper is formed using one of two different methods. The first is *tamezuki* (the accumulation method). Here the pulp is scooped up only once and then strained through the screen, producing thicker papers. Thought to have been introduced to Japan first, this method originated in China and travelled to the rest of the world from Samarkand to Fabriano and Philadelphia. When observed through transmitted light, examples of paper from the Nara period (710–794) to the Heian period (794–1185), even though they present different characteristics and technical standards, usually have a random fibre distribution. This indicates that they were made with the *tamezuki* method.

The second method is *nagashizuki* (the flowing method), which was probably developed at the Kamiyain paper mill set up by the government of Kyoto in 807. In this case, the process starts with *neri* (mucilage), a thick viscous substance obtained from the root of *Hibiscus manihot* – known as *tororo aoi* – or from the bark of the *Hydrangea paniculata* – known as *nori utsugi*. It is added to the vat to maintain the fibres in suspension and to slow the speed of drainage, which is essential when forming uniform and thin, sometimes almost transparent, sheets. The mould is dipped into the vat several times, and the pulp is scooped up and shaken repeatedly back and forth and from side to side until the sheet becomes uniform and excess solution is thrown off. At every successive dip the sheet of paper is slowly laminated, becoming thicker with a predominant fibre orientation along the chain lines, according to the fibres' flow and the screen motion at the time of papermaking.[10]

The sheets of paper are laid down on a board one after the other. The pile is progressively pressed, then each sheet is peeled off and brushed gently onto wooden boards to dry outdoors. Once the sheet is dry the side that was placed against the board will have a smooth surface with a wood-grain pattern, whilst the exposed side will be rough and may bear faint brush marks. With the increasing use of heated metal boards, the surface of the paper started to lack this quality.

The main stages of papermaking are the subject matter of *Kami o tsukuru hitotachi* by the artist Serizawa Keisuke (1895–1984), a book published in 1950 as a limited edition of fifty copies. Serizawa was part of the *Mingei* movement, which began in the 1920s to highlight the value of traditional crafts. Serizawa played a leading role in the revival of stencil dyeing (*katazome-e*), which he used in this book's six powerful illustrations. Papermaking is a recurrent theme in his work, showing his admiration for this craft while acknowledging its place in the Japanese cultural landscape.

Another figure associated with the revival of handmade Japanese paper was Gotō Seikichirō (1898–1989). Gotō practised papermaking and travelled extensively across the country to study this craft. The results of his journeys and research are described in *Kami no Tabi*, a comprehensive book with coloured stencil illustrations (*katazome-e*) and samples of Japanese paper, published in 1964 in a limited edition of 300 copies (FIG. 52).

In recent times the Japanese government has recognized the production of a number of papers as 'intangible cultural heritage' (to use UNESCO terminology), and has designated as its skill holders, or Living National Treasures, the papermakers

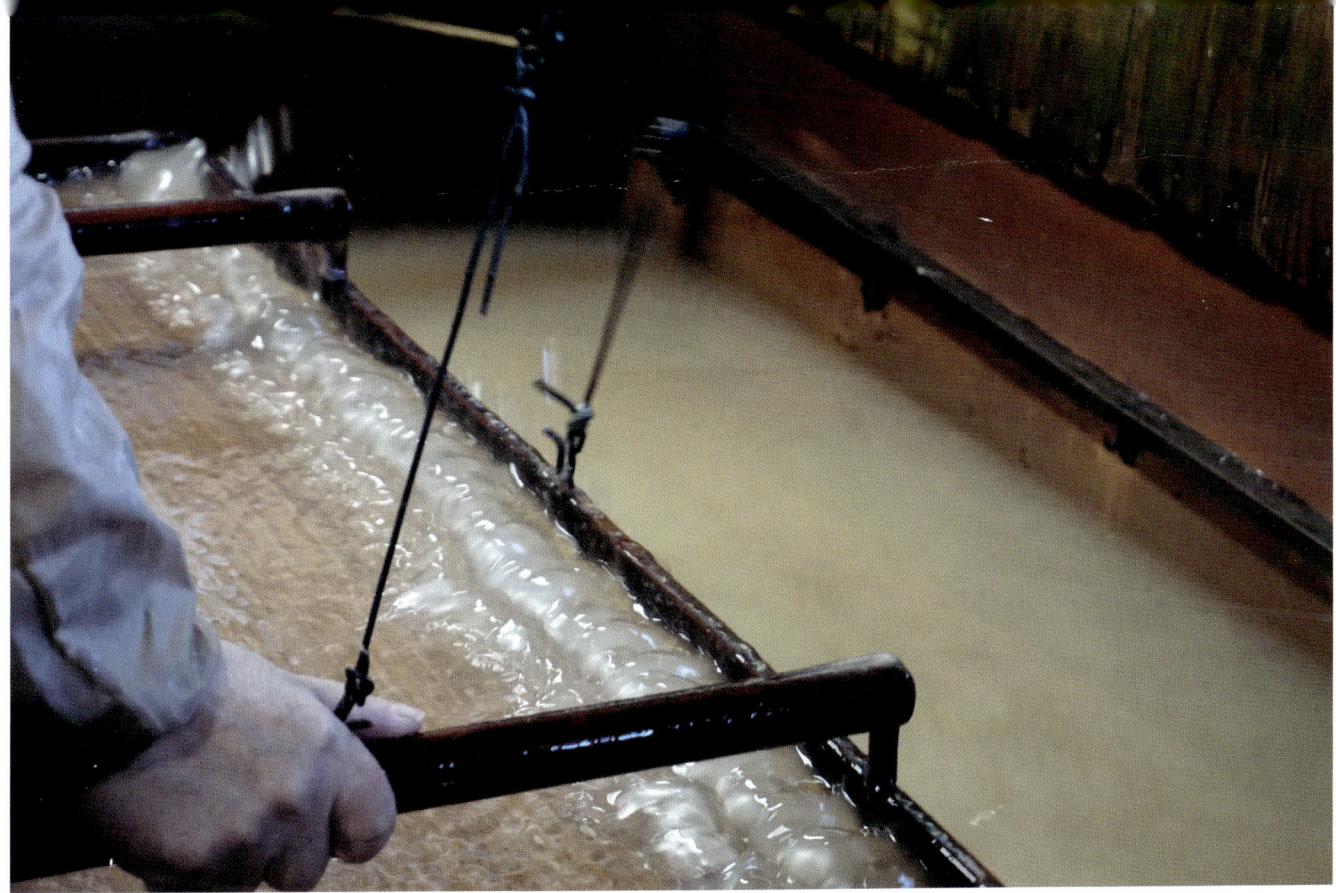

53 Papermaking at Izumo Mingeishi, Izumo, Japan, March 2023.

who have given new energy to the transmission of this craft. For example, the late Living National Treasure Abe Eishirō (1902–1984) received broad recognition for his *gampi* paper, and his mill Izumo Mingeishi in the Shimane Prefecture continues to produce paper using his methods (FIG. 53). Like Serizawa, he was also part of the *Mingei* movement,[11] creating folk art papers and bringing back the colourful *kumogami*, a cloud-patterned paper used for writing. A range of samples of Abe's *gampi* paper are included in the *Mingei* magazine *Kogei*, in a 1933 issue dedicated to the topic of *washi*.[12] Japanese hand papermaking has continued to create papers of exceptional qualities and long-term stability. In 2014 the production of *Sekishū hanshi*, *Minogami* and *Hosokawashi* has been recognized as intangible cultural heritage of humanity by UNESCO.

The appearance and properties of paper can be modified through simple treatments or elaborate processes. Burnishing or hammering the paper's surface increases the density of the sheet, giving it a smooth and glossy texture on which it is not only easier to write but ink is prevented from bleeding. A similar surface texture is obtained by coating paper with a solution of glue sizing, which reduces its porosity. Beyond these basic methods, a wide range of original techniques was developed to

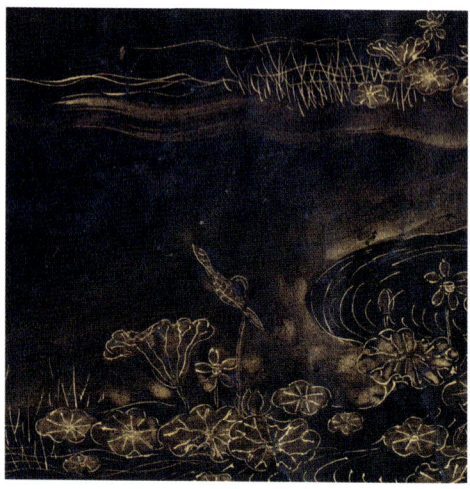
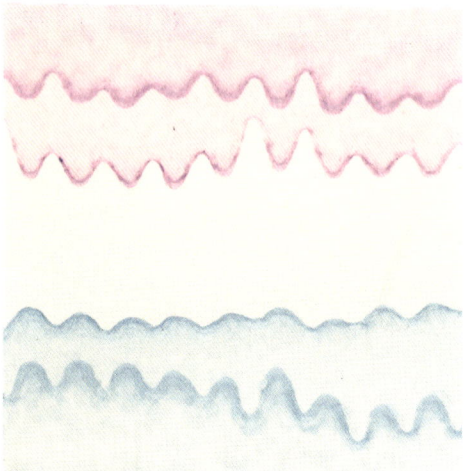
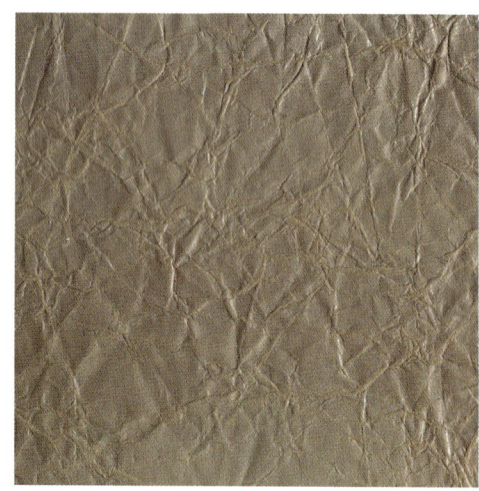

54 Details showcasing a range of techniques commonly used for dyeing and decorating paper. LEFT TO RIGHT (a) *konshi*, a paper dyed with indigo by immersion, (b) a marbled cloud-pattern paper, (c) a pattern obtained by crumpling a paper coated with paint, (d) scattered flecks of silver leaf of different shapes and sizes seen under calligraphic work, (e) a lustrous pattern obtained by rubbing gilded paper against a woodblock, (f) decorations painted in gold seen under calligraphic work. MS. Jap. d.30-50; Woudhuiysen b. 13; Nipponica 1001; MS. Jap. c.4 (R); MS. Jap. d.30-50; MS. Jap. c.8 (R).

produce attractive papers which were in demand for writing poetry, for endpapers, book covers and other applications.

Noteworthy dyeing and decorative methods can be identified across the Bodleian Japanese collection (FIG. 54). Examining these examples of paper brings to life the skills at play. Sometime the fibres are dyed before they are made into paper. Other times the paper surface is dyed by brush, either uniformly with barely visible brush strokes or with prominent brush strokes obtained with dented brushes, which are deliberately used to form simple patterns from stripes to grids. Paper can also be dyed by blowing colours on it, or by immersing the paper sheets in a dye solution. A typical example of the last practice is *konshi*, a strong and durable dark indigo blue paper, produced since the Heian period for copying sutras with gold ink (FIG. 54a). Through a sequence of carefully timed immersions in the indigo dye, the paper reaches the desired shade. After being rinsed and dried it can be coated with a mixture of alum and glue sizing, or beaten with a mallet or polished with a shell to give it a smooth and glossy surface. Further dyeing methods include stencil dyeing and *suminagashi*, a marbling technique where patterns formed by ink flowing on water are transferred onto fine papers such as *hōsho* or *torinoko*.

More intricate techniques are found adorning papers used for calligraphy and copying.

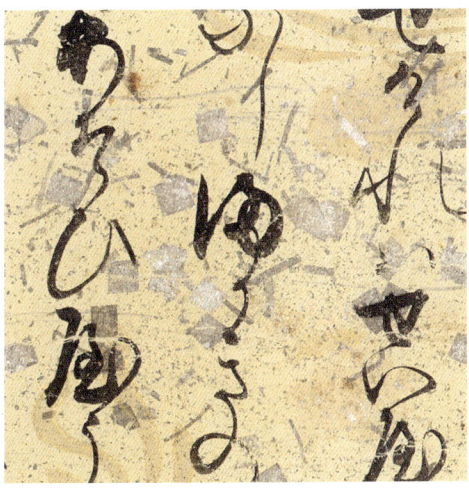
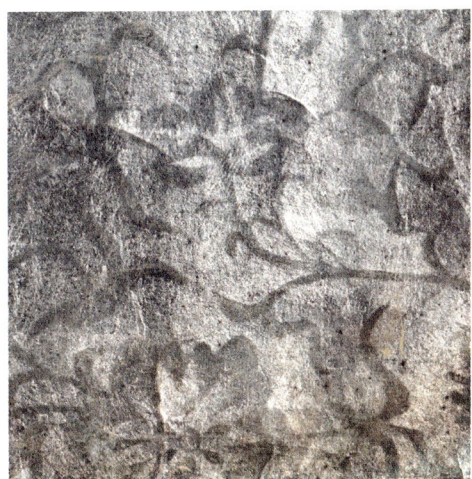
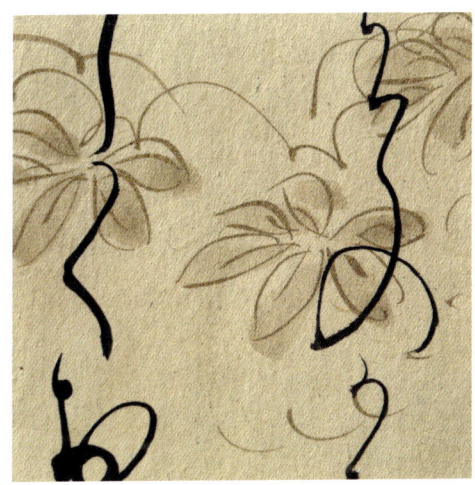

Distinctive patterns were obtained by adding dyed fibres to a newly formed sheet in many ways. Fibres coloured mostly in indigo or purple were laid at the top and bottom of a newly formed sheet of paper, or tossed onto it to form cloud patterns. A marbled cloud design was obtained by dipping the bottom edge of the mould with a newly formed sheet of paper into a vat of coloured fibres, and repeating this process several times (FIG. 54b). A pattern resembling drops of water was the result of flicking a leaf dipped into water over a wet sheet of paper; the drops form shallow holes on the sheet just deep enough to create a decoration.

Wrinkled papers were also in demand, ranging from *momigami* (a thick, good-quality *kōzo* paper repeatedly crumpled by hand) to paper coated with opaque pigments and crumpled to obtain a crackle design, used primarily as covers for books (FIG. 4.9c). The aforementioned *danshi* is a paper with a finely wrinkled surface, with the thickest being the most wrinkled to the thinnest having slight creases, made by pressing a number of wet *kōzo* papers on top of one another and then lifting them together at an acute angle while still slightly wet.

Precious metals were added to make elegant papers with shimmering effects. Gold and silver, transformed into powder, flakes or thin square leaves, were respectively sprinkled, scattered or applied to paper prepared with glue (FIG. 54d). Paper was coated with a layer of paint made with either mica or *gofun*, a white pigment from oyster shells, often mixed with other pigments to create muted colours. Gilded or coloured papers were at times further decorated using wood blocks either to print or emboss patterns. Extraordinary lustrous patterns were realized by rubbing gilded or coloured papers against carved woodblocks with an animal tusk (FIG. 54e). The paper used to write or cover luxury books was often decorated with motifs such as birds and plants painted in gold and silver (FIG. 54f). The ways to embellish paper through colours and textures were countless.[13]

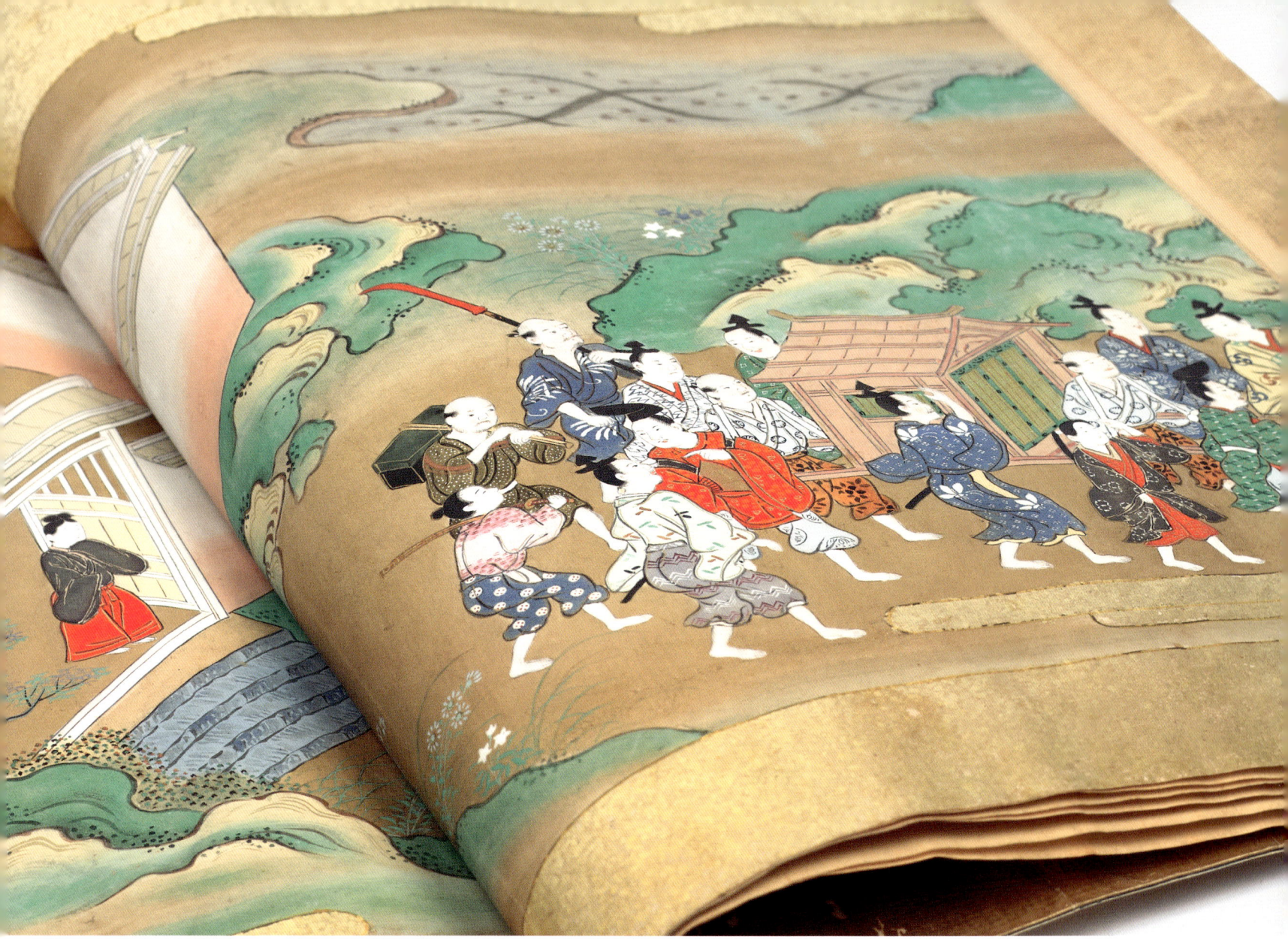

55 A page from *The Tale of Akimichi*, eighteenth-century manuscript. The pigments identified here are: carbon for the black, smalt or indigo for the blue, vermilion for the red, red lead for the orange, *gofun* for the white, malachite for the green, organic red mixed with *gofun* for the pink, and others. A delicate layer of gold paint has been applied over the ground, whilst the clouds in the foreground are executed with scattered flecks of gold leaf. MS. Jap. d. 65.

## COLOUR AND LUSTRE

Colours are created by transforming raw ingredients into paint. They have either been extracted from natural sources – from roots to flowers, from insects to sea shells, from precious minerals to natural earths – or have been artificially made, and occasionally discovered by chance, during scientific experiments. The introduction and use of pigments in Japan is described in early chronicles such as the *Nihon shoki*, the aforementioned history of Japan written in the eighth century where facts and mythology merge. Historical records indicate that most pigments were made in Japan, but they were also procured from China and later Europe.[14]

Any desired colour can be obtained with a wide range of rare or familiar pigments (FIG. 55). It can be the result of a single unadulterated pigment, or of mixtures of pigments. For example, blue indigo and gamboge were combined to make green. More intriguingly, pigments of the same colour, such as indigo and Prussian blue, were mixed to obtain the right hue of blue or for economic reasons. Colours that look very similar to the eye can be obtained using very different ingredients – the only way to know their composition with certainty is by scientific investigation. In recent years, the development of scientific methods to identify pigments with great accuracy has provided information of invaluable assistance to the study of pigments found in Japanese books. Complementary analysis has helped to ascertain the artists' preferences or simply what was available to them when creating the work, as well as to establish whether any colour alteration has occurred over time since the work's execution. The results of the analysis are often the only resource, as historical records illustrating the use of colours are scarce or inadequate to provide an accurate overview of pigments used at a specific time and place. Selected areas of the paint layer from books in the Bodleian Japanese collection have been analysed to illustrate the characteristics of most of the pigments described below.[15]

The quality of the raw materials sourced, the method perfected to create the pigment, as well as the dimension and shape of the pigment's particles, all determine the appearance and ultimately stability of the paint layer. For example, a paint with fine pigment particles penetrates through the fibres of the paper substrate and tends to be far more stable than one with coarse particles. Even though pigments are the main components of the paint layer, there are other factors which play a significant part in its appearance and stability, such as the amount of binder present, the mode of application, the type of paper support and how the paint penetrates into it.

The colour red is obtained from a variety of inorganic and organic materials (FIG. 56). Mellow red pigments, varying in hues and shades, have been made by grinding and refining natural earths coloured by iron oxide. A vigorous red is reached with vermilion obtained directly from the mineral cinnabar, or by recombining artificially, at a high temperature, cinnabar's main constituent elements – mercury and sulphur. However, within the pages of a book this pigment can darken and reconvert into the black form of mercuric sulphide. Even though deposits of cinnabar are found across Japan, the best vermilion was imported from China. Another source of inorganic red was red lead. Made by heating lead white pigment or metallic

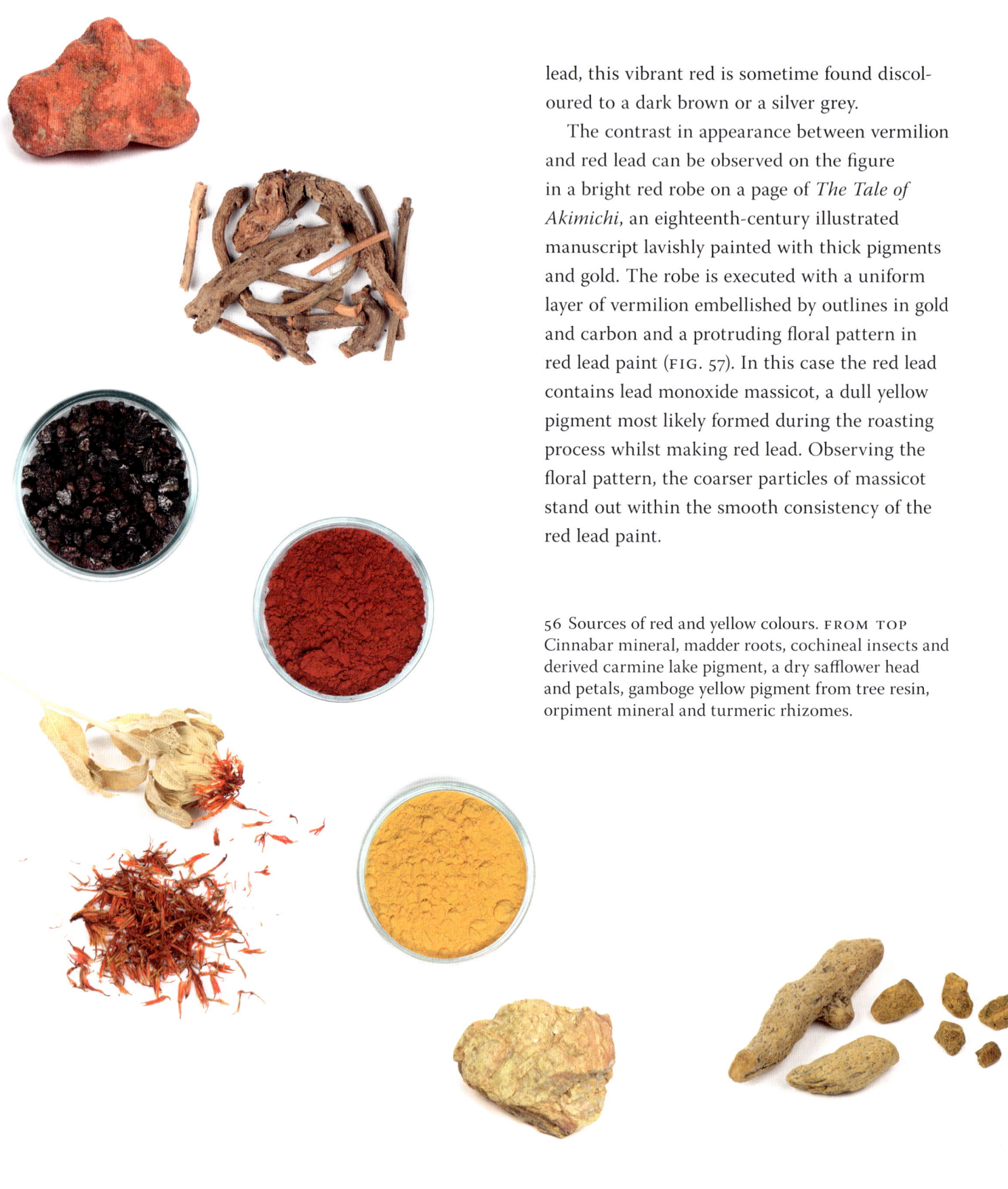

lead, this vibrant red is sometime found discoloured to a dark brown or a silver grey.

The contrast in appearance between vermilion and red lead can be observed on the figure in a bright red robe on a page of *The Tale of Akimichi*, an eighteenth-century illustrated manuscript lavishly painted with thick pigments and gold. The robe is executed with a uniform layer of vermilion embellished by outlines in gold and carbon and a protruding floral pattern in red lead paint (FIG. 57). In this case the red lead contains lead monoxide massicot, a dull yellow pigment most likely formed during the roasting process whilst making red lead. Observing the floral pattern, the coarser particles of massicot stand out within the smooth consistency of the red lead paint.

56 Sources of red and yellow colours. FROM TOP Cinnabar mineral, madder roots, cochineal insects and derived carmine lake pigment, a dry safflower head and petals, gamboge yellow pigment from tree resin, orpiment mineral and turmeric rhizomes.

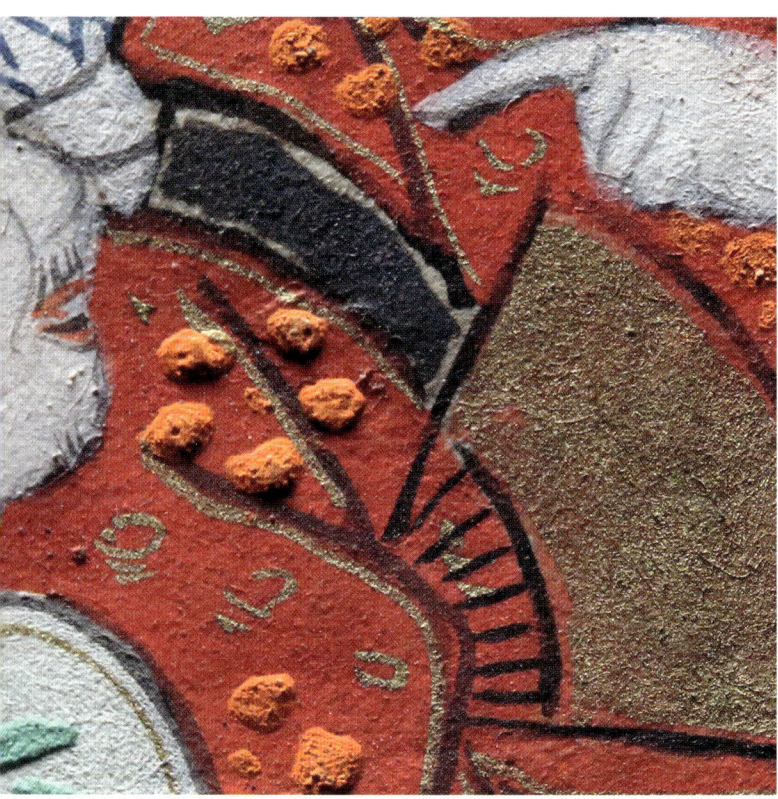

57 (& PAGE 126) Detail from *The Tale of Akimichi*, eighteenth-century manuscript. The robe is painted in vermilion, while the protruding flower pattern is executed in red lead containing massicot, a dull yellow pigment. MS. Jap. d. 65.

A diversity of rich reds derives from organic sources. Vast amounts of petals from the bright orange flowers of the safflower (*Carthamus tinctorius L.*) are collected, dried and crushed to create expensive reds. First the petals are rinsed with water to remove the yellow colorant, then they are treated with a solution of alkaline ash to extract the red colorant carthamin, and finally an acid is added to precipitate the colorant into a beautiful red powder. An important region of production of safflower in Japan is the Mogami River valley

of Yamagata Prefecture. Other organic sources of red are concealed in the roots of Japanese madder (*Rubia akane Nakai*), and the following two scale insects known since the late Edo period: the lac insect (*Laccifer lacca*), imported from India and Southeast Asia, which produces a resinous pigment; and the desiccated bodies of the female cochineal (*Dactylopius coccus*), native to Mesoamerica and yielding carmine. Carmine was first imported into Europe in the sixteenth century, later reaching China and Japan. Its crimson red colour was a suitable alternative to safflower red, and by 1869 it had largely replaced it, having become readily available at increasingly lower costs. Analysis shows that reds are often the result of admixtures containing any of these red pigments.

In Europe, besides the traditional sources of red, an astounding range of red and violet dyes were synthetized from coal tar, following the accidental invention of mauve in 1856. These bright 'aniline colours' were gradually introduced to the Japanese market, probably by foreign merchants in Yokohama. Their use coexisted with most of the traditional colorants of the late Edo period, with the exception of safflower and dayflower blue, both of which proved unstable and prone to fading.[16] These modern synthetic colours were transforming the artist's palette not only in Japan but across the world.

An important source of yellow colour is a toxic and glittery pigment obtained by grinding orpiment, an arsenic sulphide mineral occurring most commonly near hot spring sites. During the late Edo period and the early Meiji period, synthetic arsenic sulphide pigments were most likely manufactured in Japan and, probably due

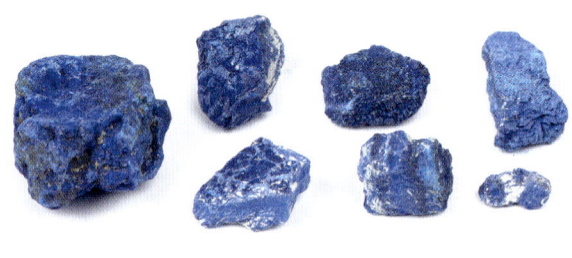

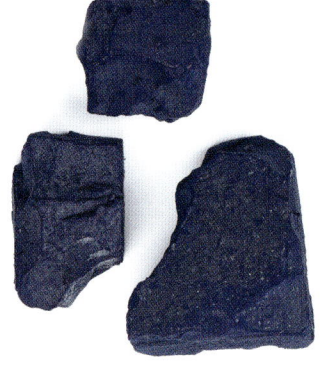

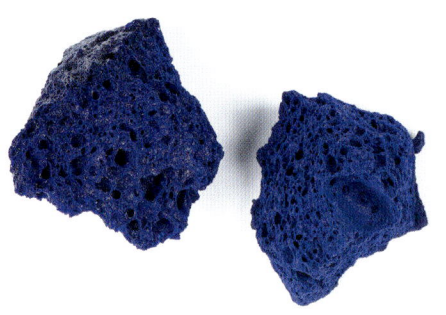

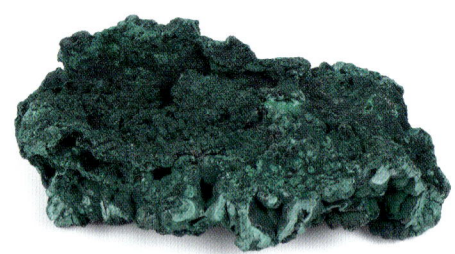

to their low price and easy availability, were commonly used in woodblock printing or for book covers.[17] Other sources of bright yellow are the following two pigments: turmeric, obtained from the orange-yellow rhizomes of the plant *Curcuma longa L.*, which is cultivated in most tropical and subtropical countries, and gamboge, an imported gum resin obtained from the trees of the *Garcinia* species growing throughout South and Southeast Asia. The latex exuding from incisions in the bark of these trees solidifies in brittle lumps, which give a transparent golden colour. Occasionally, natural yellow earths are also used.

The predominant source of green is the pigment from the semi-precious stone malachite, a basic copper carbonate found in several locations in Japan (FIG. 58). Like most mineral pigments it is prepared by pounding, grinding, sieving, washing

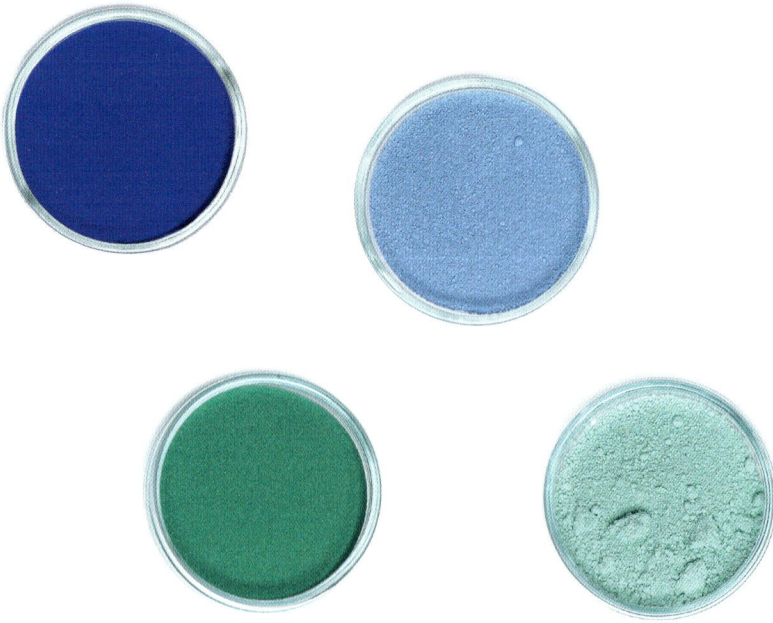

58 Sources of blue and green colours. FROM TOP Lumps of azurite mineral, pressed indigo cakes, artificially made smalt, malachite mineral, coarsely and finely ground azurite pigment, coarsely and finely ground malachite pigment.

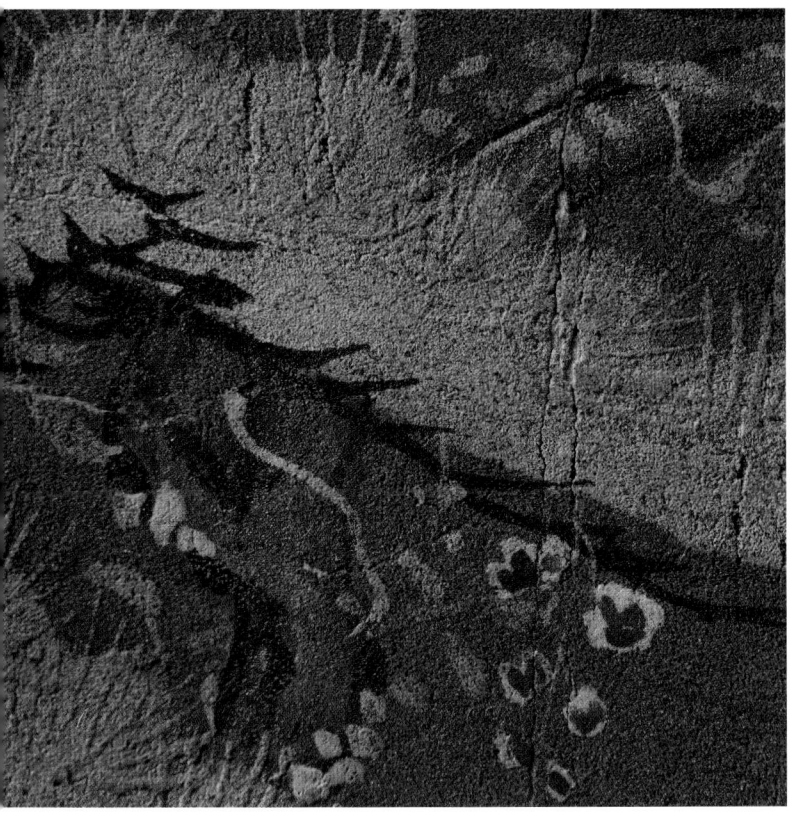

59 Detail from *The Legend of Urashima Tarō*, seventeenth-century painted handscroll. Both the azurite used to paint the river and the malachite used for the Japanese pines have a granular texture. The coarseness of these two pigments complements the sheen of the red flowers, painted in an organic red glaze of fine particles. MS. Jap. c.4 (R).

away any impurities, and grading. During the last process, also known as 'levigation', the ground pigment is dispersed in water with the larger heavier particles settling first and the finest remaining in suspension the longest. In this way the pigment can be separated by particle size, from coarser to finer grades, obtaining different textures and a variety of shades – the more finely ground

material being lighter in colour. Malachite, as with other copper-based pigments, is a well-known cause of degradation and brown discolouration of the paper substrate. Other common greens are obtained, as mentioned, by mixing indigo blue and yellow pigments.

A familiar blue colour is prepared from selected lumps of the basic copper carbonate mineral azurite in the same way as malachite – by grinding, washing and levigation. Coarsely ground azurite gives a dark blue whilst the lighter shades are obtained by the finely ground pigment. Azurite is found in deposits across Japan together with malachite. The painted panels in *The Legend of Urashima Tarō* (FIG. 59) make abundant use of various grades of azurite from dark to light blue, which complement the grades of malachite.

The petals of the Asiatic dayflower (*Commelina communis*) yield a moisture-sensitive blue. This rare colourant is stored in the form of dyed pieces of paper.[18] Another organic source of blue, with far-reaching applications, is indigo. It is obtained from several species of plants, of which dyer's knotweed (*Persicaria tinctoria*) is indigenous to Japan. As attested by objects amongst the thousands of artefacts stored in the *Shōsōin* repository, it was used in Japan at least from the eighth century. Since the Edo period or earlier, the area around the stream of the Yoshino River and the town of Mima, in the Tokushima Prefecture of Shikoku Island, has been an important centre of indigo production. Today only a small number of traditional workshops still remain. The leaves of the indigo plant are treated with a protracted fermentation process by keeping them wet in large heaps and regularly turning them over. The fermented material is mixed with alkaline ash for further fermentation, and after three months the indigo colourant is ready.

An artificially made blue pigment derives from coarsely ground smalt, a potassium-rich glass, coloured blue by the incorporation of cobalt oxide during manufacture. A modern synthetic source of deep blue is Prussian blue, which was inadvertently discovered in Berlin in 1704. This ferric ferrocyanide blue spread rapidly throughout the world. Imported by Dutch and Chinese traders, it was increasingly available in Japan after the 1820s when it started to become a dominant colour for Japanese woodblock printing.[19]

The main source of black is *sumi*, a carbon ink composed of fine soot and animal glue. Two kinds of carbon black ink have been produced: one made from burning pinewood, and the other from burning vegetable oil. The latter has been produced for centuries in various workshops, many of which were located in the Nara area. In sheltered rooms workers tend earthenware pots burning vegetable oil, and remove the soot that forms on the lids (FIG. 60). The soot is then kneaded together with animal glue and fragrant spices and essences, and pressed into decorative wood moulds. The solid ink is gradually dried over many months, first in wood ash and then hanging indoors (FIG. 61). Finally, it is washed, coated with glaze, scorched with charcoal, polished with a clam shell, and decorated. Carbon black is a ubiquitous pigment found in books, prints and paintings. *Ukiyo-e* artists used this pigment of very fine particles for the rendition of

60 Earthenware pots burning vegetable oil, to generate soot on the pot lids from which ink sticks are made. Kobaien Nara, Japan, March 2023.

61 Ink sticks hanging indoors to dry. Kobaien, Nara, Japan, March 2023.

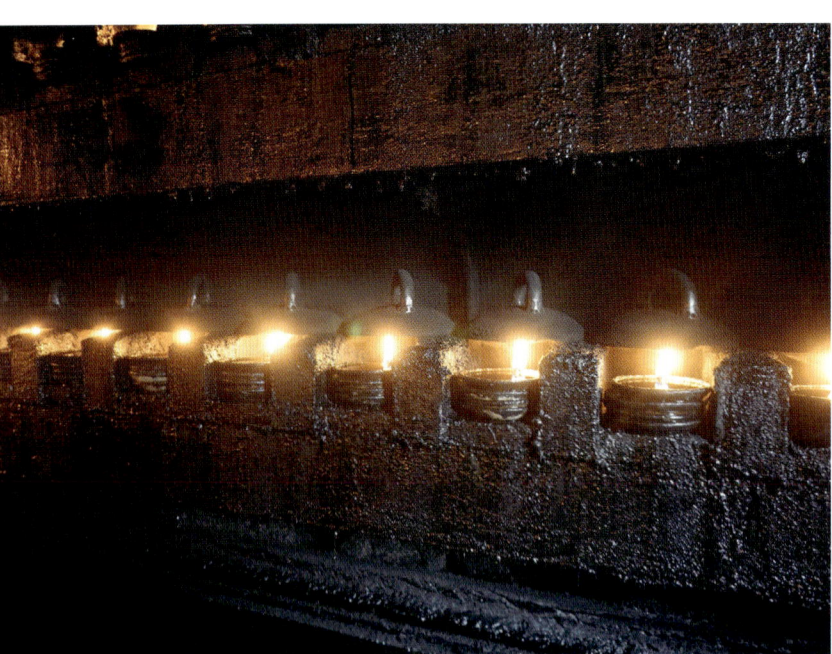

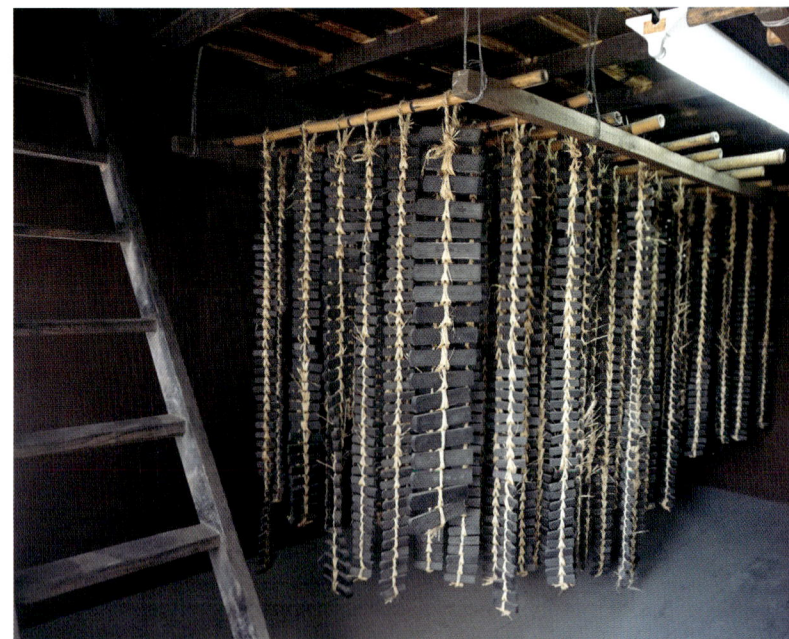

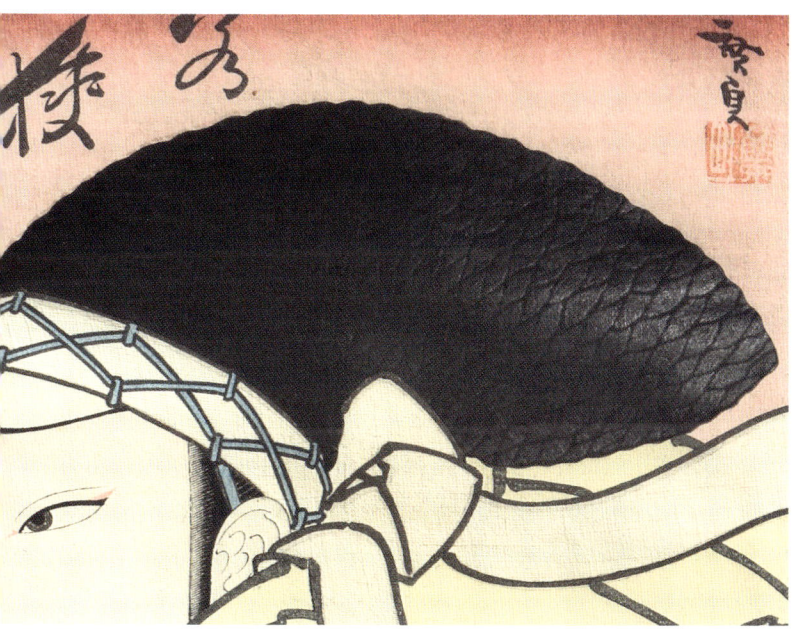

62 Detail from an album of *ukiyo-e* prints, Nipponica 372. The thick paper substrate, with its smooth surface, is possibly *hōsho*. Special woodblocks were prepared to emboss the paper. This technique, known as 'blind printing', was used to create three-dimensional effects, which here emphasize the actor's hairstyle, forehead and woven headband. A special block was also employed to polish the carbon black paint layer of the hairstyle to obtain the juxtaposition of a matt and glossy finish.

delicate details, or for staggering effects such as in this image from an album of prints, Nipponica 372 (FIG. 62).

Early sources of white colour are white clay and the noxious lead-based whites. The conventional lead white pigment is artificially made by exposing metallic lead to acetic acid vapour, produced by heating up vinegar over a fire. The white coating formed over the metal is then removed and reduced

to fine particles by levigation. Another source of white is *gofun*, a pigment made of crushed oyster shells. The shells are gathered in piles and left outdoors to break down for a protracted period of time – up to fifteen years can elapse to obtain the best quality. Afterwards the shells are reduced to fine calcium carbonate particles by the usual process of washing, grinding and levigation. From the sixteenth century onwards, *gofun* became the predominant white and an important constituent of pigment mixtures to obtain lighter colour tones. It can create a smooth layer ideal to delineate the minute details of a face (FIG. 63). However, this pigment tends to flake off over time, since it forms a thick layer that does not penetrate well into the paper substrate.

Sources of various colours, from mica to precious metals, are used to impart lustre to the book. Mica includes a number of silicate minerals, of which the white muscovite is predominantly used in Japan – when ground into a pigment, it creates subtle glittering effects. Gold, found in mines in mountain regions or in alluvial sediments such as the ones of Mutsu Province at the northern end of Honshu, can be easily hammered between sheets of paper until it is transformed into very thin leaves. Leaves of gold, or silver, can in turn be ground into pigment or be applied in whole squares, cut strips, scattered flecks or sprinkled powder, enlivening the surface of the book and gleaming in the light. Copper, silver or colourants are sometimes added to gold to create a variety of tones. Gold can also be polished to obtain various degrees of brightness, with beautiful results. The cover of the Bodleian's copy of *The Tale of Akimichi* makes the most of the shimmering effects of different tones of gold,

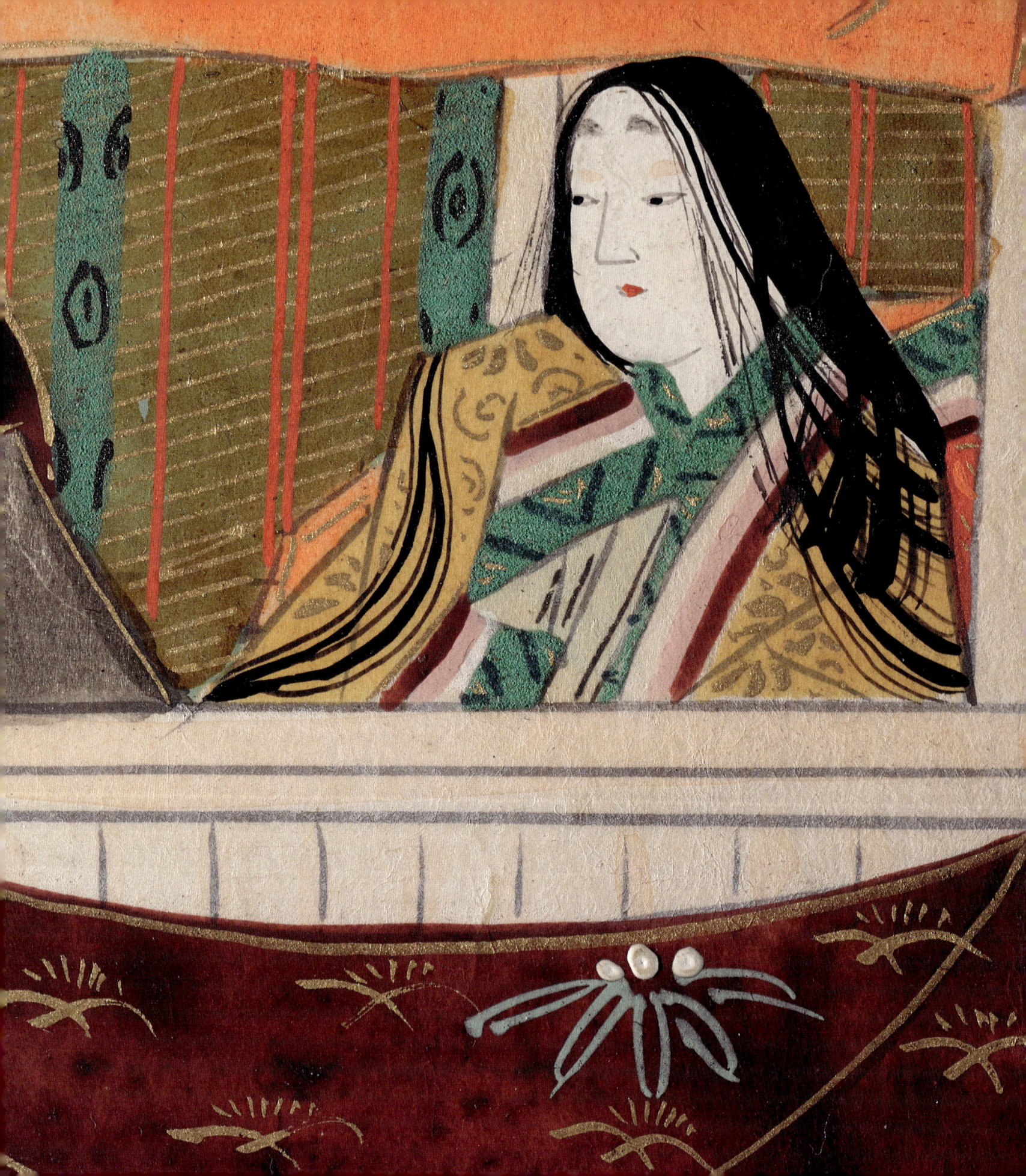

used as paint, sprinkled powder and scattered flecks on *konshi*, the durable dark indigo blue paper described earlier in this chapter (FIG. 65). Silver, whether in leaf form or flecks, soon loses part of its original shine, often appearing tarnished as a dark grey colour. This deterioration effect derives from its sensitivity when exposed to atmospheric contaminants.

Any of the colorants above, whether from traditional sources or newly discovered, require a binder to turn them into usable paint. In Japan the customary binder is *nikawa*, a glue made from various animal tissues, mostly skin. The skins are generally sprinkled with lime and kept in piles for a period of time before being washed and cooked in hot water for several hours, at increasing temperatures. This protein solution is then cooled in trays, and cut up and dried into a glassy solid amber product. When needed as a binder, it is dissolved in hot water.

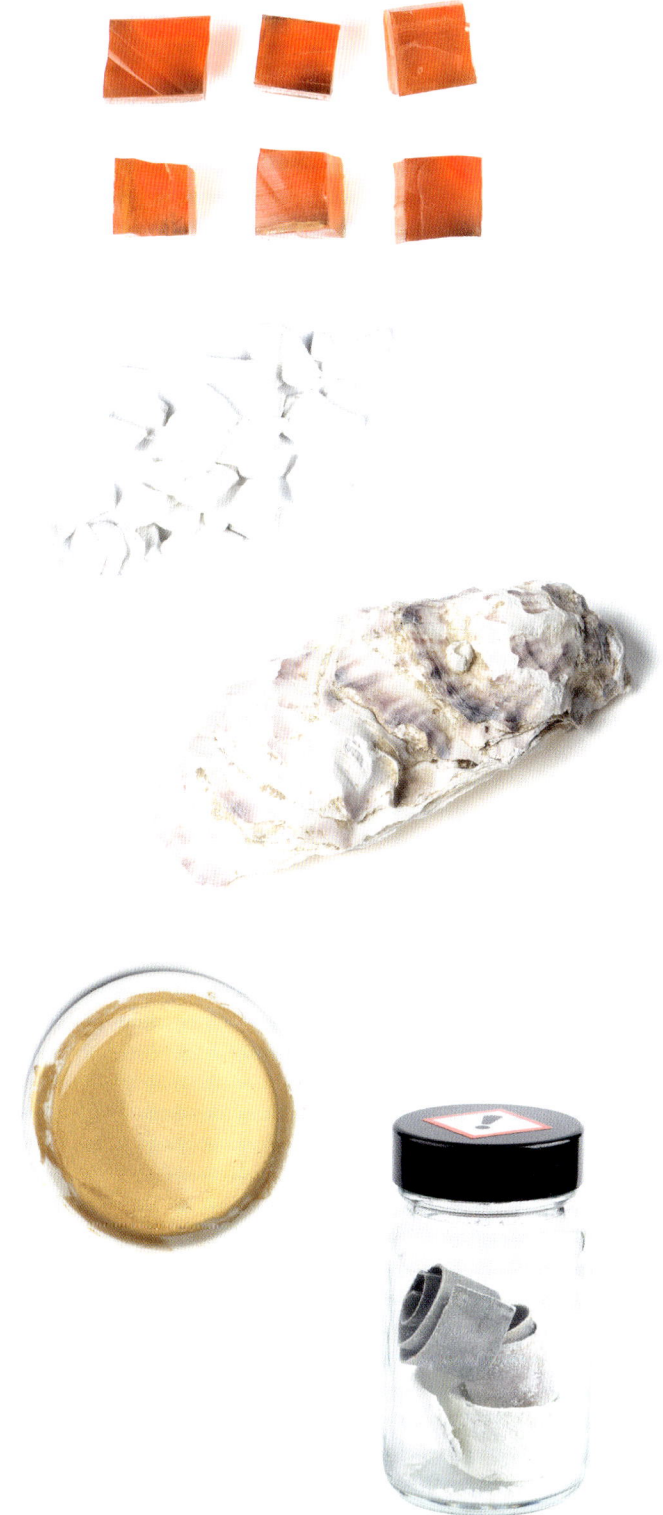

63 Detail from *Sumiyoshi Monogatari*, seventeenth-century painted handscroll. The face has been painted with *gofun*, a white pigment made of crushed oyster shell. Its typically smooth texture contrasts with the coarsely ground malachite pigment used for the green collar of the kimono. MS. Jap. c.8.

64 FROM TOP Cubes of dry *nikawa* glue from animal tissue traditionally mixed with pigments as a binder, white *gofun* pigment from oyster shell, gold pigment and white lead pigment from coils of lead metal.

A solution of glue and alum is generally used to coat the paper in order to create a surface suitable for painting. Another adhesive is rice paste, made by heating up rice flour and water. It is primarily used in woodblock printing as a colour thickener to help transfer the colour from the block to the paper without any colour bleeding. A different paste, made with wheat starch rather than rice, is commonly used for attaching backing paper and joining together separate parts of the book, whether in scroll or bound format.

## UNDERSTANDING THE JAPANESE BOOK

Looking at the materials and the practical skills that lay behind the making of Japanese books has many benefits. It widens the ways in which this type of collection can be studied and interpreted, it helps to find suitable conservation treatments and long-term preservation strategies, and it shows the part played by the makers, a story often neglected. Acknowledging the craftsmanship present in Japanese books requires shifting the focus to the papermakers at work with the mould in their hands, to the ink makers, mixing soot with gelatine and aromatic spices, to the alchemist and later the chemist, creating colours with unassuming ingredients – and the list goes on.

65 (& PAGE 124) Detail from *The Tale of Akimichi*, eighteenth-century manuscript. The shimmering gold effects are emphasized against the dark and glossy indigo of the *konshi* paper. The flowers and leaves are painted with a warm tone of gold; the sprinkled decorations are in a cooler tone. MS. Jap. d. 65.

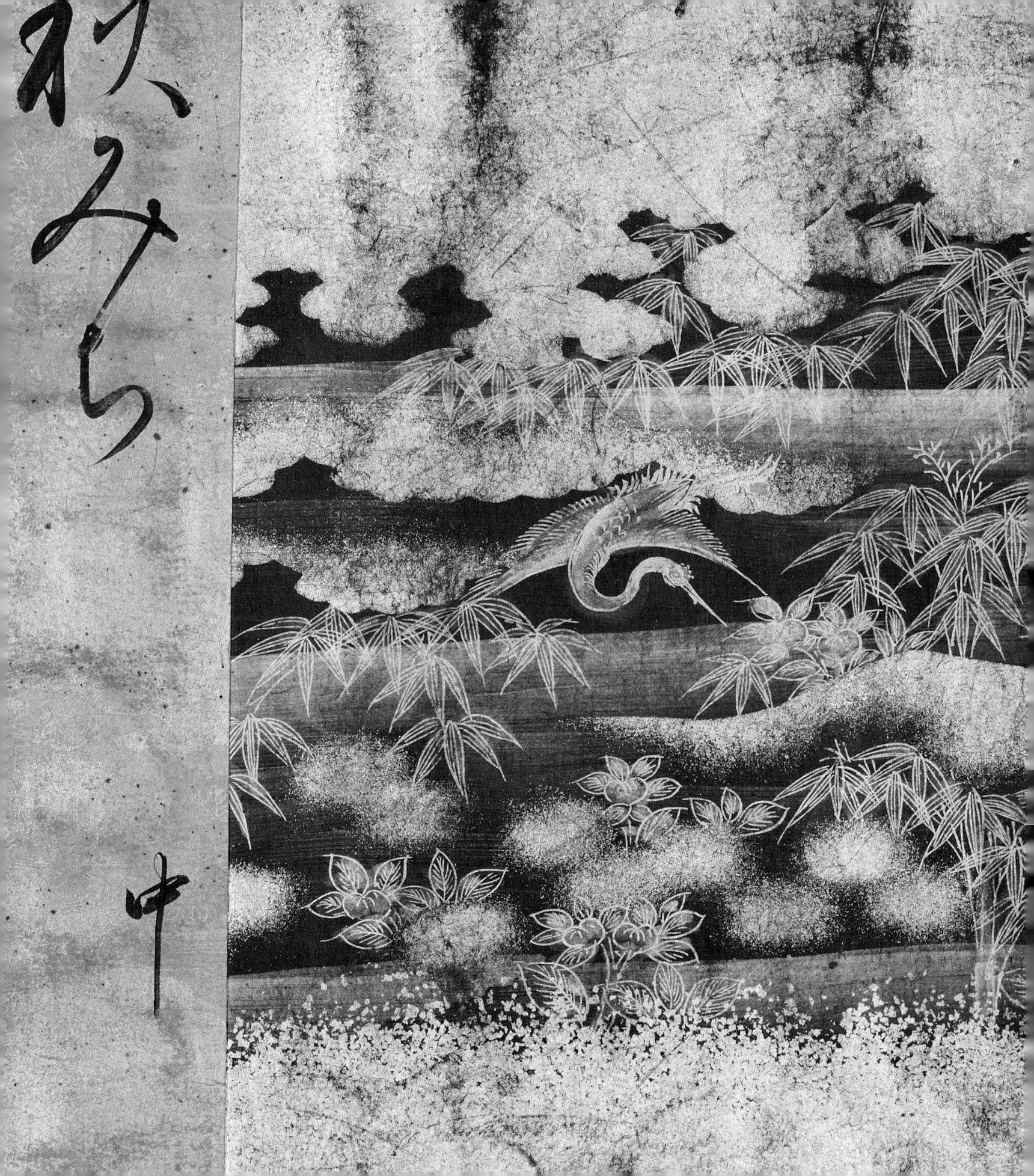

初みら

叶

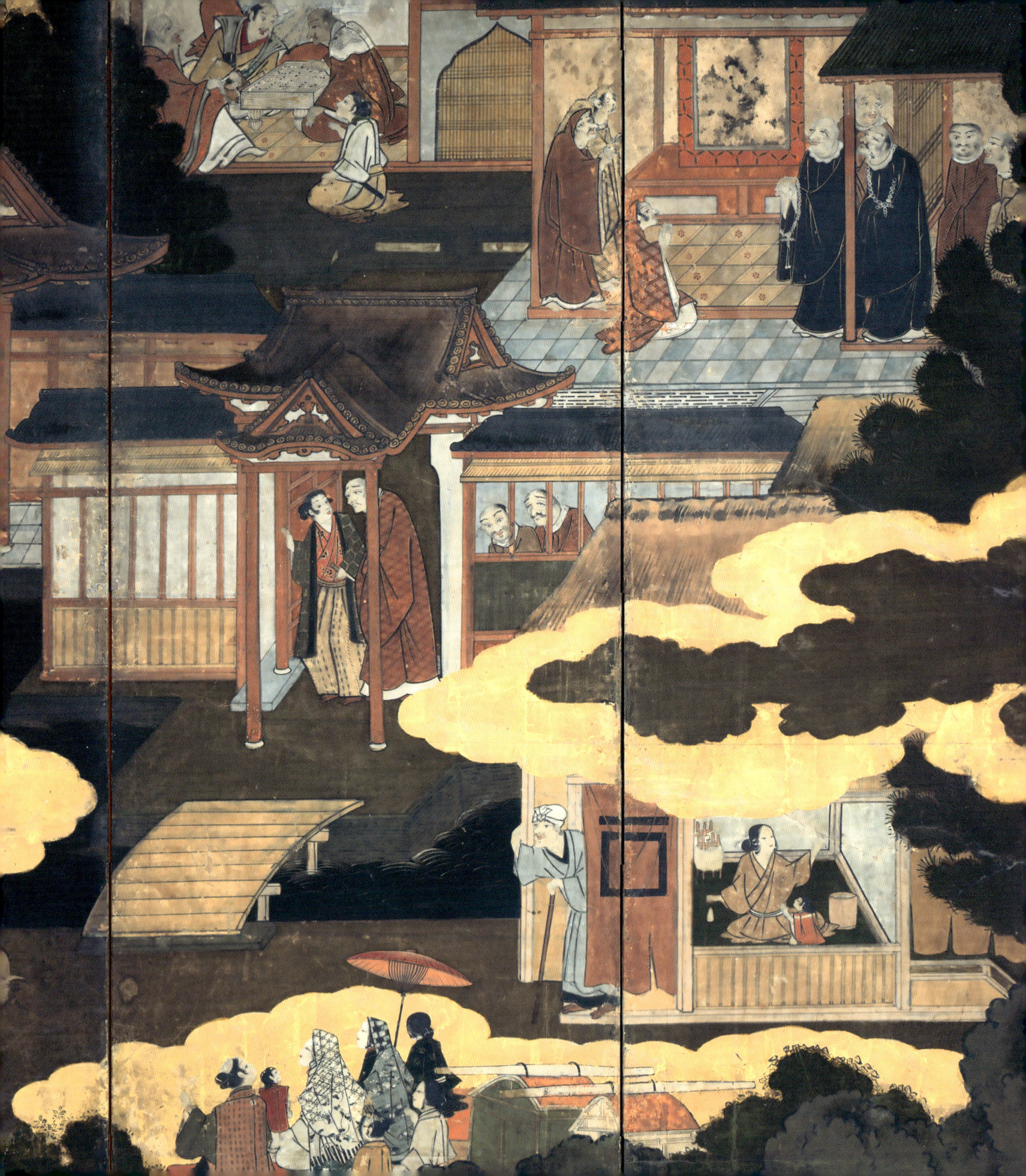

# 5

# Typography and
# Jesuit mission prints

## KATJA TRIPLETT

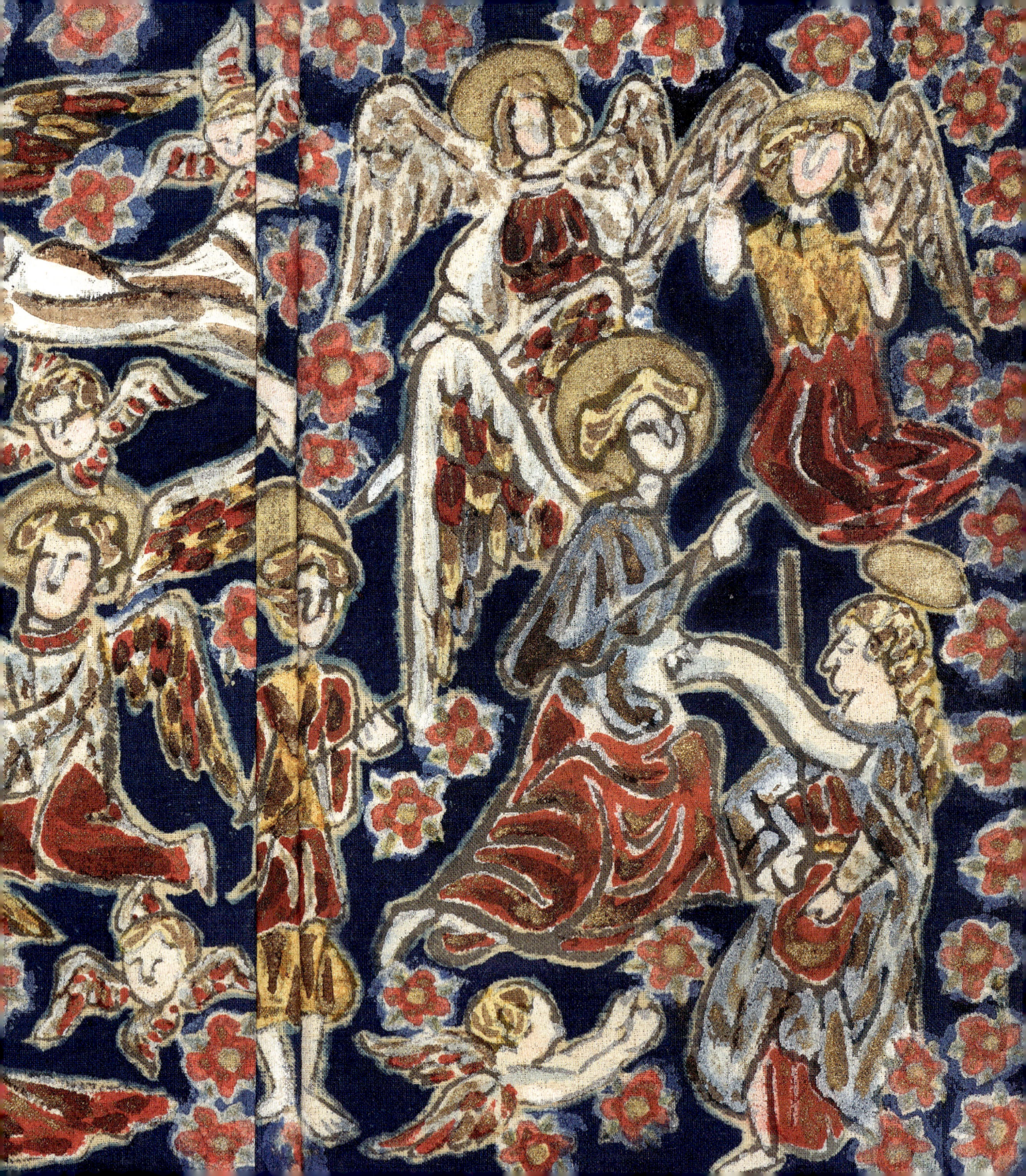

B Y THE TIME the modern Japanese artist Kawakami Sumio (1895–1972) published his charming book of woodcuts entitled *Haraiso* (*Paradise*) in 1951, the presence of a Christian tradition in Japan was almost four hundred years old. Kawakami's *Haraiso*, written entirely in Japanese but printed in Roman letters, is reminiscent of a much earlier tradition of printing Christian works in Japan. We know today that the Jesuits and their teams printed about forty-one different works during the early Jesuit mission, from 1590 to 1614. Their print-runs often amounted to several thousand.

## THE EMERGENCE OF CHRISTIAN BOOK CULTURE IN JAPAN

While Kawakami printed his *Haraiso* using woodblocks, into which he had carved images and texts, the Jesuits printed their early books on a European printing press, which they had laboriously shipped from Portugal via Goa in India and Macao in China. These two harbour towns in Asia were the location of important Portuguese enclaves for trade and the Catholic mission.[1]

The press was considered at the time to be the pinnacle of printing technology in Renaissance Europe. It was responsible for the first ever printed books using movable type in Japan, and served the Counter-Reformation for at least thirty years. When the Japanese government started to systematically implement their prohibition of the Christian mission in Japan in 1614, the press was moved back to Macao. Nearly all materials and books from that press were destroyed, such that only about ninety printed books are known to exist today, most of them in overseas collections. Given the extreme rarity of Japanese Jesuit mission printed books, the Bodleian Library's collection of six so-called *Kirishitan-ban* (Christian books) is of supreme importance for scholarship and religion alike (FIG. 68).

The title of Kawakami's book of woodcuts, *Haraiso*, derives from the Portuguese word for paradise; similarly the term *Kirishitan* links back to the Portuguese *cristaõ*, meaning Christianity or Christian.[2] During the period of persecution and suppression of Christianity in Japan, *Kirishitan* people were regarded as dangerous, and thus the

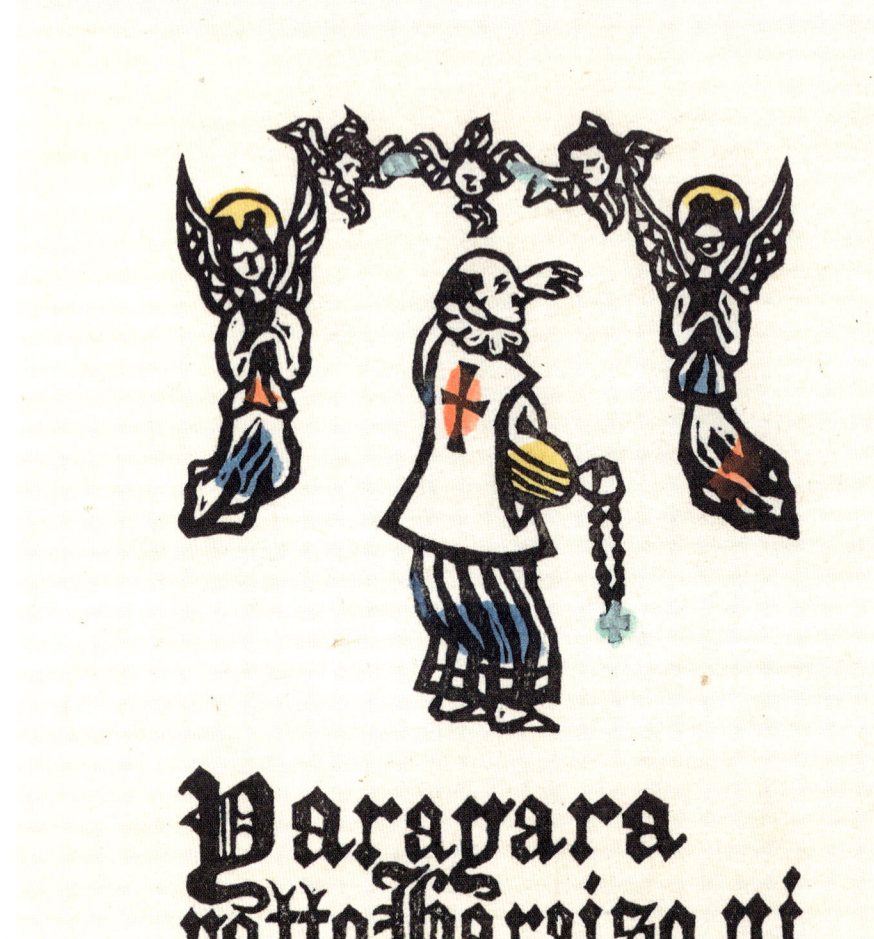

**Yarayara patto Haraiso ni tsuki marashita. Haraiso no Mon wa Hari no Ana no goto karu ya.**

expression developed a pejorative meaning. Still, many *Kirishitan* individuals and families continued to practise their faith in secret, and passed on, at least orally, the prayers they had learned from the missionaries. They continued to baptize their children covertly, and to celebrate Holy Mass. The Japanese government must have been acutely aware of hidden *Kirishitan*, as attested to by the confiscations of Christian books and arrests of suspected Christians during the centuries following the end of the mission. The existence of this underground Christian community in Japan was unknown in Europe, however. When the French priest and missionary Bernard Petitjean (1829–1865) oversaw the building of a church in Nagasaki, just after the end of the government's seclusion policy, he was amazed to find himself approached by a number of *Kirishitan* from the area. They were descendants of Catholics from the sixteenth and early seventeenth centuries. He wrote in a letter to the superior of the Japanese mission:

> Urged no doubt by my guardian angel, I went up and opened the door. I had scarce time to say a Pater when three women between fifty and sixty years of age knelt down beside me and said in a low voice, placing their hands upon their hearts: 'The hearts of all of us here do not differ from yours.'[3]

67 (& PAGE 154) Detail of a folding screen, first quarter of the seventeenth century. Japan, ink, colour, gold and gold leaf on paper. In the upper right-hand corner, Jesuits and Franciscans greet the ship's captain and members of his crew in the main hall of a Christian church. Metropolitan Museum of Art, New York.

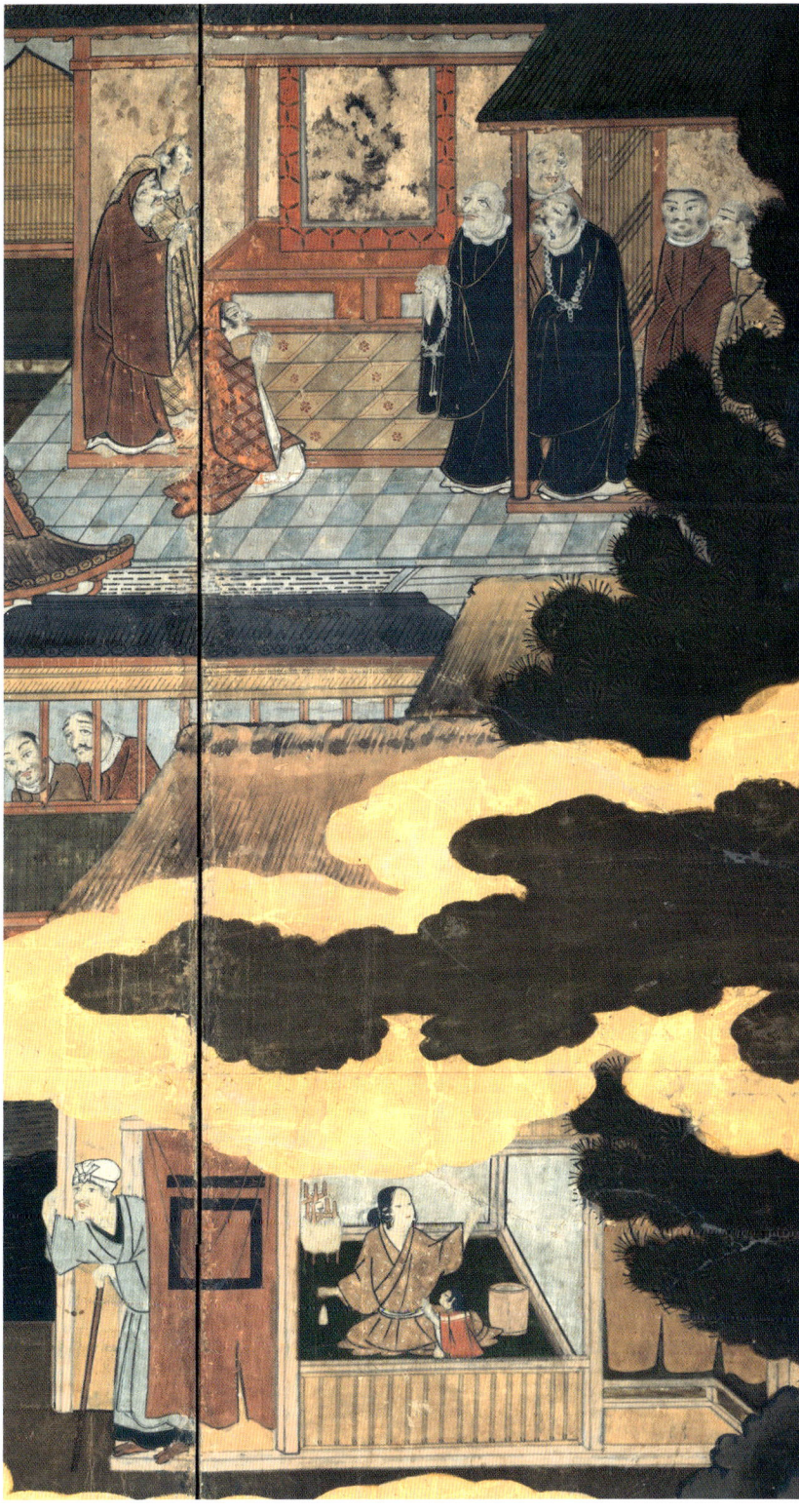

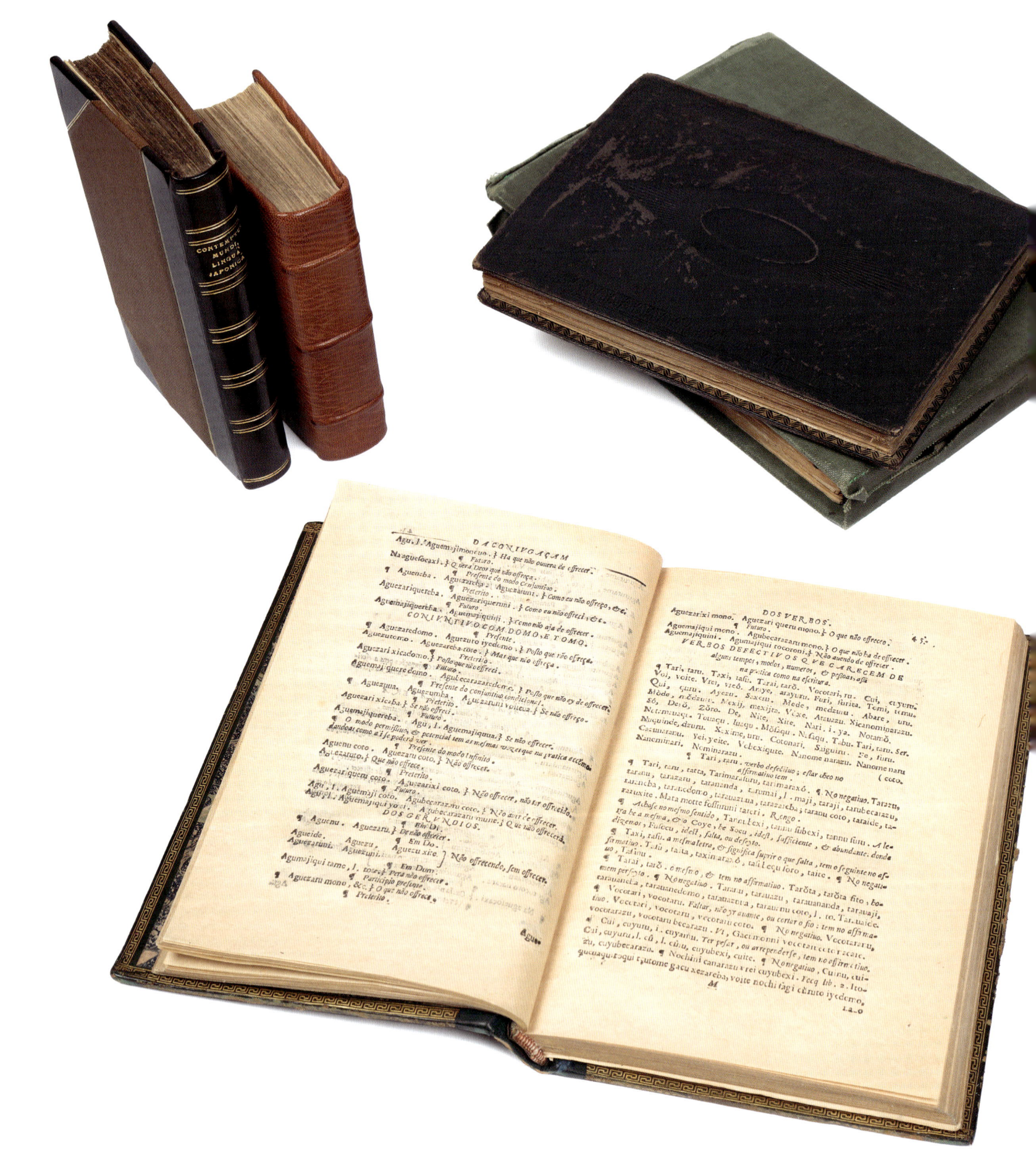

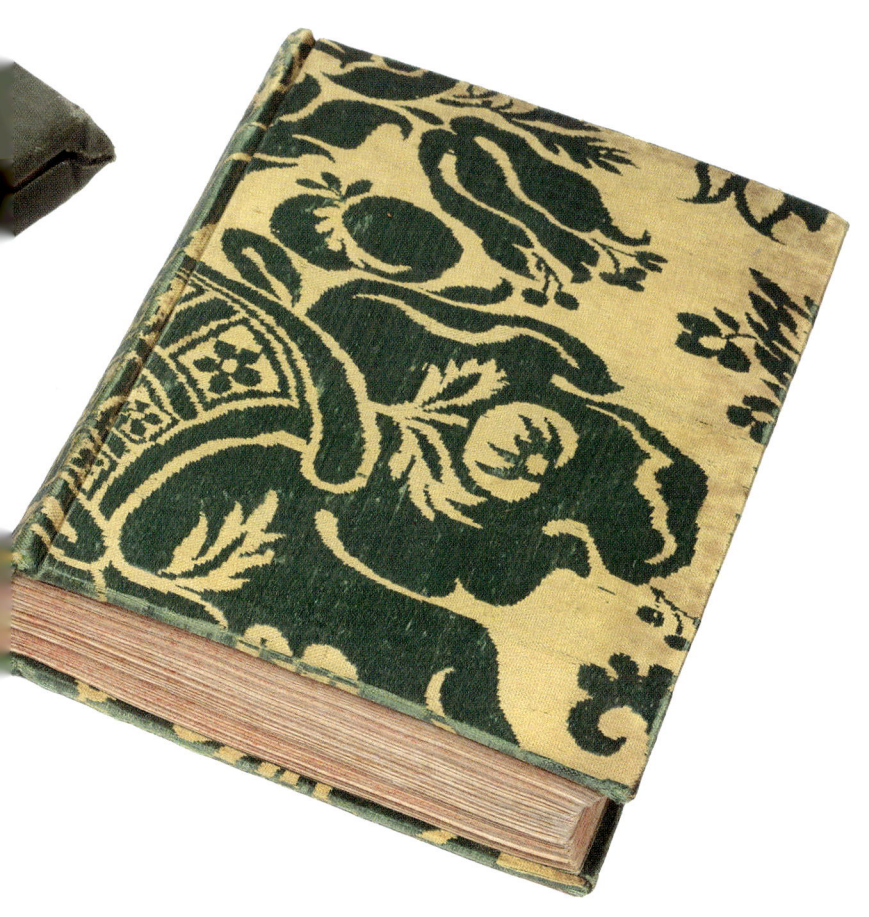

The ban on the religion and its spread was lifted in 1873, at which point the persecutions of the *Kirishitan* ceased. Those who met the *Kirishitan* were astonished to find them reciting their daily prayer with portions in still recognizable sixteenth-century Portuguese, which had been the language of most of the early modern Jesuit missionaries. They also sang songs in Latin with a distinct Portuguese pronunciation, as their ancestors had learned hundreds of years before. Today, the term *Kirishitan* has been rehabilitated as a name for the Japanese indigenous Christians and their culture, including their print culture.

Jesuit missionaries created a wide range of books, calendars, images, religious objects and spaces during the so-called Christian century, with the aim of fully and permanently establishing their creed in Japan. Looking back from the perspective of the modern age, it seems incredible that the printing press took several years to reach the Japanese shore in Nagasaki.[4] Along with it were also shipped printing tools and the matrices used for making the type; however, the matrix for the italic type was not of the desired quality, and the Jesuits and their teams of skilled craftspeople ultimately created a new one in Japan. They also created a new set of Roman type. The Bodleian

68 The Bodleian Library collection of Jesuit mission books from the late sixteenth and early seventeenth centuries. The six rare books contain texts in romanized Japanese, Portuguese and Latin, all produced on a printing press painstakingly imported from Europe. Arch. B e.22, Arch. B f.69, Arch. B e.42, Arch. B e.41, Arch. B d.13, Arch. B d.14.

# PROLOGO.

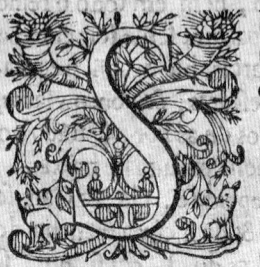

SENDO o Vocabulario meyo tam neceſſario, & importante pera aprender qualquer lingoa, ha muito tempo que os Padres da Companhia, que eſtamos em Iapão, deſejauamos ſair com elle impreſſo pera os Padres, & Irmãos que vem de nouo a cultiuar, & augmentar eſta Chriſtandade, terem algũa maneira de guia, & ajuda pera aprender eſta lingoa: mas porque pera iſto ſe requeria muita noticia, & experiencia do vſo deſta lingoa, & mais exacto exame dos vocabulos, não ſe podia em breue tempo fazer tam grande obra, poſto que ja ha annos auia algũs Vocabularios, & Artes de mão de que ſe ajudauão os que de nouo a aprendião, & principalmente hũ Dictionario da lingoa Latina impreſſo com a declaração em Portugues, & em Iapão, de que ſe ajudauão muito aſſi os de Europa pera aprender a lingoa de Iapão, como ós meſmos Iapões Irmãos, & Dôjicos pera aprender a Latina. Agora que com as muitas perſeguições deſta Chriſtandade vagou algum tempo mais aos Padres, & Irmãos Iapões pera reuer, & examinar melhor os Vocabularios, que eſtauão ja ha annos feitos poſto que imperfeitamente: alguns dos que melhor ſabião a lingoa de Iapão, com a ajuda tambem de alzuns naturaes entendidos nella nos aplicamos com diligencia por alguns annos a examinar, acrecentar, & aperfeiçoar eſte Vocabulario, o qual ſe não ſair tam perfeito como ſe deſeja, por ſer a lingoa de Iapão mui abundãte, & varia no vſo, ſendo hum o eſtillo das cartas, outro o dos liuros, outro o da pratica familiar, & outro o das pregações; & tendo eſta lingoa encorporadas em ſi muitas palauras da China, cuja declaração depende muito dos meſmos liuros, & caractéres da China: todauia ſegundo a diligencia, & exame, que ſe tem feito he obra de que os noſſos ſe ajudarão muito, & ainda os Iapões: Por que ſe declara nella não ſomente o ſentido cotrente, & vſo ordinario dos vocabulos, mas tambem o extraordinario, & metaphorico, & muitos, mui varios, & elegantes modos de falar que tẽ aſſi na pratica, como na eſcritura. E poſtoque nelle ſe poẽ muitas palauras Cobitas mais correntes, & vſadas aſſi na pratica, como nos liuros, & cartas: todauia de propoſito ſe deixarão os nomes proprios de lugares, homens, & outros impertinentes por não ſerem tã neceſſarios pera aprender a lingoa.

## Algũas aduertencias neceſſarias pera o vſo, & intelligencia deſte Vocabulario.

NA colocação, & ordem dos vocabulos ſeguimos o modo que ſe teue no dictionario Latino ja impreſſo, não indo pollas cabeças, & deriuação das palauras, mas pella ordem do Alphabeto Latino, por que aſſi ſe acha melhor, & mais depreſſo o vocabulo que ſe buſca.

Ordinariamente quando o vſo da palaura nãs partes do Cami he differente do de cá,

deſtes

Library collection contains books printed with both the old and the new type, and the difference is easily discernible (FIGS 69 & 70).

The greatest technical challenge for the printers was to create type for printing in the *kanji* (Chinese characters) and *kana* (syllabaries derived from Chinese characters) that make up the Japanese writing system. The printers succeeded, and some copies of their printing in Japanese script have survived, too. Little known is that the printers in Japan also used the cherished European printing press to print musical scores (FIG. 71) for requiems and other liturgical songs, a first in Japanese printing history. The score shown here looks as if it is the result of double-printing – using two successive print-runs – but is in fact the outcome of a triple-printing process, according to scholar and Jesuit print culture expert Toyoshima Masayuki.[5]

69 Prologue of the *Vocabulario da lingoa de Iapam.* The Jesuits and their teams printed the dictionary in 1603–04 with the new Roman printing type cast in Japan. Arch. B d.13.

70 Vol. 1, page 64 of the *Sanctos no gosagueô no vchi nuqigaqi,* with the beginning of the apostle Saint James the Minor's hagiography. This 1591 book was printed using Roman type imported from Europe. Arch. B f.69.

71 OVERLEAF *Manuale ad sacramenta ecclesiae ministranda,* Nagasaki, 1605, pp. 258–9. Shown here is an antiphon, or short chant, for the repose of the soul: *In paradisium deducant te angeli (May the angels lead you into paradise).* After the printing of the main text in black, all the parts of the book seen in red – rubrics, headline text and five-line staves for the music – were printed next. A third printing, again in black, was done for the song lyrics, the neumes (musical notation), the folios and the keyline around each page. Arch. B e.22.

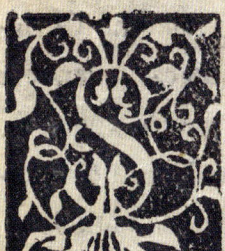

64.  S . A N D R E N O

Sancti tomoni itçumademo facaye tamŏ vareraga von aruji Iefu Chrifto banmin ni tattomare tamŏ mono nari .

## SANCTO IACOBE
### Menor Apoftolo no gofa-
GVEO, NARABINI SONO MAR-
tyrio no yŏdai. Core Eufebio Cefa-
rienfe toyũ gacuxŏ no qirocu
nari .

ANĉto Iacobe Menor ua Euange-
lio ni miyetaru gotoqu , iũninin no Apoftolo no vchi no go ichi-nin nari . Menor to nazzuĝeraru-ru coto ua, ima go ichinin S . Io-an Euangelifta no go qiŏdai ni Santiago Mayor to mŏfu ni maguiracafaru maiqi tame to nari.Go cu-docu, gojenxin no votoritaru toyũ niua arazu : tada Santiago Mayor yori mo nochi ni Apoftolo ni na-ri tamŏ ni yotte , Menor toua mŏfu to zo .
Go-

Antiphona.

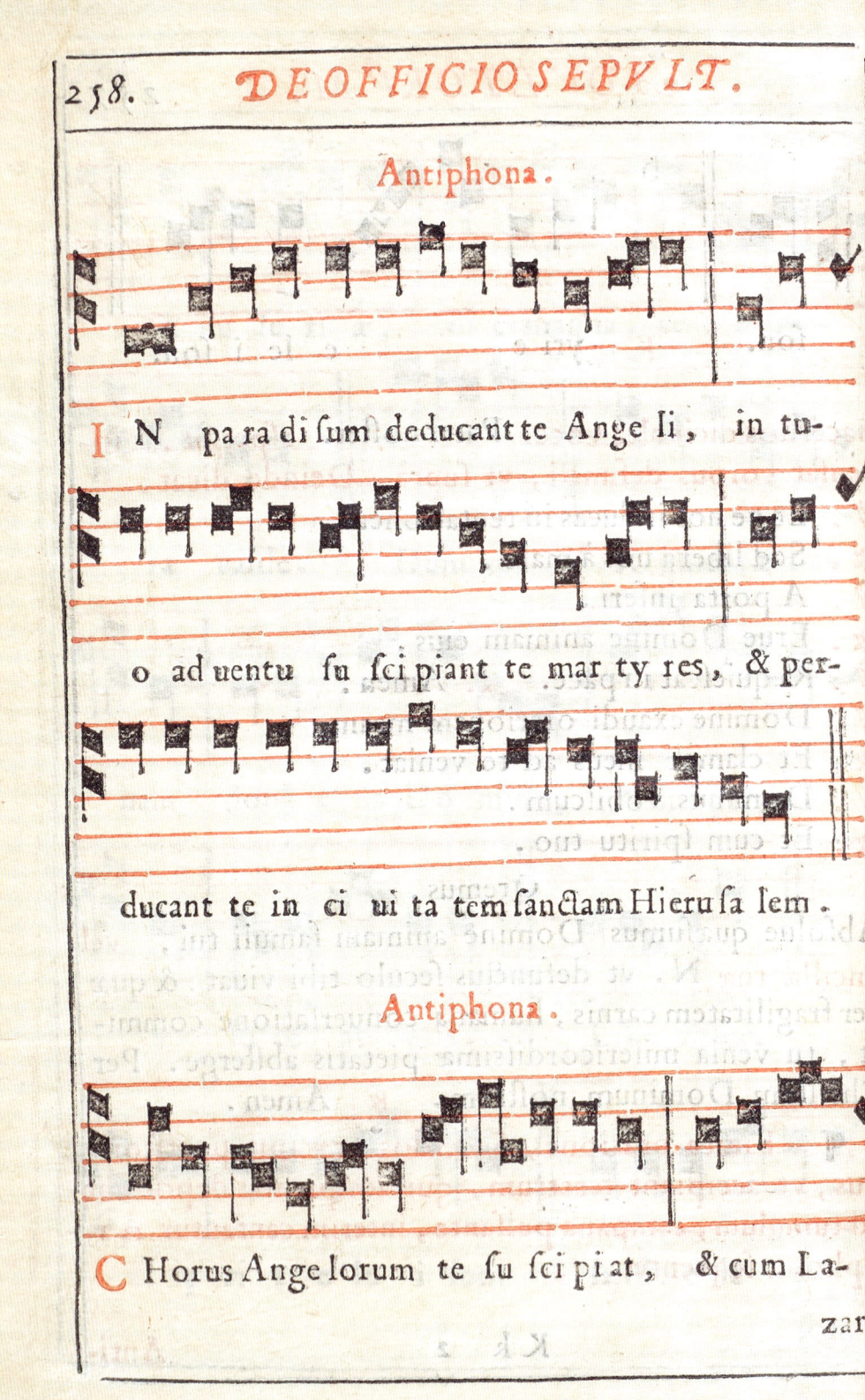

IN pa ra di ſum deducant te Ange li , in tu-

o ad uentu ſu ſci piant te mar ty res , & per-

ducant te in ci ui ta tem ſanctam Hieruſa lem.

Antiphona.

C Horus Ange lorum te ſu ſci pi at , & cum La-

zaro

K k 2

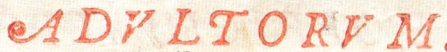

zaro quódam paupere    æternam ha be as requié.

**Mox dicatur Antiphona ad Benedictus.**

**Antiphona ad Benedictus.**

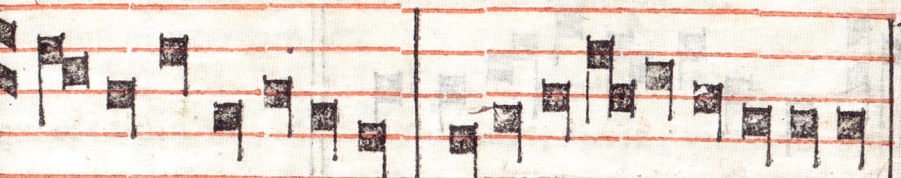

E Go sum    re surre cti o, &    vi ta,    qui

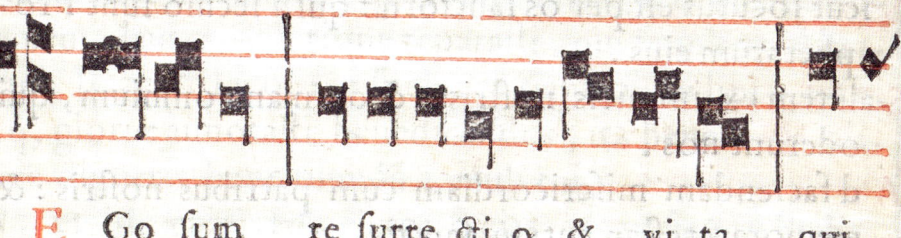

credit in me, e tiam si mortuus    fu erit vi-

uet: & omnis qui viuit, & credit in me nó

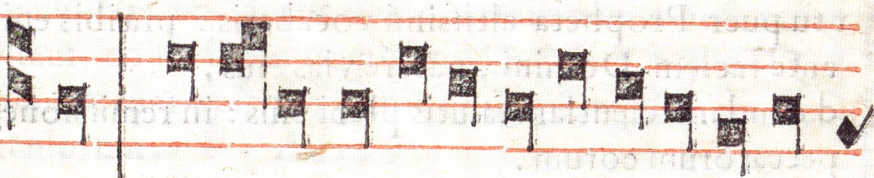

mori-

# SANCTOS
## NOGOSAGVEONO
### VCHINVQIGAQI
quan dai ichi .

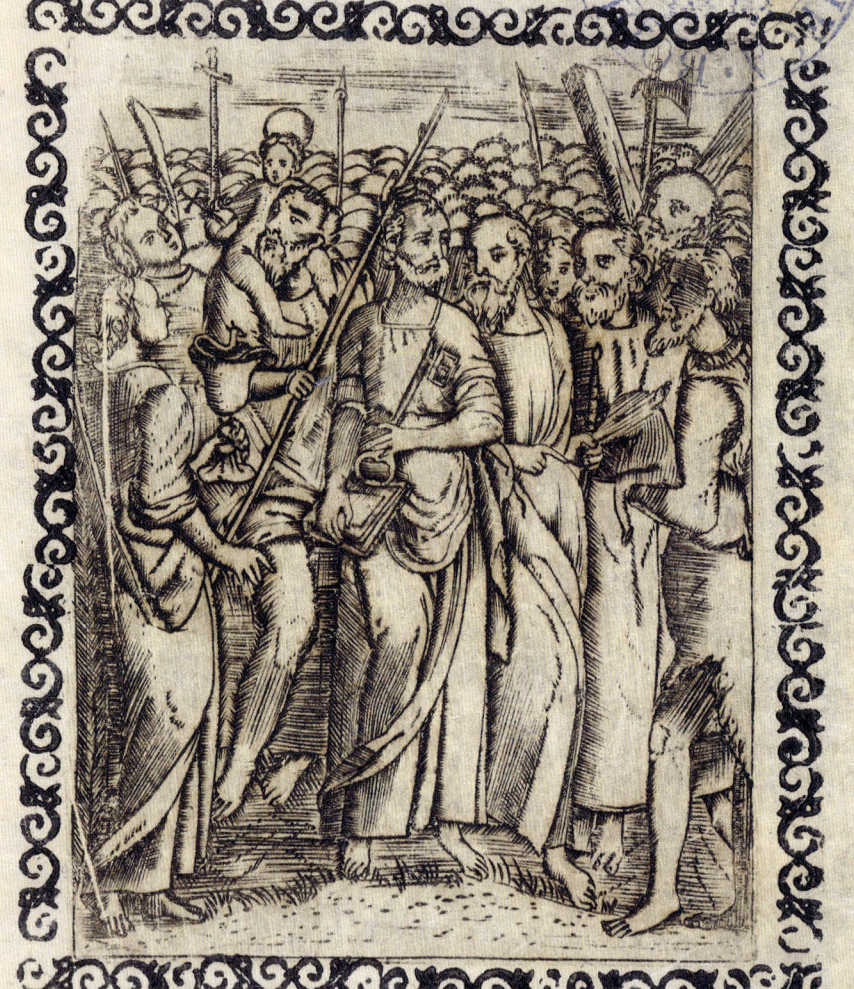

FIIENNOCVNITACACVNOGVN
IESVSNOCOMPANHIANOCOLLEGIO
Cazzufa ni voite Superiores no von yuruxi uo cò
muri core uo fan to nafu mono nari. Goxuxxe irai
## MDLXXXXI.

## TRANSLATIONS AND TRANSLATORS

Pupils in Jesuit schools and seminaries learned to etch copper plates, which were used to print on the press as well as for woodblock printing.[6] The title page of a collection of saints' and martyrs' hagiographies, *Sanctos no gosagueô no vchi nuqigaqi* (hereafter *Sanctos*), printed in 1591, might well be an example of their efforts (FIG. 72).[7] This was probably the first book printed with movable type in Japan. The book is of a small and therefore handy size (9 × 14 cm), and served to edify and teach people in Japan about the saints and martyrs of the early church.

The title page was produced using a two-step printing process, as evidenced by an edition of *Sanctos* now in the Bibliothèque nationale de France, recently described in detail by Yoshimi Orii.[8] The printers began by producing the title in romanized Japanese, along with a decorative frame with a floral pattern. On the Bibliothèque nationale edition's title page, the etching of the image of a host of saints and martyrs partly overlaps the surrounding decorative frame, indicating that the image was printed after the frame. The printers therefore performed a second step – using the *intaglio* process (inking an engraving or etching) – to print the image. The engraving/etching was done with very fine lines and is of a high quality overall.

72 Title page, *Sanctos no gosagueô no uchi nuqigaqi*, Kazusa, 1591. A small and therefore handy size, this book served to edify and teach people in Japan about the saints and martyrs of the early church. Arch. B f.69.

In the print, we see barefoot men and women, simply or poorly clad. Some of those depicted at the front of the vast crowd of saints and martyrs are recognizable by what they are carrying: Saint Peter holds his characteristic key and, to his right, Saint Christopher carries the infant Jesus. Peeping out from the edge is Saint John the Baptist, with a lamb in his arms. Interestingly, they do not have the halos that would normally indicate sainthood. This perhaps tells us that we should understand this book to be about their lives as humans, as was popular among the humanist Jesuit order of Renaissance Europe. The image signifies that all past saints and martyrs will welcome one's soul into Heaven.

The didactic nature of *Sanctos* and other devotional mission printed books is also made apparent by the appendices, containing glossaries of key words and terms considered difficult to understand. In the case of *Sanctos*, such a glossary in Japanese has only been found in manuscript versions, whereas a printed list of terms and explanations is provided in the appendix of a 1596 translation of Thomas à Kempis's *Contemptus mundi* (*Contempt of the World*, also known under the title *Imitation of Christ*) (see FIGS 76 & 77).

*Sanctos* explains the meaning of martyrdom to newcomers to the Catholic religion, giving many examples. It also tells the story of Barlaam and Josaphat, which, perhaps unbeknownst to the early modern translators and the compiler of *Sanctos*, ultimately derives from the hagiography of the Buddha Shakyamuni. When the legend of Barlaam and Josaphat[9] was recounted to an audience socialized in a culture that had been deeply shaped by Buddhism, the story must have

# RELATIONI
# DELLA VENVTA
## DEGLI AMBASCIA-
## TORI GIAPONESI

à Roma fino alla partita di Lisbona.

Con le accoglienze fatte loro da tutti i
Principi Christiani, per doue
sono passati.

Raccolte da Guido Gualtieri.

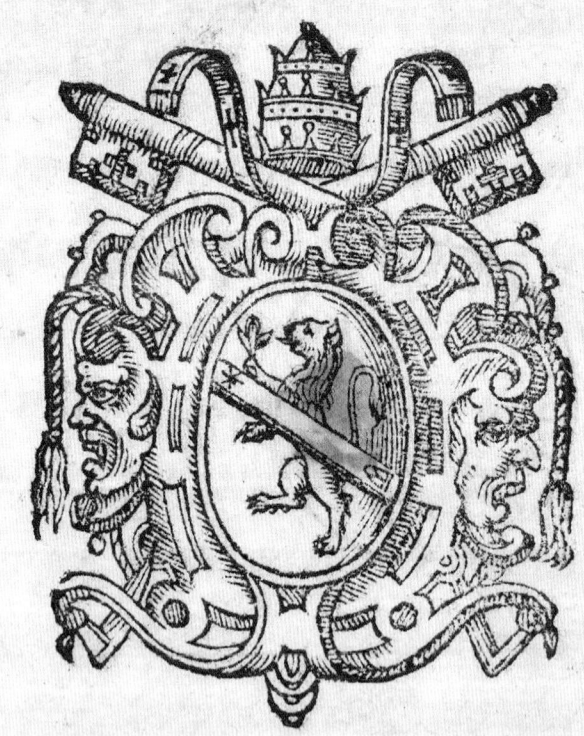

IN ROMA. Per Francesco Zannetti.
M. D. LXXXVI.

Con licentia de i Superiori.

been recognizable. We can say that at one point the hagiography of the Buddha Shakyamuni left its Indian context, entered Christianized lands where it morphed into a Christian story, and then re-entered a Buddhist country via the Christian mission.

While names of compilers or authors are sometimes mentioned in the Jesuit mission printed books, it is of utmost interest to also see the names of the translators. For example, in *Sanctos* we find mentions of some hagiographies' translators, such as Brothers Yōfo Paulo and Hōin Vincente, who were father and son. Both were educated men, and were well versed in classics and the Buddhist teachings before they converted to Christianity. Another outstanding translator in the mission's service was Hara Martinho (*c.*1569–1629), who spent some years in Europe in his youth. He was one of four adolescent men who were sent by Christian local rulers of provinces in Kyushu to accompany European Jesuits to form an embassy in Europe. The so-called Tenshō Embassy departed Nagasaki in 1582, and was well documented at the time, such that we know about their travel route and their encounters with Catholic leaders, including the pope and members of the ruling elite in Europe (FIG. 73).[10]

73 Guido Gualtieri, *Relationi della venuta degli ambasciatori giaponesi a Roma fino alla partita di Lisbona*, Francesco Zennetti, 1586. This account, written four years after their departure from Nagasaki, details the experiences of four young Japanese Catholics sent to Europe to strengthen the Jesuit mission in Japan. Zennetti created decorative initials that the Jesuits and their teams copied and used, for example in the very first Jesuit print in Japan (1591). 8° T 183 Art.

During their time in Europe, the Jesuits purchased the printing press and letter types for the Japanese mission press. Because of the long distance between the two regions, the prospect of having to import printing paper from Europe was quite daunting. As a result, they apparently performed a test print on Japanese torinoko paper (*torinokogami*), a high-quality eggshell-coloured paper that they had brought with them from Japan, to see whether it could withstand the high pressures of the printing process. The paper was (and is to this day) primarily made of fibres of the plant *Wikstroemia sikokiana*, aptly referred to as the paper tree (see chapter 4 on the materiality of Japanese books). Fortunately, the torinoko paper served this purpose extremely well, as we can see from the excellent condition of the Bodleian Japanese mission printed books.

All four young men eventually returned to Japan, in 1591, taking with them the disassembled printing press and additional equipment. Of the four, Hara was the most accomplished in European languages, and is known to have edited an abridged version of the 1596 translation of *Contemptus mundi*. This version was printed in Japanese script in a Christian layman's printshop in Kyoto in 1610, probably using wooden type or the woodblock printing technique. Only one copy has survived. Whether Hara was also involved in the translation that was printed in 1596 is unclear, but we do know that the text had circulated in manuscript form for many years before it was made into a printed book. Jesuit letters report on the convert Hosokawa Gracia, a samurai lady, who studied an early handwritten translation of the work.

## MULTILINGUAL BOOKS FOR THE MISSION

The printed books had many functions for the Jesuit mission, ranging from the edification of the Jesuit brothers and fathers, to education in the schools, seminaries and colleges that they established during the Christian century, and communication with converts. Works such as the manual for ministering the sacraments, the *Manuale ad sacramenta ecclesiae ministranda* (FIG. 74), were produced to serve the practical running of the mission. This text is printed with movable type, using both black and red ink – another first in the history of printing in Japan. As was customary in European religious and legal works, the red (*rubrica* in Latin, from the word for the red earth that was used to produce red-coloured ink in ancient times) was used for the explanatory parts of a text. The resulting rubrics in the *Manuale* alert the minister how to administer the sacraments, and instruct him, among other things, to preach in the vernacular – whether in Japanese for a Japanese audience, or in Portuguese for a speaker of that language. The *Manuale* provides several examples printed in romanized Japanese and in Portuguese respectively. We learn from words to an

74 *Manuale ad sacramenta ecclesiae ministranda*, Nagasaki, 1605, pp. 118–19. Instructions are given here for celebrating the Eucharist in the presence of an infirm brother, printed in red (rubrics). The words to be said during the service are printed in black ink. Arch. B e.22.

75 OVERLEAF Kyushu is the island coloured pale blue on this map of Japan by the Jesuit cartographer Abraham Ortelius, from *Theatrum Orbis Terrarum*, London, 1606. The Jesuit mission press was moved to several different locations in the south-west area of Kyushu. Douce O subt. 15.

*118.* DE SACRAM

℣. Mitte ei Domine auxilium d
Sion tuere eum.
℣. Nihil proficiat inimicus in co
quitatis non apponat nocere ei.
℣. Esto ei Domine turris fortit
inimici.
℣. Domine exaudi orationem me
meus ad te veniat.
℣. Dominus vobiscum. ℟. E
Oremus.
Deus infirmitatis humanæ singula
tui super infirmum nostrum osten
misericordiæ tuæ adiutus Ecclesa
repræsentari mereatur. Per Chri
trum. ℟. Amen.

¶ Finita hac oratione, accede
vbi decumbit ægrotus, cuius con
audiuit, rogabit an, & cui sit c
alicuius alterius peccati recordetur
dari, audiet illum ex confessione se
sita pœnitentia absoluat. Quara
ab aliquo (si quem forte offender
petere, aut vt ipse Sacerdos eius no
tibus generaliter petat. Exquirat
dispositus sit corporaliter ad sus
tiam, an verò timeatur vomitus,

¶ Post quàm hæc, & alia, qu
iudicauerit, cum ægroto breuiter
ce intelligibili circunstantibus co

### Si infirmus fit Iaponius.

Coconi vareraga qiŏdai naru bŏnin ari : taxicanaru Chriftanno gotoqu vareraga vŏn tafuqete Iefu Chrifto no tattoqi fontaiuo vqe tatematçuri taqu nozomaruru nari : cono vŏn arujiuo yoqi cacugo nite vqe tatematçuru graçauo ataye tamai , tocuto naru yŏni vonouono ima Pater nofter , Aue Maria ippenzzutçu tanomaruru nari. Mata tareni taixitemo fumajiqi cotouo xexi coto araba, Iefu Chriftoni taixi tatematçuri yuruxite tamauareto tanomaruru nari . Mata fono mini taixi rŏjequuo xexi fito araba, Chriftanno taixetno vye yori cocoro yori xamen furuto nari .

### Si infirmus fit Lufitanus.

Aqui jaz hum noffo Irmão enfermo , & como fiel chriftão quer receber o fanctifsimo corpo de Noffo faluador IESV Chrifto: pedeuos que por elle rezeis hum Pater nofter , & hũa Aue Maria , pera que Noffo fenhor lhe dee graça com que dignamente receba o feu fanctifsimo corpo . Pede perdão por amor de Noffo fenhor a qualquer peffoa aque tiuer feito coufa algũa , que não deueffe fazer . E fe poruentura alguém o tem offendido, elle có boa vótade, & charidade chriftãa lhe perdoa .

¶ His dictis Sacerdos priùs facta reuerentia Sacramento, parunéque ad partem recedens, conuerfus ad ægrotum dicat fimul cum illo in lingua vulgari, Confiteor Deo, clarè , diftinctè, & deuotè .

¶ Finita confefsione dicat Sacerdos. Mifereatur tui omnipotens Deus , & dimifsis omnibus peccatis tuis perducat te ad vitam æternam . ℞. Amen .

Q                                               Indul

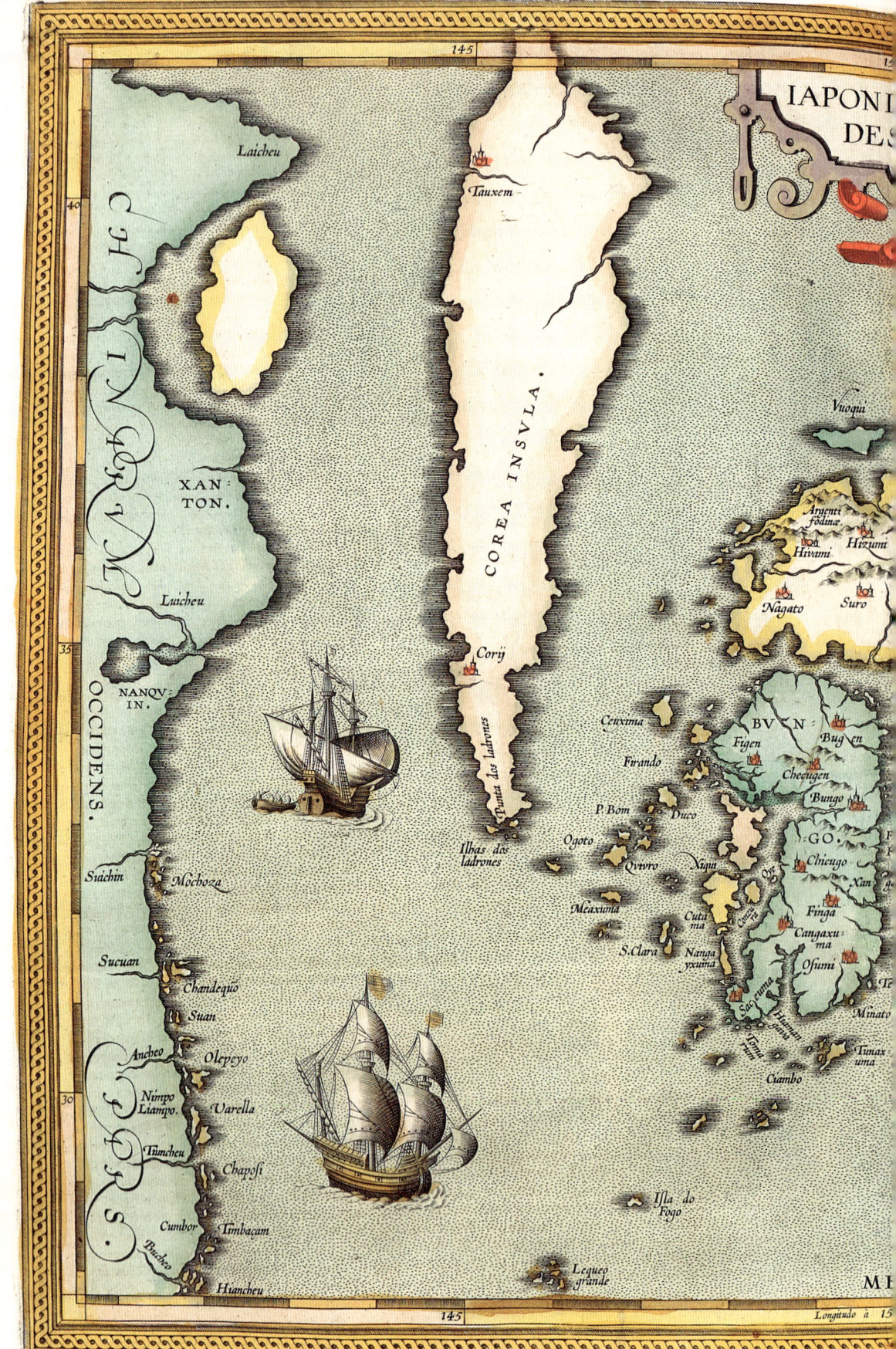

IAPONI
DES

Laicheu

XAN-
TON.

Luicheu

OCCIDENS.

NANQU-
IN.

Suachin

Mochoza

Sucuan

Chandequo

Suan

Ancheo

Olepeyo

Nimpo
Liampo.

Varella

Trimcheu

Chaposi

Cumbor

Timbacam

Bucheo

Huancheu

Vuoqua

Argenti
fodina

Hizumi

Hivami

Nagato

Suro

COREA INSVLA.

Corij

Punta dos ladrones

Ilhas dos
ladrones

Ceuxima

Firando

P. Bom

Ogoto

Quiro

Meaxuma

S.Clara

Nanga
yxuma

BVN
GO.

Figen

Bugen

Cheeugen

Bungo

Duco

Xiqu

Chicugo

Xan

Finga

Cangaxu
ma

Cuta
ma

Ofumi

Minato

Timax
uma

Ciambo

Isla do
Fogo

Lequeo
grande

ME

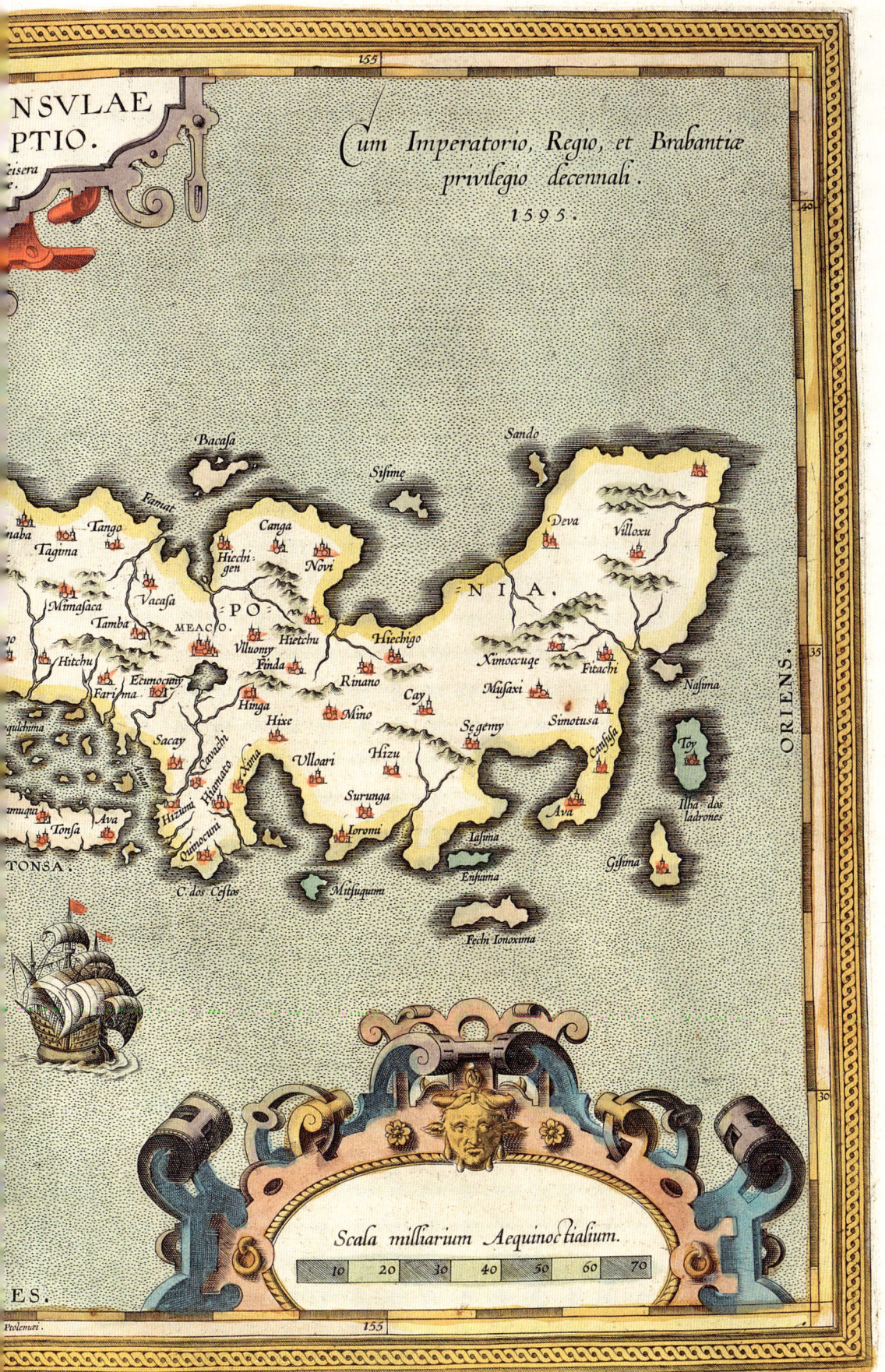

NSVLAE
PTIO.

*Cum Imperatorio, Regio, et Brabantiæ*
*privilegio decennali.*
1595.

Bacaſa

Sando

Siſimę

Deva
Villoxu

Famar

Tango
Taguma

Canga

N I A .

Hiechi
gen
Novi

naba

Mimaſaca

Vacaſa

Tamba

PO

Hiechu
MEACO.

Vlluomy
Finda

Hiechu

Hiechigo

Ximoccuqe

Fitachi

Naſima

Eeunociny
Fariſma

Rinano

Muſaxi

Hinga

Hixe

Mino

Cay

Segemy

Simotuſa

Toy

Sacay

Cay

Vlloari

Hizu

Canfuſa

Ava

Cervachi

Xeuu

Ilha dos
ladrones

muqui
Tonfa
Ava

Hizum
Hiſmuara

Surunga

Iſima

Gifima

Quinocum

Ioromi

TONSA.

C. dos Ceſtus

Mitſuquam

Enſuma

Fechi Ionoxuma

ORIENS.

ES.

Ptolemæi.

*Scala milliarium Aequinoctialium.*

10  20  30  40  50  60  70

infirm brother during the Eucharist that, by 1605, there were Japanese speakers among the Jesuit brothers.

Today, we are used to reading romanized Japanese words such as sushi, or place names such as Nagasaki and Hirado, but this system of romanization was only developed in modernity. Because language skills and the production of authoritative texts were of paramount importance to the early modern Catholic mission in Japan, the Jesuits and their teams created a system of romanization based on Portuguese pronunciation. In the transcription scheme established by the early modern missionaries, used only for a century, sushi, Nagasaki and Hirado would be spelled *suxi*, Nangasaqui and Firado.[11] Once familiar with this early romanization system, it is easy to read a Japanese text written in the refined style of the highly developed indigenous literary culture, without having to struggle with the complex Japanese script. Another advantage, on top of circumventing the complexity of using *kanji* and *kana*, was that the many loanwords from Portuguese and Latin could be effortlessly incorporated into a fully romanized Japanese text, producing a homogenous-looking text.

Most of the six Bodleian Library Japanese mission-printed books specify the place of their publication. All the printing locations are on the southernmost Japanese island of Kyushu. The earliest is labelled as being from Kazusa (1591), followed by a book from Amakusa (1595), one with no indication of place (1596), and three from 1603 to 1608 from Nagasaki. One might assume that these labels signify the existence of three different print workshops, but we have ample evidence to the contrary. Jesuit letters and reports show that

the missionaries moved their one and only press from their college in Kazusa to Amakusa, then to a secret location (probably also in Amakusa) because of the unsafe political situation for the mission at the time, and finally to Nagasaki, where it was set up in the Christian hospital. We know that the operators of the press dismantled it in 1614 when they were forced to leave Japan. At this point, they shipped it to Macao, where it was used until at least 1620.

## READING AND SALVATION

We can gain a rare insight into the work of the printers by comparing three editions of the Japanese translation of the popular devotional book *Contemptus mundi*. The original work was compiled in Latin in the medieval period by Thomas à Kempis (*c.*1380–1471). Like *Sanctos*, and many other *Kirishitan-ban*, *Contemptus mundi* was written entirely in romanized Japanese. When we compare the three extant copies, all from 1596,[12] we notice slight differences. It seems that the printers and editors constantly checked the newly printed books, and corrected errors such as simple typos by adjusting the typesetting right away.

Of the six Bodleian Jesuits mission printed books, the copy of *Contemptus mundi* (1596) shows the most traces of use (FIGS 76 & 77). It is

76 & 77 Title page & flyleaf, Japanese translation of Thomas à Kempis' *Imitation of Christ*: *Contemptus mundi jenbu*: *core youo itoi, Iesu Christono gocŏxequio manabi tatematçuru michiuo voxiyuru qiŏ*, Collegio de Japão, Amakusa (?), 1596. The handwritten dedication, written in the sixteenth century, is by an unknown hand. Two other copies of this edition are known to exist: one in the Ambrosiana Library in Milan, the other in the Bibliotheca Augusta in Wolfenbüttel. Arch. B e.42.

# CONTEMPTVS

mundi jenbu.

CORE YOVO ITOI, IESV CHRIS-

tono gocŏxeqiuo manabi tatematçu-

ru michiuo voxiyuru qiŏ.

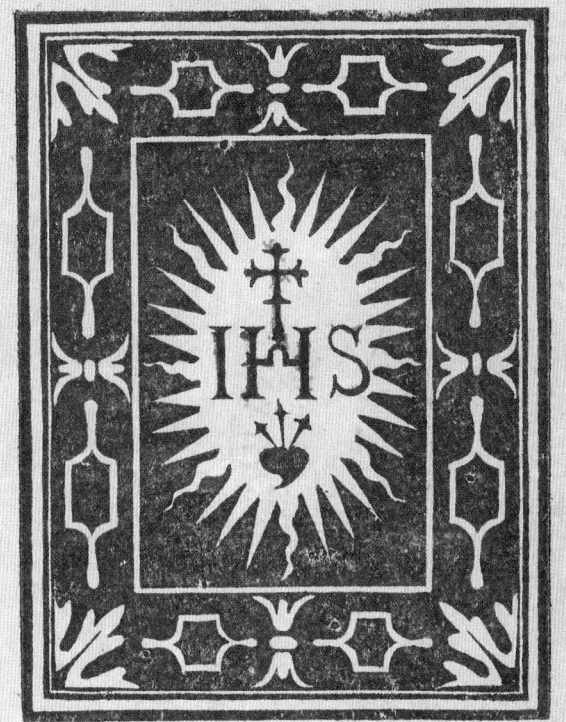

NIPPON IESVS NO COMPANHIA

no Collegio nite Superiores no goguegiuo

motte coreuo fanni firaqu mono nari.

Toɉini goxuxxeno nenqi. 1596.

---

Goxuxxe iray xengo fiacu fachiɉũ
gonen meni papa Sixto ypri Nippon no Companhia no padre com-
bŏ ni yotte sazz uqetamŏ gocuriqi
no cŏto.

Tarenitemo are cono qiŏ no vchii-e-
ragiŏ uo yomu tabigoto ni ɉũnen
no Indulgencias uo cŏmuru nari.

Beatiſſima Maria tattomare tamaye.

also the only one to boast a contemporary note, handwritten in romanized Japanese: 'Goxuxxe iray xengofiacu fachijǔ gonen meni papa Sixto yori Nippon no Companhia no padre combǒ ni yotte sazzuqetamǒ go curiqi no coto. Tarenitemo are con qiǒ no vchi iccagiǒ uo yomu tabigoto ni jǔnen no Indulgencias uo cômuru nari. Beatissima Maria tattomare tamaye.' A translation into modern English is as follows: 'Merit granted by Pope Sixtus in Anno Domini 1585, at the earnest request of the fathers of the society in Japan; whoever shall read a single chapter of this book shall on each occasion receive ten years' Indulgences. Hail Most Blessed Mary.'

Interestingly, Pope Sixtus granted the merit more than ten years before the book was actually printed. It may have been granted during the visit of the Tenshō Embassy, when the young Japanese men who formed the embassy presented a preliminary Japanese translation of Luis de Granada's Spanish translation of the book. It is not clear whether a Japanese convert wrote the note on the flyleaf. One of the Jesuit fathers may have written it on behalf of a convert, as it is debatable whether those educated in Japan would have written using the romanization system. Also, the note appears to have been written with an ink quill, and not, as was customary, with a brush.

The note indicates that people did not only read the book for edification or education, but that they also expected or hoped that on reading even a single chapter they would be granted remission of the punishment of their sins. This is reminiscent of practices related to reading Buddhist sutras. Reading or reciting even the sutra's title was thought to be a highly meritorious practice, ensuring this-worldly benefits, a good birth, and ultimately liberation from all suffering.

Three of the Bodleian's six Jesuit mission printed books are related to language acquisition and knowledge about Japan. They served as reference works, not least to enable communication with men and women of high social status. Members of the mission worked on them for many years prior to their actual printing, and in one case the work was printed in several parts over a period of four years.

## MONUMENTS OF LEARNING

The *Dictionarium Latino Lusitanicum, ac Iaponicum*, a trilingual dictionary with translations of Latin words into both Portuguese and (romanized) Japanese, is the earliest language-learning work in the collection (FIG. 78). The book was modelled after the popular Latin lexicon by Ambrosius Calepini (*c.* 1440–1510), and was printed in Amakusa in 1595. With this substantial publication, the Jesuit mission introduced to Japan the contemporary Renaissance European trend of returning to the use of classical Latin, a trend fervently supported by the Jesuit order.

An extensive bilingual lexicon followed in 1604, and was published in Nagasaki after the printing press was moved there. The *Vocabulario da lingoa de Iapam, com adeclaracão em portugues, feito por*

78 *Dictionarium Latino Lusitanicum, ac Iaponicum ex Ambrosii Calepini*, Amakusa, 1595. Entries of Latin words are followed by translations and explanations of their meaning in Portuguese and Japanese, in romanized script. Arch. B e.41.

# DE INCIPIENTI
## BVS A LITERA.

### A

NOMEN est literæ pri
mæ Hebræis, Græcis, & La
tinis, quæ à Cicerone falu-
taris litera dicitur, quòd no-
ta effet abfolutionis, vt, C,
condemnationis.

A, I, AB, I, ABS, præpofitio. Lufitanicè, de,
da, do. Iaponicè, yori, cara, ni.

A, I, Ab, fignificat motum à loco, vt redeo
ab agro. Lus. Torno do campo. Iap. No
yori modoru. ¶ Item, Significat tempus, vt
à puero. Lus. Defde menino. Iap. Yô
xô yori. Interdum poft. Lus. De pois.
Iap. Nochi, cara, yori, fuguite. Vt à pran-
dio. Lus. De pois de jantar. Iap. Afamexi
no nochi. ¶ A rege fecundus. Lus. Pri
meira peffoa depois del Rey. Iap. Xex
xô, Quambicu. ¶ Item, fignificat, Pro,
vt ab aliquo facere, ftare &c. Lus. Aju
dar, ou defender a alguem. Iap. Fitouo fi
qi furu, catôdo furu, tayorini naru. ¶ A
teftibus, à voluntate, &c. Lus. Defenfor
de teftimunhas, ou vontade alhea. Iap.
Taninno zonbunuo fome cacaguru, I, xô
cominuo fijqi furu mono. ¶ Ab aliquo
foluere, numerare, &c. Lus. Fazer alguem
q̃ outrẽ pague por elle, ou em feu nome.
Iap. Vaga fumotuo tani fenben faturu.
¶ Item, A, I, ab, officiorum, & dignitatum
nominibus præpofitũ, eos fignificat, qui
ijs, aut officijs, aut dignitatibus fugutur,
vt A rationibus. Lus. Contador. Iap.
Sancata. ¶ A manu, vel à manibus. Lus.
Efcriuão do principe, ou fenhor. Iap.

Goyũfit, vôxegaqi. ¶ A pugione. Lus.
Pagem du eftoque. Iap. Tachimochi.
Aliquãdo ponitur pro Côtra, vt defédere fe
à frigore. Lus. Defenderfe côtra o frio. Iap.
cáuo fuxegu, fayeguiru. Aliquãdo, pro Per,
vt ab fe cantat. Lus. Canta defi, & de fua
vontade. Iap. Vonoreto, I, cocoroto v-
tõ. ¶ Item, pro Præter, fiue Contra, vt
ab re. Lus. Sem proueito, ou fora de pro
pofito. Iap. Muyacuni, niauzu. ¶ Itẽ, Pro
eo quod dicimus, quod pertinet ad, vt à
pecunia imparatus fum. Lus. Quanto ao
que pertéçe a dinheiro eftou defapercibi
do. Iap. Caneno bunua bucacugo nari, I, fu
nhoi nari. ¶ Item, à parte, vel verfus aliquã
partem, vt ab oriente. Lus. Da parte do
oriente. Iap. Figaxi yori, I, figaxini. ¶ Itẽ,
Cum ablatiuo perfonæ, domicilium figni
ficat, vt à iudice venio. Lus. Venho de
cafa do juiz. Iap. Qendanninno xucuxo
yori qitaru.

### A ANTE B.

Ab, præpofitio, vide fuprà.

Ábaces. Lus. Vafos em q̃ fe guardaõ peças ri
cas, & preciofas. Iap. Cojiqi naru mono
no iremono, iye.

Abaciõ diminut. ab Abax. Lus. Mefa peque
na de contar. ¶ Iap. Guinxenuo cazoyuru
chijfaqi ban. ¶ Itẽ Mefa, ou banca peque
na, em q̃ fe poem pratos, ou outros vafos
femelhantes. Iap. Cojendana.

Abactor, oris. Lus. O que furta gado. Iap
Guinuba, fitçuji, nadono nufubito.

Abactus, us. Lus. Empuxaõ, ou o lançar fo

Nuſumitori, u, otta. Furtar.

Nuta. Certa maneira de ſalſa, ou eſcaueche, com que concertão Namaſu, &c. ¶ Nutanamaſu. Namaſu feito cõ eſte eſcaueche.

Nutaaye. Certa iguaria feita com eſte eſcaueche. ¶ Nutaayeni ſuru. Concertar o comer deſta maneira.

Nutana. l, nutanamono. Peſſoa cuja, mal compoſta, deſcuidada, ou priguiçoſa.

Nutanamaſu. Vide, Nuta.

Nuxi. Dono, ſenbor, ou ſenhora de qualquer couſa.

Nuxi. Vos, ou tu, falando com gente baixa.

Nuxi. Official de charoar com Vruxi.

Nuxiya. Caſa onde ſe faz eſta obra de Vruxi.

Nuye. Paſſaro aſſi chamado.

### DE ALGVNS ADVERBIOS QVE COMEÇAM POLLA LETRA, P.

#### P ANTES DO A.

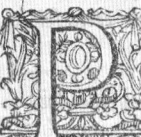

**P**Appato. Adu. Modo de ſe aleuantar pò, ondas, labareda, &c.

Pararito. l, fararito. Adu. Modo de ſoar algũa couſa que ſae como grãos, &c. ¶ Itẽ, Totalmente, ou ſem ficar nada. Vt, Pararito tatta. Aleuantaráoſe todos ſem ficar nenhum.

Pararito vchicuzzuſu. Deſtruir totalmente ſe ficar nada.

Patto. Adu. Modo deſe leuantar, & eſpalhar algũa couſa como ſumo. Vt, Chiqemuriga patto tatta. Yax. O ſumo, ou va por do ſangue ſe aleuantou, & eſpalhou.

Paxxito. Adu. Modo de acertar com a ſeta, ou com lança, &c. Vt, Paxxito atatta. Deu, ou acertou bem no aluo, &c.

#### P ANTES DO I.

**P**Inpin. Adu. Modo de dar couces a beſta. ¶ Vmaga pinpinto fanuru. O caualo da couces.

Pixxito. Adu. Modo de eſtar muito juſta, apertada, ou metida algũa couſa.

#### P ANTES DO O.

**P**Onpon. l, poponto. Adu. Modo de ſoar o tabaquinho de Iapão, ou eſpingardas quãdo deſparão, &c.

Poppoto. Adu. Modo de ſubir a flamma, &c. Vt, Fonouoga poppoto tachinoboiu. Subir a flamma, ou labareda com furia.

### DOS VOCABVLOS QVE COMEÇAM POLLA LETRA, Q.

#### Q ANTES DO E.

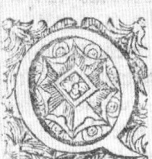

E. Vt, Qeiuru. Transfigurarſe, ou aparecer noutra forma, ou figura, como o Demonio no corpo bumano, &c. ¶ Fotoqe fitoto qe xitamŏ. O Fotoque apareceo em figura bumana.

Qe. Cauſa, ou achaq dalgũa couſa. Vt, Sono qe ni varucatta. Por iſſo ſoy mal, ou mao. B.

Qe. Riſca. Vt, Qeuo fiqu. Riſcar.

Qe. Couſa ordinaria, ou de cote: não ſe vſa ſem compoſição. Vt, Qeno qirumono. Veſtido de cote, & ordinario. ¶ Qefare. Tẽpo ordinario ſem feſta, & concurſo de gente, & tempo feſtiual, &c. ¶ Qeno fucu. Veſtido ordinario: bæc vide infrà ſuo loco.

Qe. Cabelos. ¶ Qega tatçu. Arripiaremſe os cabelos. ¶ Qeuo ſuru. Mudarem as aues a pena, ou animaes os cabelos.

Qe. Eſcama de peixe. ¶ Qeuo toru. Eſcamar o peixe. Palaura que ſe vſa em algũas partes do Cami.

Qe, ru, eta. Dar com o pè para diante. Vt, Axiuo motte fuxitaru inacuiauo fattatozo qetariqeru. Taif. Lib. 2. Deu, ou botou com o pè a almofada que eſtaua no chão derepente. ¶ Mariuo qeiu. Iugar à pella com o pè como he cuſtume em Iapão.

Qeague, uru, eta. Dando com o pè aleuantar, como

*alguns Padres e Irmaõs da Companhia de Jesus* was, according to its extended title, put together by 'a group of Jesuit fathers and brothers' who spoke Portuguese in their daily lives. The proficient interpreter of the mission, João Rodrígues (1558/62–1633), may have served as one of the compilers of this Japanese–Portuguese lexicon. It is a colossal volume, containing about 32,000 entries, ordered alphabetically, with the translations often accompanied by examples of use (FIG. 79). The *Vocabulario* also provides some grammatical explanations, but these are very limited.

While it is possible that more extensive grammar notes and textbooks circulated in manuscript form among the Jesuit community, the first Japanese grammar book printed by the mission press was João Rodrígues' *Arte da lingoa de Iapam*, a three-part compendium on the Japanese language and culture (FIG. 80). This work is therefore of the utmost importance for the modern study of Japanese linguistics. Rodrígues starts the first part of his work by analysing verbs, as was customary in European grammatical works, and then goes on to explain syntax in detail. The second part contains a discussion on morphology, such as the challenge of using 'Christian' lexemes, and an intriguing chapter on Chinese and Japanese poetry (FIG. 81).[13] At this time, such poetry was discussed and practised by the men and women of the educated elite in Japan, and so knowledge of it was seen as beneficial to the mission. The author describes

79 *Vocabulario da lingoa de Iapam*, Nagasaki, 1603–04. This page lists Japanese words under the letters *P* and *Q*, using the romanization system developed by the early modern Jesuit missionaries and their teams. Arch. B d.13.

both *uta* and *renga* poetry in great detail. The third and final part provides chapters on literary cultures, natural philosophy, political and cultural history and, significantly for the mission, on the writing of letters, with many examples. Among the examples are some provided by Japanese brothers such as Hōin Vincente.

Overall, the compendium provided much material for regional, linguistic and cultural studies for the foreign missionaries. But it also contains comparisons between Japanese cultural or intellectual expressions and 'ours' – often meaning those from Rodrígues' native Portugal, or Europe in general, though he had departed for East Asia as an adolescent. The *Arte da lingoa de Iapam* informs its readers about both cultural translation and linguistic translation, while its author must have been more familiar with Japanese than with European culture at that point. Interestingly, the *Arte da lingoa de Iapam* does not contain a single instance of Japanese script, although Rodrígues was able to consult original texts and read them fluently. Even the model letters to dignitaries, ladies of rank and Buddhist monks are all in romanized Japanese. However, in this simplified form, Rodrígues introduced many subjects to his readers for the first time. The compendium comprises knowledge that those from a European background had never encountered before.

In his treatise on poetry, Rodrígues quotes many poems in Japanese, but only provides a translation of one single verse into Portuguese – a couplet from an *uta* poem about a mother mourning the death of her son. In his capacity as a diplomat and interpreter to the mission, Rodrígues travelled constantly through Japan in critical and turbulent

porque as palauras da China estam diuisas nestes dous generos de accentos. ſ. So
cu, Fiŏ, de modo que a collocaçam destes pes, & sua ordem depende toda do
segundo pè do primeiro verso.

¶ E pera se entender esta ordem porei aqui estes sinais como elles fazem dos
quais os brancos significam, Fiŏ, os pretos, Socu, & os meos brancos, & meios
pretos significam que naquelle lugar podem estar indifferentemente, Fiŏ, ou
Socu. Como se ve nas figuras seguintes.

¶ 1. ○ ○ ○ ● ● ○ ○ Xi. 1.
                                    Exem-
2. ○ ● ○ ○ ○ ● ○ plo.
3. ○ ● ○ ○ ○ ○ ●
4. ○ ○ ○ ○ ○ ○ ○

¶ 1. ○ ● ○ ○ ○ ○ ○ Xi. 2.
                                    Exem-
2. ○ ○ ○ ○ ○ ○ ○ plo.
3. ○ ● ○ ○ ○ ○ ○
4. ○ ● ○ ○ ○ ● ○

¶ 1. ○ ○ ○ ○ ○ Rengu. 1.
                                    Exemplo.
2. ○ ● ● ○ ○

¶ 1. ○ ● ● ○ ● Rengu. 2.
                                    Exemplo.
2. ○ ○ ○ ● ○

## DO VERSO DE IAPAM.

¶ A poesia de Iapam por nome geral se chama Vta, Cadŏ, Vacano
michi. E ao poeta chamam, Cadŏxa, Vacanotaxxa, Vtayemi. E o com-
por versos se diz, Vtauo yomu, Xirenguuo tçucuru. Fazer verso da China. Caxo, liuro de versos.

¶ O verso de Iapam he lingoa muyto branda & elegante de certas syllabas, ou pes como o nosso verso exametro & pentametro, & he propriamte como
disticos: porque nam contam historia continuada em verso mas em hum distico
se comprende a sentença, ou a cousa que querem dizer.

¶ Este verso, ou distico consta como digo de dous versos: o primeiro se chama Camino cu, o qual tem tres pes, o primeiro de cinco syllabas, o segundo de
sete, & o terceiro de cinco. O segundo verso se chama, Ximeno cu, que tem

Z 3                                                                dous

times, making it a wonder that he brought the monumental *Arte da lingoa de Iapam* to publication at all.

The first poem Rodrígues mentions in his treatise on poetry is 'Cuzŏxi',[14] which comprises the first stanza of a nine-stanza Buddhist work that the Jesuits were fascinated with. In another book they published a full version, albeit stripped of any reference to Buddhism, as a *memento mori* – a reminder of the inevitability of death.[15] In Buddhist Japan, the nine stanzas were originally a meditation on the nine stages of the decomposing body, to teach about the impermanence of life. The poem in the *Arte da lingoa de Iapam* serves as an example of a Chinese poem. Remarkably, the compiler provides the reading of the Chinese poems in the Japanese language, not, as one could expect, in the Chinese-derived reading of the characters:[16]

Feijeino ganxocuua biochŭni votorŏ.   Cuzŏxi
Fŏtai nemuruga gotoxi, xinxino sugata.
Von ay mucaxino tomo, todomatte nauo ari.
Fiyŏ xequicon: satte idzucunica yuqu.
Ganqua tachimachini tçuqu faru sanguet.
Meiyô vochiyasuxi, aqui ixxi.
Rŏxô guanrai sadamareru sacai naxi.
Gojen nogaregataxi, socuto chito.

80 João Rodrígues, *Arte da lingoa de Iapam*, Nagasaki, 1604–08. This chart from the poetry chapter in part three shows patterns representing the metre of Chinese-style poems. Such diagrams appear in contemporary Japanese works on Chinese poetry. White circles indicate level tones (*hyō*) of feet (syllables), black circles oblique tones (*soku*). Half-white, half-back circles indicate that either tone could be placed in the composition. In the Jesuit mission print, the circles were printed using special types, but some may have been filled in by hand later using *sumi* ink – incorrectly in several places. Arch. B d.14.

A translation of the stanza into English reads:

> During your illness your usual countenance
>      grew pale;
> The appearance of the recently dead is like
>      a beautiful sleeping body.
> Affection for an old friend persists,
>      as if she were still alive.
> The spirit flies away in the evening –
>      whither does it go?
> The third month of spring is the flower-viewing
>      season but abruptly ends;
> The leaves of life so easily fall
>      in an autumn moment.
> By their nature neither young nor old
>      have any lasting abode.
> Sooner or later, whether early or late,
>      it is impossible to flee death.[17]

Part three also contains chapters on numbers and measurements. Folio 231 has a diagram of the cardinal directions and animals of the zodiac according to the Sino-Japanese tradition on the right-hand page, and another, similar chart printed exactly aligned on the following left-hand page. Leafing through the book, this creates a surprising effect because the diagram on the other side of the page shimmers through the thin but sturdy torinoko paper.[18]

### THE LEGACY OF JESUIT BOOK PRINTING

Despite the Japanese ban on Christianity *de facto* ending the mission's publishing enterprise in the archipelago, the Jesuit fathers continued printing books on Japanese language and culture from outside of Japan, and their legacies lived on. The Jesuits printed an abbreviated and revised edition of the *Arte da lingoa de Iapam* in Macao in 1620, still hoping to return to Japan. Similarly, a later edition of the *Vocabulario* was printed in Manila in 1630. But the situation did not improve for the Christian mission for another two centuries, until the official lifting of the ban in 1873. Some years before the end of the ban, the French priest Bernard Petitjean obtained a version of the *Dictionarium Latino Lusitanicum, ac Iaponicum* in Manila, where many Christians had sought exile in the early seventeenth century. Under Petitjean's supervision, a new edition was published for missionary purposes, with some important changes. The Portuguese was left out completely, turning the *Dictionarium* into a bilingual lexicon. Portuguese, the *lingua franca* of the Jesuits, lost its significance in the late nineteenth century, and was therefore dropped from the new edition. Also, the corrections and additions listed at the end

81 João Rodrígues, *Arte da lingoa de Iapam*, Nagasaki, 1604–08. This diagram shows the cardinal directions and animals of the zodiac. It conflates cardinal directions and the passage of time by means of the Sino–Japanese twelve animals classification system. On top is the cardinal direction north, which corresponds to the night hours and is represented by 'rat' (*ne*), south to the hours of the day, represented by 'horse' (*uma*) etc. The numerals in the centre ranging twice from 4 to 9 indicate how the hours of the day were counted: for example, 9 for 'the ninth hour' corresponding with 'rat' is midnight, whereas 'the ninth hour' corresponding with 'horse' is midday. Because of this tradition, the modern word for *ante meridiem* in Japanese, *gozen*, literally means 'before (the hour of) the horse'. Arch. B d.14.

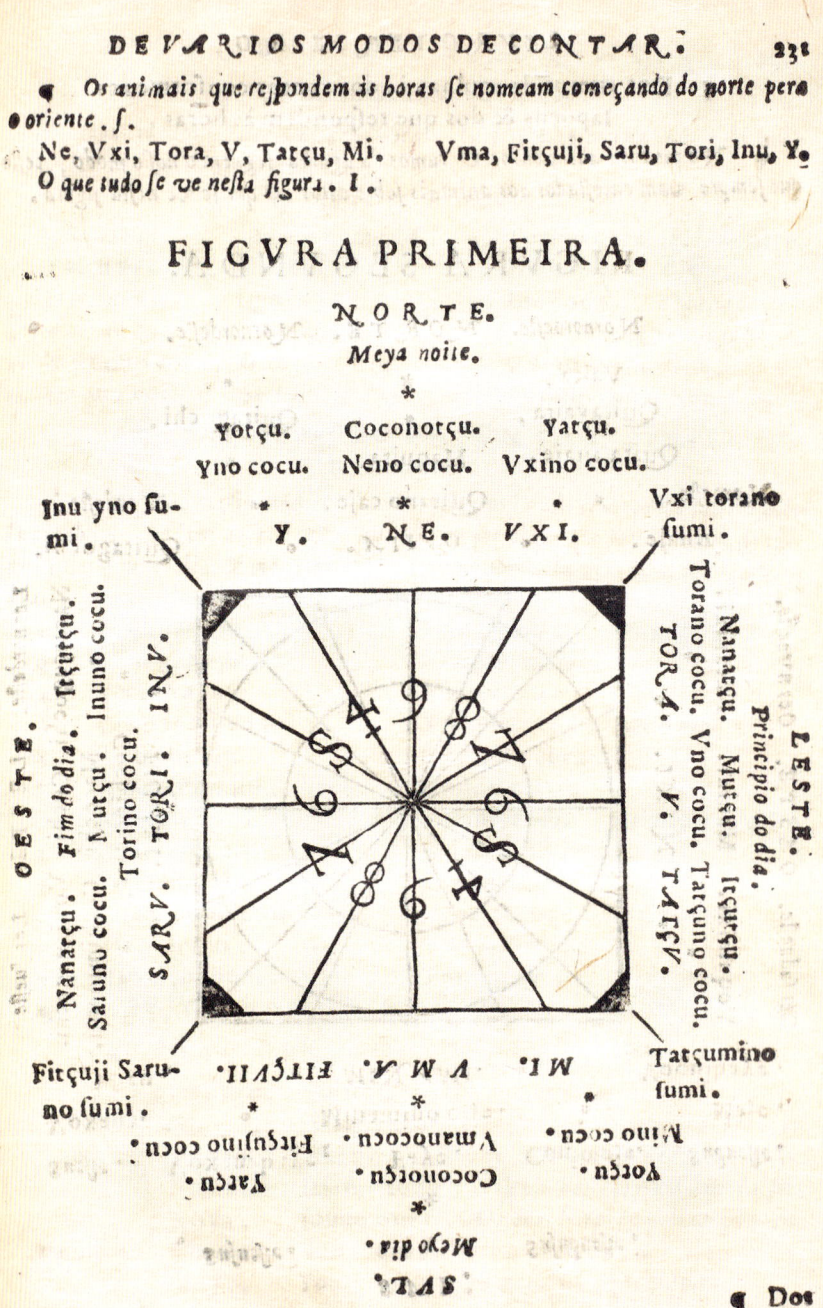

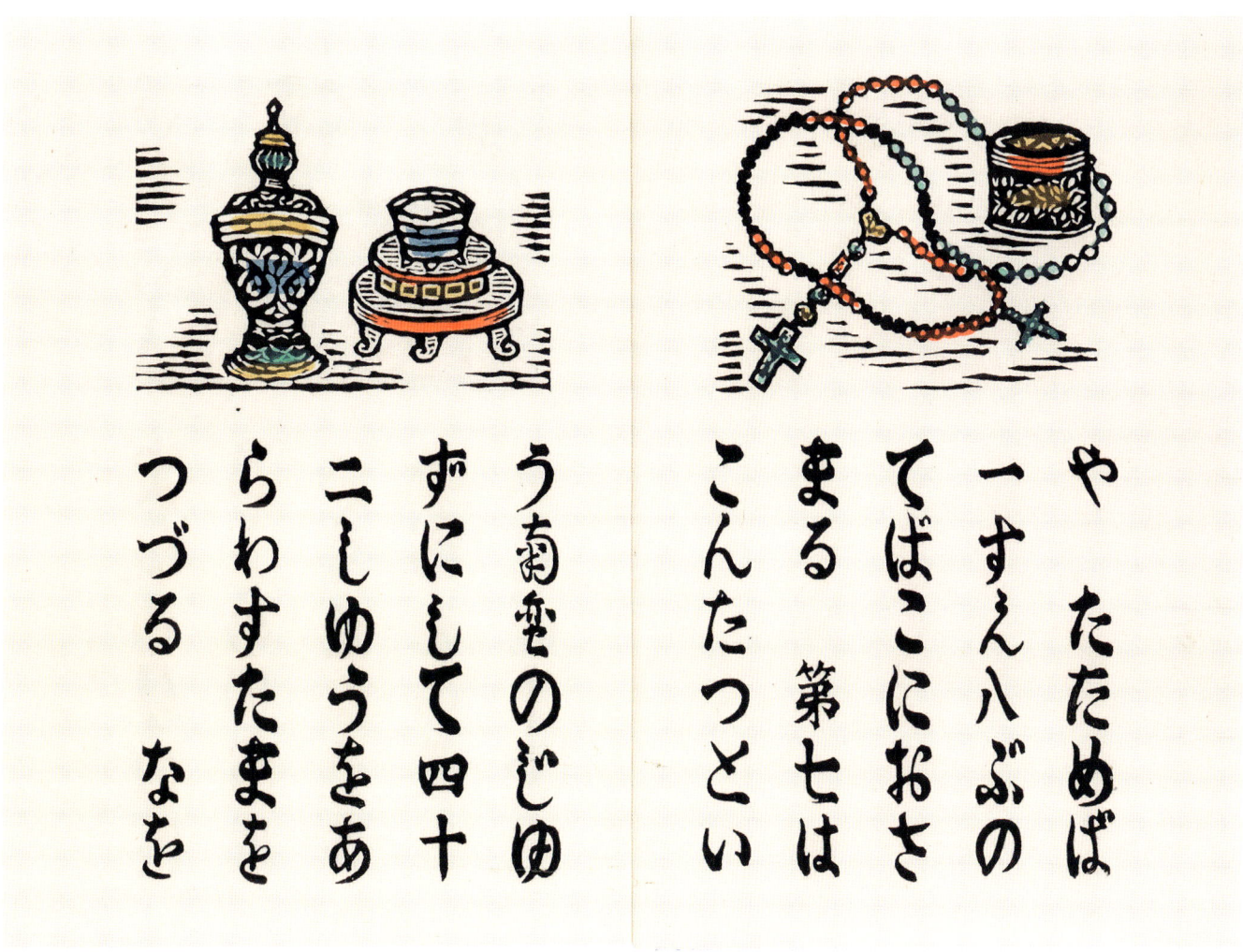

やたためば
一すゑ八ぶの
てばこにおさ
まる　第七は
こんたつとい

うゑ窒のじゅ
ずにもて四十
ニしゅうをあ
らわすたまを
つづる　なを

of part three of the 1608 work were incorporated into the main body of the lexicon. In this way, the early Jesuit mission printed books continued to exert some influence on the mission.

All three language and culture reference works described are of key importance for comprehending and translating other romanized texts from the Japanese Jesuit mission press today. Modern research on the Japanese mission and their books is, to a large extent, based on the six printed books held at the Bodleian Library. *Kirishitan-ban* helps us better understand not only

82 Kawakami Sumio, *Bansen Nyūshin*, 1969. Wood-block print on paper, hand-coloured. The title of the book means '(Southern) Barbarian ships entering the port'. The illustrations show a small caddy, two rosaries and other items that European trading ships brought to Japan in the late sixteenth and early seventeenth centuries. Nipponica 1002.

the language and culture of Japan at the time, but also the translational and cross-cultural relations. In cases of works such as the book of woodcuts by Kawakami, the now rare volumes can even contribute to more fully appreciating modern and contemporary arts.

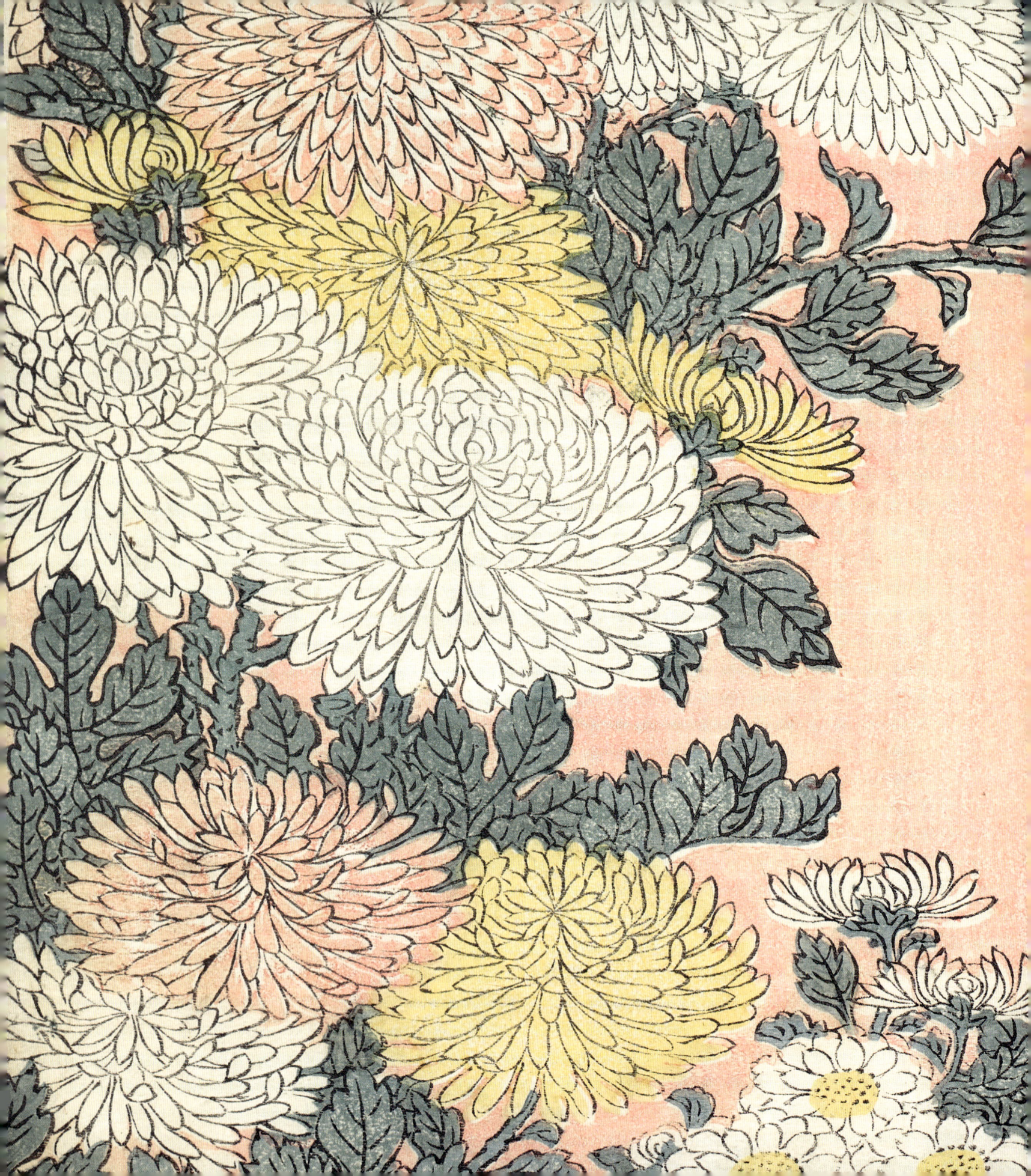

# 6

# Commercial publications
# in Tokugawa
# and Meiji Japan

LAURA MORETTI

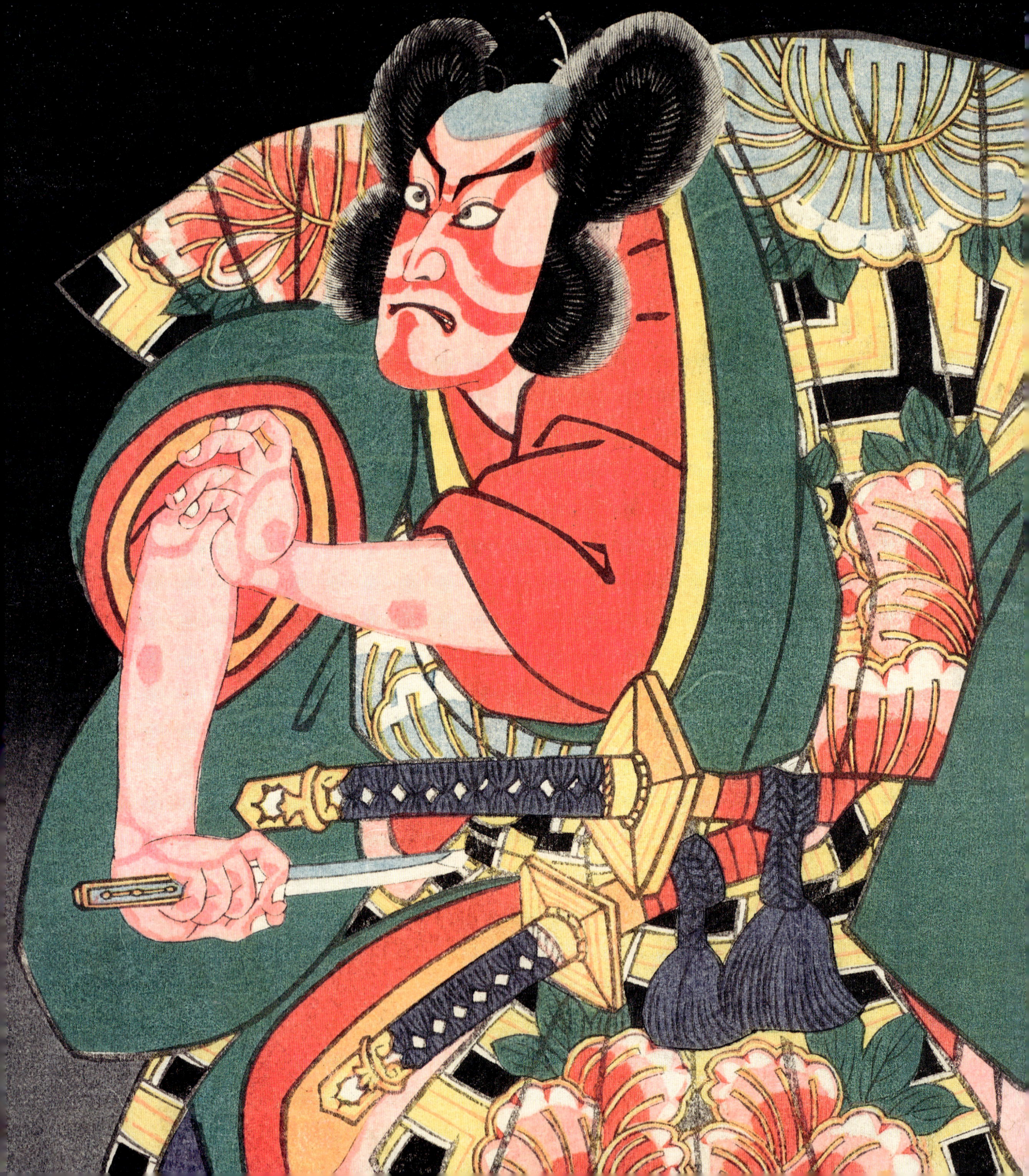

ITAMURA HIKOGORŌ (fl. eighteenth century) was an avid reader and collector of early modern graphic narratives (*kusazōshi*). He must have been still young when he started buying books around 1762, yet little is known about him or his family. The scant traces that this young man left in the books he owned – usually his signature (FIG. 84), possibly a date, and only rarely information about his acquisitions – tell a compelling story of a thriving publishing business. Hikogorō has been saved from oblivion by Kimura Yaeko's meticulous research on eighteenth-century picture books, which has shown that the books Hikogorō owned are now scattered in various collections throughout Japan and the United Kingdom, including his copy of *Hachiman Tarō ichidaiki* (*The Life of Hachiman Tarō*, FIG. 83).[1]

This chapter looks at key features of the world of Japanese commercial publications across the seventeenth, eighteenth and nineteenth centuries (FIG. 85). It first delves into an exploration of the publisher–bookseller Tsuruya Kiemon (fl. eighteenth century), who issued *Hachiman Tarō ichidaiki* and whose shop Hikogorō possibly visited for his purchase. It demonstrates the core traits of early modern commercial publishers, their business model, and the complexity of the space that they created – both physical and metaphorical. The focus then shifts to the technologies employed for the publication of books, particularly xylography and copperplate, which allowed for great flexibility. Finally, it addresses the culture of migration that characterizes much of the commercial publishing, ranging from the reuse of blocks in the production of new texts to the repackaging of textual materials in new formats. This brief journey across a complex universe made of books, publishers, authors, artists and readers is also conceived as a journey of discovery of the early modern and Meiji-era materials owned by the Bodleian Libraries.

83 OVERLEAF Covers for graphic narrative *Hachiman Tarō ichidaiki* (*The Life of Hachiman Tarō*), mid-eighteenth century. Published by Tsuruya Kiemon, Edo. This edition comprises five volumes. Nipponica 1009.

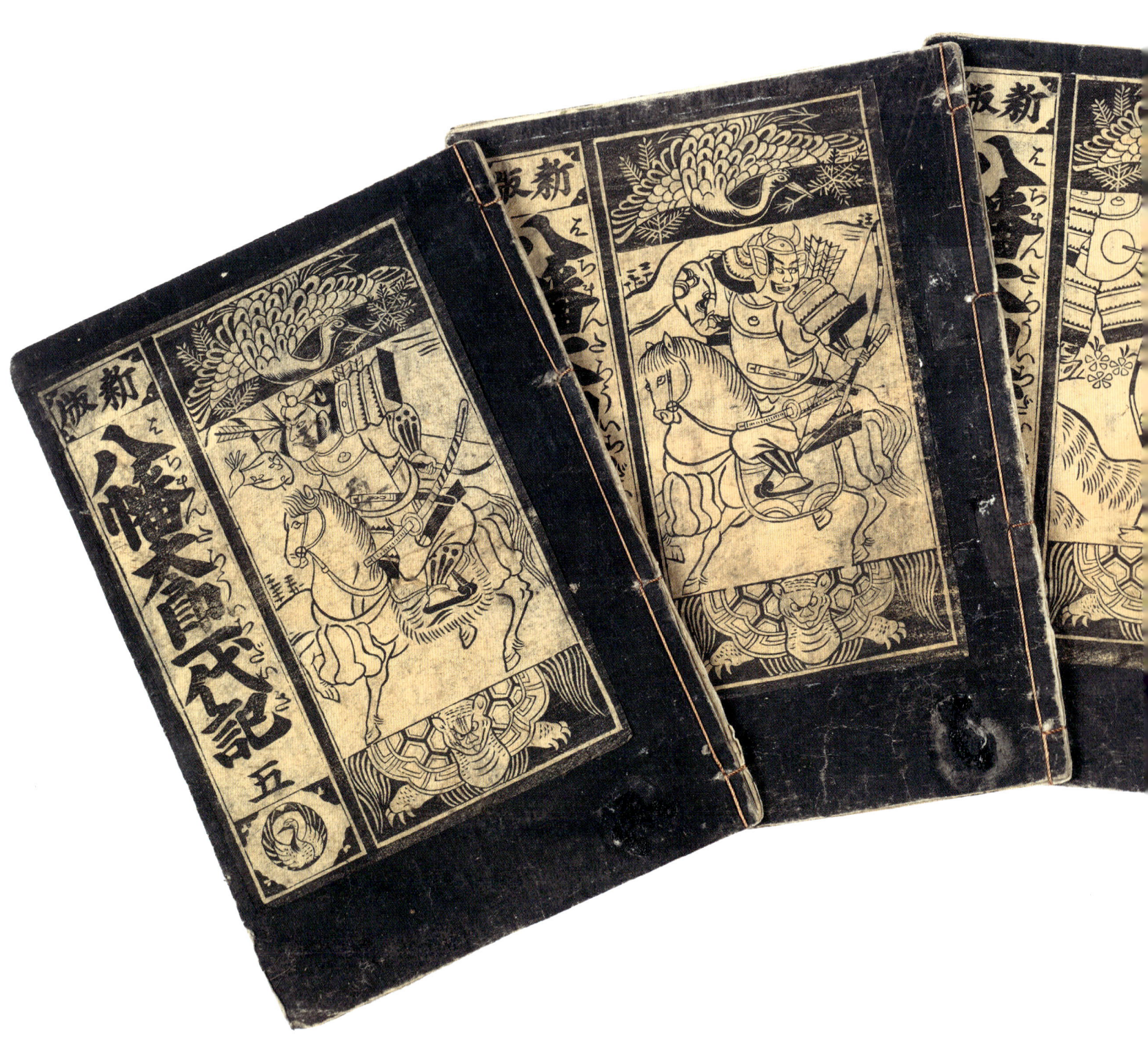

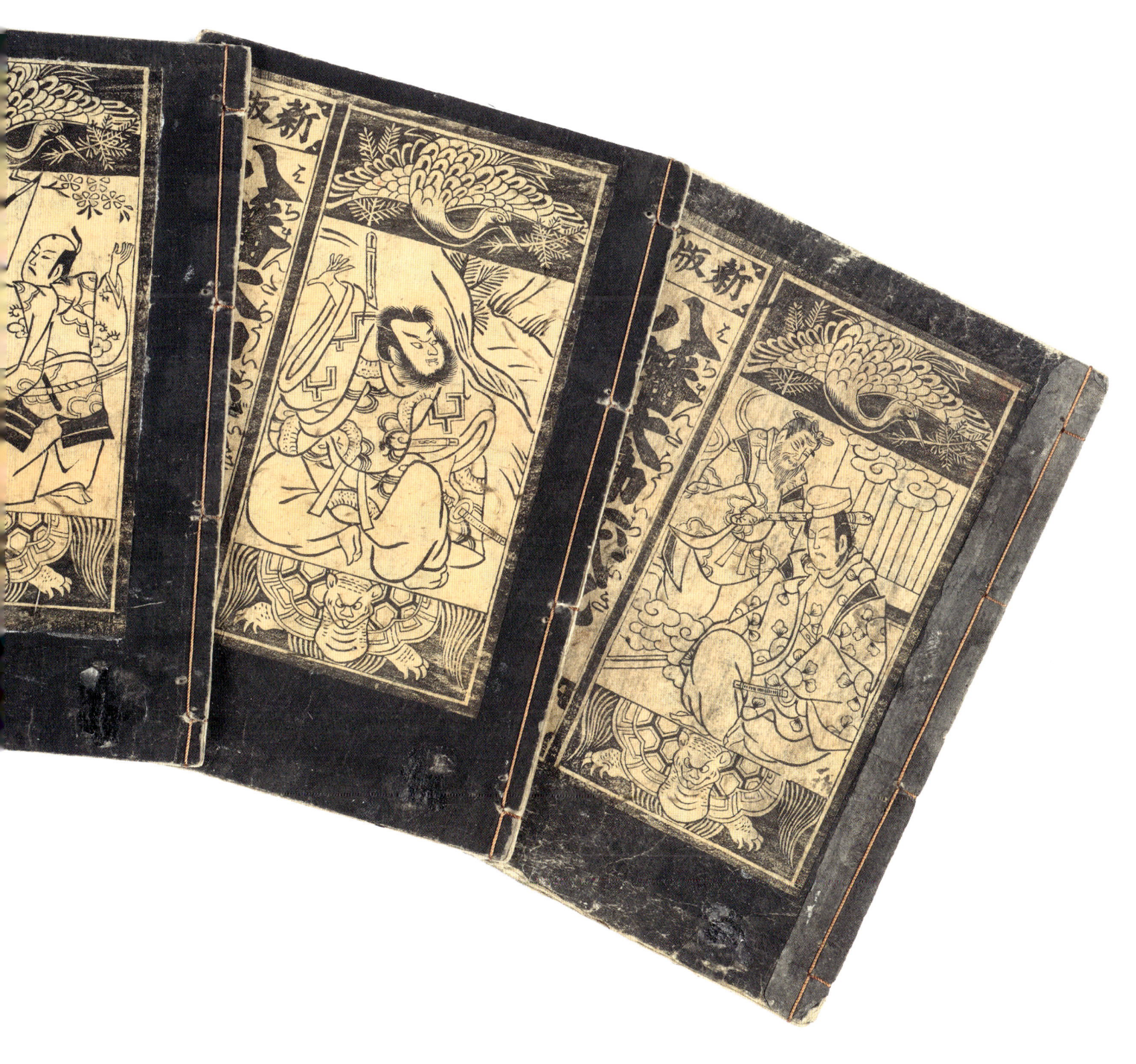

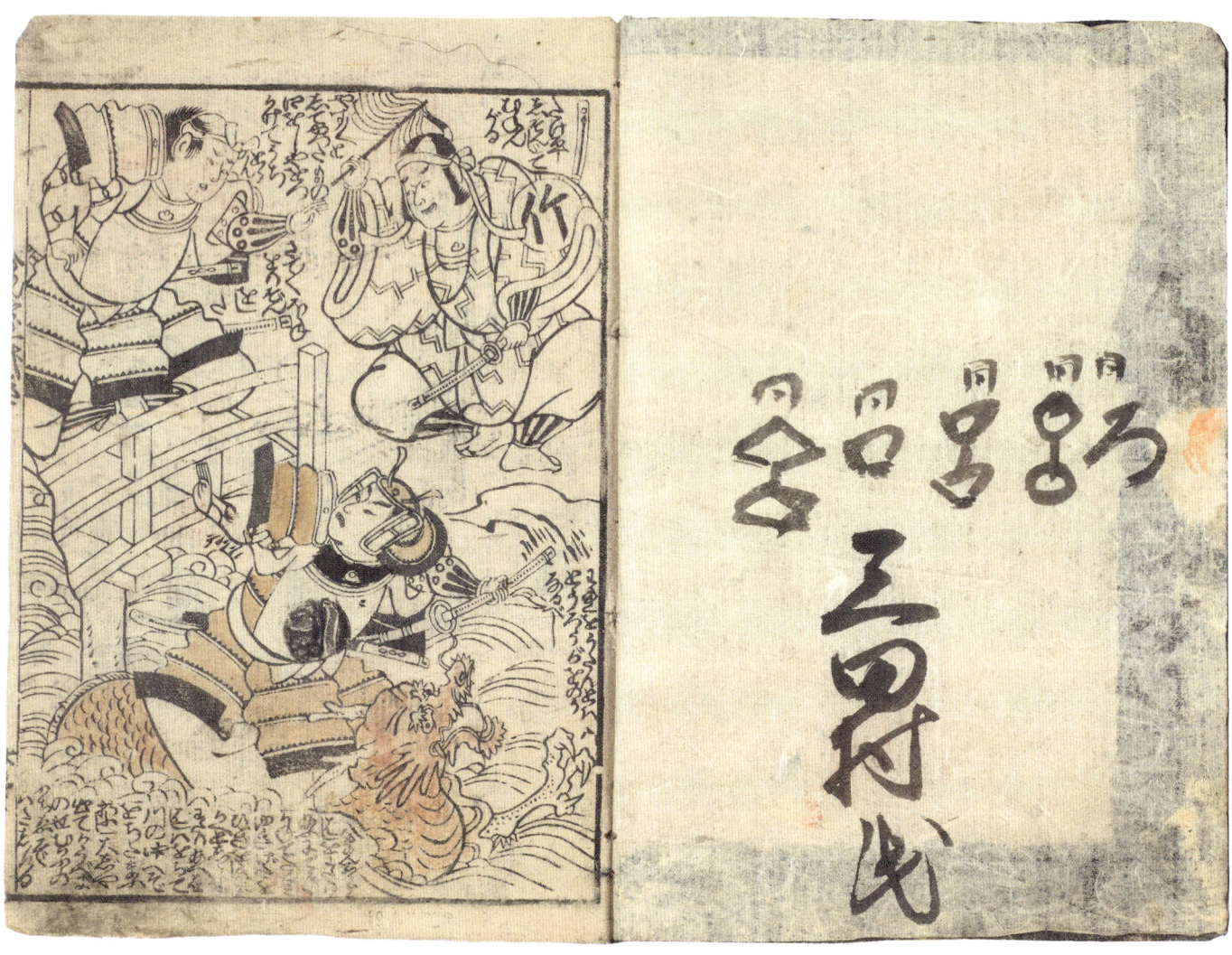

## THE ENTREPRENEURIAL MIND

By the end of the seventeenth century Kyoto had a well-established network of publishers, with around 1,500 names listed in the colophons of the myriad of books that were available on the market.[2] By the eighteenth century, Edo (today's Tokyo) and Osaka had joined what had become a burgeoning industry, with Edo gaining prominence from the second half of the eighteenth century. Tsuruya Kiemon – also known as Senkakudō – well exemplifies the successful career that a talented entrepreneur could secure. Tsuruya Kiemon's company started in Kyoto, as early as 1631 when we witness the birth of Japanese commercial publishing.[3] This is just seventeen years after the almanacs discussed in chapter 1 (see FIGS 14 & 15), some of the oldest Japanese woodblock-printed materials from the Tokugawa period held at the Bodleian Libraries. The Kyoto firm focused on the publication of librettos for the puppet theatre, and we know that it was still active at least until 1837.[4] In 1672 the Tsuruya Kiemon name also appears in conjunction with a book issued in Edo: *Buke hyakunin isshu* (*One Hundred Poets, One Poem Each by Warriors*).[5]

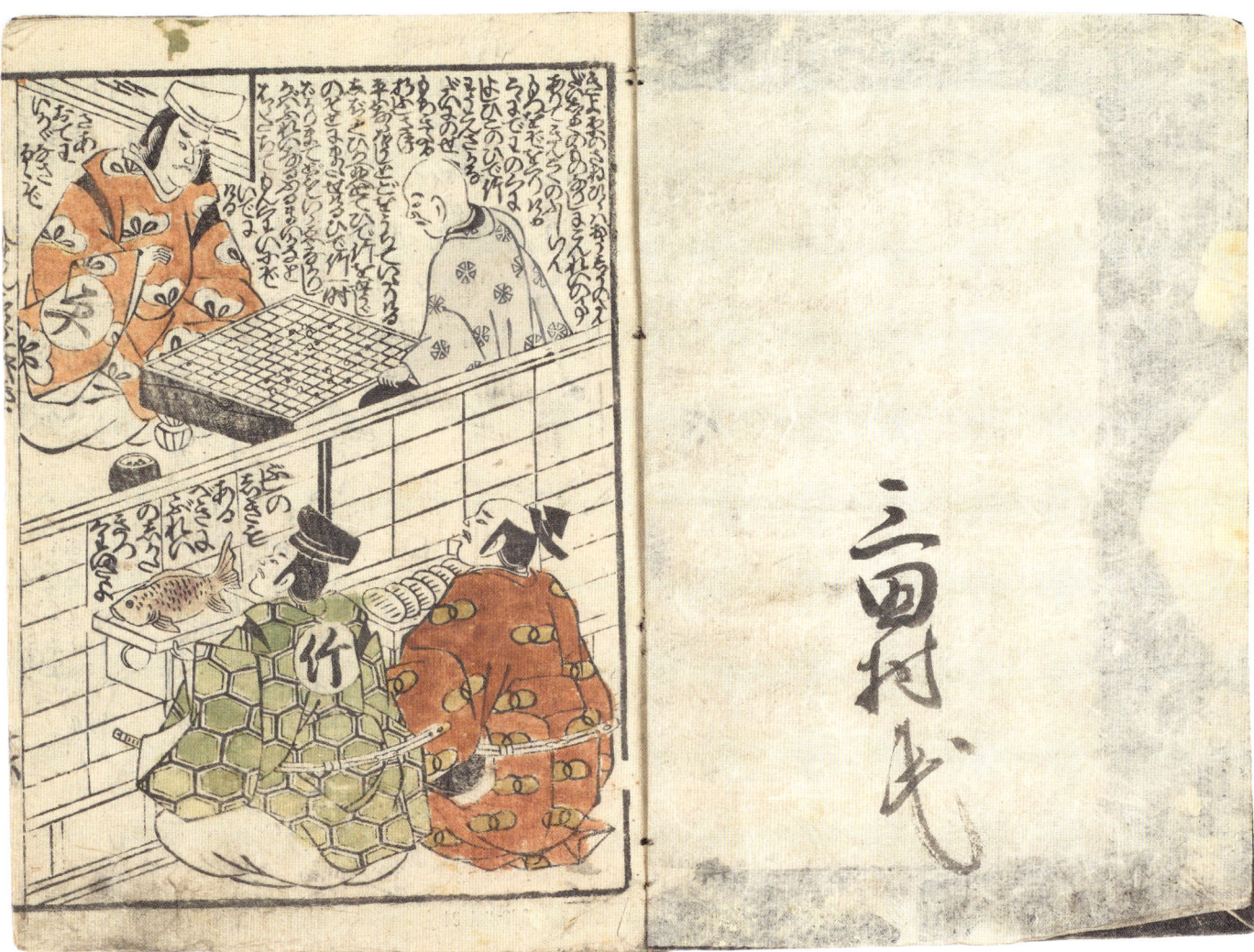

How the two Tsuruya Kiemon brands were connected is yet to be clarified. Located in the area of
Nihonbashi, the beating heart of the consumeristic
megacity of Edo and an area where several book-
shops converged, the Edo firm continued to trade
into the Meiji era.[6]

The Edo shop features in a number of contemporary materials, which allows us to form a better
image of how the company operated. It appears in
an oft-quoted 1824 business directory in association
with two words: *shomotsu* and *jihon*.[7] The former
was the label for more serious reading matter, while

84 Inside front cover and recto of the first folio from
RIGHT volume 4, and LEFT volume 5 of *Hachiman
Tarō ichidaiki* (*The Life of Hachiman Tarō*), showing the
signature of Mitamura Hikogorō (fl. eighteenth century).
Nipponica 1009.

the latter identified light-hearted booklets and
ephemera. This differentiation did not work as a
strict dichotomy, in particular during the seventeenth century, yet it became more apparent as the
publishing business started to feature guilds (*hon'ya
nakama*). In 1716, the Kyoto publishers of *shomotsu*
(or *shomotsuya*) united to regulate the publications

85 These pages show a snapshot of the variety of commercial products issued by publishers in early modern Japan. BOTTOM a later imprint of the 1655 *Kana retsujoden* (*Biographies of Women in the Vernacular*), possibly issued in Kyoto – a Japanese translation of a Han dynasty collection of the lives of exemplary and virtuous women. Kornicki 113. TOP LEFT The 1815 *Ehon jōruri zekku* (*Mixed Verses on Puppet Theatre*), issued in Edo and Nagoya, displays the virtuosity of Hokusai's brush and delights readers with a selection of poems and quotations from plays, using multifarious calligraphic hands. Kornicki 316. TOP RIGHT A charming collection of poetry published in 1801 by leading publisher Nishimuraya Yohachi: *Nyōbō Sanjūrokkasen (Thirty-Six Immortal Women Poets)*. Kornicki 1003. OVERLEAF, LEFT Books written in Chinese also constituted an important part of the book market, as the 1660 medical book titled *Jūshikei hakki* shows. It explains the locations of meridians and acupuncture points. Kornicki 15. OVERLEAF, TOP RIGHT & BOTTOM A map of the main road connecting Kyoto to Edo: *Tōkaidō gojūsan-eki shōkei (Beautiful Views of the Fifty-Three Stations along the Tōkaidō Highway)*, bound in a concertina book, dated 1860, and surviving with its original wrappers. Nipponica 353.

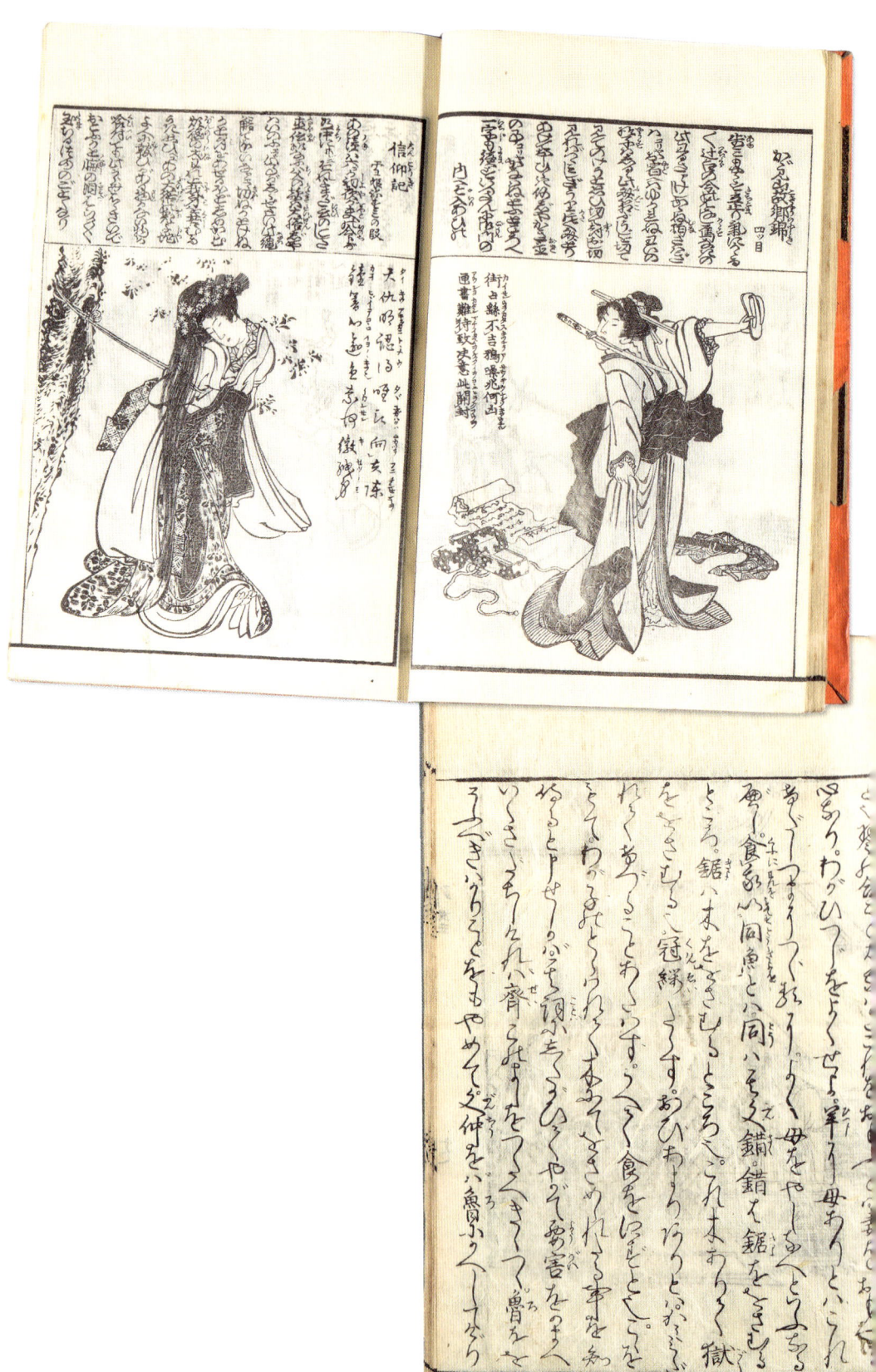

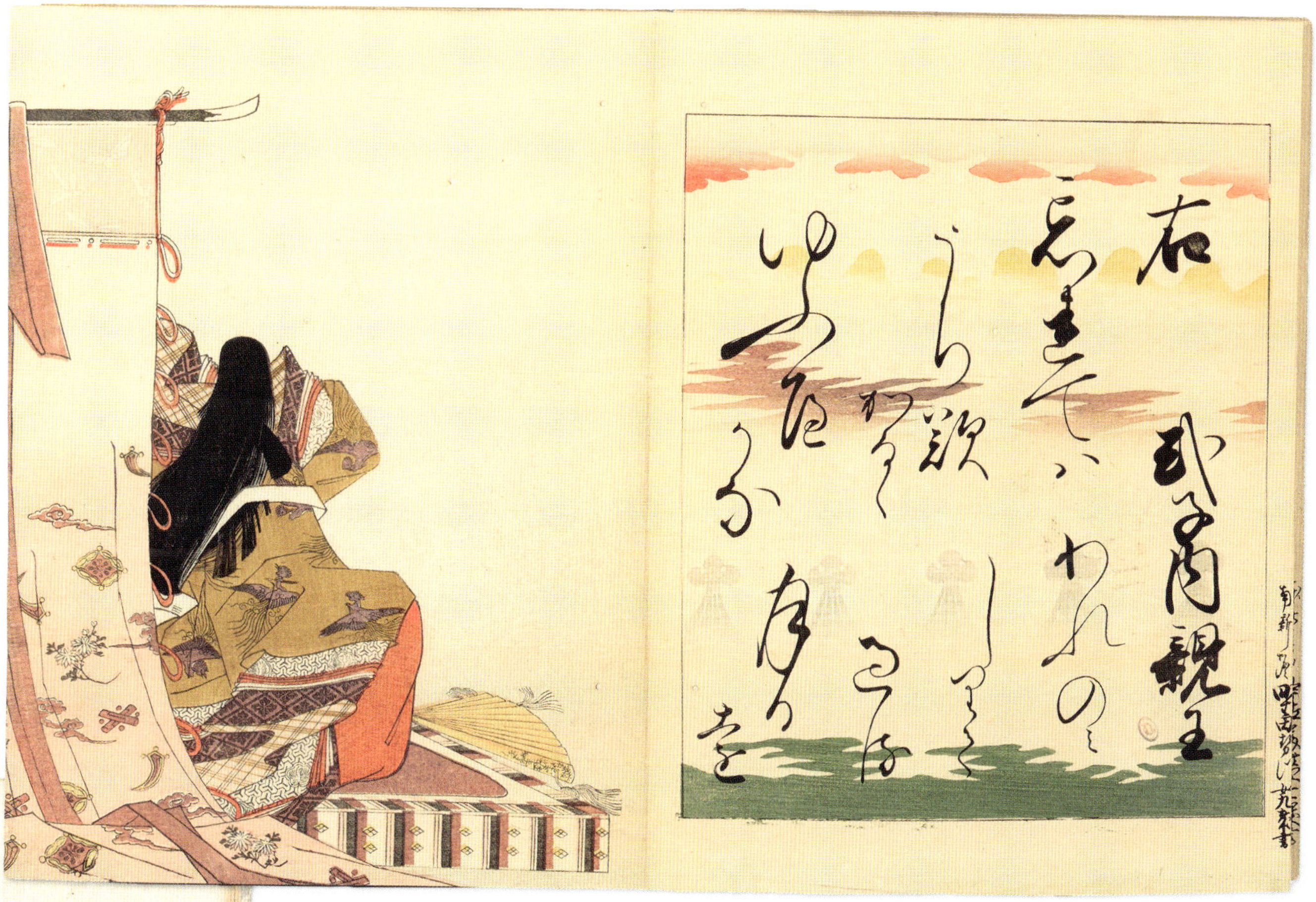

右

武蔵鐙

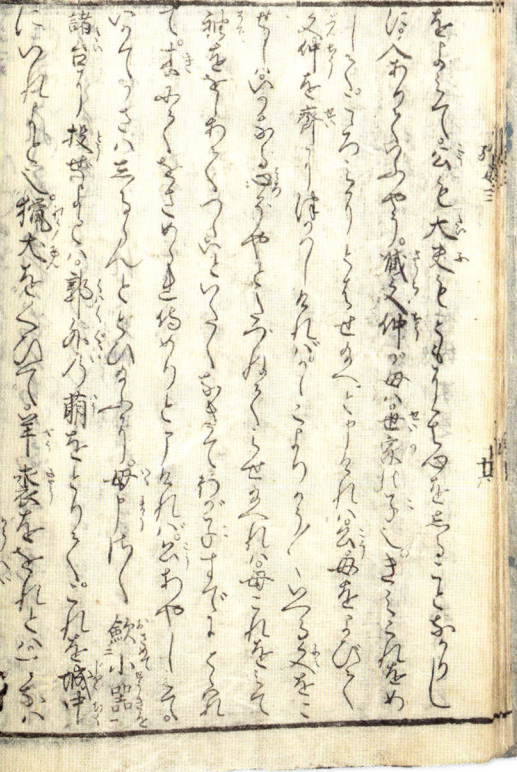

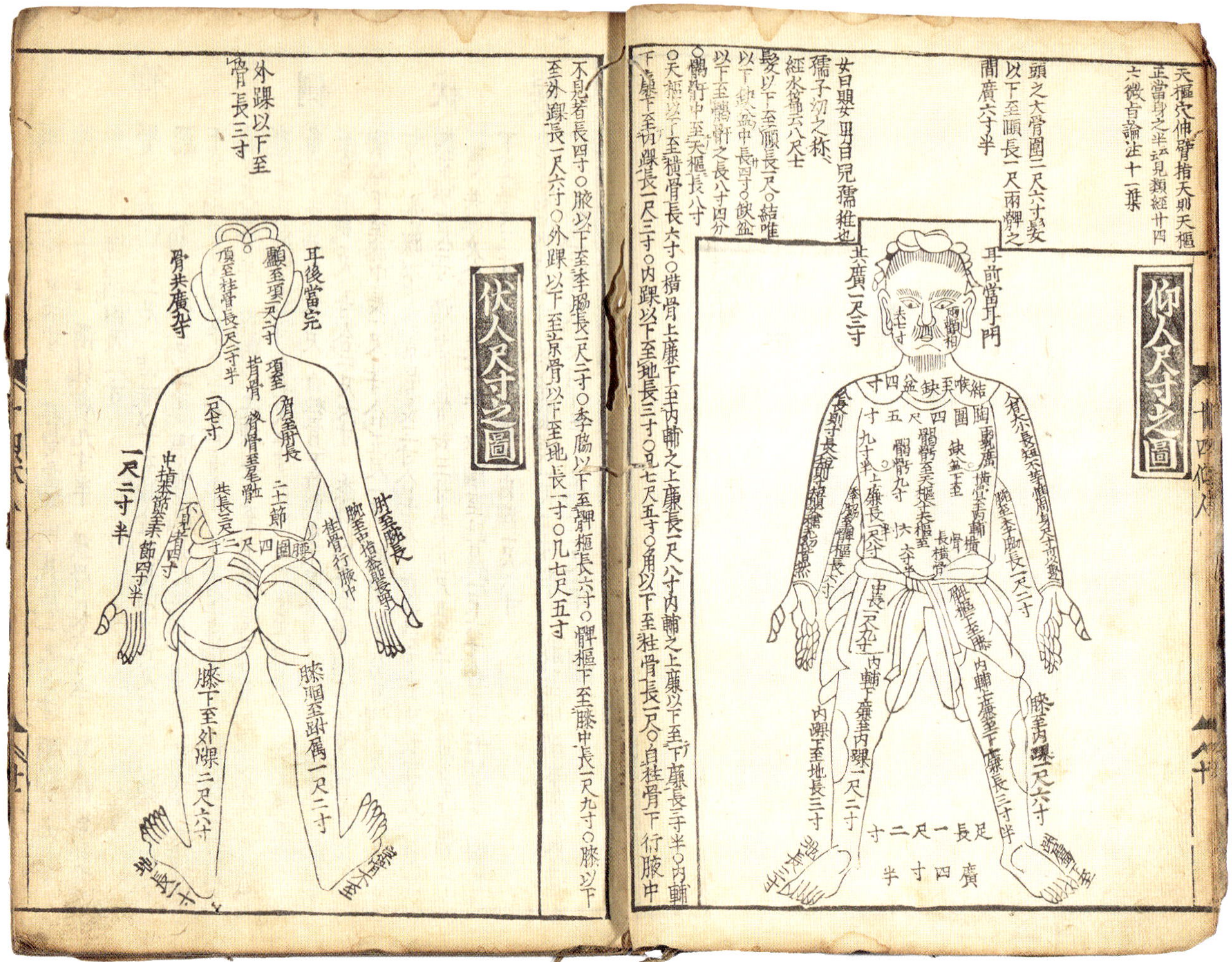

仰人天寸之図

伏人尺寸之図

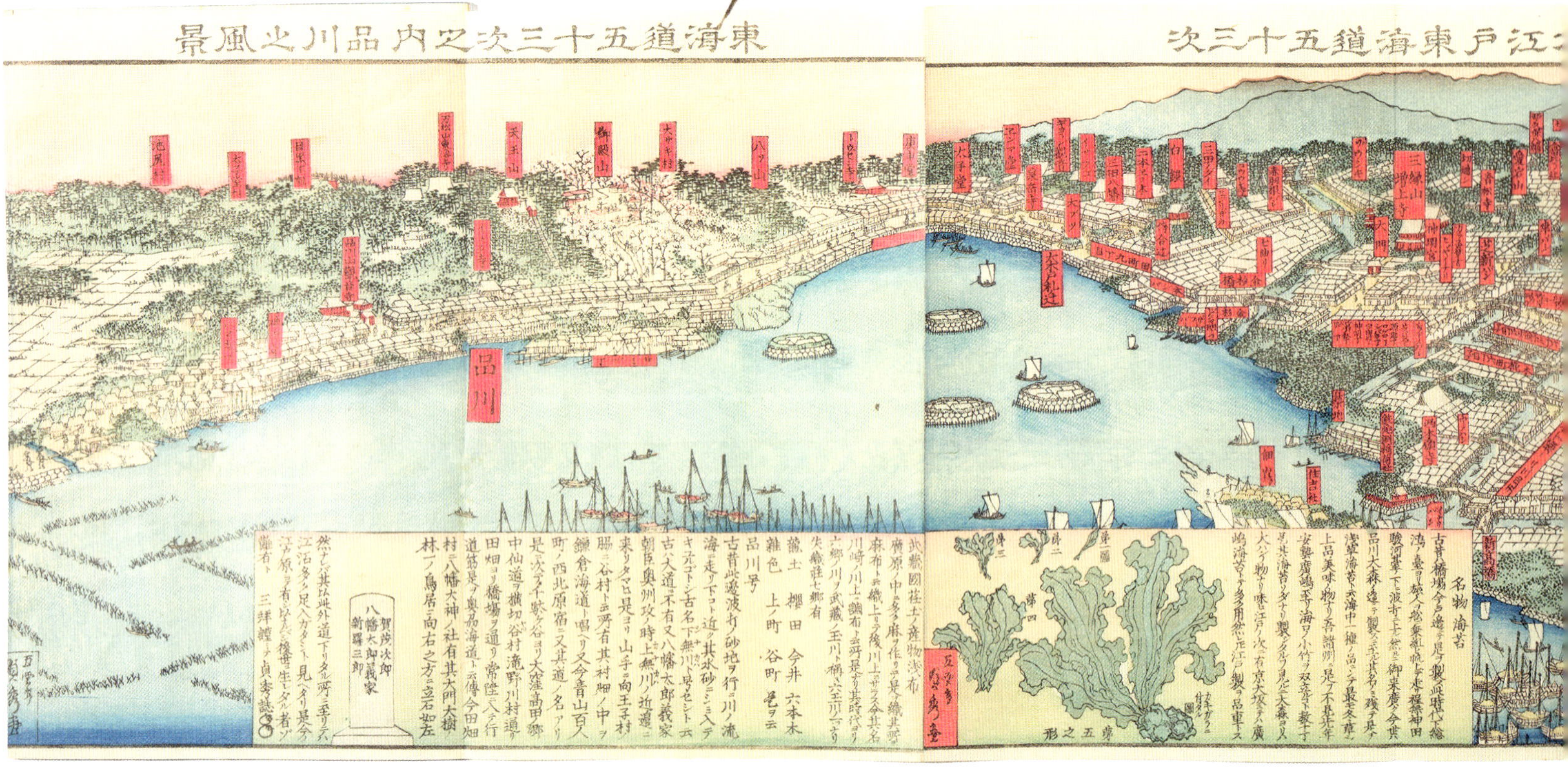

東海道五十三次之内　品川　止風景

江戸東海道五十三次

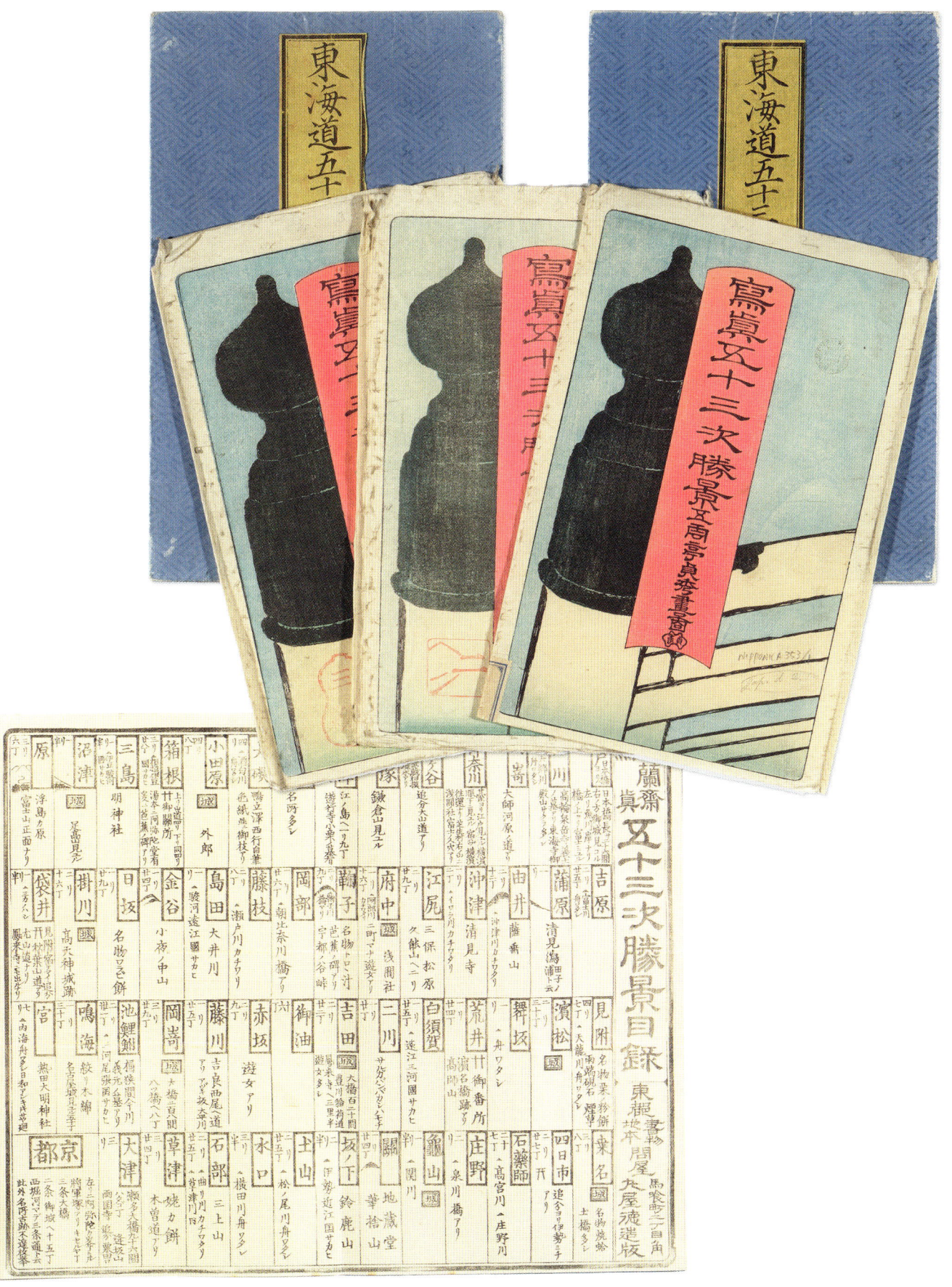

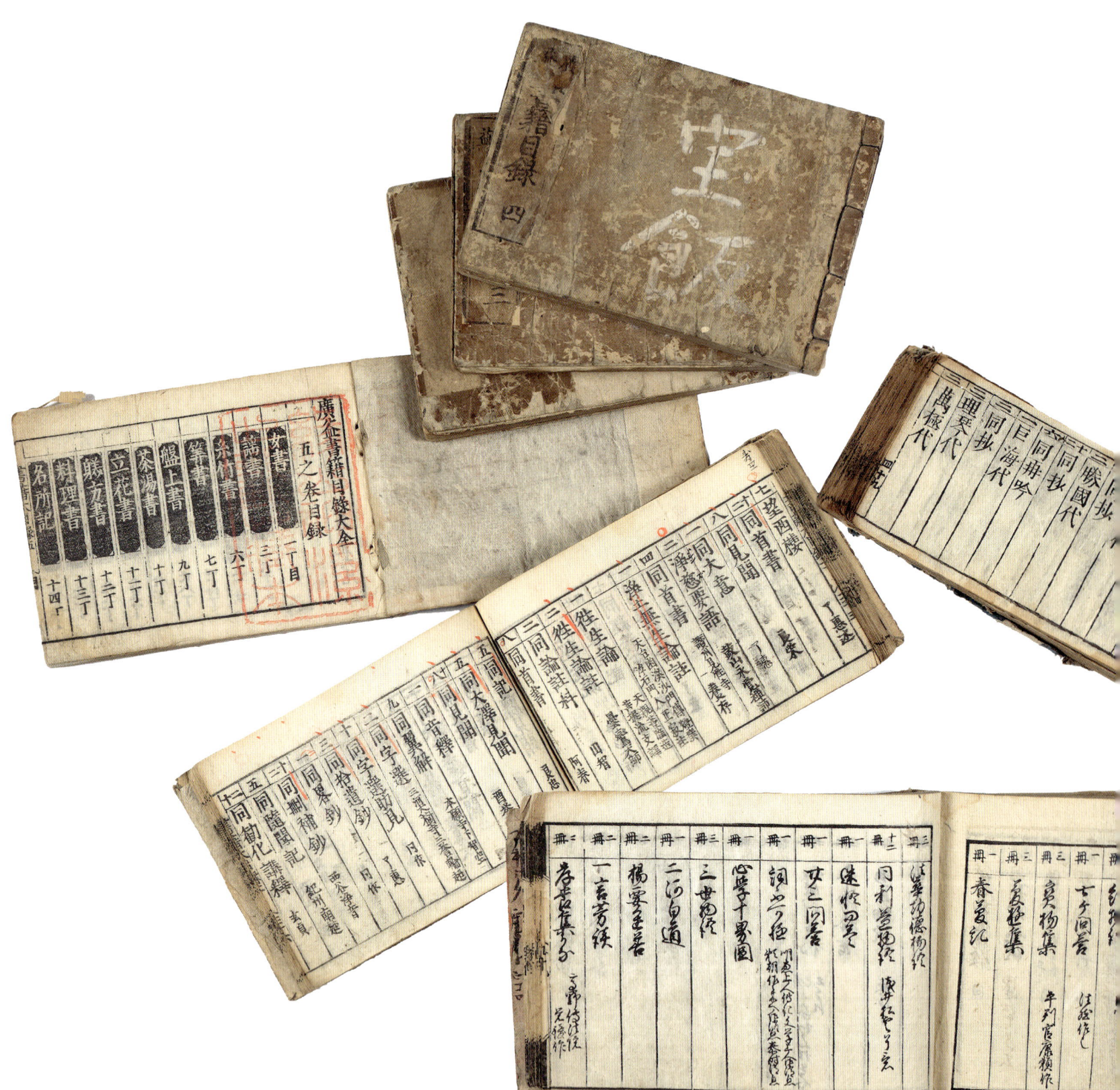

of books, in an attempt to prevent cannibalistic duplications of their printed matter. The same happened in Edo in 1721, and in Osaka in 1723. However, there seems to have been no apparent equivalent organization for publishers of *jihon* (also known as *jihon'ya* or *sōshiya*). The Tsuruya shop in Edo undertook both types of enterprise, thus maximizing the chance of profit. The same business directory offers a list of some of Tsuruya's products: calendars in booklet format (*Edo-goyomi*), picture books (*ezōshi*) of the type that Hikogorō used to buy, fully coloured woodblock prints (*nishiki-e*), and various types of printed paper.

The range of textual typologies that the company's stock covered over the centuries is impressive. The Union Catalogue Database of Japanese Texts lists 590 titles connected to the name Tsuruya Kiemon. As well as the products listed above we find textbooks (*ōraimono*), including maths books and calligraphy manuals, along with travel literature

86 Selection of *shojaku mokuroku* (book-trade catalogues) published in 1674 and 1692. They list titles of books that were available on the market at that point in time, organized according to publishing genres. Kornicki 48, Kornicki 49, Kornicki 50.

and guidebooks, jestbooks, poetry anthologies of linked poetry (*haikai*), mad-verses (*kyōka*) and Chinese poetry, non-fictional essays (*zuihitsu*), theatre playbills, and fictional genres that literary histories normally subsume under the label of *gesaku* (literally 'playful work', often translated as 'playful literature' or 'frivolous literature'). One of their most notable genres was that of graphic narratives. The firm worked in tandem with celebrated authors and illustrators to package delightful books where texts and illustrations collaborate in the creation of meaning.[8] The publication of the best-selling *Nise Murasaki inaka Genji* (*A Fraudulent Murasaki's Bumpkin Genji*) – comprising seventy-six individual volumes, published from 1829 to 1842 – is certainly the jewel in Tsuruya's crown.[9]

The study of titles published by early modern publishers in Japan is assisted by book-trade catalogues (*shojaku mokuroku*) and publishers' catalogues (*zōhan mokuroku*). *Shojaku mokuroku* were issued from 1667 into the nineteenth century as stand-alone publications that listed the books available on the market in a specific area (FIG. 86). *Zōhan mokuroku* refers to the list of titles published by a specific publisher at a specific point in time, usually included at the back of their publications.[10] To anyone wishing to reconstruct the phenomenal output of Tsuruya Kiemon, the publisher's catalogues are a source of precious information that complements that in the Union Catalogue. For instance, the catalogue that comes at the end of a six-volume graphic narrative issued in 1826 includes publicity about calendars, travel-related materials, manuals of instruction and education for women, and books about kabuki actors, with the last half-folio zooming in to the array of the graphic narratives issued that year. The crest displaying a crane (the *tsuru* in Tsuruya's name) and the address are followed by an invitation to visit the shop.[11] From other sources we learn that cosmetic products were also on sale.[12]

Tsuruya Kiemon's stock showcases the magnitude of the business of commercial books in Edo-period Japan. From the seventeenth century onwards the publishing industry catered for all sorts of interests and literacy abilities, inundating the market with a wide range of printed materials that quenched the thirst for knowledge, information and entertainment. It is a dazzling metaphorical space made of words and images packaged in exquisite and affordable products, printed by savvy entrepreneurs.

What about the physical space of Tsuruya's shop? Figure 87 helps us form a mental picture of what Hikogorō would have seen, although it is dated a few decades later. It is taken from the influential guidebook *Edo meisho zue* (*Guide to Famous Places in Edo*), published between 1834 and 1836.[13] Despite being issued by publisher Suharaya Mohee and

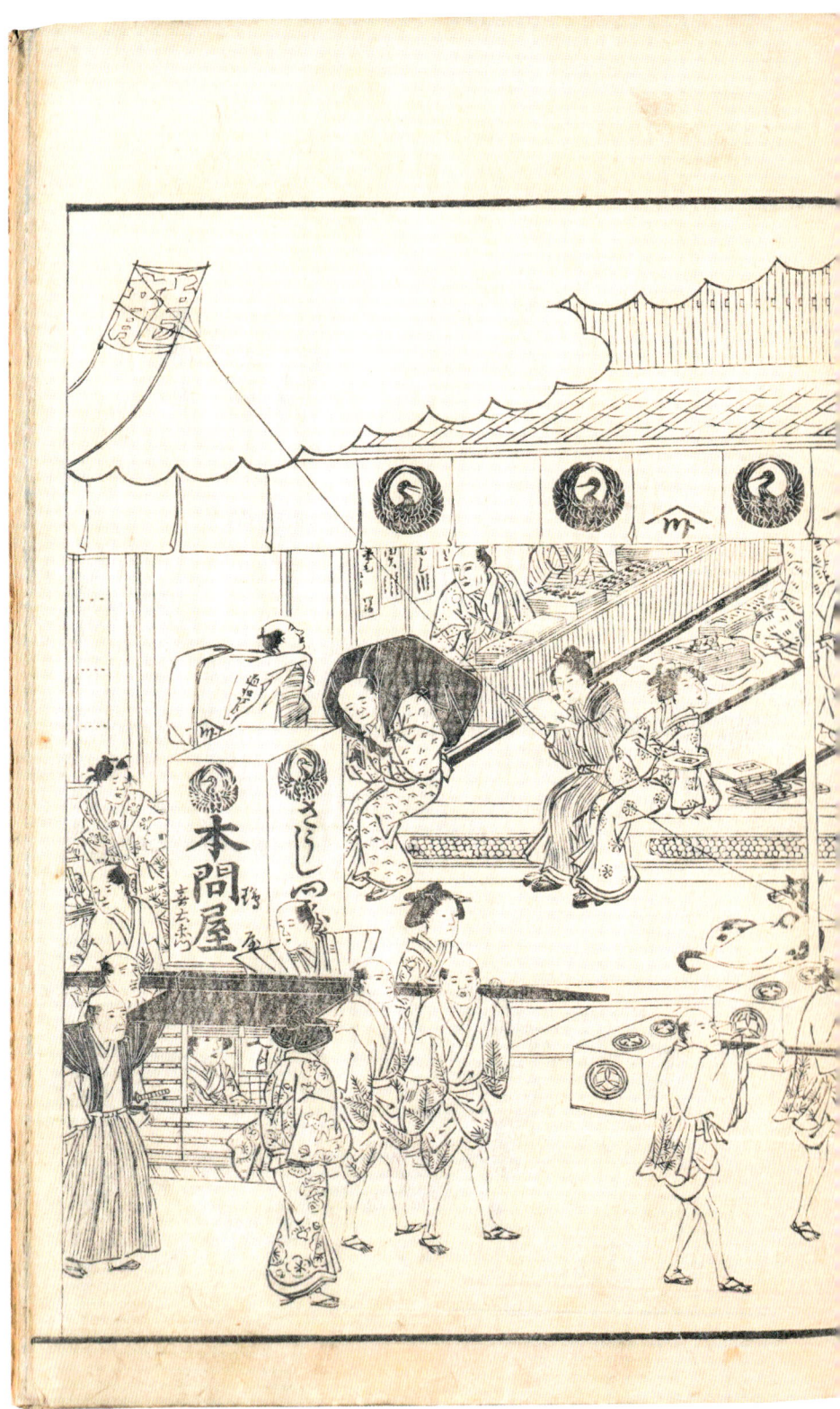

87 Double-page illustration of Tsuruya Kiemon's bookshop in Edo, from Saitō Chōshu (author), Hasegawa Settan (illustrator), *Edo meisho zue* (*Guide to Famous Places in Edo*), 1834–36. Published by Suharaya Mohee, Edo, vol. 1, 61v–62r.

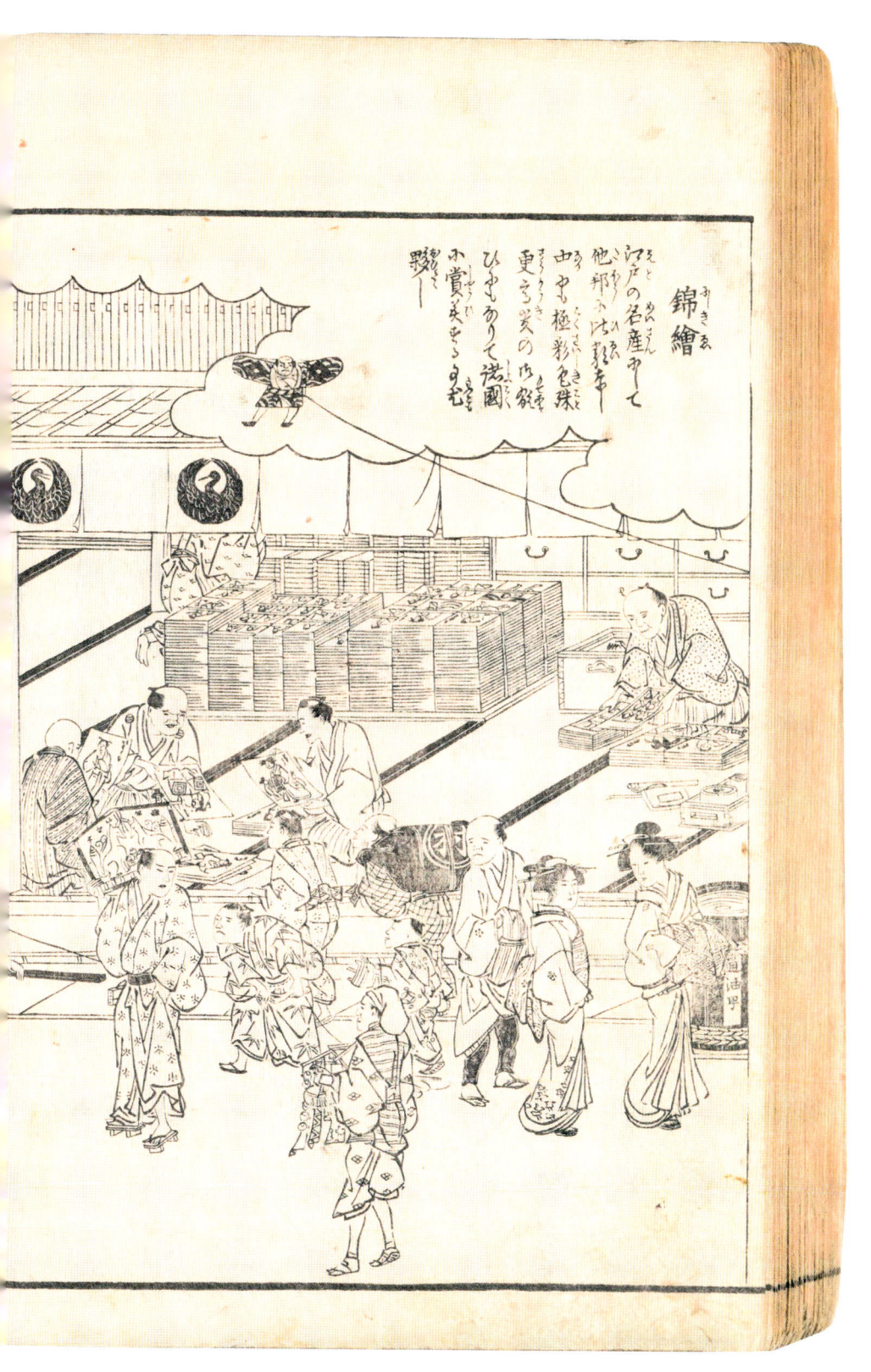

錦繪

錦繪は江戸の名産にして
他邦に比類なく
由て極彩色珠
更に美の巧緻
ひとしくありて諸國
小賞に美ちる事
歟

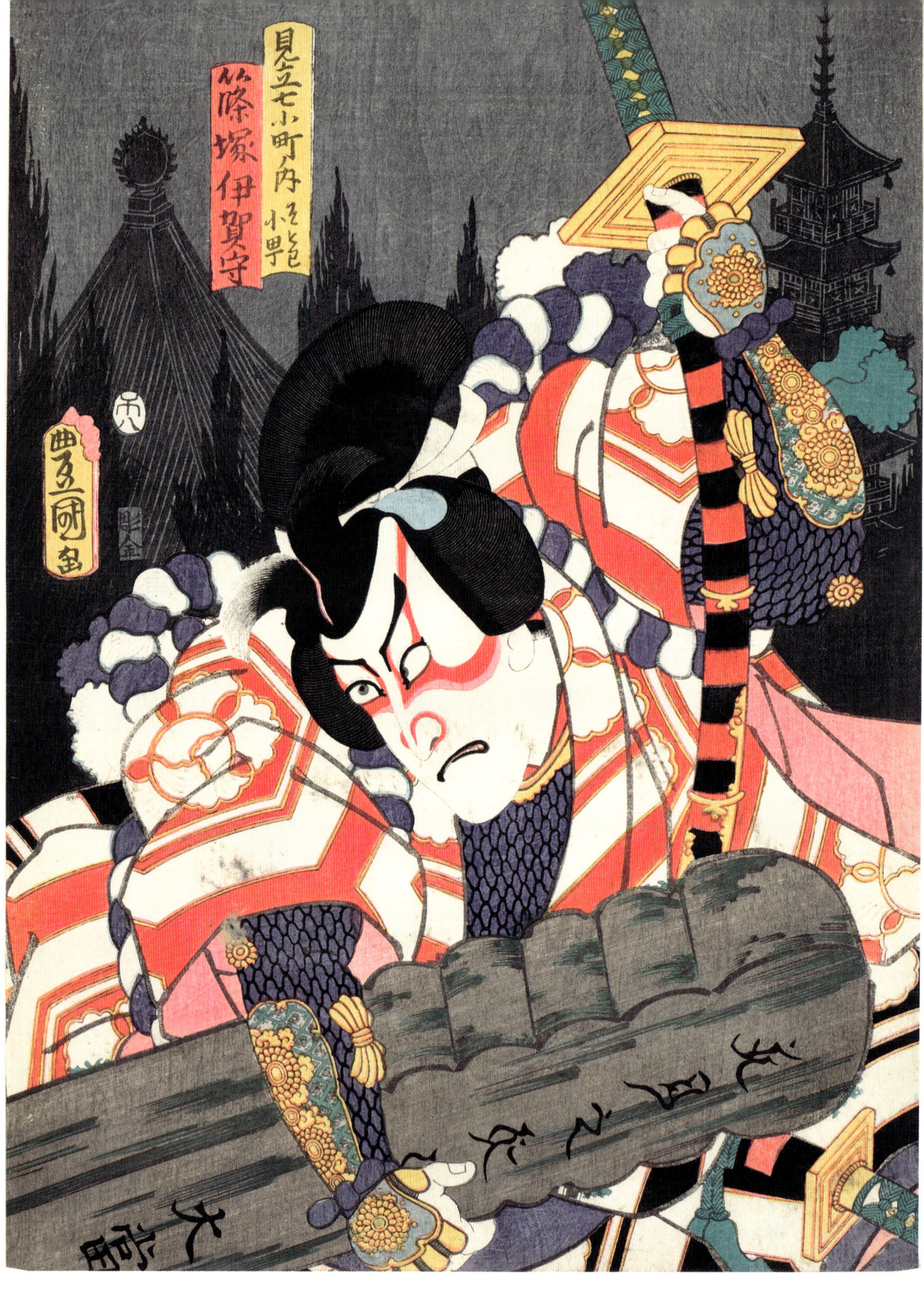

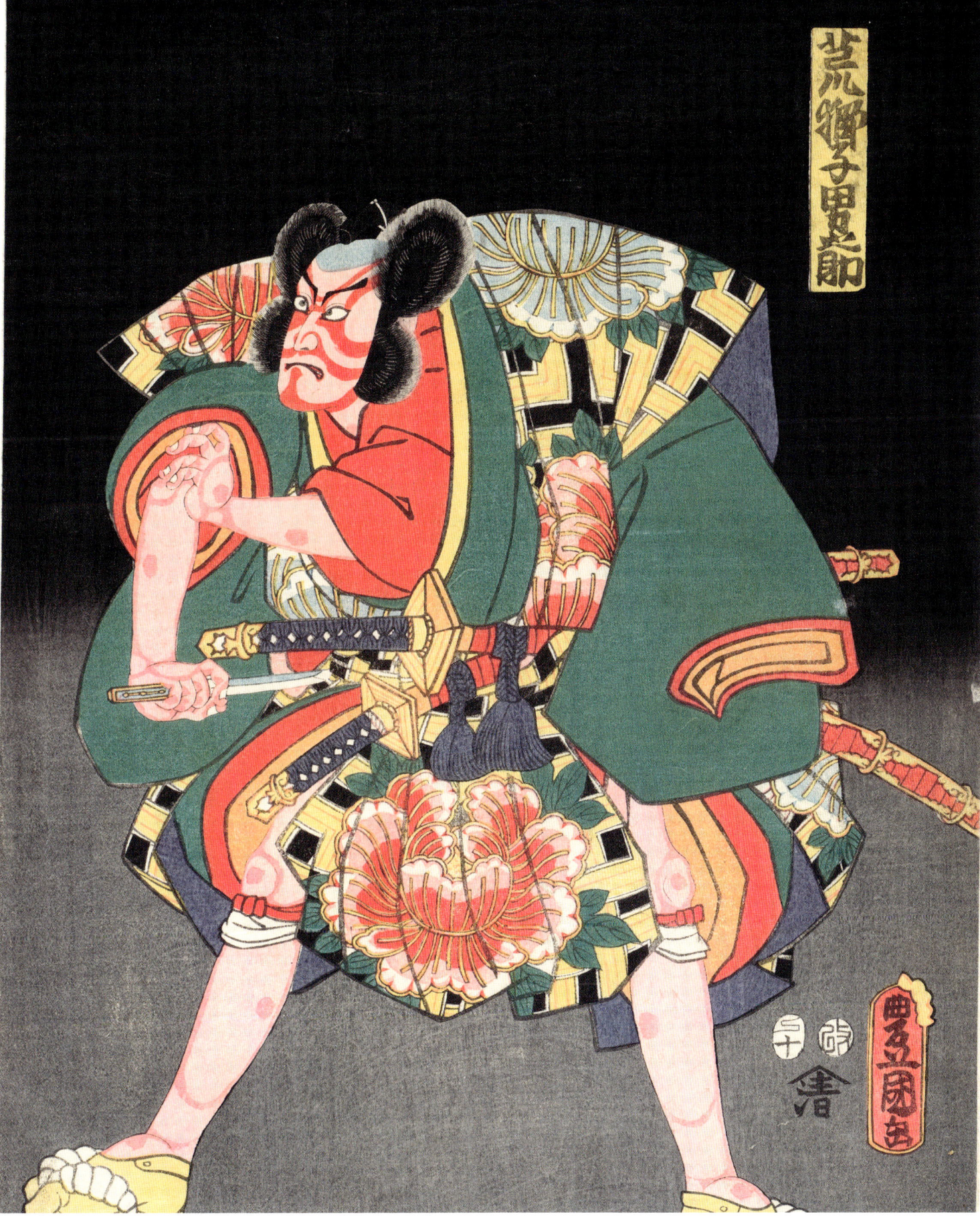

being distributed in fourteen shops – crucially, not at Tsuruya's – this guidebook celebrates Tsuruya Kiemon's success by displaying the shop on a double-page spread. A pile of prints, most likely fully coloured woodblock prints, dominates the right side of the shop, visually reinforcing the message conveyed by the caption on the right: *nishiki-e* prints are the centrepiece of urban Edo and its publishing culture, admired and desired across the country. Such prints presented the charms of the contemporary world – landscapes, the kabuki stage (FIGS 88 & 89), contemporary beauties, warriors, humorous and playful images, and much more – in a reasonably priced item that could be purchased in any shop like Tsuruya's. *Nishiki-e* prints, illustrated books and ephemera shared an osmotic space where fertile cross-pollination was the norm.

Tsuruya Kiemon is paraded as *the* must-go-to shop if one wishes to purchase such an iconic product. This is not to say that books are absent from Tsuruya's shop. Two female customers are foregrounded on the left, absorbed in reading two booklets that share the physical qualities of graphic narratives, just like *Hachiman Tarō*

88 PREVIOUS SPREAD, LEFT *Nishiki-e* print (*ōban* size) by Utagawa Toyokuni III (1786–1865), depicting a kabuki actor in the role of Shinozuka Iganokami. From the series *Mitate nana Komachi no uchi* (*Matches for the Seven Komachi Plays*). Issued in 1858 by Shimizuya Naojirō, Edo. Nipponica 363.

89 PREVIOUS SPREAD, RIGHT (& PAGE 186) *Nishiki-e* print (*ōban* size) by Utagawa Toyokuni III (1786–1865), depicting a kabuki actor in the role of Arajishi Otokonosuke. Issued in 1857 by Shimizuya Naojirō, Edo. Nipponica 363.

*ichidaiki* (see FIG. 84). Outside, on the far left near the shop sign, are two young boys who look deeply satisfied at their purchases. Inside, at the back of the shop on the left, is the clerks' desk with abacus and account books as a reminder that this was a quintessentially commercial enterprise, organized for the publisher–bookseller to enjoy financial profit. The two men carrying voluminous bundles on their shoulders bring to the fore another facet of Tsuruya Kiemon's business model: that of wholesaler, distributing goods to other retailers. This means that our Hikogorō could have purchased his book at a different shop. It is widely assumed that Tsuruya would also sell goods purchased from other publishers.[14]

Early modern Japanese publisher–booksellers provided customers with a wonderfully interactive space in which to sample printed products and socialize, whilst fuelling the distribution of books and printed matters to retailers within and outside the capital Edo. They shaped a complex business network that extended to Japan at large and that still awaits full investigation. Everyone was welcome to the early modern Japanese bookshop: men, women and children from across different sectors within Japanese society. A charming *senryū* (seventeen-syllable poem) even suggests that one could visit Tsuruya's shop at night:

> *ko o omou*　　　　子を思ふ
> *yoru no Tsuruya e*　夜るの鶴やへ
> *kusazōshi*　　　　艸さうし
> Thinking about the children / Tsuruya is open till late / with his graphic narratives [15]

A sketch of the same shop delighted Western readers in the 1870 *Le Japon illustré* (FIG. 90).

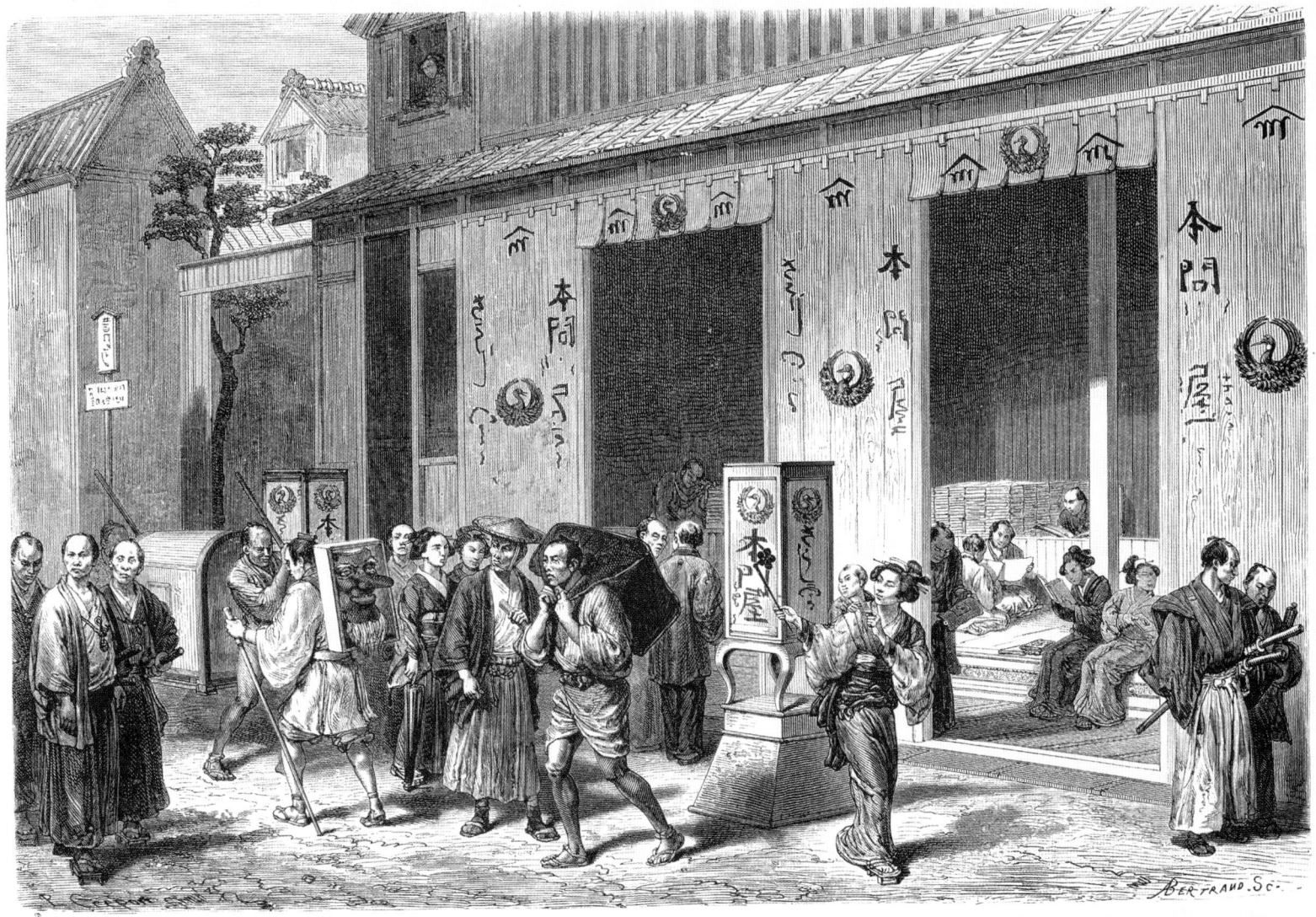

Although the artist might have been inspired by the image in the guidebook to Edo discussed above, it would not be impossible to imagine some fidelity to how the Meiji-era shop of Tsuruya Kiemon might have looked. If Henry Moseley had had a chance to visit bookshops other than the ones in Osaka (see the introduction to the present volume),

90 Tsuruya Kiemon's bookshop. Engraving from Aimé Humbert, *Le Japon illustré*, Hachette, Paris, 1870, p. 5. 247192 c.3.

he would have almost certainly stumbled upon this establishment, one that thrived from the very beginning of the book industry in Japan.

## COMPLEX PAGE LAYOUTS

Let us take a look at *Hachiman Tarō ichidaiki*, the book issued by Tsuruya Kiemon that Hikogorō purchased. On the recto of the first folio (FIG. 91) we read that the warrior Minamoto no Yoriyoshi laments the lack of a male heir and goes on a pilgrimage to the Iwashimizu Hachimangū shrine in Kyoto. Moved by the man's deep faith, the deity enshrined there reassures the man that he will be blessed with the birth of a son and gifts him a sword, with the promise that this will ensure the continuation of the family line.

Within the printed frame, at the top of which we note Tsuruya's crest, the page effortlessly accommodates text and images. At the bottom right, asleep, is Yoriyoshi; the first logographic character of his name (頼) is visible in the middle of his chest. Sitting next to him is probably a retainer, not mentioned in the verbal text. The visual and the verbal dimensions work in tandem to co-create meaning. Looming over them is a cloud that supports the apparition of the deity, who carries the promised sword. The text occupies the empty spaces of the page. Narration and speech (with the deity's words) mix in the two blocks of text at the bottom of the page, whilst the text at the top rehearses once more the god's words, with a different speech line. The text contains few logographic characters and is mainly recorded in phonetic script, making reading accessible also to novice readers with limited literacy.[16] The choice of cursive, with multiple variants for each phonetic syllable, was the norm in texts in the vernacular at the time. Colours were added by hand, a technique known as *hissai*, but whether this was done by Hikogorō himself is difficult to ascertain.

This printed page is the result of a harmonious combination of multiple components: text, calligraphy and images. To make such a complex page layout at all possible, xylography (printing from woodblocks) was the chosen technology for commercial publications in the Tokugawa period. This is not to say that early modern Japan did not flirt, albeit for a relatively short period of time in the first half of the seventeenth century, with moveable type.[17] As the *sagabon* specimens discussed in chapter 1 showcase, moveable type could be employed to produce exquisite products. Yet, commercial publishers soon reverted to the use of woodblock printing. Peter Kornicki's seminal work has identified several reasons for the shift from moveable type to xylography, including the need to incorporate phonetic glosses and diacritic marks to aid comprehension of texts written in literary Chinese and/or with many logographic characters.[18]

The flexibility that woodblock printing enabled cannot be readily discarded. A woodblock is, after all, akin to a blank page. It can be cut with anything that an author and/or artist wishes to see in the final product. An example of an early modern Japanese woodblock (*hangi*), owned by the Bodleian Libraries (FIG. 92), displays thick text written in literary Chinese employing non-cursive logographic characters. But block-cutters could cut anything that was on the block-ready maquette

91 Recto of the first folio in volume 1, *Hachiman Tarō ichidaiki* (*The Life of Hachiman Tarō*), mid-eighteenth century. Published by Tsuruya Kiemon, Edo. Nipponica 1009.

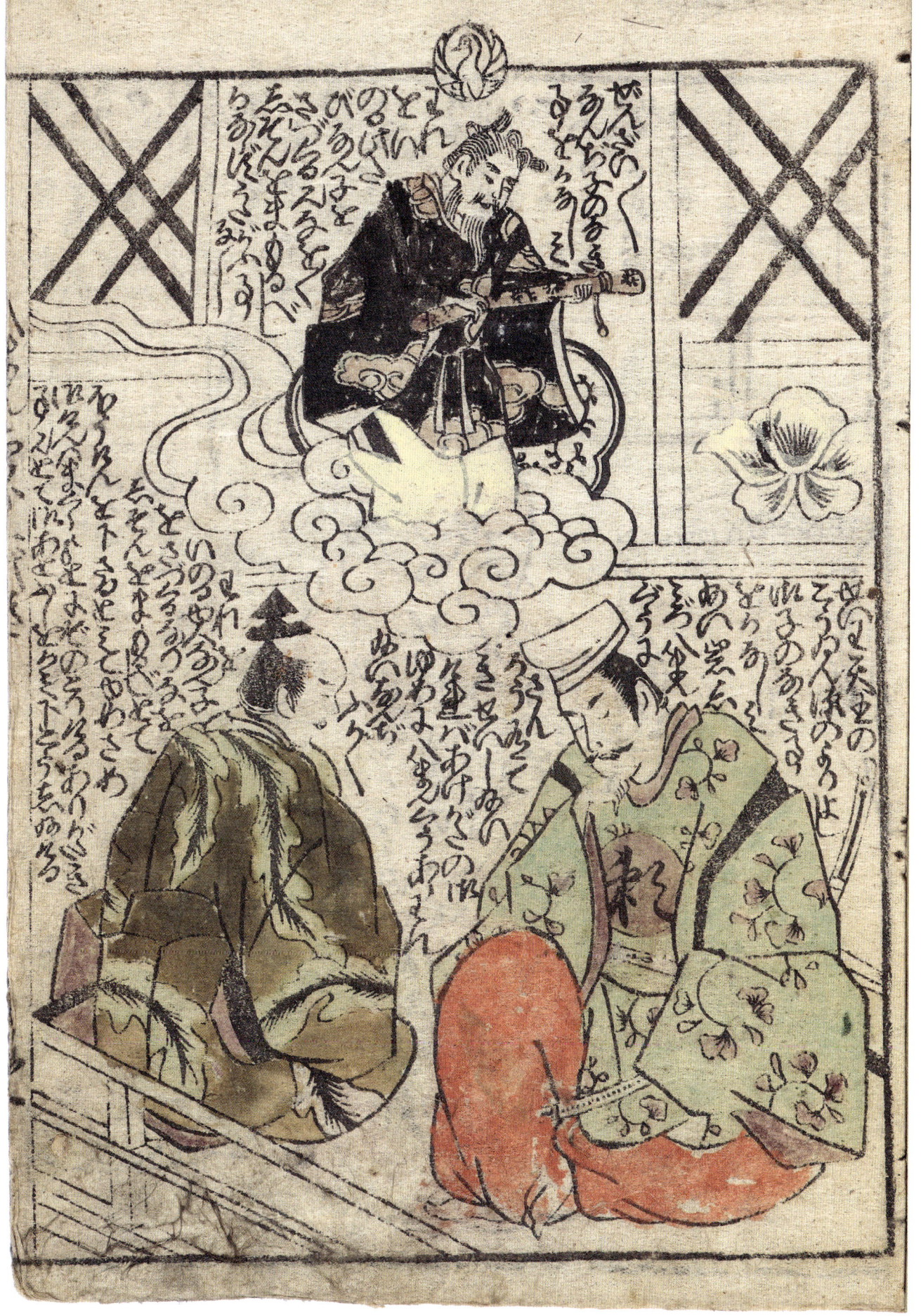

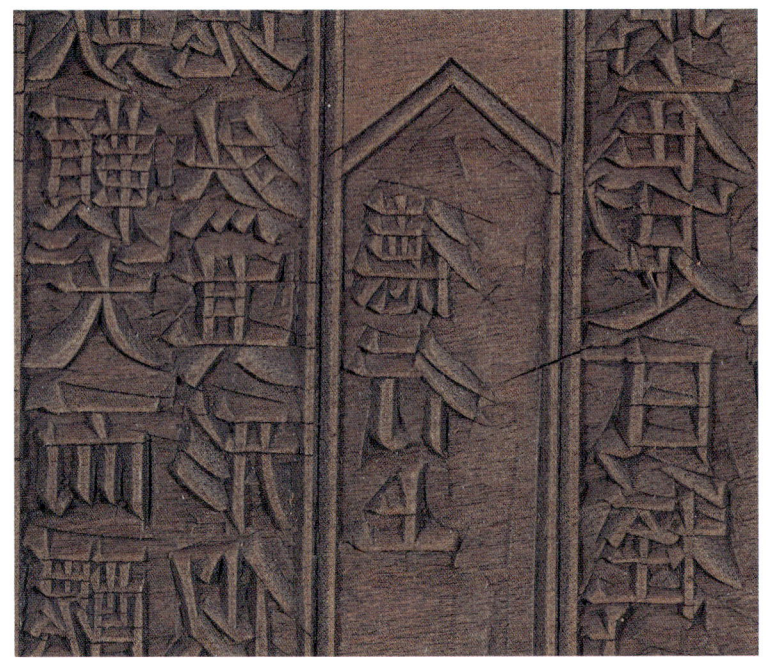

92 An early modern Japanese woodblock. The block-heart title ABOVE reads 徳行, a compound included in several early modern book titles. Nipponica 1014.

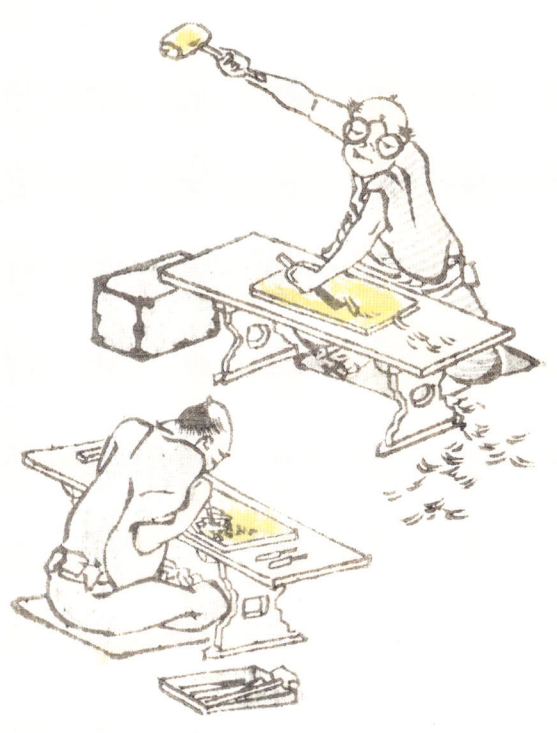

93 Image showing two block-cutters preparing new printing blocks, from *Hokusai Manga*, vol. 1, 1814–18. Nipponica 439.

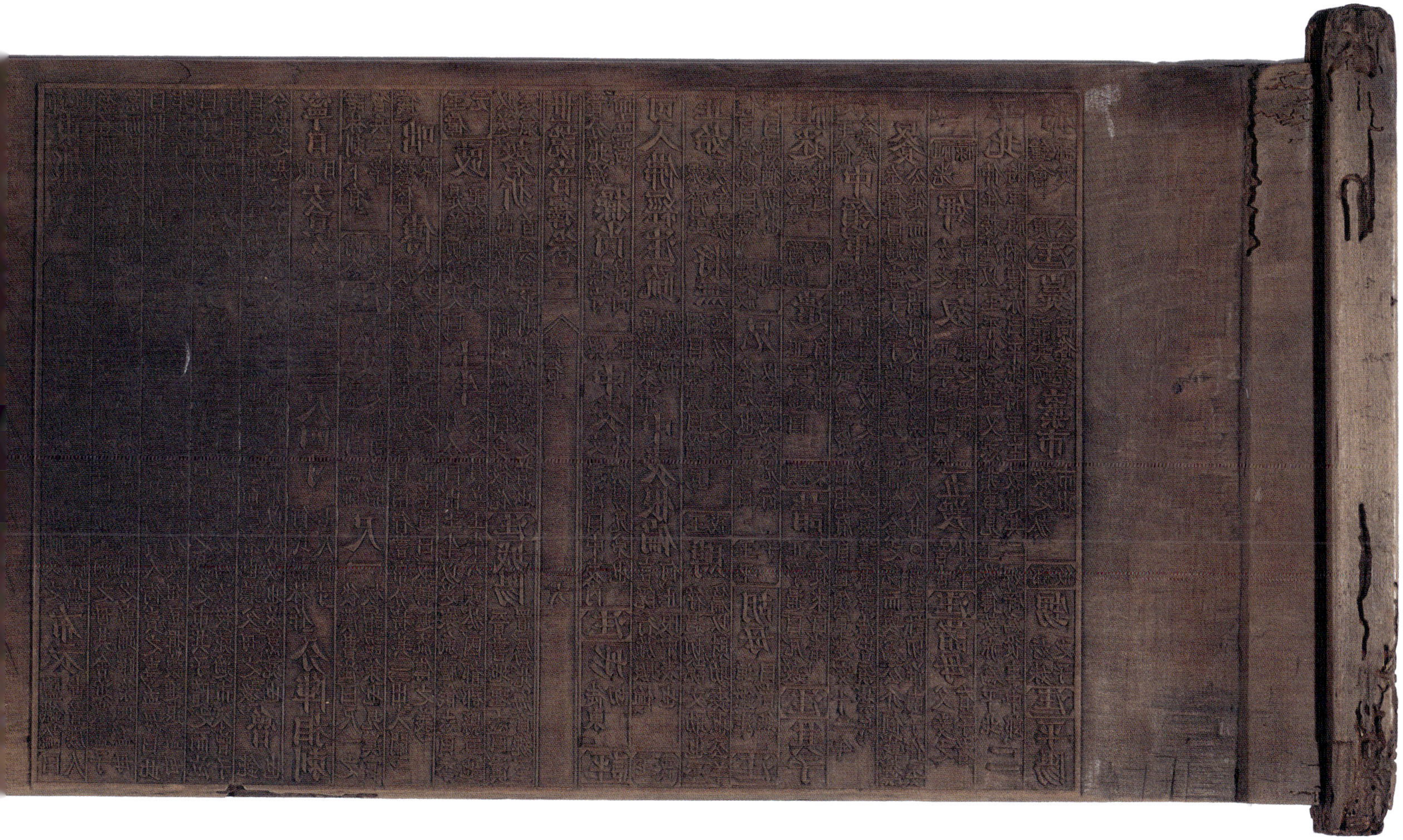

(*hanshita*), be it text (in all sorts of calligraphic styles), images, or a mixture of both.

If we go back to *kusazōshi* – the type of books collected by Hikogorō – we have clear records about the bookmaking process. The author would create a draft (*sōkōbon*), which contained text and a rough outline of the illustrations, at times with specific requests to the artist. The artist would create block-ready drawings which would then be passed to a calligrapher, whose job was to inscribe the cursive text in a polished hand. The block-ready maquette would then reach the block-cutter (*horishi*, FIG. 93). The cutting would be done in relief. Then the printer (*surishi*) would come in, applying ink on the woodblock, placing a sheet of paper on it, and rubbing with the object known as a *baren*.[19] As Cynthia Brokaw puts it when discussing xylography in China, we are dealing with cheap, portable technology, which does not require much capital or overheads.[20] What is more, it is a technology that allows for great flexibility in book design. Alessandro Bianchi, in his current research on what he calls 'the architecture of design', is investigating the immense variability of borders, calligraphy and *mise en page*, and asserts the crucial role that woodblock printing played to enable such creativity.[21]

A point in case can be found in a charming book owned by the Bodleian Libraries (FIGS 94, 95, 96). This untitled work is one example of a vast gamut of books produced for women in early modern Japan. These publications covered various topics, but customarily included useful encyclopaedic contents complemented by instructions on wedding ceremonies, specimens for letter writing, and poetic collections such as *The Thirty-Six*

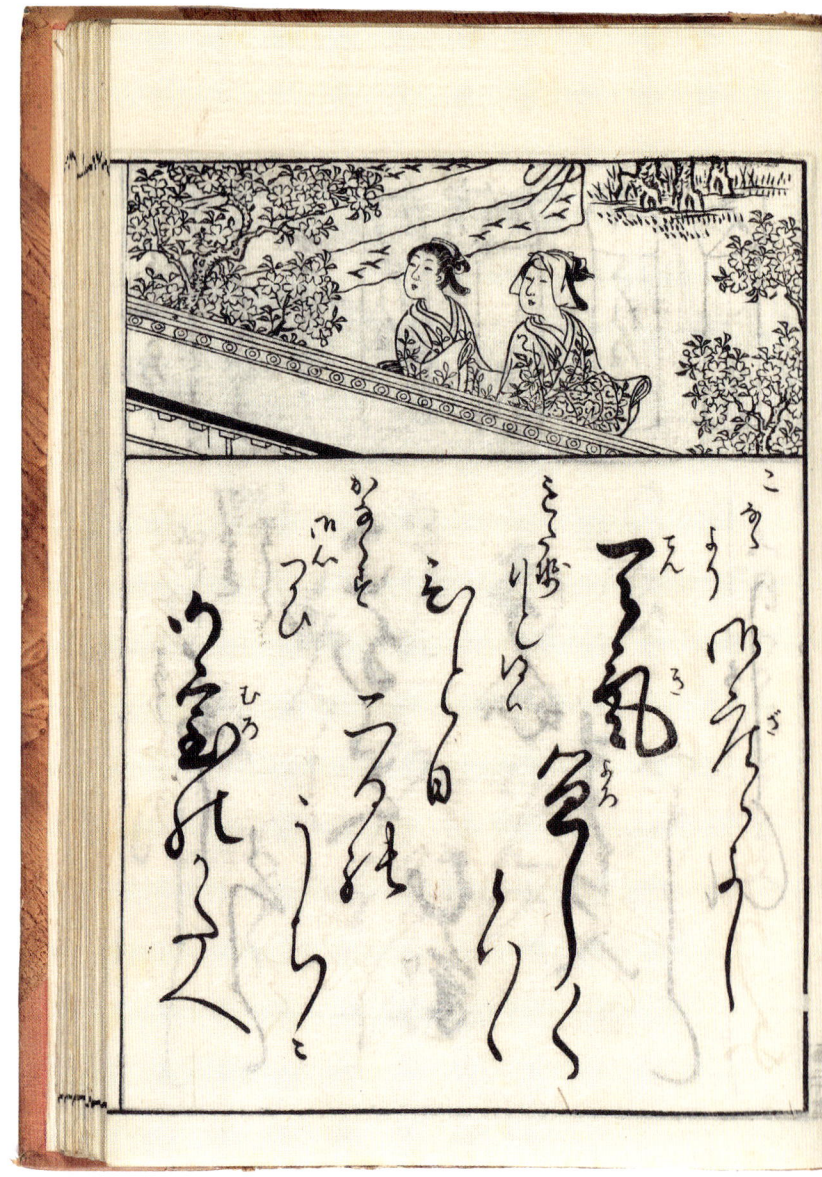

94 Double-page spread showing the complex page layout of a book thought to be *Jokyō fūki dai*, 1785. Published by Yoshinoya Tamehachi, Kyoto. Douce Jap. d.2.

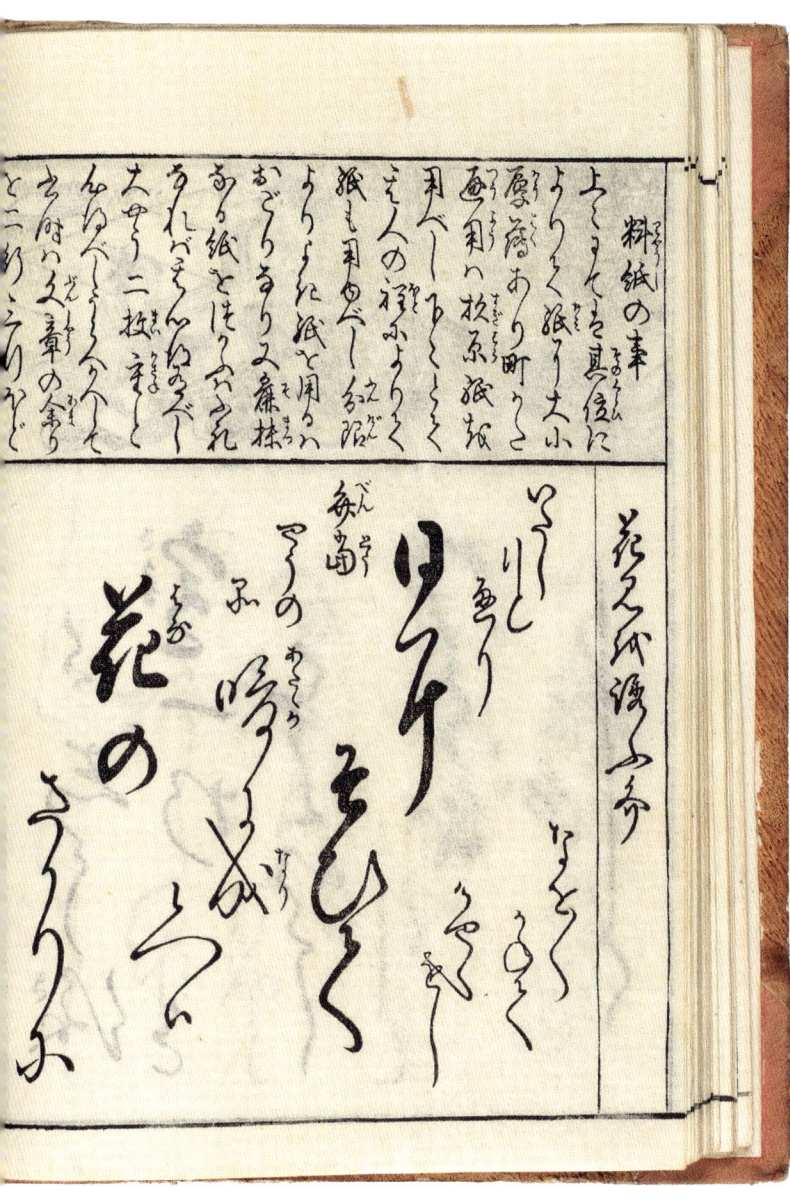

Immortal Poets and One Hundred Poets, One Poem Each.[22] The identification of the book is akin to a thrilling hunt, as its title is not recorded anywhere. It is most likely connected to the wrapper of Jokyō fūki dai (Teachings for Women: The Base of Wealth and Fame) (FIG. 97), as the Bodleian purchased them from the same auction (see Introduction).[23] The page layout of this book is exquisitely complex, as can be evinced from the double-page spread in FIG. 94. Two thirds of the page is dominated by an example of a letter to be sent when inviting someone to view the cherry blossoms in bloom. The spacious calligraphy is organized in what is known as scattered writing (chirashigaki). It adopts conventions typical of the linguistic and visual register known as nyohitsu. Although nyohitsu translates as 'the woman's brush,' it referred to a type of written language and visual codes that could be applied in communication between women, with women, or with men.[24] Key here is the reproduction of the hand of an expert calligrapher. This can be easily accommodated by means of xylography. The upper banner presents a different text. On this page it is related to letter writing, with explanations of what paper to use. The image on the left visualizes how the flower viewing might take place.

Whilst the majority of the book is printed from relief blocks in a single shade of black ink, the first ten double-page spreads are in colour, which is added using three different techniques. The first spread (FIG. 95) gifts readers with an eye-catching image of chrysanthemums in yellow, pink, green and white. The black outlines of the flowers were printed from the keyblock. On the right is the name of the Osaka artist Katsura

95 OVERLEAF (& PAGE 184) The first colour spread in a book thought to be Jokyō fūki dai, 1785. Published by Yoshinoya Tamehachi, Kyoto. On the right is the signature of the artist Katsura Munenobu, printed white on pink using the hidariban technique. Douce Jap. d.2.

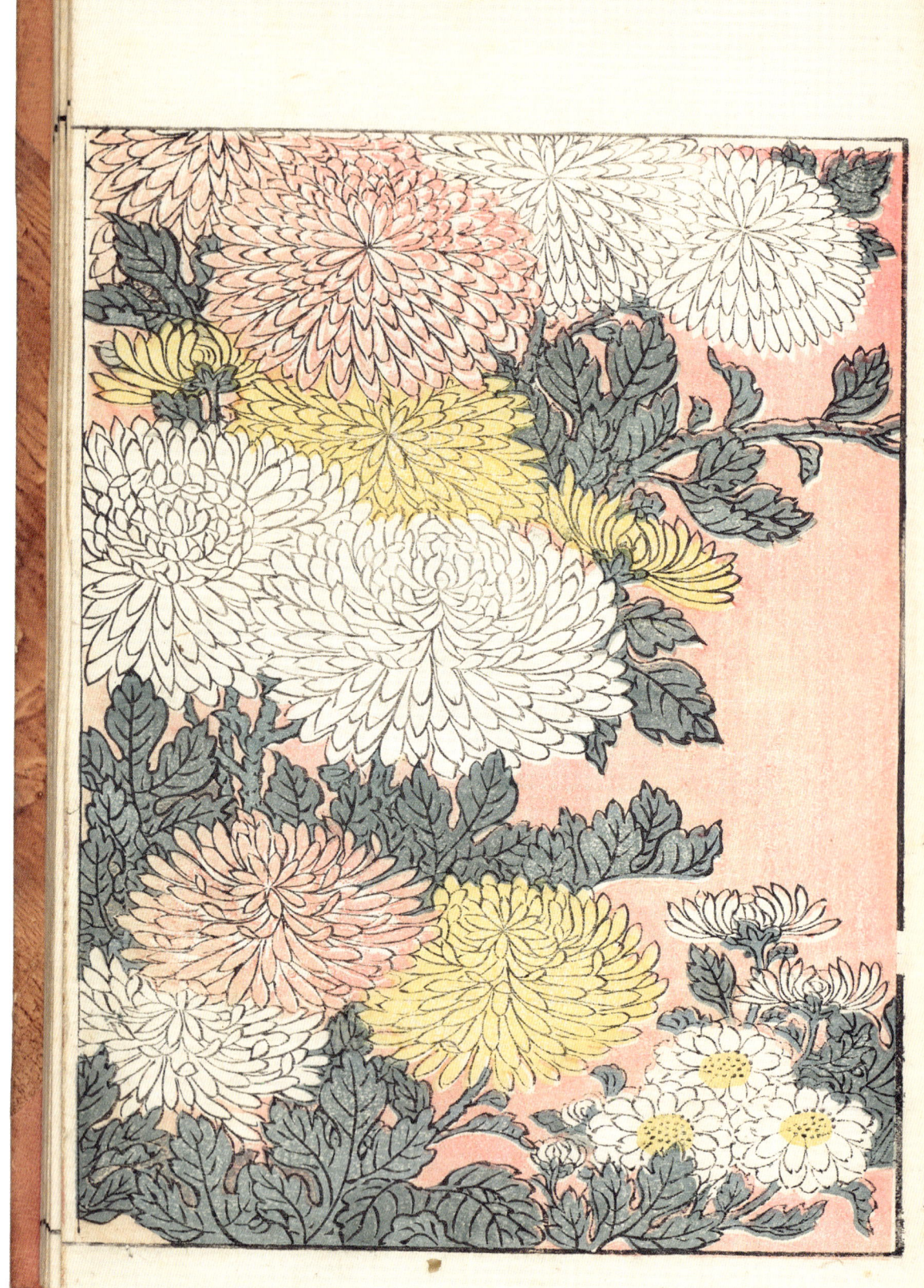

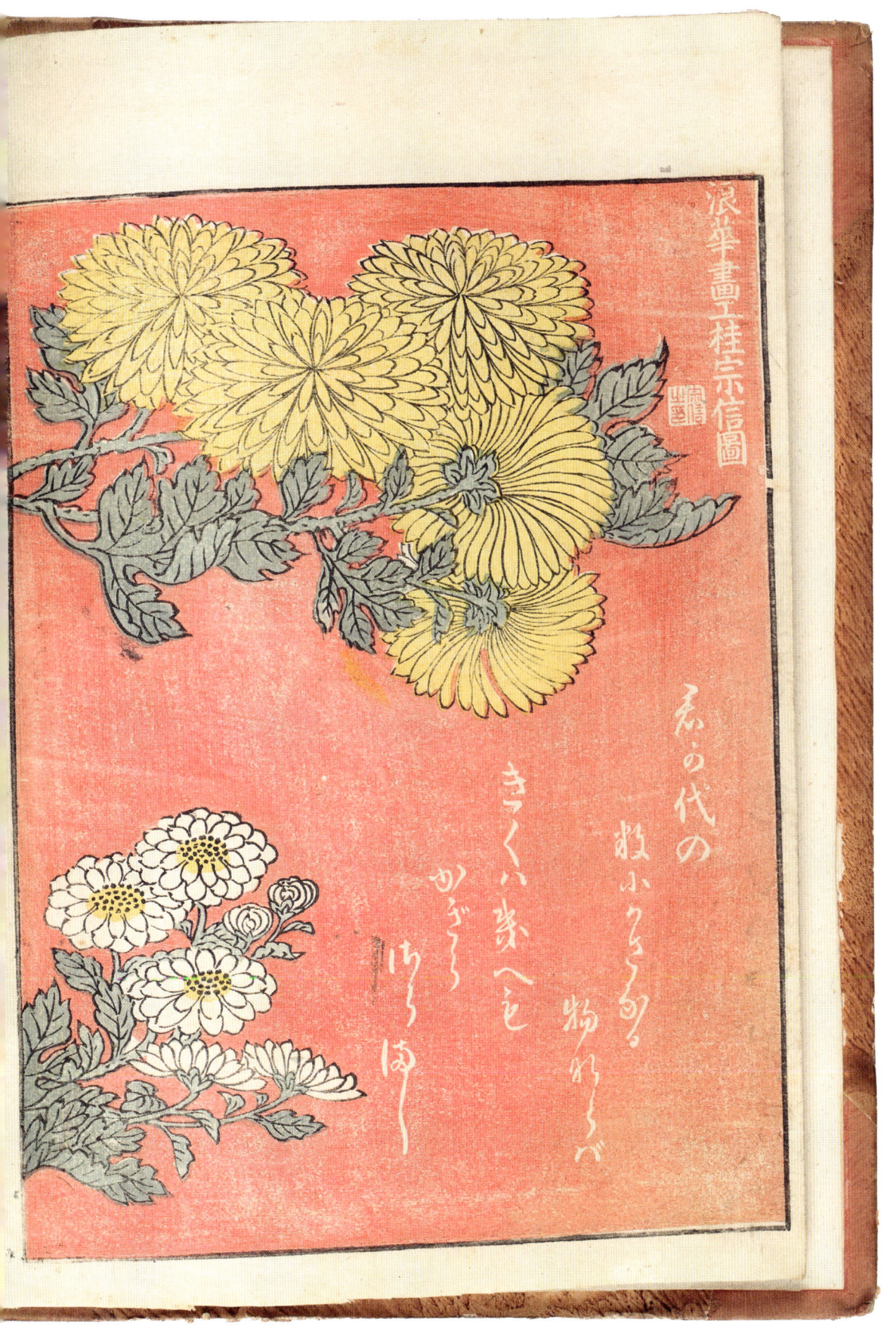

浪華畫工桂宗信圖

君か代の
　　救ふくきく
　　　　　　物ぐさぶ
きくハ栄へを
　　　かぎ
　　　　　くるゆく

かきをさとついま川を
らふまよ八伊勢抄紙よ
から人れけてまこと
やきぬえて八れ
しちうづきふかさゝて
ゆりやれがゝき近のさゝ
すつゝわれのさゝしく
わみさえと出八く
まさあか坂の実八
下のるをかゝてく
しろゝ松のすゝゝゝ
下れる戒つきしゝり
すのへ下もとりゝ
すとつねきりとしひ
あゝけしをしゝとそ

こゑちん

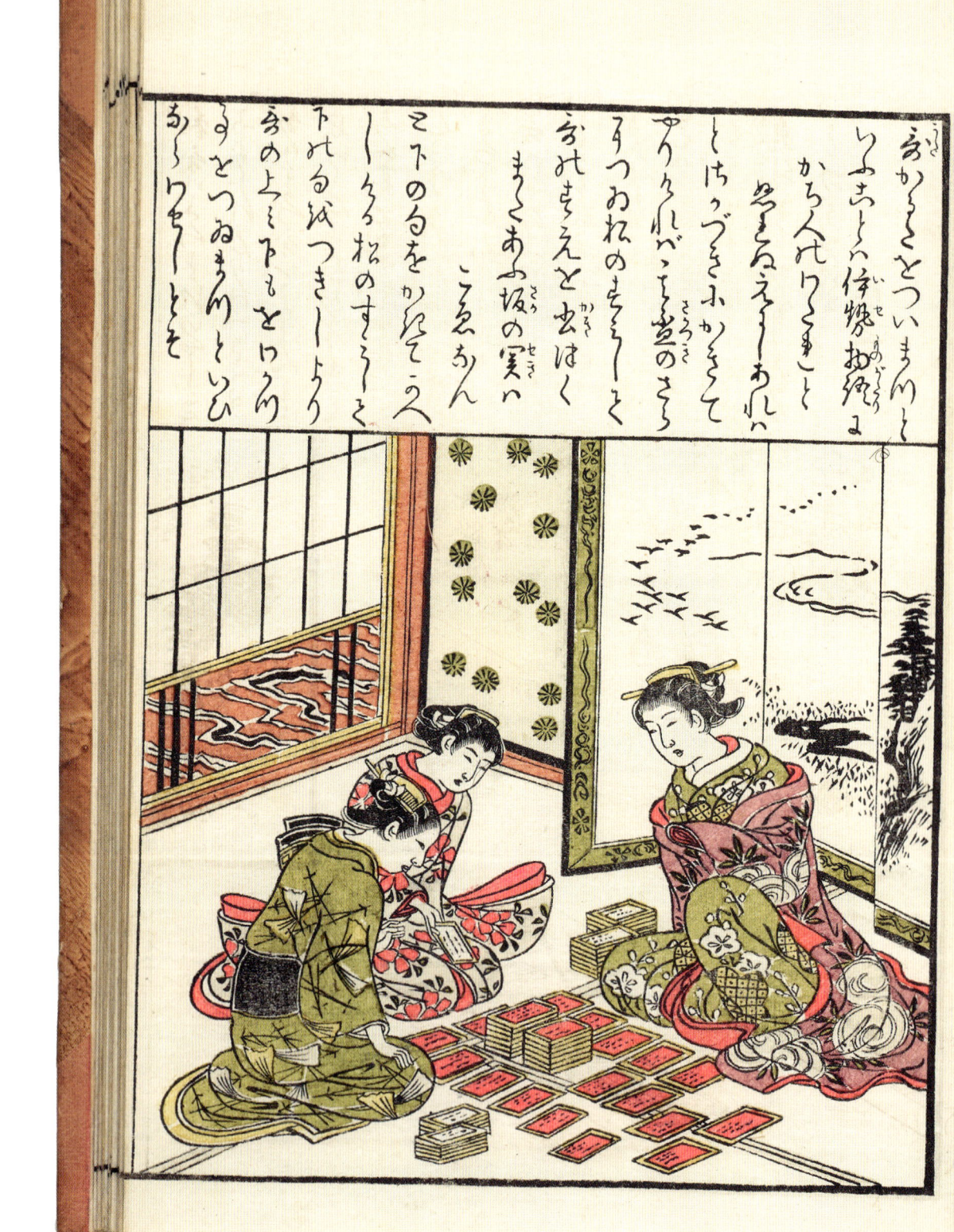

和歌はこゝろをたねとして
よろづにんげんできる
ありもづ方とよまんと
思げんをかゆくて
ちん哀をわたるすみ一に
んきよろれが分のすぐに
よろしんさりくれば
分のさ也もいゝ自然
とを合うわんある
きとかり也とて入
きず〳〵ああ先つらを
もうごし目うえを
鬼神ともかんずるも
とつゝみれも
れぬて

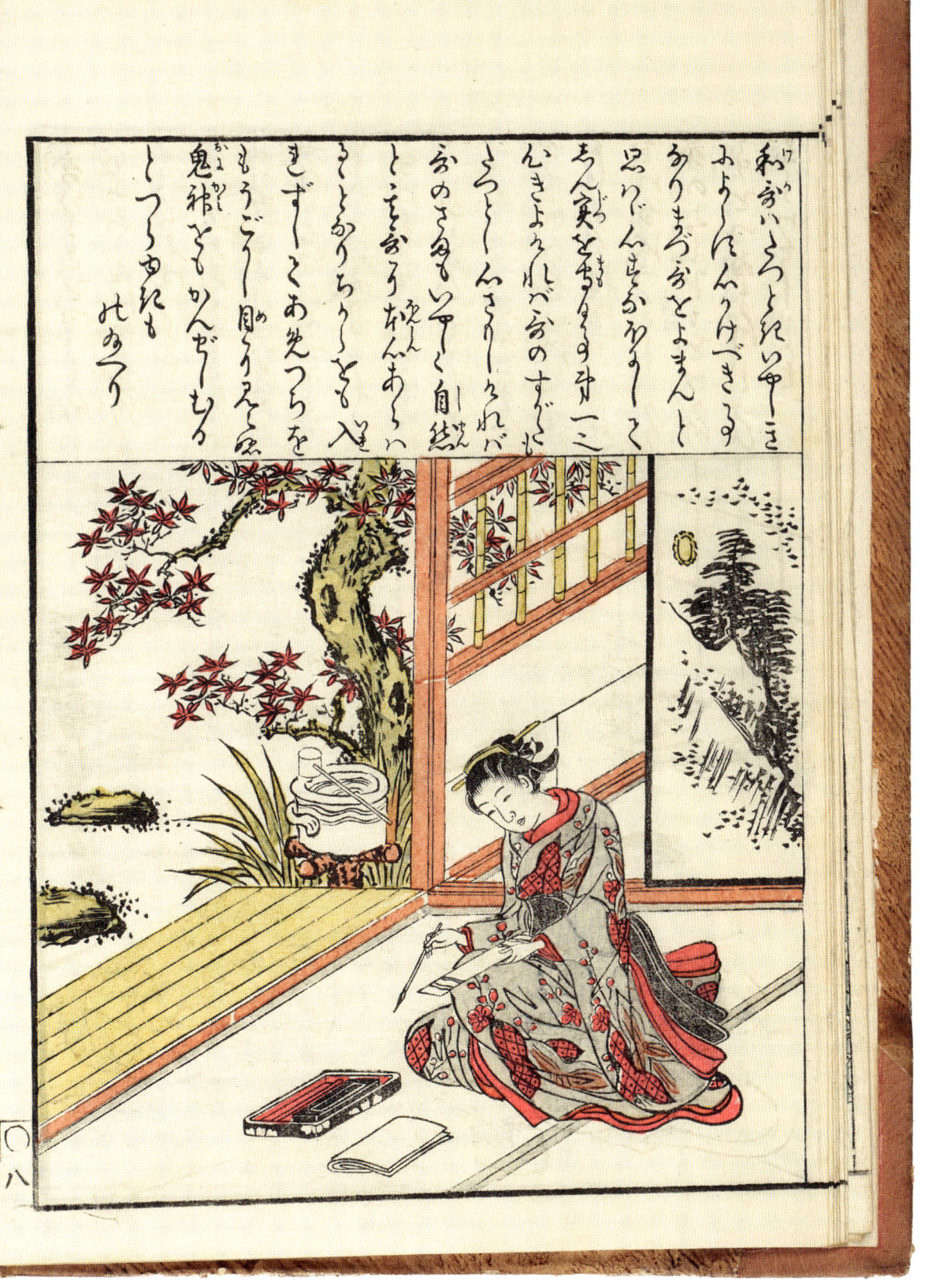

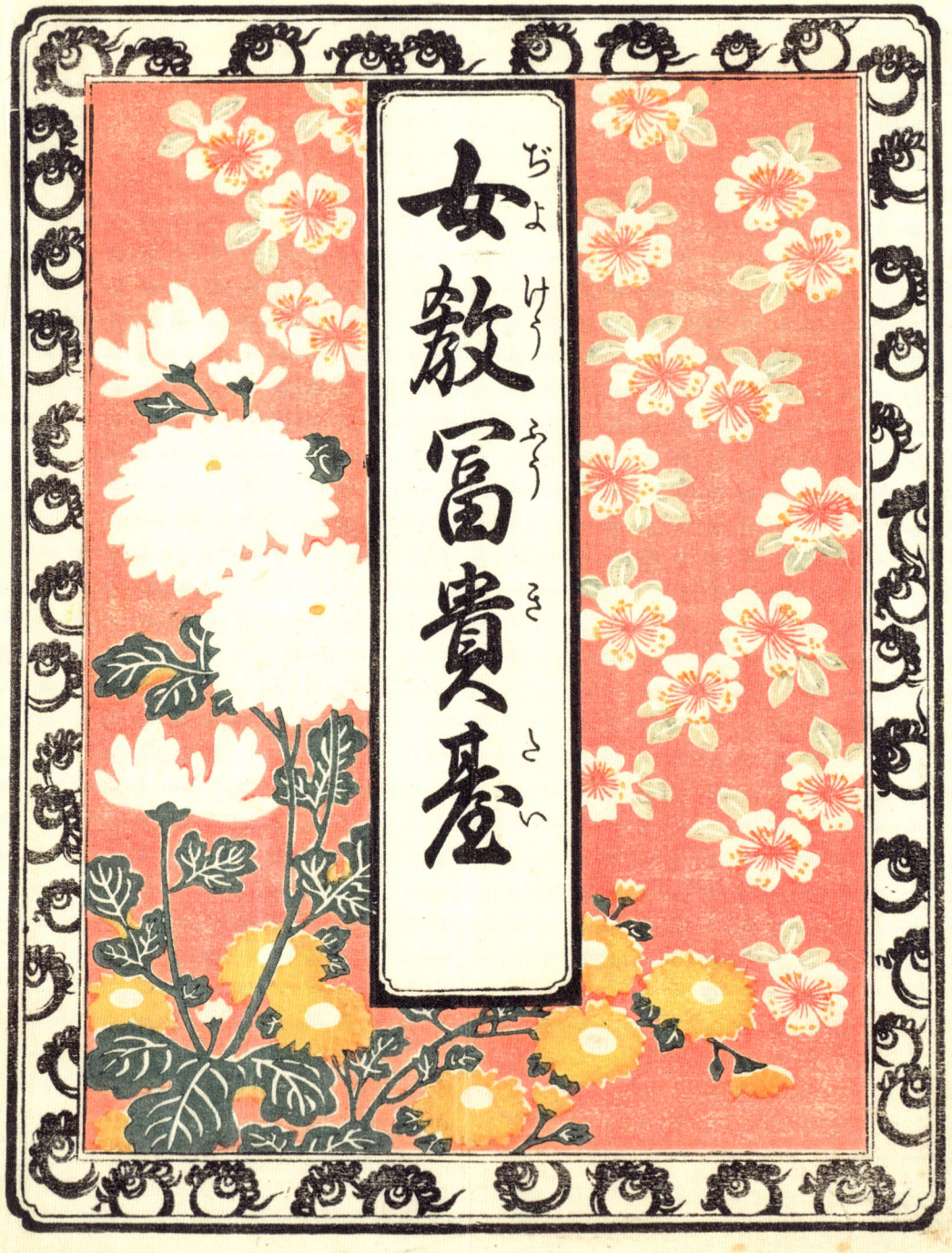

女教ふうきさい　天明新版

女教冨貴蔵
ぢょ　けう　ふう　き　さい

Munenobu (1735–1790).[25] His signature, as well as the poem, are printed with the technique known as *hidariban*, with the block cut to produce white-on-black text – in this case, white-on-pink (FIG. 95, right). This would have required a separate block from the keyblock. The other colours would have been applied using other relief blocks, one for each colour, a technique known as *tashokuzuri*, in which each colour is added by means of a separate block.[26] Once we turn the page, we realize that the remaining nine spreads display the technique of *kappazuri*: colours are applied to the outline illustrations by brush-over stencils (FIG. 96). This technique was particularly cherished in the Kamigata region (Kyoto and Osaka) from the 1730s, and indeed the book in question was issued in 1785 by the Kyoto publisher Yoshinoya Tamehachi (fl. eighteenth century), who probably hired the artist Katsura Munenobu from Osaka. *Kappazuri* was, however, a rather rare technique, and *tashokuzuri* was used to produce the majority of polychrome illustrations in books as well as prints.

96 PREVIOUS SPREAD An illustration with colours applied using stencils (*kappazuri*), from a book thought to be *Jokyō fūki dai*, 1785. Douce Jap. d.2.

97 LEFT Wrapper for *Jokyō fūki dai* (*Teachings for Women: The Base of Wealth and Fame*). It records the date as Tenmei era (1781–89). Douce Jap. d.8.

## MIGRATIONS

The commercial book in early modern Japan and, to a certain extent, in the Meiji era, shows a propensity to migrate. The first type of migration is of blocks from one publisher to another. Yoshinoya Tamehachi's book on women's education, briefly explored in the previous section, is a case in point. The pagination points to a book that is conceived as an assemblage of separate sets of blocks. The first fifty-five folios display the folio number on the verso, towards the gutter. They run from 1 to 55, with the fourth folio apparently missing. Except for seven folios, all the numbers are preceded by the mark ●. We expect to find folio number 56 at the end of this section. The pagination, however, starts anew from number 1, this time preceded by a different mark: ○. This starts the section containing the *One Hundred Poets, One Poem Each*, and continues until number 50. What follows are three folios numbered 18, 19 and 20. This composition, not particularly unusual for this type of book, suggests a composite publication that combines sets of woodblocks that were not necessarily conceived for one specific book, but could be – and were – mixed and matched.

Furthermore, the blocks used to print the section entitled *Onna yō chiyo no tomo* ('A Woman's Companion for All Generations') migrated at least once. They were used as part of another composite volume for women titled *Onna yō shotsū anmon* (*Letter Templates for Women*), issued in Osaka by Kawachiya Tasuke.[27] That this is a later impression of the same blocks can be evinced from the quality of the printed surface – there are cracks in the printing frames and in the lines of the cursive writing, combined with a general

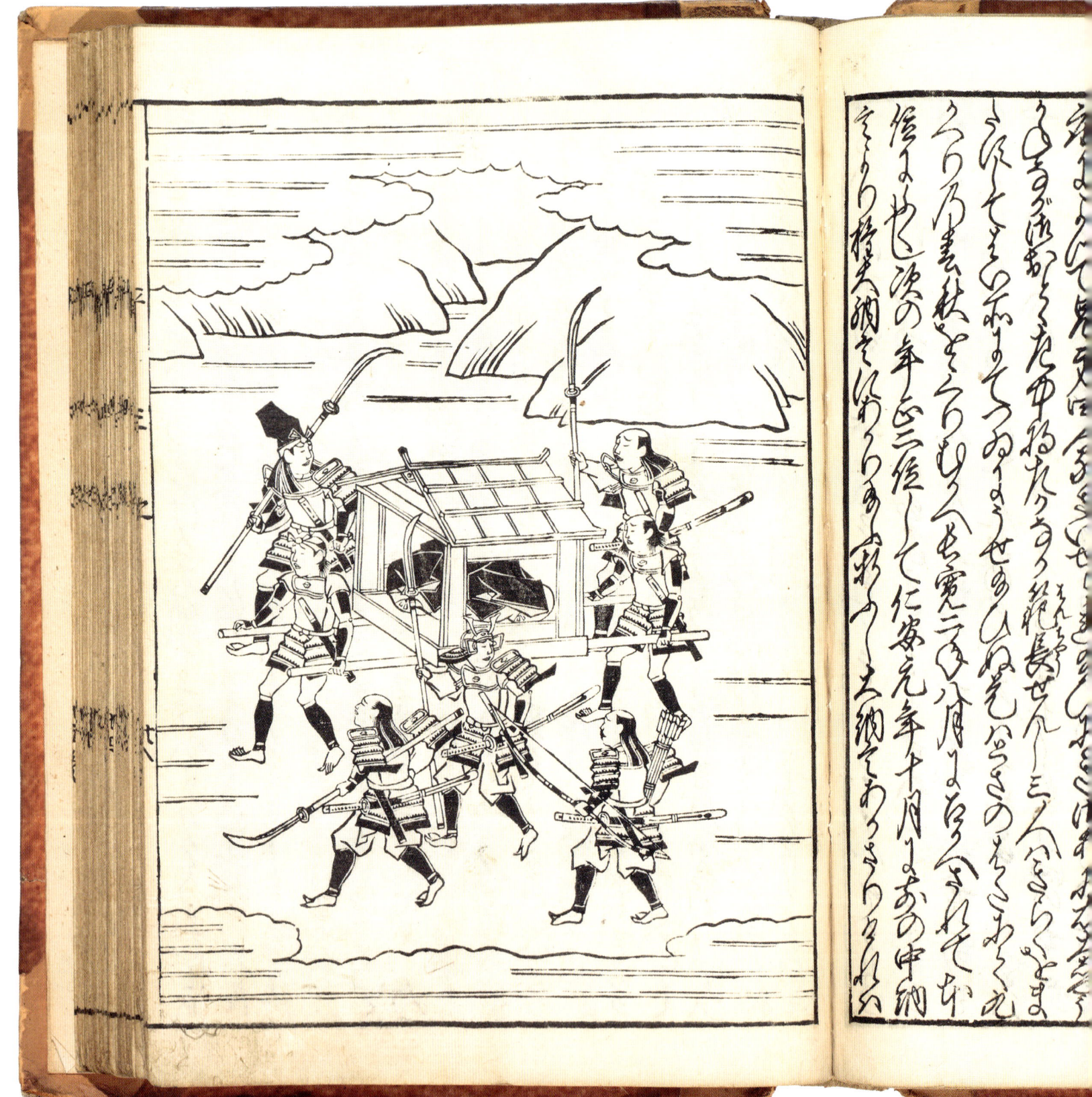

ろうとして仁安元年十月よりおの中納
言よりせ次の年正三位して仁安元年十月よりおの中納
くりの書杜をくりむとも是をくれそて
さりなきのうちをこそのらきてありき
ますりませのおへらくうまをくうりく
ぎしてまのそれのやうよりのをくくえ
うくたのもうてへ給やうするせんよくくえ
うくもれんなかてそれくよこれるるうのは
けきそかへらくうらやかくよらのけん
さりくり程生納をしくりくるくるを
さりくり程生納をしくりくるくるを

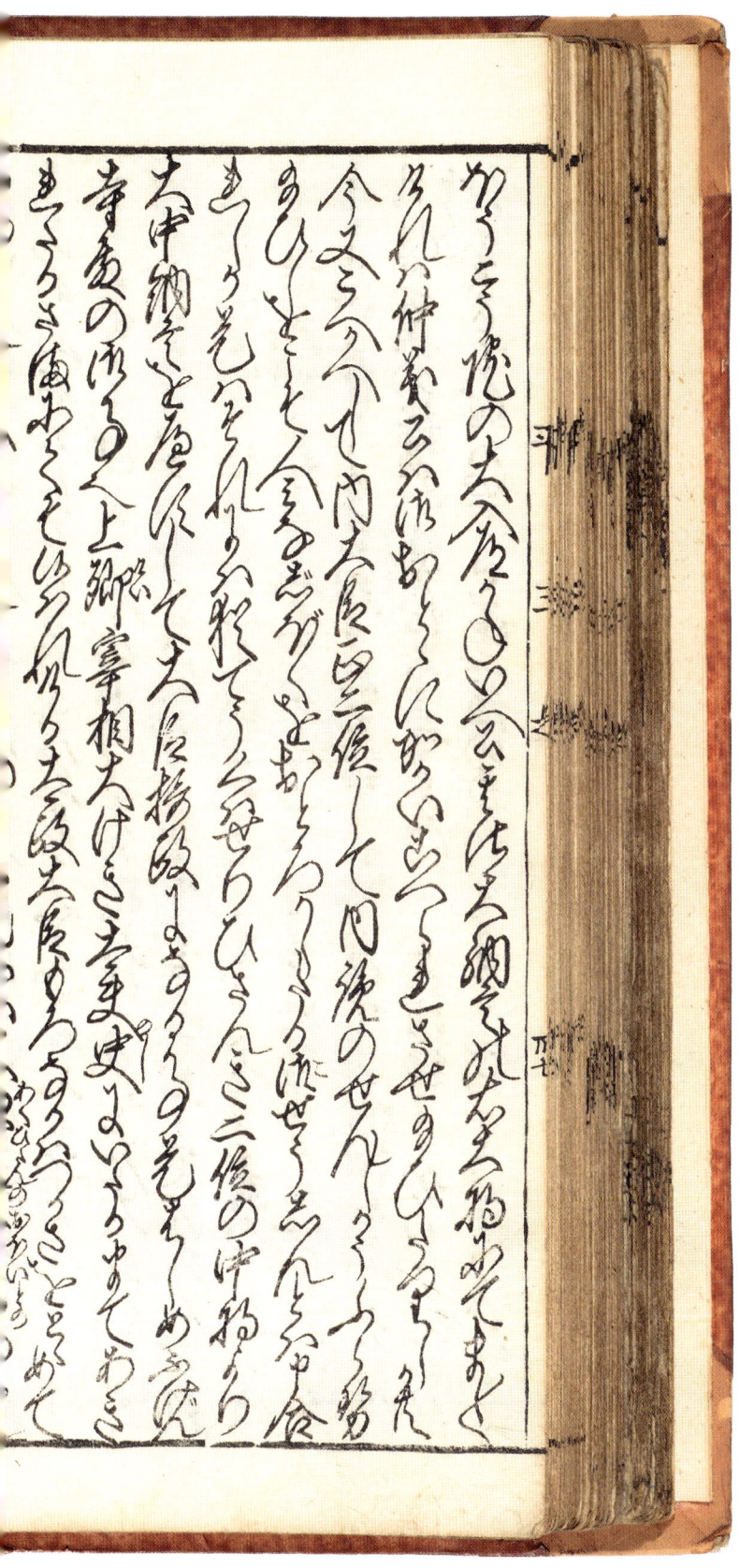

lack of crispness in the printed lines. Yoshinoya's backmatter (a half folio pasted onto the back cover) is another example of block migration. The same backmatter can be found at the end of *Joyō fuku judai* (*Women's Essentials: The Base for Wealth and Longevity*), a book dated 1785 and issued by the same publisher.[28] At a certain point the blocks also migrated from Kyoto to Osaka, featuring in a later edition of the same book issued by different publishers.[29]

The circulation of woodblocks described here speaks of a complex network of publishers that developed over time and across space. If a publisher could not lay their hands on a specific set of blocks, they could revert to producing facsimiles. Facsimiles were issued despite attempts by *shomotsuya*-type publishers to protect rights on their own woodblocks, through the guild's checks.

It was not only a matter of blocks migrating. Contents that struck a chord with contemporary readers were often appropriated, repackaged and/or adapted. This process was eased by the absence of copyright law and intellectual property. This is not to say that early modern Japan lacked originality. This concept was, however, framed in different terms. As Kyoto writer Miyako no Nishiki (1675–?) once put it, 'to create the new out of the old is what brilliant writers do'.[30]

*Hachiman Tarō ichidaiki* is a telling example. As research by Kuroishi Yōko has shown, a number

98 A example of *gunsho*. Text and illustration from *Heike Monogatari* (*Tale of the Heike*), vol. 3, 37v–38r. Douce Jap. d.3.

of scenes are inspired by the war tale *Zen Taiheiki* (*Earlier Chronicle of the Great Peace*), which was possibly issued for the first time around the 1680s.[31] Whilst living in a period characterized by sustained peace, early modern Japanese readers had a fascination for the world of samurai. *Gunsho* – comprising not only war tales but also etiquette manuals inspired by the secret traditions of the military elite, biographies of warriors, manuals for horse riding and much more – constituted a rich and multifarious publishing genre in bookseller's catalogues (FIG. 98). The narratives were packed with action and human drama. They were also framed as a sort of history curriculum, helping to shape something akin to a historical consciousness. Alongside these publications, warriors and their stories also infused popular entertainments. Lectures on *Taiheiki* (*The Chronicle of the Great Peace*) were delivered on the streets, reaching all social strata. The kabuki theatre and the puppet theatre staged stories related to historical warriors, and warrior prints dazzled the eyes with images full of colour and dynamism. Board games and graphic narratives translated complex stories into products that could be enjoyed by adults and children alike.

The tale of Hachiman Tarō must have resonated with readers, as Tsuruya Kiemon himself published two different editions of the same story, both packaged in the form of graphic narrative. Whether Tsuruya lost the blocks of the edition owned by Hikogorō, perhaps in a fire, or whether the keyblocks of the previous edition were so worn out because of too much use, is a matter of speculation. But the fact that a publisher decided to invest capital in cutting a new set of blocks is evidence of the popularity enjoyed by the story. At an even later stage, possibly at the beginning of the nineteenth century, Tsuruya reissued Hachiman Tarō's adventures in a new edition, with text by renowned author and scholar Morishima Chūryō (1754–1810) and illustrations by Kitao Masayoshi (1764–1824), under the title *Ōshū gunki* (*Military Record of Ōshū*). A bigger sized version was titled *Hachiman Tarō ichidaiki: E-zukushi* (*The Biography of Hachiman Tarō: With Illustrations*). A later impression of the same blocks was issued by Tsuruya together with another Edo-based publisher, Chōjiya Heibee. There are twenty-one early modern publications listed in conjunction with Hachiman Tarō in the Union Catalogue.

The story of this warrior continued to charm readers in the latter part of the nineteenth century. This is when the Tokyo-based publisher Maki Kinnosuke comes to the fore. The National Diet Library records hundreds of titles issued in Tokyo by Maki between 1884 and 1895, including editions of the life of Hachiman Tarō.[32] The 1895 edition owned by the Bodleian, titled *Ehon Hachiman Tarō* (*The Illustrated Hachiman Tarō*), has a polychrome cover (FIG. 99) which still uses the *tashokuzuri* printing technique, with multiple woodblocks. The colour scheme is quintessentially of Meiji-era flavour. Everything that follows, however, is printed with what appears to be copperplate (*dōban*). More work needs to be conducted to fully understand how the book was produced and printed, including whether we are dealing with etching, engraving or lithography. What we can

99 Cover of *Ehon Hachiman Tarō* (*The Illustrated Hachiman Tarō*), Maki Kinnosuke, Tokyo, 1895. Nipponica 1011.

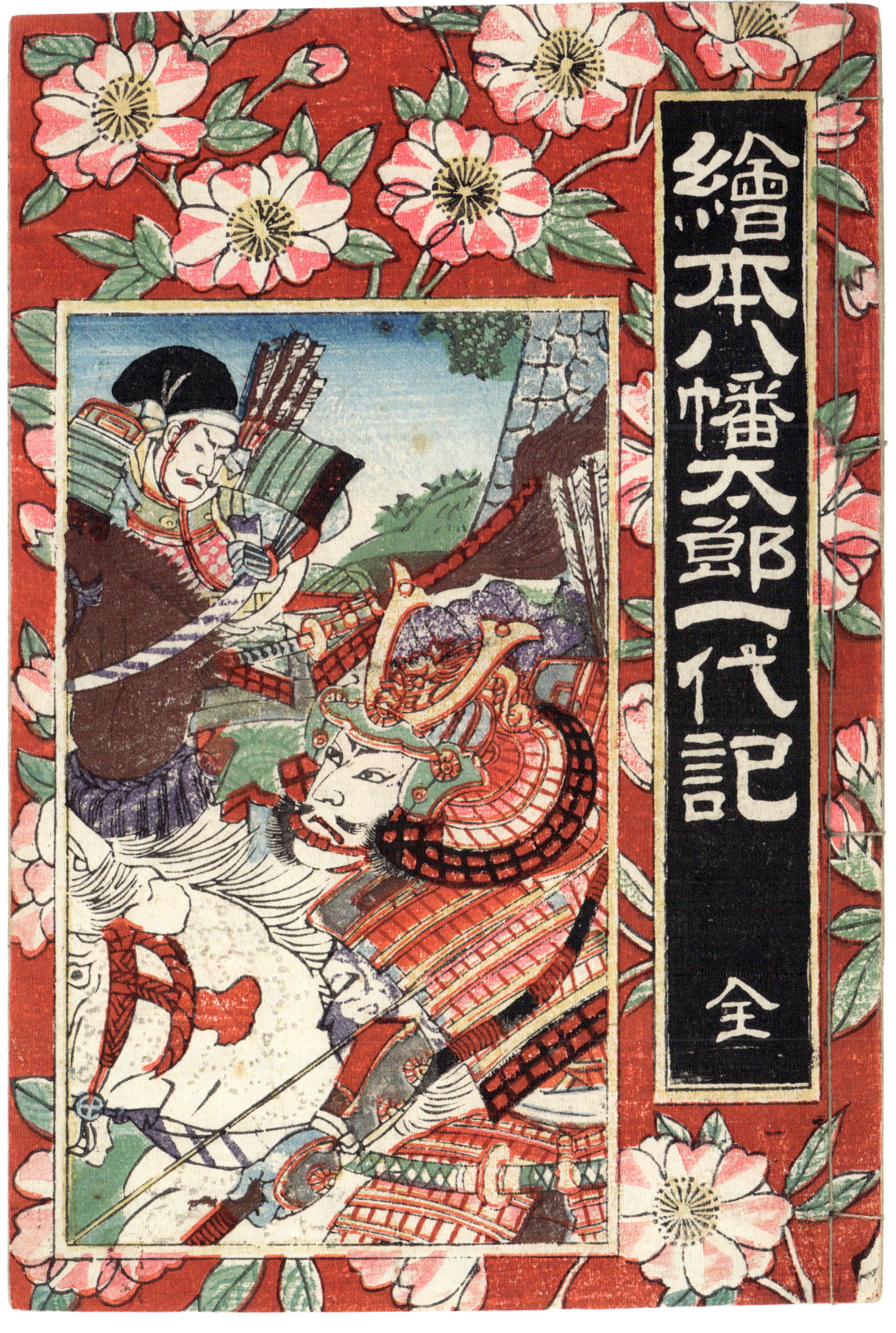

繪本八幡太郎一代記

全

say is that the book makes clever use of the visual potentialities usually associated with copperplate printing in Japanese materials. The use of fine lines in varying degrees of thickness and density enables interesting three-dimensional effects and a heightened sense of realism. This particular edition also makes use of a quirky visual trick that was cherished in copperplate-printed graphic narratives: flaps. The second double-page spread gives us Minamoto no Yoriie fighting against Abe no Sadatō. One warrior is on the right flap, the other on the left (FIG. 100). This is the episode in Hachiman Tarō's biography that Maki's edition focuses on. The flaps are opened to reveal a dynamic scene, most probably the battle of Koromo River (FIG. 101). Flaps and other movable features had appeared already in early modern books, often in sexually explicit materials. Here the same device is appropriated to increase the sense of excitement in adults and children alike. By operating the flaps, the reader enables movement and action on the printed page, adding an extra layer to the charm of this book.

It might be tempting to view the use of copperplate printing in the Meiji era as a choice that naturally goes hand-in-hand with a general fascination with Western technology.[33]

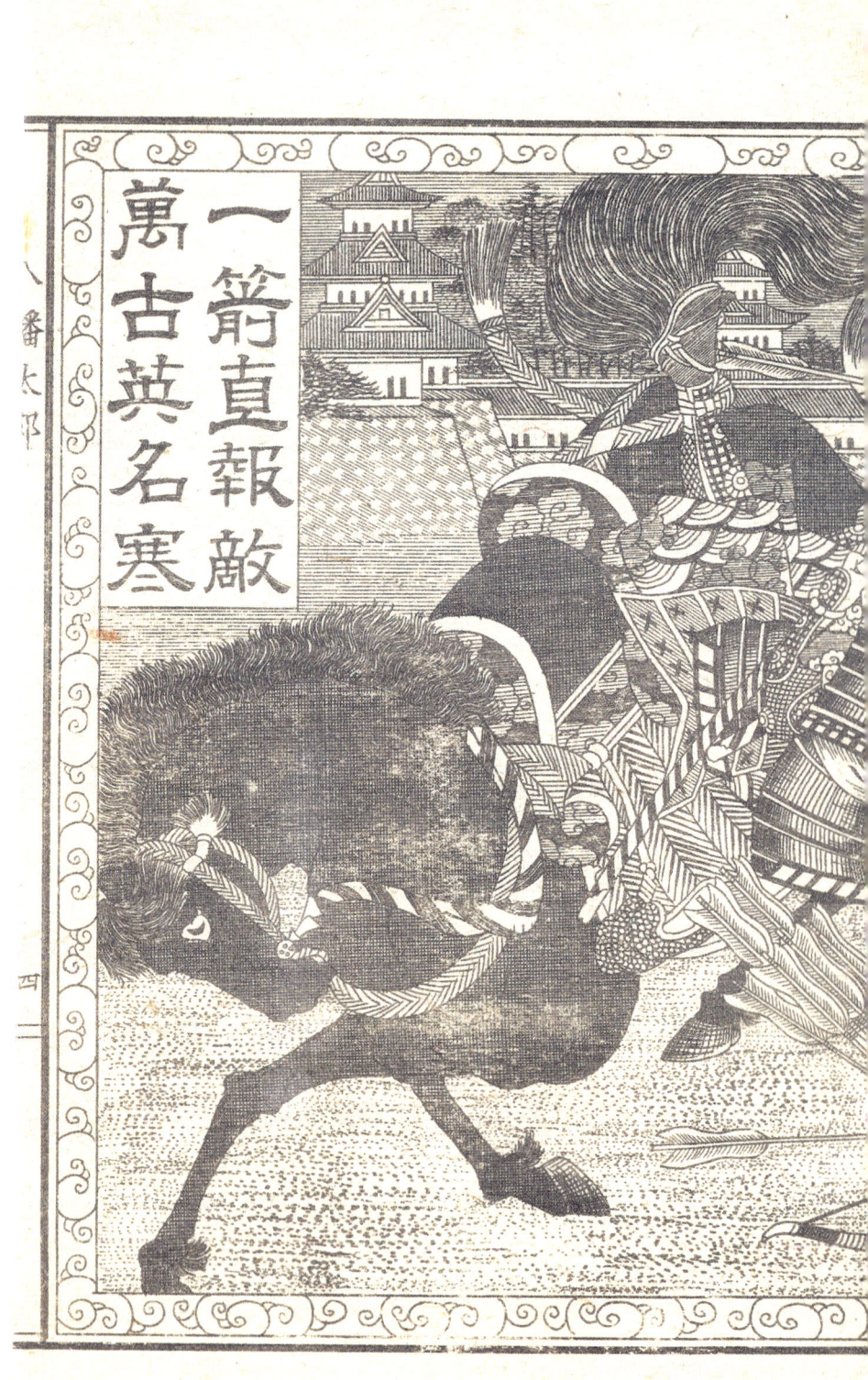

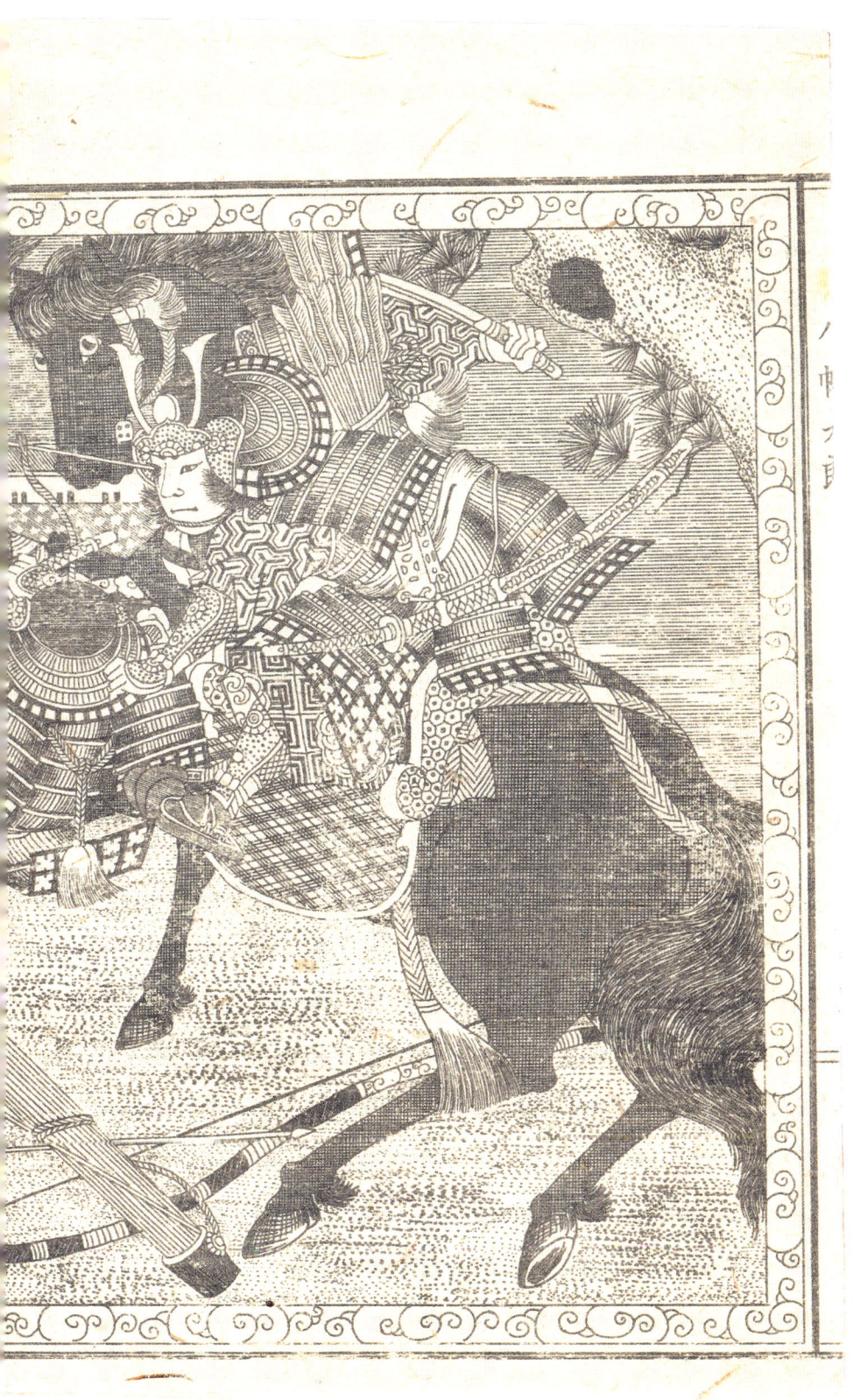

100 Second double-page spread with flaps in *Ehon Hachiman Tarō* (*The Illustrated Hachiman Tarō*), Maki Kinnosuke, Tokyo, 1895. Nipponica 1011.

101 OVERLEAF Flap now open, from second double-page spread in *Ehon Hachiman Tarō* (*The Illustrated Hachiman Tarō*), Maki Kinnosuke, Tokyo, 1895. Nipponica 1011.

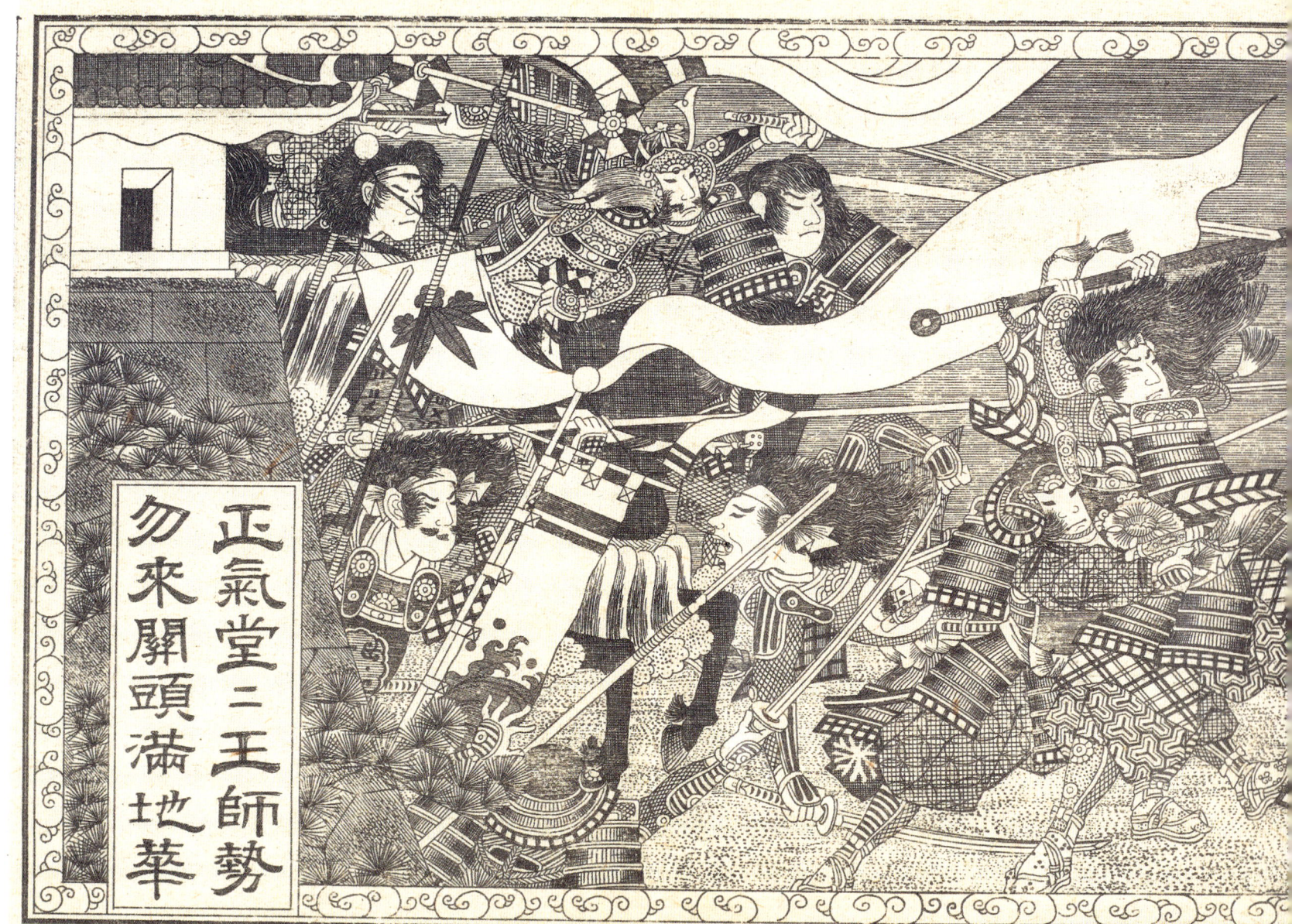

正氣堂三王師勢
勿來關頭滿地華

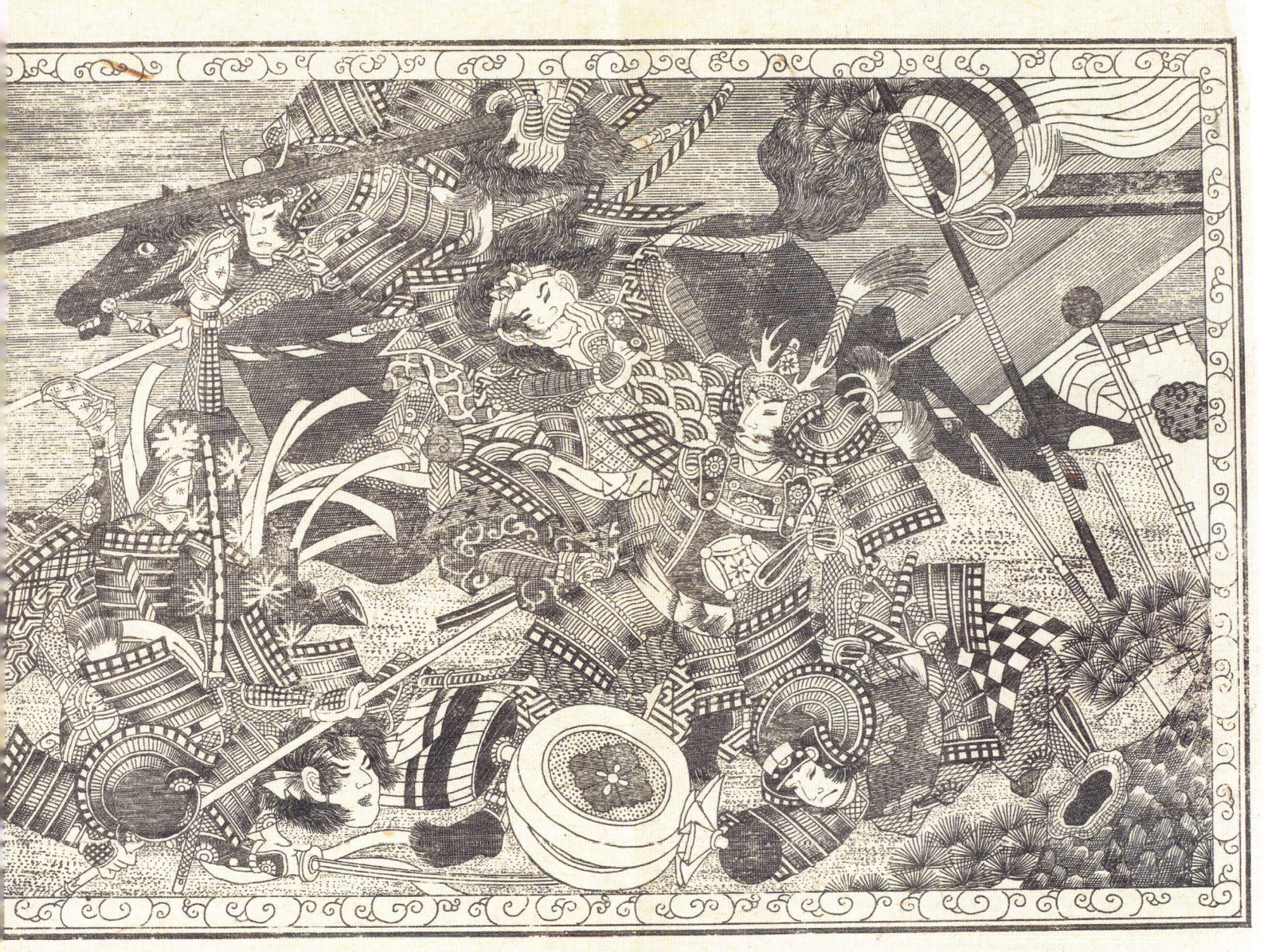

Seminal work by Isobe Atsushi, however, complicates this seemingly easy equation.[34] Focusing on the production of copperplate-printed *kusazōshi* (graphic narratives), Isobe notes that they became particularly popular from around 1882, at a time when typesetting started being used for transcriptions of early modern books into non-cursive script. Typesetting was ideal for bibliographic translations of early modern Japanese books into Western-looking books, with text taking precedence over images. Typesetting, however, was not suited to retaining a flexible page layout where text and images enter into dialogue with each other to co-create meaning. Since graphic narratives were still issued by *jihon'ya* and were catering for the needs of aficionados of this kind of books, copperplate printing was viewed as a suitable alternative to woodblock printing. Visual continuity with early modern products was enabled, while at the same time giving a frisson of a modern look.[35]

In discussing the migrations of printing blocks and content, we should mention another book owned by the Bodleian Libraries titled *Tanoshimi sōshi* (*A Booklet of Delights*). This curious book has a publishing history rooted in a complex web of multiple migrations. It all started around the early 1840s with *Naniwa miyage* (*Souvenirs of Osaka*), issued by Osaka publisher Shioya Kihee. This was advertised in 1842 as 'a sizeable collection of small-sized *banzuke* [ranking charts] of highbrow and lowbrow matters; a source of laughter'.[36] The advertisement hints at the intrinsically hybrid nature of *Naniwa miyage*. Each volume, in fact, assembles small-sized single-sheet prints (16.5 × 22.5 cm), comprising a great number of ranking charts as well as other ephemera. If we take a close look, we realize that each sheet bears a title and a colophon, despite being bound in one volume. This implies that each sheet was printed so that it could be sold also as a separate, discrete title. Yet *Naniwa miyage* was also a book. It comprised volumes of multiple sheets bound together, with a title on the covers and a colophon at the end of a volume or of an instalment. However, as a book *Naniwa miyage* is unusual. Firstly, the binding is different from the ordinary *fukurotoji* (pouch-binding) used in Japan at this time, having something more akin to what we would view as an album. Secondly, no copy of the same volume contains the same single-sheet prints, in the same order. In other words, *Naniwa miyage* as a book lacks the kind of stability that books used to have by this time in the world of Japan's commercial publishing. It is a delightful hybrid – a book that is ephemeral in nature and that collects ephemera.

The scale of the first edition of *Naniwa miyage* was impressive. The first two instalments alone included more than 300 single-sheet prints. Analysis of the content has shown that pre-existing materials were displaced from their original context to be incorporated into this collection. In other words, *Naniwa miyage* was a site of migration. First is a movement of printing blocks. Shioya Kihee acquired a minimum of thirty-seven woodblocks of similar small-sized single-sheet materials from at least nine other publishers, mostly based in Osaka. Second, Shioya Kihee refashioned the contents of previously published books to fit his hybrid printed medium and his publishing project.

Whilst being conceived as a site of appropriation of ephemera and books, *Naniwa miyage* itself enjoyed several migrations. At some point in time before 1861, the neighbouring publisher–bookseller Kawachiya Heishichi (fl. nineteenth century) got his hands on Shioya Kihee's woodblocks. Whether he acquired them or was given them is at present impossible to determine. Kawachiya Heishichi systematically cut out Shioya Kihee's colophons from each sheet, but otherwise kept most of the single-sheet prints intact. There are traces of a few amendments as well as a negligible addition of some new sheets. Overall Kawachiya's *Naniwa miyage* is a later impression of Shioya's keyblocks. Kawachiya's *Naniwa miyage* further migrated a few yards away, landing in the hands of the prolific nineteenth-century publisher Wataya Kihee. It was issued in five volumes. For the first time the title was changed to *Tanoshimi sōshi*, and the sheets were newly cut facsimiles of a selection from *Naniwa miyage*, also with some additions. This is what the Bodleian owns (FIG. 102). If we take a look at Wataya Kihee's colophon, we learn that he was in charge of cutting the blocks of *Tanoshimi sōshi* – and therefore owned the blocks – but we also realize that twenty-three other publisher–booksellers joined in marketing *Tanoshimi sōshi* across Japan. Crucially seven were based in the east, in Edo.

*Tanoshimi sōshi* differs from its predecessors in that it has lost any hybrid nature, with the contents remaining the same in all the surviving specimens. In other words, *Tanoshimi sōshi* was reconceptualized as a book. All was set for this text to migrate to this new region, to Edo, taking multiple new lives in at least three collections. *Azuma miyage* (*Souvenirs from the East*) and *Ume no kotobuki* (*Auspicious Plum Blossoms*) retain the majority of the contents of *Tanoshimi sōshi*, but again cutting

fresh woodblocks as facsimile. *Edo jiman* (*Edo Pride*) introduces a substantial number of new materials. In the second half of the nineteenth century, single sheets à la *Naniwa miyage* navigated the exciting world of modernity in terms of contents, printing technology and binding, in several publications.

The copy of *Tanoshimi sōshi* held at the Bodleian is by no means rare, but its bibliographic meaning is significant. It sits at the centre of the complex textual rhizome reconstructed above, allowing a publishing project that originated in Osaka to migrate physically to Edo and further in time into modern Japan. The study of these materials has the potential to contribute to the most recent trends in research on the second half of the nineteenth century in Japan, which calls into question any easy division between the early modern and the modern when it comes to popular publications.

### UNLOCKING THE ARCHIVE

This is just a tiny fraction of a much wider field of study that sits at the intersection of textual scholarship, literature and art history. The publishing industry in Tokugawa and Meiji Japan, made of thousands of titles of books and ephemera, remains an exciting intellectual arena that calls for more research. Key to unlocking the complexities of such fields remains the archive, with collections like the one housed in Oxford inspiring more work.

102 OVERLEAF A sheet from *Tanoshimi sōshi* (*A Booklet of Delights*), Wataya Kihee, Osaka, *c.* 1860s? The title of the sheet reads 'Dai shinpan / Donji-zukushi' and points to the contents: a list of fake radicals that playfully stretch the logic of Japanese writing. Nipponica 209.

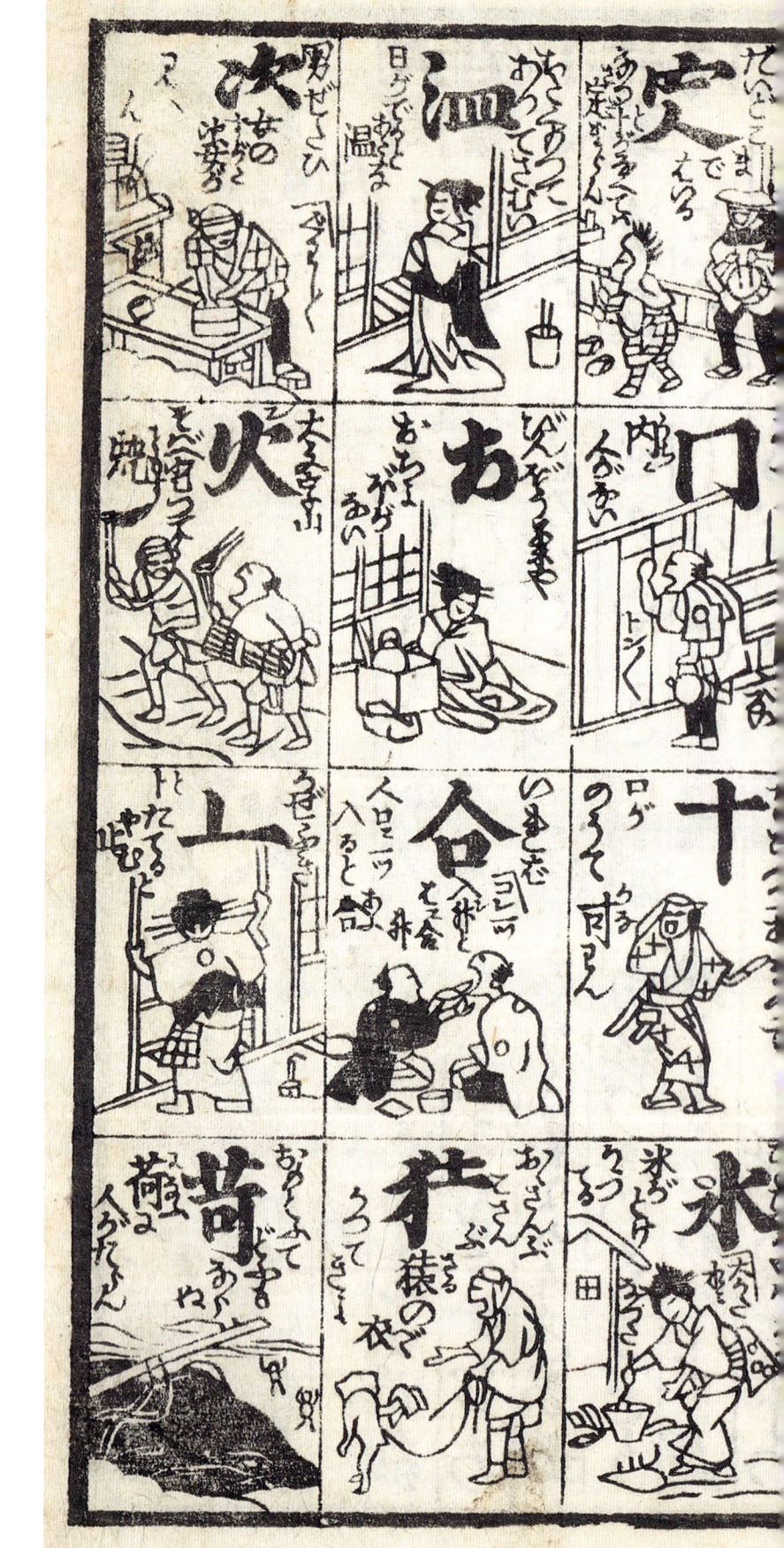

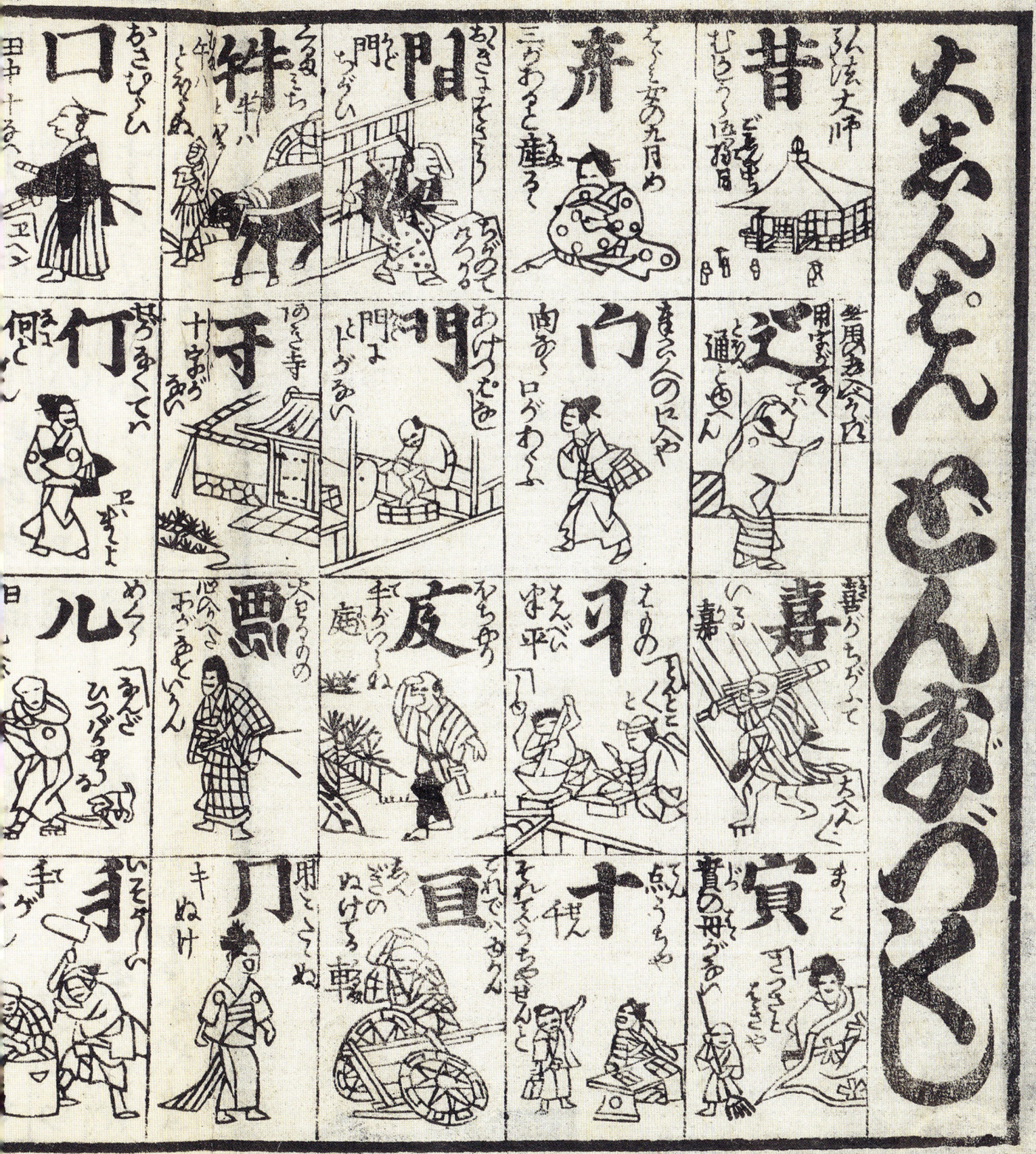

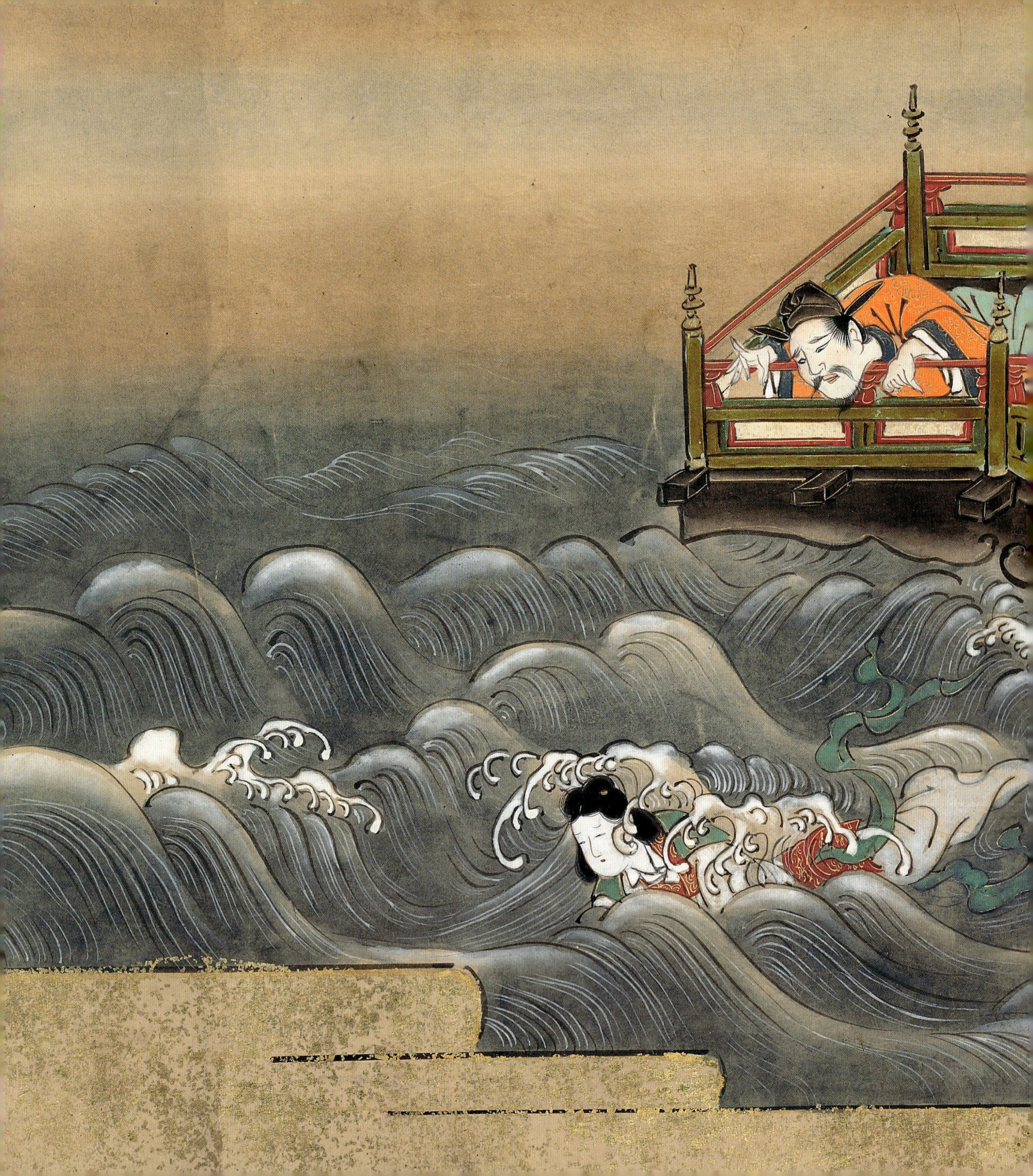

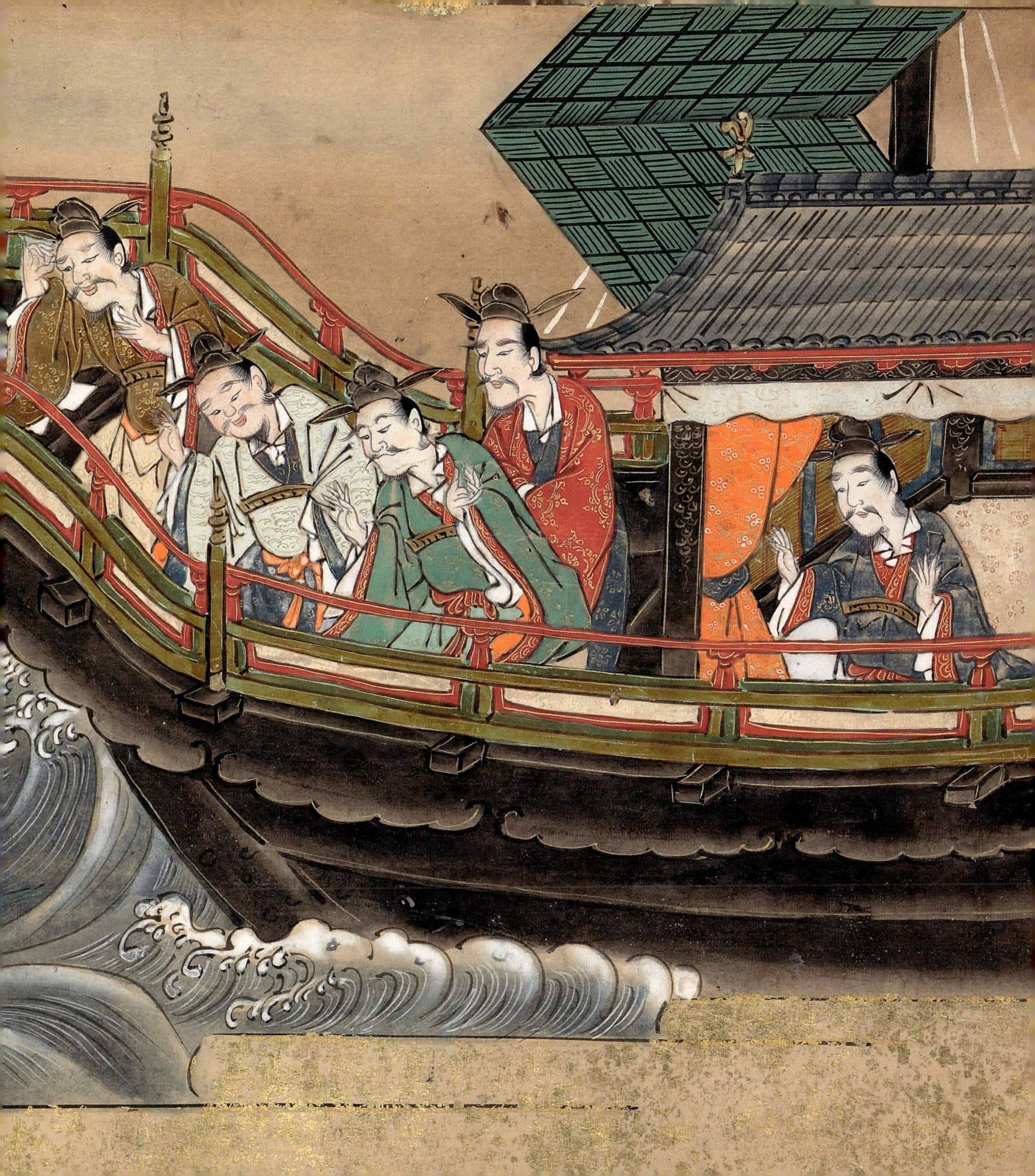

# NOTES

## INTRODUCTION

1. This introduction was written by examining original documentation pertaining to the building of the Japanese collection, and is based on published works such as Izumi Tytler, 'Zōsho o tōshite miru Nihon to no deai', *Shomotsugaku* 18, 2020, pp. 44–51; Gregory Walker et al., *The Bodleian Library: A Subject Guide to the Collections*, Bodleian Library, Oxford, 2004, pp. 145–7; Izumi Tytler, 'The Japanese Collections in the Bodleian Library', in Yu-Ying Brown (ed.), *Japanese Studies: Papers Presented at a Colloquium at the School of Oriental and African Studies*, British Library Occasional Papers 11, 1990, pp. 113–22. Although this historical sketch makes no claim to completeness, it complements earlier scholarship by outlining the history and provenance of the Japanese collection up to the present day.

2. Thomas James, *Catalogus Librorum Bibliothecæ Publicæ*, Apud Iosephum Barnesium, Oxoniæ, 1605, pp. 320, 595, 604.

3. Thomas Hyde, *Catalogus Impressorum Librorum Bibliothecæ Bodlejanæ in Academia Oxoniensi*, 1674, E Theatro Sheldoniano, Oxonii, p. 171.

4. Jeremiah Carter's donation is recorded in William Dunn Macray, *Annals of the Bodleian Library, Oxford: With a Notice of the Earlier Library of the University*, 2nd edn, enlarged, and continued from 1868 to 1880, Clarendon Press, Oxford, 1890, p. 428. Robert Ward's donation is registered on p. 148.

5. Derek Massarella and Izumi K. Tytler, 'The Japonian Charters: The English and Dutch Shuinjō', in *Monumenta Nipponica*, vol. 45, no. 2, Summer 1990, p. 196.

6. William Dunn Macray, *Annals of the Bodleian Library*, 2nd edn, Clarendon Press, Oxford, 1890, pp. 315–16.

7. Louis Langlès, *Catalogue des livres, imprimés et manuscrits, composant la bibliothèque de feu M. Louis-Mathieu Langlès*, Paris, 1825. Participation in the sale is discussed and authorized in the signed curators' minutes of 1 March 1825, in which the Bodleian commissioned the Parisian dealer 'M. Renouard' – possibly Antoine-Augustin Renouard (1765–1853) – to handle the acquisition on behalf of the Library. See Bodleian Library Records d. 12, f. 54r.

8. Wolfgang Michel, 'A Naturalist Lost – C.P. Thunberg's Disciple Johan Arnold Stützer (1763–1821) in the East Indies', in Josef Kreiner (ed.), *Japanese Collections in European Museums III: Reports from the Toyota-Foundation-Symposium Toyota-Foundation-Symposium Königswinter 2003*, Bier'sche Verlagsanstalt, Königswinter, 2015, pp. 147–62.

9. Douce left to the Bodleian an annotated copy of the sale catalogue (Douce CC 298.1) of the auction, which took place at 38 King Street, Covent Garden, on 24 April 1823. While no comprehensive list of his acquisition is given, Douce noted the purchase of 'Several curious and rare Japanese books with cuts' in an entry of his *Collecta* (see MS. Douce e. 68). On Douce and Triphook, see John Feather, 'Robert Triphook and Francis Douce: A Bookseller and One of His Customers', in *Bodleian Library Record*, vol. 15, no. 5/6, October 1996.

10. David Helliwell, *A Catalogue of the Old Chinese Books in the Bodleian Library*, Volume 2: *Alexander Wylie's Books*, Bodleian Library, Oxford, 1985, p. iii.

11. Nanjō Bun'yu, *A Catalogue of Japanese and Chinese Books and Manuscripts Lately Added to the Bodleian Library*, Clarendon Press, Oxford, 1881.

12. *Oxford University Gazette*, vol. 19, supplement to no. 646, 15 May 1889, p. 436. Ibid., vol. 27, supplement to no. 894, 18 May 1897, p. 508. Ibid., vol. 32, supplement to no. 1049, 13 May 1902, p. 506. Ibid., vol. 34, supplement (1) to no. 1111, 10 May 1904, p. 584.

13. The Japanese-language cataloguer was given the sum of £6 10s. See *Oxford University Gazette*, vol. 39, supplement to no. 1269, 11 May 1909, p. 644. For Satow's donation, see ibid., p. 638.

14. Diego Zancani, 'Una biblioteca di cent'anni fa: la "Dante

collection" di Paget Toynbee (1855–1932)', in *Bibliofilia* 100, 1998, pp. 495–512.

15. See MS. Toynbee. d. 23 b, fols. 20.

16. Excerpt from a letter in Library Records. e. 388, f. 28.

17. Excerpt from a letter dated 31 January 1913, in MS. Toynbee d. 25, f. 19.

18. *Oxford University Gazette*, vol. 45, supplement (1) to no. 1456, 10 March 1915, p. 474. On the Moseley donation, see also Keta Keiko, 'Okkusufōdo Daigaku Thoshokanzō Mōzuriī korekushon', in *Nihon Bungaku*, vol. 50, no. 9, September 2000, pp. 29–39.

19. Henry Nottidge Moseley, *Notes by a Naturalist on the Challenger*, Cambridge University Press, Cambridge, 2014, p. 493.

20. Ibid. p. 484.

21. On the development of Japanese Studies in Oxford, see Roger Goodman and Arthur Stockwin, 'Oxford University', in Hugh Cortazzi and Peter Kornicki (eds), *Japanese Studies in Britain: A Survey and History*, Amsterdam University Press, Amsterdam, 2016, pp. 148–65.

22. *Annual Report of the Curators of the Bodleian for 1950–51*, University Press, Oxford, 1951, p. 16.

23. Kit Brook, 'Contextualizing Yoshimura Yoshio's Newspaper Self-portraits: Ah, Un and Bitter', *Bodleian Library Record*, vol. 35, nos 1–2, 2022, pp. 178–84.

24. Peter Kornicki, 'Catalogue of Japanese and Korean Books Acquired by Professor Peter Kornicki and Donated to the Bodleian Library', in *Bodleian Library Record*, vol. 35, nos 1–2, 2022, pp. 111–49.

## ONE

I am indebted for their kind assistance to Alessandro Bianchi, David Helliwell, Margaret Makepeace, John Morgan, William Poole, Sasaki Takahiro and Timon Screech.

1. Anthony Farrington, *The English Factory in Japan, 1613–1623*, British Library, London, 1991, pp. 795, 1048–74, 1110–27, 1141–6, 1153–72.

2. *Catalogue universalis librorum in bibliotheca Bodleiana omnium Librorum, Linguarum, & Scientiarum genere refertissima*, Iohannes Lichfield, & Iacobus Short, Oxford, 1620, paragraph 11.

3. Oxford, Bodleian Library, MS. Jap. b.2 (*shuinjō*) and MS. Savile 48 (log-book). Derek Massarella and Izumi K. Tytler, 'The Japonian Charters: The English and Dutch *shuinjō*', *Monumenta Nipponica* 45, 1990, pp. 189–205; Timon Screech, *The Shogun's Silver Telescope: God, Art and Money in the English Quest for Japan, 1600–1625*, Oxford University Press, Oxford, 2020, pp. 151–3.

4. *Purchas his Pilgrimage, or Relations of the World and the Religions Observed in All ages and Places discovered, from the Creation unto this Present*, 1617; facsimile published by Kessinger, Whitefish MT, 2003, p. 669. This observation was, Tim Screech informs me, omitted from Purchas's *Hakluytus Posthumous* of 1624. Farrington, *The English Factory in Japan*, p. 239.

5. A diary of the visit to Japan in 1673 can be seen in Bodleian Library, MS. Rawl. a. 191, ff. 69–76.

6. Screech, *The Shogun's Silver Telescope*, pp. 84–5.

7. Derek Massarella, 'The Early Career of Richard Cocks (1566–1624), Head of the English East India Company's Factory in Japan (1613–1623)', *Transactions of the Asiatic Society of Japan* 20, 1985, pp. 1–46; Screech, *The Shogun's Silver Telescope*, pp. 83–4.

8. Farrington, *The English Factory in Japan*, pp. 251, 254, 259–60, 262–65. Cocks' letters to Wilson are contained in the State Papers (Spain) in The National Archives (SP 94/8–16).

9. Adam Clulow, 'From Global Entrepôt to Early Modern Domain: Hirado, 1609–1641', *Monumenta Nipponica* 65, 2010, pp. 1–35.

10. Bodleian Library, Nipponica 379 and 466.

11. Watanabe Toshio, *Nihon no koyomi*, Yūsankaku, Tokyo, 1984, pp. 73, 148–55, plate 79.

12. Bodleian Library, MS. Ashmole 1787(2). Farrington, *The English Factory in Japan*, p. 1566. Peacock's hand may be seen in a damaged letter he wrote in 161[?]: British Library, IOR E31 f.214. See the following article on the muster: Peter Kornicki and Alessandro Bianchi, 'Edo shoki no eibun bukan', *Nihon kenkyū* 67, 2023, pp. 167–84.

13. Farrington, *The English Factory in Japan*, p. 753. Derek Massarella, '"The Loudest Lies": Knowledge of Japan in Seventeenth-century England', *Itinerario* 11, 1987, pp. 52–71.

14. Edward Bernard, *Catalogi librorum manuscriptorum Angliae et Hiberniae in unum collecti cum indice alphabetico*, Sheldonian Theatre, Oxford, 1697, pp. 61, 153.

15. Tōkyō Daigaku Shiryō Hensanjo (ed.), *Igirisu shōkanchō nikki*, genbunhen, 3 vols, Tōkyō Daigaku shuppankai, Tokyo, 1978–80, vol. 1, p. 343; Kornicki, *Umi o watatta Nihon shoseki – Yōroppa e, soshite Bakumatsu Meiji no Rondon de*, Heibonsha, Tokyo, 2018, pp. 10–15.

16. Bernard, *Catalogi*, pp. 151, 153. Probate was granted on Viney's estate in December 1687 but there is no mention of books: The National Archives PROB 4/15642. Viney's hand can be seen in Parliamentary Archives, HL/PO/JO/10/1/295, 'Main papers', 17 July 1660.

17. Cambridge, Sidney Sussex College, Muniment Room Bb.7.2. J.A. Venn, *Alumni Cantabrigenses*, Cambridge University Press, Cambridge, 1922–54, vol. 4, p. 305.

18. Bodleian Library, Nipponica 131–133.

19. Kyoko Kinoshita, 'The Advent of Movable Type Printing: The Early Keicho Period and Kyoto Cultural Circles', in Felice Fischer (ed.), *The Arts of Hon'ami Kōetsu, Japanese Renaissance Master*, Philadelphia Museum of Art, Philadelphia PA, 2000, pp. 56–73.

20. Ejima Ihee and Akira Omote (eds), *Zusetsu Kōetsu utaibon*, Yūshūdō, Tokyo, 1970.

21. *Paribon Nippo jisho = Vocabvlario da lingoa de Iapam*, Benseisha, Tokyo, 1976, p. 166; Patrick Schwemmer, 'Japanese Jesuit Literature and the Kōwaka Ballad', in Teresa Ciapparoni La Rocca (ed.), *Il grande viaggio: la missione giapponese del 1613 in Europa*, Scienze e Lettere,

Rome, 2019, pp. 41–5. Takahashi Tsuyoshi, 'Makao Korejio shozō no Nihongo gakushū shoseki ni kansuru ikkōsatsu', *Sōdai Chūgoku ronshū*, vol. 19, 2016, pp. 1–23.

22. William Foster (ed.), *The Journal of John Jourdain, 1608–1617*, Hakluyt Society, Cambridge, 1905, pp. lxxv, 207, 314; Farrington, *The English Factory in Japan*, pp. 245–9, 355–7, 421–2, 472, 543–4, 729, 1529; for Jourdain's will, see The National Archives PROB 11/136 sig. 87. The word 'Manophon' resembles the hand of Wickham, who wrote with large flourishes, but the initial M differs from his.

23. On Shen's travels and his knowledge of Latin, see Theodore Nicholas Foss, 'The European Sojourn of Philippe Couplet and Michael Shen Fuzong, 1683–1692', in Jerome Heyndrickx, *Philippe Couplet, S.J. (1623–1693): The Man Who Brought China to Europe*, Institut Monumenta Serica, Sankt Augustin, 1990, pp. 121–42.

24. ODNB, *sub* Shen Fuzong (by Robert K. Batchelor); William Poole, 'The Letters of Shen Fuzong to Thomas Hyde, 1687–88', *eBLJ*, 2015, article 9, pp. 1–2, 25–6; Bodleian Library, Sloane MS. Or.853a 'Catalogus librorum Chinensium in Archivo', fol. 44v.

25. Farrington *The English Factory in Japan*, p. 781.

26. *Collections of the Massachusetts Historical Society*, fifth series, vol. 1, 1871, pp. 278–9; Judith Farrington, 'The First Twelve Voyages of the English East India Company', *Indonesia and the Malay World*, vol. 29, no. 85, 2001, p. 158; Tōkyō Daigaku Shiryō Hensanjo (ed.), *Igirisu shōkanchō nikki*, vol. 3, p. 4. Farrington, *The English Factory in Japan*, pp. 168 n. 1, 1552 – Farrington suggests that Copland left Japan in 1620.

27. David Helliwell, 'Chinese Books in Europe in the Seventeenth Century' and 'The Bodleian Library's Chinese Collection in the Seventeenth Century', unpublished (https://serica.ie/17thcent); Bert van Selm, 'Cornelis Claesz's 1605 stock catalogue of Chinese books', *Quarendo*, vol. 13, 1983, pp. 247–59.

28. *Imperii Sinensis Nomenclator geographicus*, contained with separate pagination in *Andreae Mülleri Greiffenhagii Opuscule nonnulla Orientalia*, Johannem Völcker, Frankfurt an der Oder, 1695.

29. Department of Plant Sciences, MSS Sherard 253–258. There is a further volume of plant drawings from Witsen's collection in the British Library (Sloane MSS 5018), and another two volumes sent to Berlin in 1685 in the Staatsbibliothek zu Berlin (Libri picturati A41–42).

30. Farrington, *The English Factory in Japan*, pp. 472, 729.

31. Thomas Lockley, '"Yong lads of very good capacitie." Christopher and Cosmus, Anglo-Japanese Pioneers', *Japan Forum* 31, 2019, pp. 86–109; Nandini Das, 'Encounter as Process: England and Japan in the Late Sixteenth Century', *Renaissance Quarterly* 69, 2016, pp. 1343–68.

32. Dinu Luca, *The Chinese Language in European Texts: The Early Period*, Palgrave Macmillan, New York, 2016, pp. 39–41, 97–8, 151–3. As Luca notes, the page on which the Chinese and Japanese 'alphabets' were to appear is blank, but in some copies (London, Middle Temple Library;

Paris, Bibliothèque Nationale) the omission is made good in pages added after the index.

33. Peter Kornicki, 'A Sad Case of Neglect: A Chinese book in New College Library', *New College Notes* 10, 2018, article 3; Farrington, *The English Factory in Japan*, p. 949; Hatch is mentioned often by Cocks in *Igirisu shōkanchō nikki*, vol. 3.

34. In 1607 Bodley wrote to Thomas James about the Chinese books. He could not give the titles so he wrote the name of the donor in each volume. G.W. Wheeler (ed.), *Letters of Sir Thomas Bodley to Thomas James*, Clarendon Press, Oxford, 1927, p. 168.

## TWO

This essay is indebted to bibliographic surveys of the Japanese manuscript collection in the Bodleian Library and research on individual works undertaken by the Library's former librarians, Ms Izumi Tytler and Dr Alessandro Bianchi, as well as by Professor Tsuji Eiko, cited herein. I wish to thank Dr Alessandro Bianchi and the staff of the Bodleian Library for the opportunity to view the collection and to present my research to the public in July 2022. This material was also presented to Harvard University's Early Modern World colloquium in September 2022.

1. Mary Elizabeth Berry, *Japan in Print: Information and Nation in the Early Modern Period*, University of California Press, Berkeley CA, 2006.

2. For the purposes of this chapter and its focus on the place of handwritten and illustrated manuscripts in early modern Japanese society, see, among the many publications by Peter Kornicki on book history in Japan, his 'Manuscript, Not Print: Scribal Culture in the Edo Period', *Journal of Japanese Studies* 32, 2006, pp. 23–52, and, more recently, Peter Kornicki, 'Japan's Hand-written Culture: Confessions of a Print Addict', *Japan Forum* 31, 2019, pp. 272–84.

3. Julie Nelson Davis and Linda Chance, 'The Handwritten and the Printed: Issues of Format and Medium in Japanese Premodern Books', *Manuscript Studies* 1, 2016, pp. 90–115.

4. Ibid., p. 92.

5. Hayashi Kōhei, 'Okkusufōdo daigaku zō emaki Urashimatarō no honkoku to kaidai', *Tomakomai Komazawa Daigaku kiyō* 27, Tomakomai, 2013, pp. 1–31.

6. This nineteenth-century term 'trousseau' is frequently used as a translation for the Japanese words *konrei chōdo*, or *konrei dōgu*, to refer to the various household items and clothing prepared on the occasion of a marriage and customarily made in the name of the bride. Although 'trousseau' can refer primarily to clothing, in the Edo-period Japanese context the bridal items included furniture, folding screens, robes and hundreds of other household items. See Haino Akio, 'Konrei dōgu', *Nihon no bijutsu* 277, 1989.

7. For comparison, see the examination of marriage as a tool of diplomacy and wedding journeys in premodern Europe

in John Watkins, *After Lavinia: A Literary History of Premodern Marriage Diplomacy*, Cornell University Press, Ithaca NY, 2017, and Patrik Pastrnak, *Dynasty in Motion: Wedding Journeys in Late Medieval and Early Modern Europe*, Routledge, Taylor & Francis, Abingdon, 2024.

8. An especially well documented example is the wedding procession through the capital streets for Tokugawa Masako (aka Tōfukumon'in, 1607–1678), the daughter of the second Tokugawa shogun Hidetada (1579–1632), upon her marriage to Emperor GoMizunoo in 1620. Elizabeth Lillehoj recounts the proceedings and Masako's entry into the imperial palace while discussing the political significance of this unprecedented union between a woman from the warrior caste and an emperor; see 'Art and Architecture for Empress Tōfukumon'in', in Lillehoj, *Art and Palace Politics in Early Modern Japan, 1580s–1680s*, Brill, Leiden, 2011, ch. 4, pp. 121–53.

9. An important study focusing on the inventory for this wedding and its 'bridal books' (*yomeiribon*), as well as the general phenomenon of books as gifts, is Hōjō Hideo, *Tokugawa Takehime no konrei to yomeiribon, Tokugawa Takehime no konrei chōdo kenjō mokuroku*, Tōkai Gakuen Joshi Tanki Daigaku Kokugo Kokubun Gakkai, Nagoya, 1971.

10. Ryūsawa Aya calls attention to the warrior tales, specifically those related to *The Tale of the Heike* (*Heike monogatari*) and other military chronicles prepared for Matsuhime, the adopted daughter of the fifth Tokugawa Shogun Tsunayoshi (1646–1709), when she married in 1708 Maeda Yoshinori (1690–1745), daimyo of the Kaga domain. Ryūsawa uses this evidence to argue for the trousseau origins of Heike-related paintings in various formats; see Ryūsawa Aya, 'Edo jidai zenki no Heike monogatari-zu senmen ni tsuite – Umi no Mieru Mori Bijutsukan shozō 'Heike monogatari senmen gachō' o chūshin ni', in Kobayashi Kenji (ed.), *Etoku, Sengoku no geinō to kaiga: egakareta katarimono no sekai*, Miyai Shoten, Tokyo, 2020, pp. 102–12. See also the excellent study by Naoko Gunji, '*Heike* Paintings in the Early Edo Period: Edification and Ideology for Elite Men and Women', *Archives of Asian Art*, vol. 67, no. 1, 2017, pp. 1–24.

11. The wedding items for brides from the noble Konoe lineage, who married into the Tokugawa Owari line of daimyo, provide an important example of preparation by the groom's family; see Yoshikawa Miho, 'Shunkyōin Sachigimi no konrei to kiku orieda makie chōdo', *Kinkō sōsho* 45, 2018, pp. 59–109.

12. Ryūsawa, 'Edo jidai zenki no Heike monogatari-zu senmen ni tsuite', p. 109.

13. Monika Bincsik, 'A Lacquer Display Shelf Reunited with a Bridal Trousseau', *Arts of Asia*, vol. 49, no. 2, 2019, pp. 98–103. Yoshikawa Miho has also painstakingly researched how individual items from trousseau were reused over generations for separate aristocratic brides marrying into the Owari branch of Tokugawa daimyo; see Yoshikawa, 'Shunkyōin Sachigimi no konrei'.

14. In addition to manuscripts, many early modern folding screens dispersed to collections around the world were likely once part of a bridal trousseau. Thirty pairs of folding-screen paintings were included in Tokugawa Masako's trousseau, and the tradition continued into the nineteenth century, albeit on a lesser scale, with records describing the great care taken in deciding the subject matter for these works; see Haino, *Konrei dōgu*, p. 38.

15. Although most research focuses on the Edo period and the feudal system that drove trousseau production and thus the creation of books and scrolls, continuities from the Muromachi and Momoyama periods need further investigation. See, for example, the early-sixteenth-century illustrated scrolls of *The Tale of Shutendōji* in the Suntory Museum of Art, discussed in Sakakibara Satoru's two-part article, 'Santorī Bijutsukan-bon Shuten dōji emaki o megutte', *Kokka* 1076, 1984, pp. 7–26; *Kokka* 1077, 1984, pp. 33–56.

16. Isaac Titsingh and Frederic Shoberl, *Illustrations of Japan: Consisting of Private Memoirs and Anecdotes of the Reigning Dynasty of the Djogouns, or Sovereigns of Japan*, printed for R. Ackermann, London, 1822. Isaac Titsingh's posthumously published English-language book contains a detailed textual description and illustrations of the nuptial process for townspeople that were taken from the Japanese woodblock printed two-volume book, *Poppy Pouch Guide to Wedding Ceremony Preparations* (*Konrei shiyō keshibukuro*), published in 1750. For a facsimile of the Japanese text, see *Edo jidai josei bunko*, vol. 28, Ōzorasha, Tokyo, 1994.

17. Titsingh's *Illustrations of Japan* (following the 1750 marriage guide) lists close to twenty separate titles of works of literature, poetry and Chinese philosophy to be selected for inclusion on the bookshelf, adding that shelves are blank in the illustration because they are to be filled according to one's own preference; Titsingh, *Illustrations of Japan*, pp. 193–5.

18. These split-level shelves (*chigaidana*) recall the long tradition of display culture within *shoin* architecture that was first codified and popularized in the Muromachi period and that featured such shelves built into the alcove wall; the bride's bookshelf resembles a portable version of this type of display.

19. Ishikawa Tōru, *Nara ehon, emaki no tenkai*, Miyai Shoten, Tokyo, 2009. Ishikawa makes the case for a more expansive view of types of book that might have been made for the bridal trousseau.

20. Delphine Mulard, *Production et réception des manuscrits enluminés japonais des XVIIe et XVIIIe siècles: le cas du 'Récit de Bunshō' (Bunshō sōshi)*, Art et histoire de l'art, Université Sorbonne Paris Cité, 2017.

21. The 1750 wedding guide used by Titsingh (see notes 16 and 17) devotes much space to explaining the protocol for monetary transactions and gift exchange during the nuptial process. This era also witnessed the increasing importance of wedding-related businesses and professional go-betweens for those of the commoner classes (townspeople and merchants).

22. Keller Kimbraugh, in 'Pushing Filial Piety: *The Twenty-Four Filial Exemplars* and an Osaka Publisher's "Beneficial Books for Women"', *Japan Review* 34, 2019, pp. 43–68, provides a systematic account of the publication history of the *Companion Library*, noting its original title and its role among other publications for women and new brides. It also supplies detailed analysis of *The Twenty-Four Filial Exemplars* (*Nijūshikō* ) and its significance to the moral education of women readers in the eighteenth century.

23. Precisely on the issue of commoners procuring wedding libraries, Kimbraugh discusses a document written by a merchant and its suggestions for volumes to supply to a bride on entry to her new home; see ibid., p. 64.

24. Shane McCausland et al., *Chinese Romance from a Japanese Brush: Kano Sansetsu's Chōgonka Scrolls in the Chester Beatty Library*, Scala, London, 2009.

25. Asai Ryōi's text incorporates much from an earlier commentary called *Chōgonka shō* by the court noble and scholar Kiyohara Nobukata (1475–1550), which was written in Chinese characters and *katakana* and which Ryōi simply rendered in easy-to-read *kana*. The full title of Ryōi's text therefore sometimes includes the title of Nobukata's commentary and is rendered as *Yōkihi monogatari, Chōgonka shō* (*The Tale of Yang Guifei, Commentary on the Song of Everlasting Sorrow*). See Kurashima Tokihisa, *Yōkihi monogatari*, Koten bunko 478, Koten Bunko, Tokyo, 1986. Kurashima summarizes previous scholarship regarding authorship and describes significant stylistic habits among works by Asai Ryōi, as in his *Mirror of Women of Our Realm* (*Honchō jokan*, or *Honchō onna kagami*, 1661), a didactic text for women featuring historical Chinese women as analogies and exemplum for Japanese women.

26. Kobayashi Kenji first called attention to this new phenomenon of the artists of handscrolls using printed books as templates for new works and drew specifically from examples of *Song of Everlasting Sorrow*; see his '"Yōkihi monogatari" to "Chōgonka emaki" – Edo jidai zenki ni okeru emaki seisaku no ichiyōsō', *Ōtani Joshidai kokubun* 16, 1986, pp. 57–67. The Bodleian manuscripts demonstrate this trend in both handscroll and deluxe book format.

27. The *Song of Everlasting Sorrow* (*Chōgonka*) scrolls in the Bodleian collection (MS. Jap.b.4(r)) consist of volumes one (33.4 × 1199 cm) and two (33.4 × 1020.9 cm) of an original three-scroll set; the two remaining scrolls contain seven and five illustrations respectively. As will be explained, one painting has been remounted in the wrong order, and one unidentified painting appears in scroll two. See Tsuji Eiko (ed.), *Zaigai Nihon jūyō emaki sen*, 2 vols, Kasama Shoin, Tokyo, 2014, for a transcription of the text (vol. 2, kenkyū hen, pp. 281–313), full colour photos of the two scrolls (vol. 1) and a comparison by Kobayashi Kenji of the Bodleian scrolls among others to that of a complete three-scroll set in the Seitoku University collection (vol. 2, kenkyū hen, pp. 696–706).

28. The *Song of Everlasting Sorrow* (*Chōgonka*) in the Bodleian collection codex manuscripts (MS. Jap.d.14–16) consist of three thread-bound volumes.

29. Kurashima, *Yōkihi monogatari*, pp. 254–5.

30. Michael Emmerich, *The Tale of Genji: Translation, Canonization, and World Literature*, Columbia University Press, New York, 2013. Emmerich argues, for example, that Ryūtei Tanehiko's multi-volume print *Nise Murasaki inaka Genji* (1829–42) was one of many 'replacements' for the eleventh-century *The Tale of Genji* for readers and consumers in the Edo period and beyond.

31. Shane McCausland, 'The Dublin Chōgonka Scrolls by Kano Sansetsu', in Shane McCausland et al., *Chinese Romance from a Japanese Brush: Kano Sansetsu's Chōgonka Scrolls in the Chester Beatty Library*, Scala, London, 2009, p. 55.

32. Translation from Stephen Owen, *An Anthology of Chinese Literature: Beginnings to 1911*, W.W. Norton, New York, 1996, p. 444, where the poem title is translated as 'Song of Lasting Pain'.

33. Another painting later inserted into the scroll appears as painting 2 in the second scroll of the set (see pp. 228–9 of the present volume). The image depicts a woman in Chinese dress having leapt from a boat into the water as several male figures look on. No such scene appears in *The Tale of Yang Guifei* woodblock printed commentary, or in the Bodleian's codex manuscript version. The style of the painting differs slightly from the others in the two scrolls; although speculation about its subject matter is possible, it must remain a topic for future research.

34. Muraki Keiko, '"Chōgonka-e" no henyō: Nara-e-kei "Chōgonka emaki" o tegakari ni', *Bigaku geijutsugaku* 25, 2009, pp. 50–69.

35. Muraki Keiko, 'Yōwain shojō ni miru "Chōgonka-zu byōbu": Genroku jūyonen no byōbu no seisaku no ichirei', *Kansai Daigaku tōzai gakujutsu kenkyū kiyō* 52, 2019, pp. 41–62.

36. Translation from Owen, *An Anthology of Chinese Literature*, p. 447.

37. For the deification and numerous literary afterlives of Yan Guifei in Japanese literature, see Masako Nakagawa Graham, *The Yang Kuei-Fei Legend in Japanese Literature*, Edwin Mellen Press, Lewiston NY, 1998, 'The Atsuta Deity Type', pp. 168–77; Wai-Ming Ng, 'The Images of Yang Guifei in Tokugawa Texts', *Journal of Asian History*, vol. 50, no. 1, 2016, pp. 117–39. Song Chunxiao has also demonstrated how even manuscript books (*Nara ehon*) of a warrior tale such as *The Chronicle of Great Peace* (*Taiheiki*) insert 'auspicious allusions' into the Yang Guifei story and emphasize her identity as an immortal; see Song Chunxiao, 'Chūsei "Hakukyoi bungei" no kenkyū: gensetsu keisei to kaiga hyōshō', Ph.D. dissertation, Keio University, Tokyo, 2023, pp. 124–43.

38. Translated by Melissa McCormick from *Song of Everlasting Sorrow* (*Chōgonka*) codex in the Bodleian collection (MS. Jap. d.16), vol. 3, p. 19 recto, lines 2–6.

### THREE

The author wishes to acknowledge Dr Yoshitaka Yamamoto of the National Institute for Japanese Literature (Kokubungaku Kenkyū Shiryōkan), for the analysis and interpretation of poems discussed here.

1. The loanword *suiito* is in use in reference to a hotel accommodation with multiple rooms, but J.S. Bach's suites for cello, for example, are *kumikyoku,* which is a calque.
2. Robert H. Brower, 'Fujiwara Teika's *Maigetsushō*', *Monumenta Nipponica*, vol. 40, no. 4, 1985, pp. 410–12; emphasis added.
3. *Shinpen kokka taikan* henshū iinkai (ed.), *Shinpen Kokka Taikan*, Kadokawa Shoten, Tokyo, 1980, vol. 5, pp. 935–40. See also Edwin A. Cranston, 'Mystery and Depth in Japanese Court Poetry', in Thomas Hare et al. (eds), *The Distant Isle: Studies and Translations of Japanese Literature in Honor of Robert H. Brower*, Center for Japanese Studies, University of Michigan, Ann Arbor MI, 1996, pp. 65–104; and Paul S. Atkins, *Teika: The Life and Works of a Medieval Japanese Poet*, University of Hawai'i Press, Honolulu HI, 2017, pp. 88–105.
4. See, for example, versions of the 'Ten Styles' attributed to Aburanokōji Takanori (1684–1746), Sono Motoka (1691–1745) and Konoe Uchisaki (1728–1785), as well as another by Prince Arisugawa Taruhito (1835–1895), in the Tokyo National Museum (call number: B-2347).
5. A complete digital reproduction is accessible in the National Institute of Japanese Literature's *Shin Nihon kotenseki sōgō dētabēsu*: public viewer DOI 100049344. The Miyagi Prefectural Library call number is 911.2001/11 (*mokuroku bangō* 2252.)
6. Although many of these poems have been previously translated in various contexts, the translations here are the author's own; however, the translations of the names of the 'ten styles' are by Robert H. Brower (see note 2).
7. Names of poets are given first as they appear in the Imperial Household Ministry text.
8. The exceptions are 4, Saigyō's poem, here serving as the example of the 'style of deep feeling', and 10, Yoshitsune's poem, chosen to exemplify the 'demon-quelling style'.
9. These records include notes within the *Kokin wakashū* and many contemporaneous and later anthologies, which provide historicizing data about the occasions on which such poems for screen projects were originally composed and the topics in the programme.
10. Haruo Shirane, *Japan and the Culture of the Four Seasons*, Columbia University Press, New York NY, 2013.
11. Both versions of this poem reproduced from the most likely source, *Dairin gushō* and its source, *Kameyamadono shichihyakushu* in *Shinpen kokka taikan*, render its third line (-*ku*) as *karenedomo* rather than *karenu to ya*. This would yield a slightly different translation: 'the green leaves *do not fade, and yet...*'
12. The roundel that visualizes poem 9 depicts mandarin ducks in a nearly frozen pond. However, in the poem the word for mandarin duck (*mizudori*) is a pillow word (*makurakotoba)* associated with 'green leaves' (*aoba)*

through their shared colour *(ao,* green, is the most striking colour of the duck's plumage.) Thus, the poem is about the perception of residual green tints in an otherwise wintry white (imagined) waterscape – ducks are not active presences in the poem per se. Still, it should be noted that *aoba* could mean both 'green leaves' (青葉) and 'green wings (青羽), further complicating the conceit of the poem. It is also true that this visualization in the Bodleian album is in keeping with iconographic conventions established in earlier renderings of this poem as one of the exemplars of the 'Ten Styles'.
13. They range from seventh- to fourteenth-century figures – again, all male. The collections in which they most prominently appear originate in a range of periods from the tenth to the fifteenth centuries, the latest being *Dairin gushō*, the likely source for poem 9.
14. Carolyn Wheelwright (ed.), *Word in Flower: The Visualization of Classical Literatures in Seventeenth-Century Japan*, Yale University Art Gallery, New Haven CT, 1989, pp. 12–51.
15. Ibid., see p. 4, figs 16–17. The author acknowledges the research conducted by Eric Jose Esteban, a doctoral candidate in Japanese literature at Yale University, on the Beinecke album. For the pair of screens by Yamamoto Soken, see Yale University Art Gallery: 1986.5.1.1.2.
16. See Estelle Bauer and Michel Vieillard-Baron, 'Album de peintures de fleurs aux bords découpés (Les Dix Styles de Teika)', in Pauline D'Abrigeon, Pauline Guyot and Catherine Tran-Bourdonneau (eds), *À portée d'Asie: Collectionneurs et marchands d'art asiatique en France 1750–1950*, Lienart Éditions, Paris, 2023, pp. 144–51. Bauer and Vieillard-Baron also cite the Bodleian, Beinecke and Metropolitan Museum of Art albums, as well as others in the Chester Beatty Library (Dublin) and Minneapolis Institute of Art, as comparable to the Colmar album.

### FOUR

1. *Nihon shoki,* Shōgakkan, Tokyo, 1994–98: https://solo.bodleian.ox.ac.uk/permalink/44oxf_inst/35n82s/alma991013117089707026.
2. John Evelyn, *Diary and Correspondence of John Evelyn, F.R.S.: To Which Is Subjoined the Private Correspondence between King Charles I and Sir Edward Nicholas, and Between Sir Edward Hyde, Afterwards Earl of Clarendon, and Sir Richard Browne*, Henry Colburn, London, 1850.
3. Bunshō Jugaku, *Paper-making by Hand in Japan.* Meiji-Shobo, Tokyo, 1959.
4. Carl Peter Thunberg, *Flora Iaponica*, I.G. Müller, Lipsiae [Leibzig], 1784.
5. Hans Schmoller, *Mr. Gladstone's Washi: A Survey of Reports on the Manufacture of Paper in Japan, 'The Parkes Report of 1871'*, Bird & Bull, Newtown PA, 1984.
6. On the process of making Japanese paper by hand, see Timothy Barrett, *Nagashizuki: The Japanese Craft of Hand Papermaking*, Bird & Bull, North Hills PA, 1979; Timothy Barrett and Winifred Lutz, *Japanese Papermaking: Traditions, Tools, and Techniques,*

Weatherhill, New York, 1983; Claire Bolton and Yasusuke Nyuko, *Awa Gami: Japanese Handmade Papers from Fuji Mills, Tokushima,* Alembic, Oxford, 1991; Sukey Hughes, *Washi, the World of Japanese Paper*, Kodansha International, Tokyo and New York, 1978; Dard Hunter, *A Papermaking Pilgrimage to Japan, Korea and China*, Pynson, New York, 1936; Yuji Kishikawa and Chosuke Taki, *Handbook on the Art of Washi*, Wagami-do K.K., Tokyo, 1991; Bunshō Jugaku, *Paper-making by Hand in Japan*, Meiji-Shobo, Tokyo, 1959; Thomas and Harriet Tindale, *The Handmade Papers of Japan*, Charles E. Tuttle, Rutland VT and Tokyo, 1952.

7. Jugaku, *Paper-making by Hand in Japan.*

8. On the history of Japanese paper and its primary sources, see ibid.

9. Jihē Kunisaki, Motokuni Tamba and Charles E. Hamilton, *Kamisuki Chōhōki; A Handy Guide to Papermaking*, Book Arts Club, University of California, Berkeley CA, 1948.

10. Han Yoon-Hee et al., 'Traditional Papermaking Techniques Revealed by Fibre Orientation in Historical Papers', *Studies in Conservation*, vol. 51, no. 4, 2006, pp. 267–76.

11. Soetsu Yanagi, *The Beauty of Everyday Things*, Penguin, London, 2018.

12. *Kogei* magazine 28, 1933.

13. On techniques to decorate paper, see Takahiro Sasaki and Makiko Shiroto, *The Art of Washi Paper in Japanese Rare Books*, FutureLearn Keio University online course; Sukey Hughes, *Washi, the World of Japanese Paper*, Kodansha International, Tokyo and New York, 1978.

14. On the making of pigments in Japan, see Toyokichi Takamatsu, *On Japanese Pigments*, Department of Science, Tokyo, 1878; Dominique Cardon and Caroline Higgitt, *Natural Dyes: Sources, Tradition, Technology and Science*, Archetype Publications, London, 2007; John Winter, *East Asian Paintings: Materials, Structures and Deterioration Mechanisms*, Archetype Publications, London, 2008. On the identification of pigments used in Japan, see Carole Biron et al., 'Probing Some Organic *Ukiyo-e* Japanese Pigments and Mixtures Using Non-invasive and Mobile Infrared Spectroscopies', *Analytical and Bioanalytical Chemistry* 410, 2018, pp. 7043–54; Sandra Connors, Paul Whitmore, Roger Keyes and Elisabeth Coombs, 'The Identification and Light Sensitivity of Japanese Woodblock Print Colorants: The Impact on Art History and Preservation', in P. Jett et al., *Scientific Research on the Pictorial Arts of Asia: Proceedings of the Second Forbes Symposium at the Freer Gallery of Art*, Archetype Publications, London, 2005, pp. 35–47; Michele Derrick, Richard Newman and Joan Wright, 'Characterization of Yellow and Red Natural Organic Colorants on Japanese Woodblock Prints by EEM Fluorescence Spectroscopy', *Journal of the American Institute for Conservation*, vol. 56, nos 3–4, 2017, pp. 171–93; Katherine Eremin, Jens Stenger and Melanie Li Green, 'Raman Spectroscopy of Japanese Artists' Materials: *The Tale of Genji* by Tosa Mitsunobu',

*Journal of Raman Spectroscopy* 37, 2006, pp. 1119–24; Robert L. Feller, Mary Curran and Catherine W. Bailie, 'Identification of Traditional Organic Colorants Employed in Japanese Prints and Determination of Their Rates of Fading', in *Japanese Woodblock Prints: A Catalogue of the Mary A. Ainsworth Collection*, R. Keyes, Allen Memorial Art Museum, Oberlin College, 1984, pp. 253–66; Elisabeth West FitzHugh, 'A Database of Pigments on Japanese *Ukiyo-e* Paintings in the Freer Gallery of Art', *Studies Using Scientific Methods: Pigments in Later Japanese Paintings*, Freer Gallery of Art Occasional Papers, NS vol. 1, Smithsonian Institution, Washington DC, 2003, pp. 1–53; Aurelie Mounier et al., 'Red and Blue Colours on 18th–19th Century Japanese Woodblock Prints: In Situ Analyses by Spectrofluorimetry and Complementary Non-Invasive Spectroscopic Methods', *Microchemical Journal* 140, 2018, pp. 129–41; Joan Wright, Michele Derrick, Richard Newman and Michiko Adachi, 'The Colors of Desire: Examination of Colorants in *Beauties of the Yoshiwara*', *The Book and Paper Group Annual* 37, 2018, pp. 149–51; Kazuo Yamasaki, 'Technical Studies on the Pigments Used in the Ancient Paintings of Japan', *Proceedings of the Japan Academy* 30, 1954, pp. 781–85; Kazuo Yamasaki and Yoshimichi Emoto, 'Pigments Used on Japanese Paintings from the Protohistoric Period through the 17th Century', *Ars Orientalis* 11, 1979, pp. 1–14, Freer Gallery of Art, Smithsonian Institution and Department of the History of Art, University of Michigan.

15. The scientific analysis has been undertaken by Prof. Andrew Beeby, Durham University, UK, using Raman spectroscopy and fibre optics reflectance spectroscopy.

16. Anna Cesaratto et al., 'A Timeline for the Introduction of Synthetic Dyestuffs in Japan During the Late Edo and Meiji Periods', *Heritage Science*, vol. 6, no. 22, 2018, pp. 1–12.

17. Yanbing Luo, Elena Basso, Henry D. Smith II and Marco Leona, 'Synthetic Arsenic Sulphides in Japanese prints of the Meiji Period', *Heritage Science* 4, 2016, pp. 17–23.

18. Shiho Sasaki and Pauline Webber, 'A Study of Dayflower Blue Used in *Ukiyo-e* Prints', *Studies in Conservation*, vol. 47, suppl. 3, 2002, pp. 185–8. Shiho Sasaki and Elisabeth I. Coombs, 'Dayflower Blue: Its Appearance and Lightfastness in Traditional Japanese Prints', in P. Jett, J. Winter and B. McCarthy (eds), *Scientific Research on the Pictorial Art of Asia*, Archetype Publications in association with the Freer Gallery of Art, Smithsonian Institution, Washington DC and London, 2005, pp. 45–57.

19. Marco Leona and John Winter, 'The Identification of Indigo and Prussian Blue on Japanese Edo Period Paintings', *Studies Using Scientific Methods: Pigments in Later Japanese Paintings*, Freer Gallery of Art occasional papers NS, vol. 1, Smithsonian Institution, Washington DC and London, 2003.

## FIVE

1. See Mia M. Mochizuki, 'The Diaspora of a Jesuit Press: Mimetic Imitation on the World Stage', in Feike Dietz

et al. (eds), *Illustrated Religious Texts in the North of Europe, 1500–1800*, Ashgate, Farnham and Burlington VT, 2014; Katja Triplett, 'Translation Policies, Material Book Culture, and the *Contempt for the World* in the Early Jesuit Mission in Japan', in Antje Flüchter et al. (eds), *Politiken des Übersetzens / Translation Policy and the Politics of Translation*, J.B. Metzler, Berlin and Heidelberg, 2024.

2. The Portuguese word *christan*, which in modern spelling is *cristão*, was rendered as *Kirishitan* in Japan.

3. English translation by Stephen Turnbull, 'Diversity or Apostasy? The Case of the Japanese "Hidden Christians"', *Studies in Church History* 32, 1996, p. 441. Petitjean's 1865 letter is quoted in Marnas's report on the Japanese mission: Francisque Marnas, *La religion de Jésus (Yaso Ja-Kyô) ressuscitée au Japon, dans la seconde moitié du XIXe siècle*, vol. 1, Séminaire des Missions étrangères, Paris, 1931 (1896), p. 530.

4. See Sadao Ōuchida et al. (eds), *Katsuji insatsu no bunkashi: kirishitanban kokatsujiban kara shin jōyō kanjihyō made*, Bensei Shuppan, Tokyo, 2009; for the evolving print culture of the *Kirishitan-ban*, see Toyoshima Masayuki, 'Nihon no insatsu-shi kara mita Kirishitan-ban no tokuchō', in Toyoshima Masayuki (ed.), *Kirishitan to shuppan*, Yagi Shoten, Tokyo, 2013.

5. See Toyoshima Masayuki, 'Kaisetsu', in Luís de Cerqueira, *Sakuramenta teiyō: Nagasaki-ban*, ed. Toyoshima Masayuki (Tōyō bunko zenpon sōsho, 4), Bensei Shuppan, Tokyo, 2014, p. 463.

6. Alexandra Curvelo, 'A Culture In-Between: Materiality and Visuality in the Christian Mission in Japan in the Early Modern Age', in Alexandra Curvelo and Angelo Cattaneo (eds), *Interactions Between Rivals: The Christian Mission and Buddhist Sects in Japan (c. 1549–c. 1647)*, Peter Lang Publishing, Berlin, 2021, p. 249.

7. See Pia Jolliffe and Alessandro Bianchi, 'Jesuit Translation Practices in Sixteenth-century Japan: *Sanctos no gosagueo no uchi nuqigaqi* and Luis de Granada', in Jieun Kiaer et al., *Missionary Translators: Translations of Christian Texts in East Asia*, Routledge, London, 2022.

8. See Yoshimi Orii, 'Furansu kokka toshokan shozō "Santosu no gosagyō" (1591-nen) ni tsuite', *Kirishitan bunka kenkyūkai kaihō* 158, 2021.

9. Keiko Ikegami, *Barlaam and Josaphat: A Transcription of MS Egerton 876 with Notes, Glossary, and Comparative Study of the Middle English and Japanese Version*, AMS Press, New York, 1999, pp. 31–65, 117–31.

10. For accounts of the journey, see Michael Cooper, *The Japanese Mission to Europe, 1582–1590: The Journey of Four Samurai Boys through Portugal, Spain and Italy*, Global Oriental, Folkestone, 2005, and Duarte de Sande, *Japanese Travellers in Sixteenth-Century Europe: A Dialogue Concerning the Mission of the Japanese Ambassadors to the Roman Curia (1590)*, ed. Derek Massarella, trans. Joseph F. Moran, Ashgate, Farnham and Burlington VT, 2012.

11. Portuguese does not use the letters *k*, *w* or *sh*.

12. They are today held by the Bodleian Library, the Biblioteca Ambrosiana in Milan and the Bibliotheca Augusta in Wolfenbüttel, respectively; for the last, see Katja Triplett, 'The Japanese Jesuit *Contemptus Mundi* (1596) of the Bibliotheca Augusta: A Brief Remark on a New Discovery', *Journal of Jesuit Studies*, vol. 5, no. 1, 2018. See also Yoshimi Orii, 'The Dispersion of Jesuit Books Printed in Japan: Trends in Bibliographical Research and in Intellectual History', *Journal of Jesuit Studies*, vol. 2, no. 2, 2015.

13. For a full translation of the poetry section into English, including the poems, see Michael Cooper, 'The Muse Described: João Rodrigues' Account of Japanese Poetry', *Monumenta Nipponica*, vol. 26, no. 1–2, 1971, pp. 55–75.

14. Today, the title 九相詩 is transcribed as *Kusōshi*.

15. See Carla Tronu, 'Memento Mori and Impermanence (Mujō): The 1600 Jesuit Mission Press Edition of Japanese Poems on the Nine Stages of a Decaying Female Body (Kusōka)', in Alexandra Curvelo and Angelo Cattaneo (eds), *Interactions Between Rivals: The Christian Mission and Buddhist Sects in Japan (c. 1549–c. 1647)*, Peter Lang, Berlin, 2021.

16. *Arte da Lingoa de Iapam*, 1604, fol. 180r. Quoted in Cooper, 'The Muse Described', p. 60. In line 1 the word 病中 should be transcribed as *biŏchŭ* and in line 5 the word 観花 should read *quanqua*. The layout here copies that in the source text, with the poem's title, *Cuzŏxi*, placed in the upper right.

17. From the *Kusōshi*; translation by Cooper, 'The Muse Described', p. 61 n.28, slightly amended.

18. Most of the prints of the Jesuit mission press used torinoko paper; the *Sanctos* held at the Biblioteca Marciana in Venice is an exception. It is printed on *kōzo*, which is Japanese tissue paper made from the bark fibre of the paper mulberry tree.

### SIX

1. Kimura Yaeko, 'Akahon kara aohon made: Shuppanbutsu no sokumen', in Kimura Yaeko, Uda Toshihiko and Koike Masatane (eds), *Kusazōshi shū* (from the series *Shin Nihon koten bungaku taikei* 83), Iwanami Shoten, Tokyo, 1997, pp. 611–12; Kimura Yaeko, *Kusazōshi no sekai: Edo no shuppan bunka*, Perikansha, Tokyo, 2009, pp. 96–8. See also Satō Satoru, '*Onna hachi no ki* nado Mitamura-bon ni miru makki akahon no shosō', *Eiribon wākushoppu XII: Shiryōshū*, Jissen joshi daigaku bungei shiryō kenkyūjo, Tokyo, 2020. For information on other more well-known collectors, see Kawase Kazuma, *Nihon ni okeru shoseki shūzō no rekishi*, Perikansha, Tokyo, 1999; Okamura Keiji, *Edo no zōshokatachi*, Kōdansha, Tokyo, 1996.

2. For details, see Laura Moretti, *Pleasure in Profit: Popular Prose in Seventeenth-Century Japan*, Columbia University Press, New York, 2020, chs 1 and 2.

3. On the early publications of the Kyoto shop of Tsuruya Kiemon, see Kashiwazaki Junko, 'Tsuruya Kiemon', *Gengo bunka* 51, 2014, pp. 21–33.

4. The name appears among others in the colophon of the

1837 libretto titled *Hana no ani tsubomi no yatsufusa*, National Institute of Japanese Literature, Iwazu Collection, shelf mark 90–117.

5. Based on Kashiwazaki, 'Tsuruya Kiemon', pp. 32–3. See original housed at the National Institute of Japanese Literature, shelf mark ナ2–578.

6. The most recent reference that I have found so far is 1887 in the English language textbook *Shōyō futsū eigo tsūben jizai*. National Diet Library, shelf mark 特 63–831.

7. Nakagawa Gorōzaemon (compiler), *Edo kaimono hitori annai*, Kawanami Shirobee and Namariya Yasubee, Kyoto; Yanagihara Mokubee, Morimoto Tasuke and Nakagawa Gorobee, Osaka; Okadaya Kashichi, Kuwamura Hanzō, Takekawa Tōbee, Yamashiroya Sahee and Nakagawa Gorōzaemon, Edo, 1824. National Diet Library, shelf mark 123–229.

8. As a testimony of Tsuruya's centrality in the world of graphic narratives (*kusazōshi*) and other *gesaku*-related publishing projects, numerous entries can be found in Kyokutei Bakin, *Kinsei mono no hon Edo sakusha burui*, 1834, critical edition in Tokuda Takeshi (ed.), *Kinsei mono no hon Edo sakusha burui*, Iwanami Shoten, Tokyo, 2014. On graphic narratives (*kusazōshi*), see Laura Moretti and Satō Yukiko (eds), *Graphic Narratives from Early Modern Japan: The World of* Kusazōshi, Brill, Leiden, 2024.

9. On this text, see Michael Emmerich, *The Tale of Genji: Translation, Canonization, and World Literature*, Columbia University Press, New York, 2013.

10. The fashion for appending *zōhan mokuroku* at the end of books started in 1716. These publishers' catalogues were produced alongside book-trade catalogues. For details, see Laura Moretti, 'The Japanese Early-modern Publishing Market Unveiled: A Survey of Edo-period Booksellers' Catalogues', *East Asian Publishing and Society*, vol. 2, no. 2, 2012, pp. 202–3.

11. Ryūtei Tanehiko (author), Utagawa Kunisada (illus.), *Karigane kōya tsukuri no hayazome*, Tsuruya Kiemon, Edo, 1826. Author's private collection.

12. See, for example, Ryūtei Tanehiko (author), Utagawa Kuniyoshi (illus.), *Tawagoto ku awase*, Tsuruya Kiemon, Edo, 1835. Waseda University Library, shelf mark へ13 02378 0117.

13. On the genre of guidebooks known as *meisho zue*, see Robert Goree, *Printing Landmarks: Popular Geography and Meisho Zue in Late Tokugawa Japan*, Harvard East Asian Monographs 437, Harvard University Press, Cambridge MA, 2020.

14. For more details, see Suzuki Toshiyuki, *Ezōshiya: Edo no ukiyoe shoppu*, Heibonsha, Tokyo, 2010, pp. 89–95.

15. *Haifū Yanagidaru*, vol. 33, 34r, Hanaya Kyūjirō, Edo, 1765–1832. Waseda University Library, shelf mark へ09 01147.

16. On the spectrum of literacies in early modern Japan, with a focus on the seventeenth century, see Moretti, *Pleasure in Profit*, ch. 1.

17. For details, see Peter Kornicki, *The Book in Japan: A Cultural History from the Beginnings to the Nineteenth Century*, University of Hawai'i Press, Honolulu, 2001, pp. 125–36.

18. Peter Kornicki, 'Fukun katsuji hon *Shoshitsu kinkōshū* to umeju no shuppan katsudō: Kokatsujiban shūen no kaimei ni mukete', *Biblia* 144, October 2015, pp. 188–72.

19. For details about the book-making process of a *kusazōshi*, see Takagi Gen, 'The Creative Process', in Moretti and Satō (eds), *Graphic Narratives from Early Modern Japan*, pp. 84–117. For more information on printing from a woodblock, see Suzuki Jun and Ellis Tinios, *Understanding Japanese Woodblock-Printed Illustrated Books: A Short Introduction to Their History, Bibliography and Format*, Brill, Leiden, 2016, pp. 33–6.

20. Cynthia Brokaw, 'Woodblock Publishing in China's First Age of Print', Panizzi lectures, British Library, 2021.

21. Alessandro Bianchi, 'The Aesthetic and Functions of Paratext: Scripts, Mise-en-page, and Book Design', Faculty of Asian and Middle Eastern Studies, University of Cambridge, East Asia Seminar Series, 22 November 2021.

22. For an introduction on books for women, see Peter F. Kornicki, 'Women, Education, and Literacy', in P.F. Kornicki, Mara Patessio and G.G. Rowley (eds), *The Female as Subject: Reading and Writing in Early Modern Japan*, University of Michigan Press, Ann Arbor MI, 2010, pp. 7–38; Marcia Yonemoto, *The Problem of Women in Early Modern Japan*, University of California Press, Berkeley CA, 2016. I extend my gratitude to Professor Koizumi Yoshinaga for the advice given in identifying the book discussed here.

23. Unfortunately, to date no copy of *Jokyō fūki dai* that would have been sold within this wrapper is known, making a definitive identification impossible.

24. For more information about this type of letter writing, see Moretti, *Pleasure in Profit*, pp. 186–90.

25. The Union Catalogue Database of Japanese Texts lists four titles in conjunction with Katsura Munenobu's name, none matching the book held at the Bodleian.

26. For details, see Suzuki and Tinios, *Understanding Japanese Woodblock-printed Illustrated Books*, pp. 33, 67.

27. Toda Gensendō (calligrapher), *Onna yō shotsū anmon*, Kawachiya Tasuke, Osaka, second half of the eighteenth century. In the personal collection of Koizumi Yoshinaga.

28. Takada Seibee (author), Takehara Shunchōsai (illus.), *Joyō fuku judai*, Yoshinoya Tamehachi, Kyoto, 1785. Original housed at Tosho bunko. Digital images available at National Institute of Japanese Literature, shelf mark DIG-TSHB-2267.

29. *Joyō fuku judai*, in the personal collection of Koizumi Yoshinaga. The name of Yoshinoya Tamehachi is here substituted by two new Osaka publishers' names – Kawachiya Ki[hee] and another Kawachiya [name illegible] – by means of a wooden plug, using the technique known as *umeki* or *iregi*. This was another advantage of xylography; amendments could easily be done by replacing sections requiring correction with wooden plugs.

30. Miyako no Nishiki, *Genroku taiheiki*, Aoyama Ihee, Kyoto,

1702. Critical edition in Nakajima Takashi (ed.), *Miyako no Nishiki shū* (from the series *Sōsho Edo bunko* 6), Kokusho kankōkai, Tokyo, 1989, p. 100.

31. Kuroishi Yōko, 'Kurohon *Hachiman Tarō ichidaiki* ni tsuite', *Sō: Kusazōshi no honkoku to kenkyū* 24, 2003, pp. 1–55.

32. A fourth edition, dated 1893, is kept in the author's collection. The one owned by the Bodleian, dated 1895, is to my knowledge the most recent.

33. On the topic, but with no reference to copperplate printing, see Seth Jacobowitz, *Writing Technology in Meiji Japan: A Media History of Modern Japanese Literature and Visual Culture*, Harvard East Asian Monographs 387, Harvard University Press, Cambridge MA, 2015. Peter Kornicki and John Clark have explored the cultural roots that enabled the acquisition of skills in printing from copperplates – the availability of Dutch books and Dutch prints after 1720 meant that artists began experimenting in this area. Kornicki, *The Book in Japan*, pp. 166–70; John Clark, *Japanese Nineteenth-Century Copperplate Prints*, ed. Tim Clark, British Museum Occasional Papers 84, Department of Japanese Antiquities, London, 1994.

34. Isobe Atsushi, 'Dōban kusazōshi kō', *Kinsei bungei* 75, 2002, pp. 107–17; Isobe Atsushi, *Shuppan bunka no Meiji zenki: Tōkyō haishi shuppansha to sono shuhen*, Perikansha, Tokyo, 2012.

35. It is worth noting that the 1895 book owned by the Bodleian is not mentioned in Isobe's work. Isobe, *Shuppan bunka*, pp. 154–93.

36. Akatsuki no Kanenari, *Wadan sansai zue*, Kawachiya Seishichi and Shioya Kihee, Osaka, 1842. Osaka Municipal Library, quotation located in the unpaginated backmatter. The analysis that follows is based on archival research conducted in Japan (thanks to a British Academy Leverhulme Small Research Grant), which has been previously presented at a number of conferences.

# FURTHER READING

Atkins, Paul S., *Teika: The Life and Works of a Medieval Japanese Poet*, University of Hawai'i Press, Honolulu HI, 2017.

Barrett, Timothy, *Nagashizuki: The Japanese Craft of Hand Papermaking*, Bird & Bull, North Hills PA, 1979.

Berry, Mary Elizabeth, *Japan in Print: Information and Nation in the Early Modern Period*, University of California Press, Berkeley CA, 2006.

Biron, Carole, et al., 'Probing Some Organic *Ukiyo-e* Japanese Pigments and Mixtures Using Non-invasive and Mobile Infrared Spectroscopies', *Analytical and Bioanalytical Chemistry* 410, 2018, pp. 7043–54.

Brower, Robert H., 'Fujiwara Teika's *Maigetsushō*', *Monumenta Nipponica*, vol. 40, no. 4, 1985, pp. 399–425.

Buckland, Rosina, *Kabuki: Japanese Theatre Prints*, National Museums Scotland, Edinburgh, 2013.

Cardon, Dominique, and Caroline Higgitt. *Natural Dyes: Sources, Tradition, Technology and Science,* Archetype Publications, London, 2007.

Cesaratto, Anna, et al., 'A Timeline for the Introduction of Synthetic Dyestuffs in Japan during the late Edo and Meiji Periods', *Heritage Science*, vol. 6, no. 22, 2018, pp. 1–12.

Clark, John, *Japanese Nineteenth-Century Copperplate Prints*, ed. Tim Clark, British Museum Occasional Papers 84, Department of Japanese Antiquities, London, 1994.

Connors, Sandra, Paul Whitmore, Roger Keyes and Elisabeth Coombs, 'The Identification and Light Sensitivity of Japanese Woodblock Print Colorants: The Impact on Art History and Preservation', in P. Jett et al. (eds), *Scientific Research on the Pictorial Arts of Asia: Proceedings of the Second Forbes Symposium at the Freer Gallery of Art*, Archetype Publications, London, 2005, pp. 35–47.

Cooper, M., *The Japanese Mission to Europe, 1582–1590: The Journey of Four Samurai Boys Through Portugal, Spain and Italy*, Global Oriental, Folkestone, 2005.

Cooper, M., 'The Muse Described: João Rodrigues' Account of Japanese Poetry', *Monumenta Nipponica*, vol. 26, no. 1–2, 1971, pp. 55–75.

Cranston, Edwin A. (trans.), *A Waka Anthology*, 2 vols, Stanford University Press, Stanford CA, 1993, 2006.

Cranston, Edwin A., 'Mystery and Depth in Japanese Court Poetry', in Thomas Hare et al. (eds), *The Distant Isle: Studies and Translations of Japanese Literature in Honor of Robert H. Brower*, Center for Japanese Studies, University of Michigan, Ann Arbor MI, 1996, pp. 88–105.

Curvelo, A., 'A Culture In-Between: Materiality and Visuality in the Christian Mission in Japan in the Early Modern Age', in Alexandra Curvelo and Angelo Cattaneo (eds), *Interactions Between Rivals: The Christian Mission and Buddhist Sects in Japan (c. 1549–c. 1647)*, Peter Lang, Berlin, 2021, pp. 239–73. www.peterlang.com/document/1190560.

Davis, Julie Nelson, et al., *Arthur Tress and the Japanese Illustrated Book*, University of Pennsylvania Libraries, Philadelphia PA, 2022.

Davis, Julie Nelson, *Picturing the Floating World: Ukiyo-e in Context*, University of Hawai'i Press, Honolulu, 2021.

Davis, Julie Nelson, and Linda Chance, 'The Handwritten and the Printed: Issues of Format and Medium in Japanese Premodern Books', *Manuscript Studies*, vol. 1, 2016, pp. 90–115.

Derrick, Michele, Richard Newman and Joan Wright, 'Characterization of Yellow and Red Natural Organic Colorants on Japanese Woodblock Prints by EEM Fluorescence Spectroscopy', *Journal of the American Institute for Conservation*, vol. 56, no. 3–4, 2017, pp. 171–93.

Eremin, Katherine, Jens Stenger and Melanie Li Green, 'Raman Spectroscopy of Japanese Artists' Materials: *The Tale of Genji* by Tosa Mitsunobu', *Journal of Raman Spectroscopy* 37, 2006, pp. 1119–24.

Feller, Robert L., Mary Curran and Catherine W. Bailie, 'Identification of Traditional Organic Colorants Employed in Japanese Prints and Determination of their Rates of Fading', in Allen Memorial Art Museum, R. Keyes, *Japanese Woodblock Prints: A Catalogue of the Mary A. Ainsworth Collection*, Oberlin College, Oberlin OH, 1984, pp. 253–66.

FitzHugh, Elisabeth West, 'A Database of Pigments on Japanese *Ukiyo-e* Paintings in the Freer Gallery of Art', *Studies using Scientific Methods: Pigments in Later Japanese Paintings*, Freer Gallery of Art Occasional Papers, NS vol. 1, Smithsonian Institution, Washington DC, 2003, pp. 1–53.

Hughes, Sukey, *Washi, the World of Japanese Paper*, Kodansha International, Tokyo, New York, 1978.

Hunter, Dard, *A Papermaking Pilgrimage to Japan, Korea and China*, Pynson Printers, New York, 1936.

Ikegami, K., *Barlaam and Josaphat: A Transcription of MS Egerton 876 with Notes, Glossary, and Comparative Study of the Middle English and Japanese Version*, AMS Press, New York, 1999.

Ishikawa Tōru, *Nara ehon, emaki no seisei*, Miyai Shoten, Tokyo, 2003.

Jacobowitz, Seth, *Writing Technology in Meiji Japan: A Media History of Modern Japanese Literature and Visual Culture*, Harvard East Asian Monographs 387, Harvard University Press, Cambridge MA, 2015.

Jolliffe, P., and A. Bianchi, 'Jesuit Translation Practices in Sixteenth-century Japan: Sanctos no gosagueo no uchi nuqigaqi and Luis de Granada', in Jieun Kiaer et al., *Missionary Translators: Translations of Christian Texts in East Asia*, Routledge, London, 2022, pp. 24–56.

Jugaku, Bunshō, *Paper-making by Hand in Japan*. Meiji-Shobo, Tokyo, 1959.

Jun, Suzuki and Ellis Tinios, *Understanding Japanese Woodblock-Printed Illustrated Books: A Short Introduction to Their History, Bibliography and Format*, Brill, Leiden, 2013.

Kamitaka Tokuharu and Hakamada Mitsuyasu, *Chōgonka gakan: The Chester Beatty Library*, Chester Beatty Library, Dublin, and Bensei Shuppan, Tokyo, 2006.

Keyes, Roger S., *Ehon: The Artist and the Book in Japan*, New York Public Library, New York, and University of Washington Press, Seattle WA, 2006.

Kokubungaku Kenkyū Shiryōkan, *Chesutā Bītī Raiburarii emaki ehon kaidai mokuroku*, Bensei Shuppan, Tokyo, 2002.

Kornicki, Peter, 'Japan's Hand-Written Culture: Confessions of a Print Addict', *Japan Forum*, vol. 31, no. 2, 2019, pp. 272–84.

Kornicki, Peter, *Languages, Scripts and Chinese Texts in East Asia*, Oxford University Press, Oxford, 2018.

Kornicki, Peter, 'Manuscript, Not Print: Scribal Culture in the Edo Period', *Journal of Japanese Studies*, vol. 32, no. 1, 2006, pp. 23–52.

Kornicki, Peter, 'Collecting Japanese Books in Europe from the Seventeenth to the Nineteenth Centuries', *Bulletin of Portuguese/Japanese Studies* 8, 2004, pp. 21–38.

Kornicki, Peter, *The Book in Japan: A Cultural History from the Beginnings to the Nineteenth Century*, University of Hawai'i Press, Honolulu, 2001.

Leona, Marco, and John Winter, 'The Identification of Indigo and Prussian Blue on Japanese Edo Period Paintings', *Studies Using Scientific Methods: Pigments in Later Japanese Paintings*, Freer Gallery of Art occasional papers, NS vol. 1, Smithsonian Institution, Washington DC, 2003.

Luo, Yanbing, Elena Basso, Henry D. Smith II and Marco Leona, 'Synthetic Arsenic Sulphides in Japanese Prints of the Meiji Period', *Heritage Science* 4, 2016, pp. 17–23.

McCormick, Melissa, 'Tokugawa-ki sōshoku shahon no miryoku: Tosa Mitsusada hitsu "Genji Suma-zu emaki" to Hābādo Bijutsukan Hōfā Korekushon no kinsei emaki', trans. Ido Misato, in Shimohara Miho (ed.), *Kinsei Yamato-e saikō*, Brücke, Tokyo, 2013, pp. 51–67.

McCormick, Melissa, *Tosa Mitsunobu and the Small Scroll in Medieval Japan*, University of Washington Press, Seattle WA, 2009.

Marnas, F., *La religion de Jésus (Yaso Ja-Kyô) ressuscitée au Japon, dans la seconde moitié du XIXe siècle*, vol. 1, Séminaire des Missions étrangères, Paris, 1931 (1896).

Mochizuki, M.M., 'The Diaspora of a Jesuit Press: Mimetic Imitation on the World Stage', in Feike Dietz et al., *Illustrated Religious Texts in the North of Europe, 1500–1800*, Ashgate, Farnham and Burlington VT, 2014, pp. 113–34.

Moretti, Laura, and Satō Yukiko (eds), *Graphic Narratives from Early Modern Japan: The World of Kusazōshi*, Brill, Leiden, 2024.

Moretti, Laura, *Pleasure in Profit: Popular Prose in Seventeenth-Century Japan*, Columbia University Press, New York, 2020.

Moretti, Laura, 'The Japanese Early-modern Publishing Market Unveiled: A Survey of Edo-period Booksellers' Catalogues', *East Asian Publishing and Society*, vol. 2, no. 2, 2012, pp. 199–308.

Mounier, Aurelie, et al., 'Red and Blue Colours on 18th–19th Century Japanese Woodblock Prints: In situ Analyses by Spectrofluorimetry and Complementary Non-invasive Spectroscopic Methods', *Microchemical Journal* 140, 2018, pp. 129–41.

Nara Ehon Kokusai Kenkyū Kaigi (ed.), *Zaigai Nara ehon*, Kadokawa Shoten, Tokyo, 1981.

Orii, Y., 'Furansu kokkai toshokan shozō "Santosu no gosagyō" (1591-nen) ni tsuite', *Kirishitan bunka kenkyūkai kaihō* 158, 2021, pp. 15–22.

Orii, Y., 'The Dispersion of Jesuit Books Printed in Japan: Trends in Bibliographical Research and in Intellectual History', *Journal of Jesuit Studies*, vol. 2, no. 2, 2015, pp. 189–207. https://doi.org/10.1163/22141332-00202002.

Ōuchida, S., et al. (eds), *Katsuji insatsu no bunkashi: kirishitanban kokatsujiban kara shin jōyō kanjihyō made*, Bensei Shuppan, Tokyo, 2009.

Sakomura, Tomoko, *Poetry as Image: The Visual Culture of Waka in Sixteenth-Century Japan*, Brill, Leiden, 2015.

Sande, D. de, *Japanese Travellers in Sixteenth-Century Europe: A Dialogue Concerning the Mission of the*

*Japanese Ambassadors to the Roman Curia (1590)*, ed. D. Massarella, trans. J.F. Moran, Ashgate, Farnham and Burlington VT, 2012.

Sasaki, Shiho, and Elisabeth I. Coombs, 'Dayflower Blue: Its Appearance and Lightfastness in Traditional Japanese Prints', in P. Jett, J. Winter and B. McCarthy (eds), *Scientific Research on the Pictorial Art of Asia*, Archetype Publications in association with the Freer Gallery of Art, Smithsonian Institution, Washington D.C. and London, 2005, pp. 45–57.

Screech, Timon, *The Shogun's Silver Telescope: God, Art and Money in the English Quest for Japan, 1600–1625*, Oxford University Press, Oxford, 2020.

Shirane, Haruo, *Japan and the Culture of the Four Seasons*, Columbia University Press, New York, 2012.

Sorimachi, Shigeo, Japanese Illustrated Books and Manuscripts in the Chester Beatty Library, Dublin, Ireland, Chester Beatty Library and Kōbunsō, Dublin and Tokyo, 1979.

Sorimachi, Shigeo, *Supensā Korekushon zō Nihon eiribon oyobi ehon mokuroku*, rev. edn, New York Public Library (Spencer Collection) and Kōbunsō, Tokyo, 1978.

Takamatsu T., *On Japanese Pigments*, Department of Science, Tokyo, 1878.

Tindale, Thomas and Harriet, *The Handmade Papers of Japan*, Charles E. Tuttle, Rutland VT and Tokyo, 1952.

Tinios, Ellis, *Japanese Prints: Ukiyo-e in Edo, 1700–1900*, British Museum Press, London, 2016.

Tokuda Kazuo, *Otogi-zōshi jiten*, Tokyodo Shuppan, Tokyo, 2002.

Tokuda Kazuo, *Otogi-zōshi kenkyū*, Miyai Shoten, Tokyo, 1988.

Trede, Melanie, *Image, Text and Audience: The Taishokan Narrative in Visual Representations of the Early Modern Period in Japan*, Peter Lang, Frankfurt am Main, 2004.

Toyoshima M., 'Kaisetsu', in Luís de Cerqueira, *Sakuramenta teiyō: Nagasaki-ban* (Tōyō bunko zenpon sōsho, 4), ed. Toyoshima Masayuki (ed.), Tokyo: Bensei Shuppan, 2014, pp. 457–64.

Toyoshima M., 'Nihon no insatsu-shi kara mita Kirishitan-ban no tokuchō', in Toyoshima Masayuki (ed.), *Kirishitan to shuppan*, Yagi Shoten, Tokyo, 2013, pp. 89–155.

Triplett, K., 'Translation Policies, Material Book Culture, and the *Contempt for the World* in the Early Jesuit Mission in Japan', in Antje Flüchter et al. (eds), *Politiken des Übersetzens / Translation Policy and the Politics of Translation*, J.B. Metzler, Berlin and Heidelberg, 2024, pp. 173–201. https://doi.org/10.1007/978-3-662-67339-3_9.

Triplett, K., 'The Japanese Jesuit Contemptus Mundi (1596) of the Bibliotheca Augusta: A Brief Remark on a New Discovery', *Journal of Jesuit Studies*, vol. 5, no. 1, 2018, pp. 123–7. https://doi.org/10.1163/22141332-00501007.

Tronu, C., 'Memento Mori and Impermanence (Mujō): The 1600 Jesuit Mission Press Edition of Japanese Poems on the Nine Stages of a Decaying Female Body (Kusōka)', in Alexandra Curvelo and Angelo Cattaneo (eds), *Interactions Between Rivals: The Christian Mission and Buddhist Sects in Japan (c. 1549–c. 1647)*, Peter Lang, Berlin, 2021, pp. 137–59. www.peterlang.com/document/1190560.

Tsuji, Eiko, *Zaigai Nihon jūyō emakisen*, Kasama Shoin, Tokyo, 2014.

Turnbull, S., 'Diversity or Apostasy? The Case of the Japanese "Hidden Christians"', *Studies in Church History* 32, 1996, pp. 441–54. https://doi.org/doi:10.1017/S0424208400015552.

Vieillard-Baron, Michel, *Fujiwara no Teika (1162–1241) et la notion d'excellence en poésie*, Collège de France, Institute des Hautes Études japonaises, 2001.

Wheelwright, Carolyn (ed.), *Word in Flower: The Visualization of Classical Literature in Seventeenth-Century Japan*, Yale University Art Gallery, New Haven CT, 1989.

Winter, John, *East Asian Paintings: Materials, Structures and Deterioration Mechanisms*, Archetype Publications, London, 2008.

Yamasaki, Kazuo, and Yoshimichi Emoto, 'Pigments Used on Japanese Paintings from the Protohistoric Period through the 17th Century', *Ars Orientalis* 11, 1979, Freer Gallery of Art, Smithsonian Institution, Washington DC, and Department of the History of Art, University of Michigan, pp. 1–14.

Zhou, Peter X. (ed.), *Collecting Asia: East Asian Libraries in North America, 1868–2008*, Ann Arbor Association for Asian Studies, Ann Arbor MI, 2010.

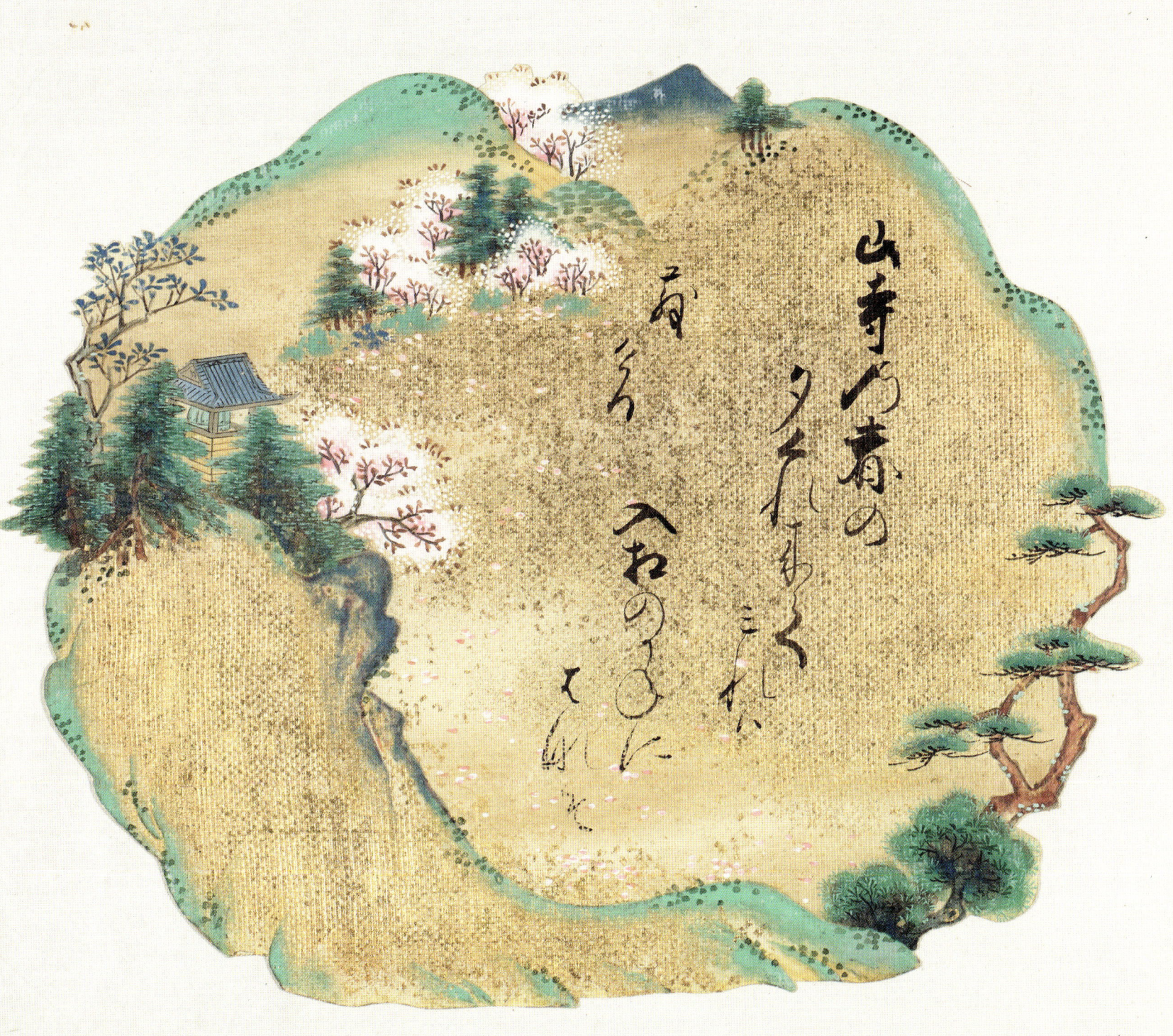

山寺の春の
夕くれ
きて見れば
入相の
かねに
花ぞ
ちりける

# CONTRIBUTORS

**EDWARD KAMENS** is Sumitomo Professor of Japanese Studies Emeritus, Yale University. He has published several books and articles about Japanese poetry, classical prose, Buddhism and literature, and the nexus of the textual and visual in Japanese culture. He directs an international team in the ongoing study of a seventeenth-century calligraphy album, known as the *Tekagamijō,* in the Beinecke Rare Book and Manuscript Library at Yale.

**PETER KORNICKI** attended Lincoln College and St Anthony's College, University of Oxford, and is emeritus professor of Japanese at Cambridge University. He has worked mainly on the history of the book in Japan and East Asia, and is the author of *The Book in Japan: A Cultural History from the Beginnings to the Nineteenth Century* (1998), *Languages, Scripts and Chinese Texts in East Asia* (2018), *Eavesdropping on the Emperor: Interrogators and Codebreakers in Britain's War with Japan* (2021), and numerous other books and articles. He was elected a Fellow of the British Academy in 2000, and in 2017 was awarded by the Japanese government the Order of the Rising Sun, Gold Rays with Neck Ribbon.

**MELISSA MCCORMICK** is the Andrew W. Mellon Professor of Japanese Art and Culture at Harvard University. Her publications examine the intersection of art, literature and history, and offer new methods for interpreting literary artefacts. Her publications include *Tosa Mitsunobu and the Small Scroll in Medieval Japan* (University of Washington, 2009), *The Tale of Genji: A Visual Companion* (Princeton, 2018), and numerous articles in English and Japanese. In 2019, she co-curated *The Tale of Genji: A Japanese Classic Illuminated* at The Metropolitan Museum of Art, and was a co-editor and author of its catalogue. Her work on book and manuscript history can also be accessed in her free online course, 'Japanese Books from Manuscript to Print' (edX).

**LAURA MORETTI** is Professor of Early Modern Japanese Literature and Culture at the University of Cambridge. Her research focuses on Japanese popular literature and culture from the seventeenth, eighteenth and nineteenth centuries. Moretti's projects are inherently interdisciplinary, placed at the intersection of literature, art history, book history, textual scholarship and palaeography. She has published widely in English and Japanese, including *Recasting the Past: An Early Modern 'Tales of Ise' for Children* (Brill, 2016), *Pleasure in Profit: Popular Prose in Seventeenth-Century Japan* (Columbia University Press, 2020) and, edited with Satō Yukiko, *Graphic Narratives from Early Modern Japan: The World of* Kusazōshi (Brill, 2024). Every year Professor Moretti runs the Mitsubishi Corporation Summer School in Early Modern Japanese Palaeography.

**Marinita Stiglitz** is Head of Paper Conservation at the Bodleian Libraries, University of Oxford, specializing in the conservation of books and large format items. Her research focuses on the comparative study of painting materials and paper in book production. Her involvement in multidisciplinary collaboration with scientists, curators and traditional craftspeople aims to bring original insight into the study of manuscripts and new approaches to their conservation. She has published on conservation practices, conservation history and technical examination of manuscripts.

**Katja Triplett,** PhD, was formerly Professor of the Study of East Asian Religions at the University of Göttingen, and is now based at Leipzig University. She is also Affiliate Professor of the Study of Religions at Marburg University. Her main field of interest is religions in Japan, exploring topics such as religious history and translation as well as visual expression and material culture. Funded by the German Research Foundation, she is currently directing a research project on translation and the early Jesuit mission in Japan. She has published widely on religions in Japan, including those of the sixteenth and seventeenth centuries.

# PICTURE CREDITS

# INDEX

Entries in **bold** refer to illustrations.

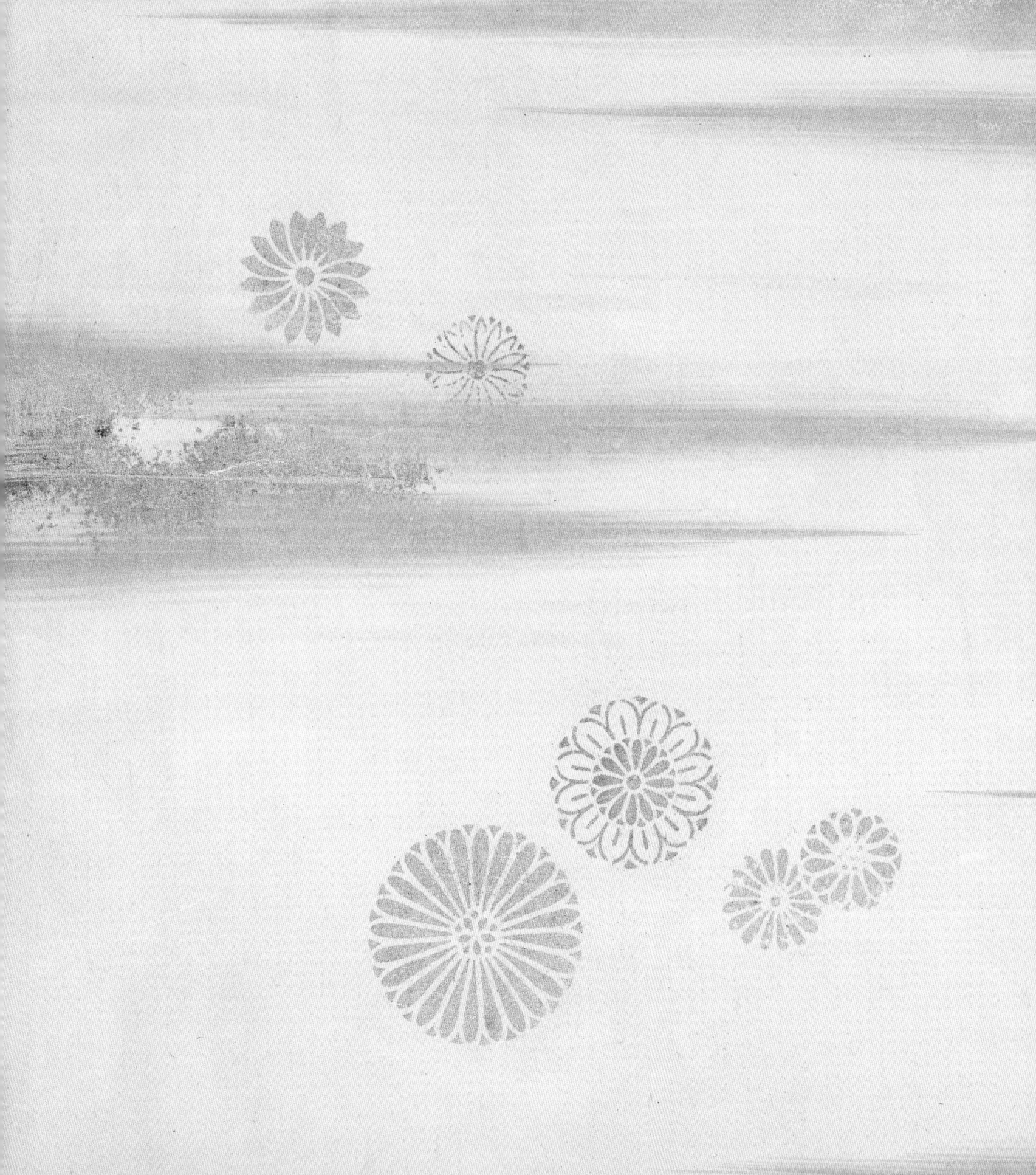

This publication has been generously supported
by the Martin J. Gross Family Foundation

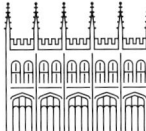

First published in 2025 by Bodleian Library Publishing
Broad Street, Oxford OX1 3BG
www.bodleianshop.co.uk

ISBN 978 1 85124 590 1

Publisher: Samuel Fanous
Managing Editor: Susie Foster
Editor: Janet Phillips
Picture Editor: Leanda Shrimpton
Cover design by Dot Little at the Bodleian Library
Designed and typeset by Lucy Morton of illuminati in 11 on 16 Warnock Pro
Printed and bound by Printer Trento S.r.l. on 150 gsm Gardamatt Art paper

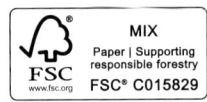

British Library Catalogue in Publishing Data
A CIP record of this publication is available from the British Library